Daniel Tyler

A Concise History of the Mormon Battalion in the Mexican War

Vol. 1

Daniel Tyler

A Concise History of the Mormon Battalion in the Mexican War
Vol. 1

ISBN/EAN: 9783337296346

Printed in Europe, USA, Canada, Australia, Japan

Cover: Foto ©ninafisch / pixelio.de

More available books at **www.hansebooks.com**

MORMON BATTALION

IN THE

Mexican War.

1846-1847.

BY SERGEANT DANIEL TYLER.

1881.

PREFACE.

After a lapse of thirty-six years from the time of the enlistment of the Mormon Battalion, no apology is required for publishing its history. Had its publication been undertaken at an earlier date, it might have been accomplished more satisfactorily to all concerned, as many important and interesting facts and incidents have doubtless been buried with the departed veterans. However, the most sanguine expectations of the author have been realized in the data collected for compiling this history, consisting of diaries written during service and numerous letters and statements from surviving members of that valiant corps.

Neither labor, pains nor expense has been spared in the effort to make this a just and authentic history. The author has not aimed at sensational effect, nor made any attempt at literary embellishment, but rather endeavored to offer a plain statement of facts and give due credit to all concerned.

Should his efforts meet the approval of his intelligent readers, his highest ambition in the publication of this work will be attained.

D. T.

CONTENTS.

INTRODUCTORY:

Martyrdom of Joseph Smith, written by President John Taylor, page 10; The "Mormons," a discourse delivered before the Historical Society of Pennsylvania, March 26, 1850, by Thomas L. Kane, page 64; The Mormon Battalion and First Wagon Road Over the Great American Desert, by Miss Eliza R. Snow, page 107.

CHAPTER I.

Causes that led to the Enlistment of the Battalion—Virtually a Requisition from the Government—Muster Roll—Servants to Officers—Families who Accompanied the Battalion. 110.

CHAPTER II.

First Orders Issued—Condition of Families and Feeling of Soldiers—Instructions of Church Authorities—A Pathetic Story of a Soldier's Wife. 127.

CHAPTER III.

Money Subscribed by the Soldiers for their Families and Poor Friends—First Death on the Journey—Out of Flour—A Prejudiced Missourian—Regrets of Mobocrats—Hurricane—Arrival at Fort Leavenworth—Anecdote of Colonel C—Dr. Sanderson appointed Surgeon—Haste to get Muskets—Character of Missouri Volunteers—More Money Subscribed by the Soldiers—Superior Intelligence and Obedience. 131.

CHAPTER IV.

Departure of Elders on Missions—Sickness—Start for Fort Leavenworth—Henry Standage Lost—News of Colonel Kane's Sickness—A Severe Storm—Feast of Honey—Ancient Ruins—Sanford Porter Healed in Answer to Prayer—Wagon Overturned in a Creek—Colonel Allen's Death—Death of Jane and John Bosco. 137.

CHAPTER V.

Question of a New Commander—Captain Hunt Elected—Arrival of Smith and Sanderson—Council of Officers—Smith Elected to take Command—Smith's Inhuman Treatment of the Sick—Repulsed by Sergeant Williams—The Sick Object to take Drugs—Sergeant Jones Protests Against their Being Forced to—Dykes' Perfidy—Letter from President Young—The "old Iron Spoon"—A Fiendish Doctor. 143.

CHAPTER VI.

A Faithful Sentinel Arrests the Colonel—The Colonel Frightened—Buffalo Meat—Military Law Read—Difficult Crossing—The Author Sick—Dread of the Doctor's Poisonous Drugs—Begs to be Left to Die—News of the Capture of Santa Fe—Dosed with Calomel—Disobey the Doctor and Recover—Doctor Claims Credit for the Cure—Camomile Tea—Who Used the Brandy—Pace's Account of Colonel Allen's Death, etc. 147.

CHAPTER VII.

Correspondence Between Sanderson and Smith and President Young—The True Version of How the New Commander should have been Selected, 153.

CHAPTER VIII.

Novel way of Catching Fish—Wagon Upset and Man Injured—Overtake Price's Regiment—Character of Price and his Men—Higgins' Detachment Sent to Pueblo—Dissatisfaction—Alva Phelps Drugged to Death—Curious Phenomenon—Suffer from Thirst—Forced Marches—Men Salivated. 157.

CHAPTER IX.

Rations Reduced—Bones of Mules Found—Ancient Ruins—The Officers and Healthy Men Push on for Santa Fe—Sick Left to Follow Without a Doctor—Style of Milking Spanish Goats—Arrival at Santa Fe—Partiality shown the Battalion by General Doniphan—Glimpse at Missouri Persecutions. 161.

CHAPTER X.

Captain Higgins' Detachment—Norman Sharp Accidentally Shot—Left to be Doctored by an Indian, and Dies—Colonel Cook Takes Command of the Battalion—His Orders. 165.

CHAPTER XI.

Detachment sent to Pueblo from Santa Fe—Death of Milton Smith—Death of Joseph W. Richards—Tributes from his Comrades, and Sister Hunt. 169.

CHAPTER XII.

Colonel Cooke's Statement of the Condition of the Battalion—Paid in Checks that could not be Cashed—Send them to Council Bluffs—Reason for Lieutenant Gully's Resignation—Condition of Animals—Strict Discipline of Colonel Cooke—An Officer the First to be Punished. 173.

CHAPTER XIII.

Mexicans too much Prejudiced to sell us Supplies—Mexican Costumes—Sergeant Elmer Reduced to the Ranks—Navajo Raids on the Mexicans—Hardships of our Journey—Animals Devoured Wholly, Except Bones and Hair—Men Have to Pull the Wagons—A Song. 178.

CHAPTER XIV.

Lieutenant Dykes resigns his Adjutancy—Dinner of Sheep's Lights—Mexican Spurs—Mexican Woman Stolen by Navajoes—Hampton Reported Well by Dr. Sanderson, and Dies a Few Hours Afterwards—Another Reduction in Rations—Rumors of Intended Revolt—Two Men Punished Through the Meanness of Dykes—Sergeant Elmer Restored to Office—Discouraging Reports of Guides—Condition of Teams. 184.

CHAPTER XV.

Lieutenant Willis Sent Back with the Sick—Only five Days' Rations for a Journey of 300 Miles—Ox Mired and Killed—Oxen Providentially Provided—Death of Elijah Freeman and Richard Carter—Wagons Exchanged for Pack Animals—Sickness of Men—Left on the Way—A Severe Journey—Snow Four Feet Deep—Arrival at Pueblo—Condition of Men—Gilbert Hunt Sent Back for the Sick—Sad Death of Coleman. 189.

CHAPTER XVI.

Detachments of Brown and Higgins—Death of Milton Kelly—Houses Completed—Death of Two Children, also John Perkins, Brother Scott. Arnold Stephens and M. S. Blanchard—Rumors of Revolt—Visit to Soda Fountain—Description of the Place—Game Killed—Pay Received. Also Orders to March to California.   195.

CHAPTER XVII.

Journey Commenced—Meeting with A. M. Lyman and Others from Council Bluffs—Emotions at Meeting—A Perilous and Severe Journey by Tippets and Woolsey—Arrival of the Detachment at Fort Laramie—Follow the Pioneer Trail—Arrival in Salt Lake Valley—Disbanded.   198.

CHAPTER XVIII.

Travels of the Main Army—Two Wagons Left—Antics of Oxen on being Packed—Muskets Used for Tent Poles—First Indian Wigwams—Ancient Earthenware and Glass—Leave the Rio Grande—Ancient Gold Mine—Goats Killed—Table Land—Road Turns to Mexican Settlements—Council Decides to go that Way—Prayers for the Colonel's Mind to be Changed—A Scare—Prayer Answered—Men March Ahead of Teams to Break the Road—Charboneaux Kills his Mule.   202.

CHAPTER XIX.

Author's Birthday—Severe Suffering from Thirst—Mirage—Reach Water—John R. Murdock Sick—Henry G. Boyle Healed in Answer to Prayer—Bear Killed—Crossing the Mountains—Wagons Lowered With Ropes—Dykes Almost Shot While Playing the Spy—Wild Cattle—Killing a Wild Bull—Return of John Allen—His Adventures.   208.

CHAPTER XX.

The Apache Indians—Jerking Beef—Loading of Guns and Firing at Game Prohibited—Order Disregarded—Author Sick—Calomel and Arsenic as Medicine—Death of Elisha Smith—Howling of the Wolves—A Song   214.

CHAPTER XXI.

Wild Horses—Game Plentiful—Wild Cattle Congregate on our Route—A Battle with them—Losses on Both Sides—One man Thrown Ten Feet in the Air—Wonderful Tenacity of Life in the Wild Bulls—Coolness and Bravery of Corporal Frost—A Song on the Bull Fight.   218.

CHAPTER XXII.

Decide to March Through Tucson—Guide held at Tucson as Prisoner—Mexican Soldiers Arrested and held as Hostages until Foster is Released—Mexicans Refuse to Surrender—Prepare for an Engagement—Mexican Soldiers Desert the Town—We March Through—Kindness of Citizens—Public Wheat Taken for Mule Feed—Primitive Mills—An Alarm—An Excited Officer—Letter to the Governor of Sonora.   224.

CHAPTER XXIII.

Long and Difficult March Without Water—Great Suffering—A Laughable Occurrence—The Pima Village—The Natives—News from Kearny—A Cruel Order—The Maricopa Indians—Their Honesty.   231.

CHAPTER XXIV.

Cross a Bend of the Gila—Brackish Water—Difficult Traveling—Boat made of two Wagon-boxes—Provisions Shipped in it—Fears for its Safety—Boating a Failure—Cargo Left—Another Reduction in Rations—Feed on Mezquit Seeds—Arrival at the Colorado—Crossing the River—Suffering of the Men sent Back for Flour—Wagon Stuck in the Middle of the River—Left there by the Colonel—His Statement Incorrect—Wagons Abandoned. 237.

CHAPTER XXV.

Troublesome Fires in the Brush—Discouraging Prospect—No Water—Alas, for Human Hopes—A Trying March—Great Suffering from Thirst—Meet fresh Mules and some Beeves—Freezing at Night and Scorching by Day—Arrival at the Cariza—Happy Relief—Good Water to Drink—Novel Style of Boots. 242.

CHAPTER XXVI.

Heavy Roads—Last Food Eaten—Messengers from San Diego—Cheerfulness of Men—News of Battles—Cutting a Road Through a Mountain Gorge—Arrival at Warner's Rancho—A Full Meal—Cheap Beef—Hot Spring—Sleeping Under Water—Flour from the Boat Disaster—March for San Diego—Beef Diet. 246.

CHAPTER XXVII.

First View of the Pacific Ocean—Arrival at San Diego Mission—Complimentary Order from Colonel Cooke—General Kearny's Entry to California—Skirmishes with Californians. 252.

CHAPTER XXVIII.

Kearny's Stubborn Defense on the Hill—Providential Stratagem of the Enemy—Desperate Resolve—Timely Relief—Sufferings of Kearny's Men—The last Decisive Battle—Civil War Feared—Fremont's Men Refuse to Deliver Public Property—Commodore Stockton's Report to the Secretary of the Navy—Commodore Stockton Refuses to treat with Jose Ma Flores—Colonel Freeman's Assumption—Articles of Capitulation—Dispute Settled—Wisdom of Stockton and Kearny—Battalion and Dragoons the only Regularly Mustered Soldiers in California. 259.

CHAPTER XXIX.

Men Visit San Diego—Precautionary Measure—March to San Luis Rey—Police Detailed—Men nearly Naked—Exorbitant Prices of Clothing—Catholic Church—Public Square about four Acres—Semi-Tropical Fruit Trees—Large Reservoir—Duties of Soldiers in Garrison—Regrets at Having to Shave—Reasons assigned—Fleas and Vermin—Only Clothing—R. N. Allred a Non-Commissioned Staff Officer—Sunday Dress Parade—The Drill Commenced—Incident of Drill—Religious Services—Seventies' Meetings—Considered Officious. 263.

CHAPTER XXX.

Company B sent to San Diego—Change of Diet—Religious Services—Sentinel Court-martialed for Sleeping at his Post—Colonel, Dissatisfied with the Meagre Penalty, Remits the Sentence — Barrowman Accepts the Result as an Answer to Prayer—Detachment Sent after Wagons—Curious Ox Yokes—Garrison Duties — Lieutenant Stoneman and Detachment sent to San Diego—Reduced to the Ranks—Unsettled Condition of Governorship—Circular from Commodore Shubrick and Proclamation from Kearny—Orders to Fremont to Disband his Forces—His Refusal. 267.

CHAPTER XXXI.

Complaints of Short Rations—Tale-Bearing Dykes—Sergeant Jones and Corporal Lane Reduced to the Ranks—March to Los Angeles—Cooke Applies for Ordnance and Fails—Four Indians Killed—Captain Hunt's Explanation—Death of David Smith—San Luis Rey Abandoned—Petition for Discharge of Battalion Treated with Contempt by Officers—Arrival of Colonel Mason—Hatred of Fremont's Men towards the Battalion—Cajon Pass Guarded. 272.

CHAPTER XXXII.

Efficiency of the Battalion—John Allen Excommunicated—Colonel Cooke Orders the Horses, Purchased by Soldiers, Sold at Auction—Fort Erected—War Imminent—Detachments all Called In—Dragoons our Champions—Privilege to Re-enlist Declined—Death of Captain Hunter's Wife—Colonel Stevenson Appointed to Supersede in Command—Letters from Families—News of a Battle—Arrival of General Kearny—He Compliments the Battalion—Skirmish with Indians—A Barbarous Practice Abolished—General Kearny's Address to the Battalion—Detachment to Accompany him to Fort Leavenworth. 277.

CHAPTER XXXIII.

Company B at San Diego—Building a Fort—Religious Services—Literary Club—Cheap Animals—"Herding Stallions"—Death of Albert Dunham—"Stocks"—Miserable Mobocrat—Fossil Remains—Wedding—Immoral Priest—Soldiers Seeking Work—News of General Taylor's Victory—Colonel Stevenson's Arrival and Address—Lieutenant Clift Appointed Alcalde—First Brick Made in California—Fourth of July Celebrated—Citizens of San Diego Petition to have the "Mormon" Soldiers Remain—Song—Return to Los Angeles. 283.

CHAPTER XXXIV.

Slaughter of Dogs—"Dancing Bill"—Detachment to San Pedro—Accident to John Spidle—Soap Factory—John Allen Drummed out of Service—Fate of Hastings' Company—Liberty Pole—Celebration of St. John's Day—Colonel Stevenson's Speech and Invitation to Re-enlist—Other Speeches Pro and Con—Conditions for Re-enlistment Rejected by Colonel Stevenson—Liberty Pole Raised—The Glorious Fourth—Bull Fight—Battalion Discharged—Paid Off—Some Re-enlist. 290.

CHAPTER XXXV.

Travels of General Kearny's Escort to Monterey—Kearny's Arrival—Fremont Under Arrest—Overland Journey Commenced—Incidents of Travel—Costume of Digger Indians—Losses in Fording a River—Visits from Brethren—Sacramento Valley—Remains of the Ill-fated Emigrants—A Horrible Scene—Bury the Bones—Accidental Shooting—Nude Indians—Boiling Springs—Pass Soda Springs and Bear Lake Valley—Meet Companies of the Saints—Arrival at Fort Leavenworth and Discharge—Fremont put in Irons. 299.

CHAPTER XXXVI.

Discharged Soldiers at Los Angeles—Their Morality, etc.—Organize for the Return Trip—Journey Commenced—A Remarkable Dream and its Fulfillment—Difficult Mountain Trail—Animals Lost—Beef Cattle Slaughtered—A Memorial of a Mountaineer's Death—The Hottest Day—Vain Search for Walker's Pass—Ecstatic Dance of an Indian—Sacramento Valley—News of the Pioneers—Some of the Men Decide to Remain and Work in California. 305.

CHAPTER XXXVII.

Get Horses Shod and Procure an Outfit—Johnson's Mill—Nude Indians—Mrs. Johnson's Story—Horrible Account of Suffering—Human Beings Living on the Flesh of their Fellows—Taste Developed for such Food—Meet Samuel Brannan Returning to California—Doleful Account of Salt Lake Valley—Captain James Brown Met—Epistle from the Twelve Apostles—Letters from Friends. 311.

CHAPTER XXXVIII.

Many Return to California—Death of Henry Hoyt—Money Providentially Provided—Clothing Lost—Pants Worn Out—Skins Purchased for a New Pair—Arrival in Salt Lake Valley—Destitute Condition of Men—Clothing Donated for Them—Seeds Brought by Battalion—Prolific Yield of Peas—Characteristics of Peas Change. 316.

CHAPTER XXXIX.

Eastward Journey Resumed—No Flour to be Obtained for the Trip—Disappointments at Bridger and Laramie—Scant Fare—Episode with Indians—Diet of Rawhide Saddle Bags—Providential Freezing of the River—Reach Winter Quarters—Kindness of Friends. 320.

CHAPTER XL.

"Mormon Volunteers"—Quartered in San Diego—Detachment Sent to San Luis Rey—Death of Sergeant Frost and Neal Donald—Extra Work Done by the Soldiers—Serve Longer than They Enlisted for—Immorality Among their Successors—Journey to Salt Lake Valley by the Southern Route. 326.

CHAPTER XLI.

Men who Returned to California for Work—Employed by Captain Sutter to Build Mills—Discovery of Gold in the Mill Race by Mr. Marshall—Other Discoveries—Effects of the Gold Fever. 332.

CHAPTER XLII.

Attempt to Explore a New Route to Salt Lake Valley—Forced to return on Account of Deep Snow—Three Men Grow Impatient and Make Another Attempt, and are Murdered by Indians—The Company Follow and Discover their Remains—Animals Alarmed—Scattered by the Firing of a Cannon. 335.

CHAPTER XLIII.

Make a Road to Carson Valley—Meet Emigrants—Their Joy at News of Gold—Enter the Valley by the Deep Creek Route—"Mormon" Enterprise in San Francisco—Adventurous Trip from San Francisco to Council Bluffs. 339.

CHAPTER XLIV.

President Young Requested by the Military Commander of California to have Another Battalion sent there—President Young's Address to the "Battalion Boys" in Salt Lake Valley—Why the Call was Made for the Battalion—Opposed to their Re-enlisting. 343.

CHAPTER XLV.

First General Festival of the Mormon Battalion in Salt Lake Valley—Speeches by Father Pettegrew, Presidents Young, Kimball and Grant, Sergeant Hyde, Captain Brown, Lieutenants Clark and Thompson and Brothers Huntington, Williams, Wilkin, King, Garner, Durphy, Hess and Hawk. 345.

CHAPTER XLVI.

Synopsis of a Lecture by James Ferguson—Correspondence Between Ferguson and Cooke—Cooke's Deference to the Mormon Battalion when Passing Through Salt Lake City in 1858—Survivors of the Mormon Battalion—Song. 364.

INTRODUCTORY.

Before entering upon the History of the Mormon Battalion, it seems necessary to offer some explanation of the previous condition of the Latter-day Saints; otherwise the reader unacquainted with those facts would scarcely be able to appreciate the situation of the people at the time of the enlistment of the Battalion.

The following sketch, written by President John Taylor, many years since, gives an excellent idea of affairs previous to the exodus of the Saints from Illinois. It is therefore republished here by the kind permission of the author. As stated in the context, it was written at a time when documentiary evidence was not available; it has, however, been since revised and compared with authentic data, and may be relied upon as true in every particular.

The historical address of General Thomas L. Kane, also inserted in this same connection, depicts in graphic terms some scenes of which he was a witness when the Saints fled from their homes in Nauvoo to journey into the wilderness.

THE MARTYRDOM OF JOSEPH SMITH.

BY PRESIDENT JOHN TAYLOR.

BEING requested by Elders George A. Smith and Wilford Woodruff, Church historians, to write an account of events that transpired before, and took place at, the time of the martyrdom of Joseph Smith, in Carthage jail, in Hancock County, State of Illinois, I write the following, principally from memory, not having access at this time to any public documents relative thereto farther than a few desultory items contained in Ford's "History of Illinois." I must also acknowledge myself considerably indebted to George A. Smith, who was with me when I wrote it, and who, although not there at the time of the bloody transaction, yet, from conversing with several persons who were in the capacity of Church historians, and aided by an excellent memory, has rendered me considerable service.

These and the few items contained in the note at the end of this account are all the aid I have had. I would farther add that the items contained in the letter, in relation to dates especially, may be considered strictly correct.

After having written the whole, I read it over to the Hon. J. M. Bernhisel, who with one or two slight alterations, pronounced it strictly correct. Brother Bernhisel was present most of the time. I am afraid that, from the length of time that has transpired since the occurrence, and having to rely almost exclusively upon my memory, there may be some slight inaccuracies, but I believe that in the general it is strictly correct. As I figured in those transactions from the commencement to the end, they left no slight impression on my mind.

In the year 1844, a very great excitement prevailed in some parts of Hancock, Brown, and other neighboring Counties of Illinois, in relation to the "Mormons," and a spirit of vindictive hatred and persecution was exhibited among the people, which was manifested in the most bitter and acrimonious language, as well as by acts of hostility and violence, frequently threatening the destruction of the citizens of Nauvoo and vicinity, and utter annihilation of the "Mormons" and "Mormonism," and in some instances breaking out in the most violent acts of ruffianly barbarity. Persons were kidnapped, whipped, persecuted, and falsely accused of various crimes; their cattle and houses injured, destroyed, or stolen; vexatious prosecutions were instituted to harass, and annoy. In some remote neighborhoods they were expelled from their homes without redress, and in others violence was threatened to their persons and property, while in others every kind of insult and indignity were heaped upon them, to induce them to abandon their homes, the County, or the State.

These annoyances, prosecutions, and persecutions were instigated through different agencies and by various classes of men, actuated by different motives, but all uniting in the one object—prosecution, persecution, and extermination of the Saints.

There were a number of wicked and corrupt men living in Nauvoo and its vicinity, who had belonged to the Church, but whose conduct was incompatible with the gospel; they were accordingly dealt with by the Church and severed from its communion. Some of these had been prominent members, and held official stations either in the city or Church. Among these were John C. Bennett, formerly mayor; William Law, Counselor to Joseph Smith; Wilson Law, his natural brother, and general in the Nauvoo Legion; Dr. R. D. Foster, a man of some property, but with a very bad reputation; Francis and Chauncey Higbee, the latter a young lawyer, and both sons of a respectable and honored man in the Church, known as Judge Elias Higbee, who died about twelve months before.

Besides these, there were a great many apostates, both in the city and county, of less notoriety, who for their delinquencies, had been expelled from the Church. John C. Bennett and Francis and Chauncey Higbee were cut off from the Church; the former was also cashiered from his generalship for the most flagrant acts of seduction and adultery; and the developments in their cases were so scandalous that the High Council, before whom they were tried, had to sit with closed doors.

William Law, although Counselor to Joseph, was found to be his most bitter foe and maligner, and to hold intercourse, contrary to all law, in his own house, with a young lady resident with him; and it was afterwards proven that he had conspired with some Missourians to take Joseph Smith's life, and was only saved by Josiah Arnold and Daniel Garn, who, being on guard at his house, prevented the assassins from seeing him. Yet, although having murder in his heart, his manners were generally courteous and mild, and he was well calculated to deceive.

General Wilson Law was cut off from the Church for seduction, falsehood, and defamation; both the above were also court-martialed by the Nauvoo Legion, and expelled. Foster was also cut off I believe, for dishonesty, fraud, and falsehood. I know he was eminently guilty of the whole, but whether these were the specific charges or not, I don't know, but I do know that he was a notoriously wicked and corrupt man.

Besides the above characters and "Mormonic" apostates, there were other three parties. The first of these may be called religionists, the second politicians, and the third counterfeiters, black-legs, horse-thieves, and cut-throats.

The religious party were chagrined and maddened because "Mormonism" came in contact with their religion, and they could not oppose it from the scriptures. Thus like the ancient Jews, when enraged at the exhibition of their follies and hypocrisies by Jesus and His apostles, so these were infuriated against the "Mormons" because of their discomfiture by them; and instead of owning the truth and rejoicing in it, they were ready to gnash upon them with their teeth, and to persecute the believers in principles which they could not disprove.

The political party were those who were of opposite politics to us. There were always two parties, the Whigs and Democrats, and we could not vote for one without offending the other; and it not unfrequently happened that candidates for office would place the issue of their election upon opposition to the "Mormons," in order to gain political influence from religious prejudice, in which case the "Mormons" were compelled, in self-defense, to vote against them, which resulted almost invariably against our opponents. This made them angry; and although it was of their own making, and the "Mormons" could not be expected to do otherwise, yet they raged on account of their discomfiture, and sought to wreak their fury on the "Mormons." As an instance of the above, when Joseph Duncan was candidate for the office of governor of Illinois, he pledged himself to his party that, if he could be elected, he would exterminate or drive the "Mormons" from the State.* The consequence was that Governor Ford was elected. The Whigs, seeing that they had been out-generaled by the Democrats in securing the "Mormon" vote, became seriously alarmed, and sought to repair their disaster by raising a crusade against the people. The Whig newspapers teemed with accounts of the wonders and enormities of Nauvoo, and of the awful wickedness of a party which could consent to receive the support of such miscreants. Governor Duncan, who was really a brave, honest man, and who had nothing to do with getting the "Mormon" charters passed through the Legislature, took the stump on this subject in good earnest, and expected to be elected governor almost on this question alone.

The third party, composed of counterfeiters, black-legs, horse-thieves, and cut-throats, were a pack of scoundrels that infested the whole of the western country at that time. In some districts their influence was so great as to control important State and County offices. On this subject Governor Ford has the following;

"Then, again, the northern part of the State was not destitute of its organized bands of rogues, engaged in murders, robberies, horse-stealing, and in making and passing counterfeit money. These rogues were scattered all over the north, but the most of them were located in the Counties of Ogle, Winnebago, Lee, and De Kalb.

"In the County of Ogle they were so numerous, strong, and well organized that they could not be convicted for their crimes. By getting some of their numbers on the juries, by producing a host of witnesses to sustain their defense, by perjured evidence, and by changing the venue of one County to another, by continuances from term to term, and by the inability of witnesses to attend from time to time at distant and foreign Counties, they most generally managed to be acquitted."†

There was a combination of horse-thieves extending from Galena to Alton. There were counterfeiters engaged in merchandising, trading, and store-keeping in most of the cities

---

*——See his remarks as contained in his History of Illinois, page 269.

†——Ford's History of Illinois, page 246.

and villages, and in some districts, I have been credibly informed by men to whom they have disclosed their secrets, the judges, sheriffs, constables, and jailors, as well, as professional men, were more or less associated with them. These had in their employ the most reckless, abandoned wretches, who stood ready to carry into effect the most desperate enterprises, and were careless alike of human life and property. Their object in persecuting the "Mormons" was in part to cover their own rascality, and in part to prevent them from exposing and prosecuting them; but the principal reason was plunder, believing that if they could be removed or driven they would be made fat on "Mormon" spoils, besides having in the deserted city a good asylum for the prosecution of their diabolical pursuits.

This conglomeration of apostate "Mormons," religious bigots, political fanatics and black-legs, all united their forces against the "Mormons," and organized themselves into a party, denominated "anti-Mormons." Some of them, we have reason to believe, joined the Church in order to cover their nefarious practices, and when they were expelled for their unrighteousness only raged with greater violence. They circulated every kind of falsehood that they could collect or manufacture against the "Mormons." They also had a paper to assist them in their infamous designs, called the *Warsaw Signal*, edited by a Mr. Thomas Sharp, a violent and unprincipled man, who shrunk not from any enormity. The "anti-Mormons" had public meetings, which were very numerously attended, where they passed resolutions of the most violent and inflammatory kind, threatening to drive, expel and exterminate the "Mormons" from the State, at the same time accusing them of every evil in the vocabulary of crime.

They appointed their meetings in various parts of Hancock, M'Donough, and other Counties, which soon resulted in the organization of armed mobs, under the direction of officers who reported to their head-quarters, and the reports of which were publishhd in the "anti-Mormon" paper, and circulated through the adjoining Counties. We also published in the *Times and Seasons* and the *Nauvoo Neighbor* (two papers published and edited by me at that time) an account, not only of their proceedings, but our own. But such was the hostile feeling, so well arranged their plans, and so desperate and lawless their measures, that it was with the greatest difficulty that we could get our papers circulated; they were destroyed by postmasters and others, and scarcely ever arrived at the place of their destination, so that a great many of the people, who would have been otherwise peaceable, were excited by their misrepresentations, and instigated to join their hostile or predatory bands.

Emboldened by the acts of those outside, the apostate "Mormons," associated with others, commenced the publication of a libelous paper in Nauvoo, called the *Nauvoo Expositor*. This paper not only reprinted from the others, but put in circulation the most libelous, false, and infamous reports concerning the citizens of Nauvoo, and especially the ladies. It was, however, no sooner put in circulation than the indignation of the whole community was aroused; so much so, that they threatened its annihilation; and I do not believe that in any other city in the United States, if the same charges had been made against the citizens, it would have been permitted to remain one day. As it was among us, under these circumstances, it was thought best to convene the City Council to take into consideration the adoption of some measures for its removal, as it was deemed better that this should be done legally than illegally. Joseph Smith, therefore, who was mayor, convened the City Council for that purpose; the paper was introduced and read, and the subject examined. All, or nearly all present, expressed their indignation at the course taken by the *Expositor*, which was owned by some of the aforesaid apostates, associated with one or two others. Wilson Law, Dr. Foster, Charles Ivins and the Higbees before referred to, some lawyers, store-keepers, and others in Nauvoo who were not "Mormons," together with the "anti-Mormons" outside of the city, sustained it. The calculation was, by false statements, to unsettle the minds of many in the city, and to form combinations there similar to the anti-Mormon" associations outside of the city. Various attempts had heretofore been made by the party to annoy and irritate the citizens of Nauvoo; false accusations had been made, vexatious lawsuits instituted, threats made, and various devices resorted to, to influence the public mind, and, if possible, to provoke us to the commission of some overt act that might make us amenable to the law. With a perfect knowledge, therefore, of the designs of these infernal scoundrels who were in our midst, as well as those who surrounded us, the City Council entered upon an investigation of the matter. They felt that they were in a critical position, and that any move made for the abating of that press would be looked upon, or at least represented, as a direct attack upon the liberty of speech, and that, so far from displeasing our enemies, it would be looked upon by them as one of the best circumstances that could transpire to assist them in their nefarious and bloody designs. Being a member of the City Council, I well remember the feeling of responsibility that seemed to rest upon all present; nor shall I soon forget the bold, manly, independent expressions of Joseph Smith on that occasion in relation to this matter. He exhibited in glowing colors the meanness, corruption, and ultimate designs of the "anti-Mromons;" their despicable characters and ungodly influences, especially of those who were in our midst. He told of the responsibility that rested upon us, as guardians of the public interest, to stand up in the defense of the injured and oppressed, to stem the current of corruption, and, as men and Saints, to put a stop to this flagrant outrage upon this people's rights.

He stated that no man was a stonger advocate for the liberty of speech and of the press than himself; yet, when this noble gift is utterly prostituted and abused, as in the present instance, it loses all claim to our respect, and becomes as great an agent for evil as it can possibly be for good; and notwithstanding the apparent advantage we should give our enemies by this act, yet it behooved us, as men, to act independent of all secondary influences, to perform the part of men of enlarged minds, and boldly and fearlessly to discharge the duties devolving upon us by declaring as a nuisance, and removing this filthy, libelous, and seditious sheet from our midst.

The subject was discussed in various forms, and after the remarks made by the mayor, every one seemed to be waiting for some one else to speak.

After a considerable pause, I arose and expressed my feelings frankly, as Joseph had done, and numbers of others followed in the same strain; and I think, but am not certain, that I made a motion for the removal of that press as a nuisance. This motion was finally put, and carried by all but one; and he conceded that the measure was just, but abstained through fear.

Several members of the City Council were not in the Church. The following is the bill referred to:

*Bill for Removing of the Press of the "Nauvoo Expositor."**

"Resolved by the City Council of the City of Nauvoo, that the printing-office from whence issues the *Nauvoo Expositor* is a public nuisance; and also of said *Nauvoo Expositors* which may be or exist in said establishment; and the mayor is instructed to cause said establishment and papers to be removed without delay, in such manner as he shall direct.

"Passed June 10th, 1844. GEO. W. HARRIS, President *pro tem*.

"W. RICHARDS, Recorder."

After the passage of the bill, the marshal, John P. Green, was ordered to abate or remove, which he forthwith proceeded to do by summoning a posse of men for that purpose. The press was removed or broken, I don't remember which, by the marshal, and the types scattered in the street.

This seemed to be one of those extreme cases that require extreme measures, as the press was still proceeding in its inflammatory course. It was feared that, as it was almost universally execrated, should it continue longer, an indignant people might commit some overt act which might lead to serious consequences, and that it was better to use legal than illegal means.

This, as was foreseen, was the very course our enemies wished us to pursue, as it afforded them an opportunity of circulating a very plausible story about the "Mormons" being opposed to the liberty of the press and of free speech, which they were not slow to avail themselves of. Stories were fabricated, and facts perverted; false statements were made, and this act brought in as an example to sustain the whole of their fabrications; and, as if inspired by Satan, they labored with an energy and zeal worthy of a better cause. They had runners to circulate their reports, not only through Hancock County, but in all the surrounding Counties. These reports were communicated to their "anti-Mormon" societies, and these societies circulated them in their several districts. The "anti-

---

*——*Deseret News*, No. 29, Sept. 23, 1857, p. 226.

Mormon" paper, the *Warsaw Signal*, was filled with inflammatory articles and misrepresentations in relation to us, and especially to this act of destroying the press. We were represented as a horde of lawless ruffians and brigands, anti-American and anti-republican, steeped in crime and iniquity, opposed to freedom of speech and of the press, and all the rights and immunities of a free and enlightened people; that neither person nor property were secure: that we had designs upon the citizens of Illinois and of the United States, and the people were called upon to rise *en masse*, and put us down, drive us away, or exterminate us as a pest to society, and alike dangerous to our neighbors, the State, and commonwealth.

These statements were extensively copied and circulated throughout the United States. A true statement of the facts in question was published by us both in the *Times and Seasons* and the *Nauvoo Neighbor;* but it was found impossible to circulate them in the immediate Counties, as they were destroyed at the post-offices or otherwise by the agents of the "anti-Mormons," and, in order to get the mail to go abroad, I had to send the papers a distance of thirty or forty miles from Nauvoo, and sometimes to St. Louis (upward of two hundred miles), to insure their proceeding on their route, and then one half or two thirds of the papers never reached the place of destination, being intercepted or destroyed by our enemies.

These false reports stirred up the community around, of whom many, on account of religious prejudice, were easily instigated to join the "anti-Mormons" and embark in any crusade that might be undertaken against us; hence their ranks swelled in numbers, and new organizations were formed, meetings were held, resolutions passed, and men and means volunteered for the extirpation of the "Mormons."

On these points Governor Ford writes: "These also were the active men in blowing up the fury of the people, in hopes that a popular movement might be set on foot, which would result in the expulsion or extermination of the 'Mormon' voters. For this purpose public meetings had been called, inflammatory speeches had been made, exaggerated reports had been extensively circulated, committees had been appointed, who rode night and day to spread the reports and solicit the aid of neighboring Counties, and at a public meeting at Warsaw resolutions were passed to expel or exterminate the 'Mormon' population. This was not, however, a movement which was unanimously concurred in. The County contained a goodly number of inhabitants in favor of peace, or who at least desired to be neutral in such a contest. These were stigmatized by the name of 'Jack Mormons,' and there were not a few of the more furious exciters of the people who openly expressed their intention to involve them in the common expulsion or extermination.

"A system of excitement and agitation was artfully planned and executed with tact. It consisted in spreading reports and rumors of the most fearful character. As examples: On the morning before my arrival at Carthage, I was awakened at an early hour by the frightful report, which was asserted with confidence and apparent consternation, that the 'Mormons' had already commenced the work of burning, destruction, and murder, and that every man capable of bearing arms was instantly wanted at Carthage for the protection of the County.

"We lost no time in starting; but when we arrived at Carthage we could hear no more concerning this story. Again, during the few days that the militia were encamped at Carthage, frequent applications were made to me to send a force here, and a force there, and a force all about the country, to prevent murders, robberies, and larcenies which, it was said, were threatened by the 'Mormons.' No such forces were sent, nor were any such offenses commited at that time, except the stealing of some provisions, and there was never the least proof that this was done by a 'Mormon.' Again, on my late visit to Hancock County, I was informed by some of their violent enemies that the larcenies of the 'Mormons' had become unusually numerous and insufferable.

"They admitted that but little had been done in this way in their immediate vicinity, but they insisted that sixteen horses had been stolen by the 'Mormons' in one night near Lima, and, upon inquiry, was told that no horses had been stolen in that neighborhood, but that sixteen horses had been stolen in one night in Hancock County. This last informant being told of the Hancock story, again changed the venue to another distant settlement in the northern edge of Adams."*

---

*———Ford's History of Illinois, page 330, 331.

In the meantime legal proceedings were instituted against the members of the City Council of Nauvoo. A writ, here subjoined, was issued upon the affidavit of the Laws, Fosters, Higbees, and Ivins, by Mr. Morrison, a justice of the peace in Carthage, the County seat of Hancock, and put into the hands of one David Bettesworth, a constable of the same place.

Writ issued upon affidavit by Thomas Morrison, J. P., State of Illinois, Hancock County, ss.

"The people of the State of Illinois, to all constables, sheriffs, and coroners of the said state, greeting:

"Whereas complaint hath been made before me, one of the justices of the peace in and for the County of Hancock aforesaid, upon the oath of Francis M. Higbee, of the said county, that Joseph Smith, Samuel Bennett, John Taylor, William W. Phelps, Hyrum Smith, John P. Green, Stephen Perry, Dimick B. Huntington, Jonathan Dunham, Stephen Markham, William Edwards, Jonathan Holmes, Jesse P. Harmon, John Lytle, Joseph W. Coolidge, Harvey D. Redfield, Porter Rockwell, and Levi Richards, of said County, did, on the 10th day of June instant, commit a riot at and within the County aforesaid, wherein they with force and violence broke into the printing-office of the *Nauvoo Expositor*, and unlawfully and with force burned and destroyed the printing-press, type, and fixtures of the same, being the property of William Law, Wilson Law, Charles Ivins, Francis M. Higbee, Chauncey L. Higbee, Robert D. Foster, and Charles A. Foster.

These are therefore to command you forthwith to apprehend the said Joseph Smith, Samuel Bennett, John Taylor, William W. Phelps, Hyrum Smith, John P. Green, Stephen Perry, Dimick B. Huntington, Jonathan Dunham, Stephen Markham, William Edwards, Jonathan Holmes, Jesse P. Harmon, John Lytle, Joseph W. Coolidge, Harvey D. Redfield, Porter Rockwell, and Levi Richards, and bring them before me, or some other justice of the peace, to answer the premises, and farther to be dealt with according to law.

"Given under my hand and seal at Carthage, in the County aforesaid, this 11th day of June, A. D. 1844.   THOMAS MORRISON, J. P." (Seal.)*

The council did not refuse to attend to the legal proceedings in the case, but as the law of Illinois made it the privilege of the persons accused to go "or appear before the issuer of the writ, or any other justice of peace," they requested to be taken before another magistrate, either in the city of Nauvoo or at any reasonable distance out of it.

This the constable, who was a mobocrat, refused to do; and as this was our legal privilege, we refused to be dragged, con-

---

*——*Deseret News*, No 30, Sep. 30, 1857, page 233.

trary to law, a distance of eighteen miles, when at the same time we had reason to believe that an organized band of mobocrats were assembled for the purpose of extermination or murder, and among whom it would not be safe to go without a superior force of armed men. A writ of *habeas corpus* was called for, and issued by the municpial court of Nauvoo, taking us out of the hands of Bettesworth, and placing us in the charge of the city marshal. We went before the municipal court and were dismissed. Our refusal to obey this illegal proceeding was by them construed into a refusal to submit to law, and circulated as such, and the people either did believe, or professed to believe, that we were in open rebellion against the laws and the authorities of the State. Hence mobs began to assemble, among which all through the country inflammatory speeches were made, exciting them to mobocracy and violence. Soon they commenced their depredations in our outside settlements, kidnapping some, and whipping and otherwise abusing others.

The persons thus abused fled to Nauvoo as soon as practicable, and related their injuries to Joseph Smith, then mayor of the city, and lieutenant general of the Nauvoo Leigon. They also went before magistrates, and made affidavits of what they had suffered, seen, and heard. These affidavits, in connection with a copy of all our proceedings were forwarded by Joseph Smith to Mr. Ford, then governor of Illinois, with an expression of our desire to abide law, and a request that the governor would instruct him how to proceed in the case of arrival of an armed mob against the city. The governor sent back instructions to Joseph Smith that, as he was lieutenant general of the Nauvoo Legion, it was his duty to protect the city and surrounding country, and issued orders to that effect. Upon the reception of these orders Joseph Smith assembled the people of the city, and laid before them the governor's instructions; he also convened the officers of the Nauvoo Legion for the purpose of conferring in relation to the best mode of defense. He also issued orders to the men to hold themselves in readiness in case of being called upon. On the following day General Joseph Smith, with his staff, the leading officers of the Legion, and some prominent strangers who were in our midst, made a survey of the outside boundaries of the city, which was very extensive, being about five miles up and down the river, and about two and a half back in the center, for the purpose of ascertaining the position of the ground, and the feasibility of defense, and to make all necessary arrangements in case of an attack.

It may be well here to remark that numbers of gentlemen, strangers to us, either came on purpose or were passing through Nauvoo, and upon learning the position of things, expressed their indignation against our enemies, and avowed their readiness to assist us by their counsel or otherwise. It was some of these who assisted us in reconnoitering the city, and finding out its adaptability for defense, and how to protect it best against an armed force. The Legion was called together and drilled, and every means made use of for defense. At the call of the officers, old and young men came forward, both from the city and the country, and mustered to the number of about five thousand.

In the meantime our enemies were not idle in mustering their forces and committing depredations, nor had they been; it was, in fact, their gathering that called ours into existence; their forces continued to accumulate; they assumed a threatening attitude, and assembled in large bodies, armed and equipped for war, and threatened the destruction and extermination of the "Mormons."

An account of their outrages and assemblages was forwarded to Governor Ford almost daily; accompanied by affidavits furnished by eye-witnesses of their proceedings. Persons were also sent out to the Counties around with pacific intentions, to give them an account of the true state of affairs, and to notify them of the feelings and dispositions of the people of Nauvoo, and thus, if possible, quell the excitement, In some of the more distant Counties these men were very successful, and produced a salutary influence upon the minds of many intelligent and well-disposed men. In neighboring Counties, however, where "anti-Mormon" influence prevailed, they produced little effect. At the same time gaurds were stationed around Nauvoo, and picket-gaurds in the distance. At length opposing forces gathered so near that more active measures were taken; reconnoitering parties were sent out, and the city proclaimed under martial law. Things now assumed a belligerent attitude, and persons passing through the city were questioned as to what they knew of the enemy, while passes were in some instances given to avoid difficulty with the guards. Joseph Smith continued to send on messengers to the governor (Philip B. Lewis and other messengers were sent). Samuel James, then residing at La Harpe, carried a message and dispatches to him, and in a day or two after Bishop Edward Hunter and others went again with fresh dispatches, representations, affidavits, and instructions; but as the weather was excessively wet, the rivers swollen, and the bridges washed away in many places, it was with great difficulty that they proceeded on their journeys. As the mobocracy had at last attracted the governor's attention, he started in company with some others from Springfield to the scene of trouble, and missed, I believe, both Brothers James and Hunter on the road, and, of course, did not see their documents. He came to Carthage, and made that place, which was a regular mobocratic den, his head-quarters; as it was the County-seat, however, of Hancock County, that circumstance might, in a measure, justify his staying there.

To avoid the appearance of all hostility on our part, and to fulfill the law in every particular, at the suggestion of Judge Thomas, judge of that judicial district, who had come to Nauvoo at the time, and who stated that we had fulfilled the law, but, in order to satisfy all he would counsel us to go before Esquire Wells, who was not in our church, and have a hearing, we did so, and after a full hearing we were again dismissed.

The governor on the road collected forces, some of whom were respectable, but on his arrival in the neighborhood of the difficulties he received as militia all the companies of the mob forces who united with him. After his arrival at Carthage he sent two gentlemen from there to Nauvoo as a committee to wait upon General Joseph Smith, informing him of the arrival of his excellency, with a request that General Smith would send out a committee to wait upon the governor and represent to him the state of affairs in relation to the difficulties that then existed in the County. We met this committee while we were reconnoitering the city, to find out the best mode of defense as aforesaid. Dr. J. M. Bernhisel and myself were appoitned as a committee by General Smith to wait upon the governor. Previous to going, however, we were furnished with affidavits and documents in relation both to our proceedings and those of the mob; in addition to the general history of the transaction, we took with us a duplicate of those documents which had been forwarded by Bishop Hunter, Brother James, and others. We started from Carthage in company with the aforesaid gentlemen at about 7 o'clock on the evening of the 21st of June, and arrived at Carthage about 11 p. m.

We put up at the same hotel with the governor, kept by a Mr. Hamilton. On our arrival we found the governor in bed, but not so with the other inhabitants. The town was filled with a perfect set of rabble and rowdies, who, under the influence of Bacchus, seemed to be holding a grand saturnalia, whooping, yelling and vociferating as if Bedlam had broken loose.

On our arrival at the hotel, and while supper was preparing, a man came to me, dressed as a soldier, and told me that a man named Daniel Garn had just been taken prisoner, and was about to be committed to jail, and wanted me to go bail for him. Believing this to be a ruse to get me out alone, and that some violence was intended, after consulting with Dr. Bernhisel, I told the man that I was well acquainted with Mr. Garn, that I knew him to be a gentleman, and did not believe that he had transgressed law, and, moreover, that I considered it a very singular time to be holding courts and calling for security, particularly as the town was full of rowdyism.

I informed him that Dr. Bernhisel and myself would, if necessary, go bail for him in the morning, but that we did not feel ourselves safe among such a set at that late hour of the night.

After supper, on retiring to our room, we had to pass through another, which was separated from ours only by a board partition, the beds in each room being placed side by side, with the exception of this fragile partition. On the bed that was in the room which we passed through I discovered a man by the name of Jackson, a desperate character, and a reputed, notorious cut-throat and murderer. I hinted to the doctor that things looked rather suspicious, and looked to see that my arms were in order. The doctor and I occupied one bed. We had scarcely laid down when a knock at the door, accompanied by a voice anounced the approach of Chauncey Higbee, the young lawyer and apostate before referred to.

He addressed himself to the doctor, and stated that the object of his visit was to obtain the release of Daniel Garn; that Garn he believed to be an honest man; that if he had done anything wrong, it was through improper counsel, and that it was a pity that he should be incarcerated, particularly when he could be so easily released; he urged the doctor, as a friend, not to leave so good a man in such an unpleasant situation; he finally prevailed upon the doctor to go and give bail, assuring him that on his giving bail Garn would be immediately dismissed.

During this conversation I did not say a word.

Higbee left the doctor to dress, with the intention of returning and taking him to the court. As soon as Higbee had left, I told the doctor that he had better not go; that I believed this affair was all a ruse to get us separated; that they knew we had documents with us from General Smith to show to the governor; that I believed their object was to get possession of those papers, and, perhaps, when they had separated us, to murder one or both. The doctor, who was actuated by the best of motives in yielding to the assumed solicitude of Higbee, coincided with my views; he then went to Higbee, and told him that he had concluded not to go that night, but that he and I would both wait upon the justice and Mr. Garn in the morning.

That night I lay awake with my pistols under my pillow, waiting for any emergency. Nothing more occurred during the night. In the morning we arose early, and after breakfast sought an interview with the governor, and were told that we could have an audience, I think, at 10 o'clock. In the meantime we called upon Mr. Smith, a justice of the peace, who had Mr. Garn in charge. We represented that we had been called upon the night before by two different parties to go bail for a Mr. Daniel Garn, whom we were informed he had in custody, and that, believing Mr. Garn to be an honest man, we had now come for that purpose, and were prepared to enter into recognizances for his appearance, whereupon Mr. Smith, the magistrate, remarked that, under the present excited state of affairs, he did not think he would be justified in receiving bail from Nauvoo, as it was a matter of doubt whether property would not be rendered valueless there in a few days.

Knowing the party we had to deal with, we were not much surprised at this singular proceeding; we then remarked that both of us possessed property in farms out of Nauvoo in the country, and referred him to the county records. He then stated that such was the nature of the charge against Mr. Garn that he believed he would not be justified in receiving any bail. We were thus confirmed in our opinion that the night's proceedings before, in relation to their desire to have us give bail, was a mere ruse to separate us. We were not permitted to speak with Garn, the real charge against whom was that he was traveling in Carthage or its neighborhood: what the fictitious one was, if I knew, I have since forgotten, as things of this kind were of daily occurrence.

After waiting the governor's pleasure for some time we had an audience; but such an audience!

He was surrounded by some of the vilest and most unprincipled men in creation; some of them had an appearance of respectability, and many of them lacked even that. Wilson, and, I believe, William Law, were there, Foster, Frank and Chauncey Higbee, Mr. Mar, a lawyer from Nauvoo, a mobocratic merchant from Warsaw, the aforesaid Jackson, a number of his associates, among whom was the governor's secretary, in all, some fifteen or twenty persons, most of whom were recreant to virtue, honor, integrity, and every thing that is considered honorable among men. I can well remember the feelings of disgust that I had in seeing the governor surrounded by such an infamous group, and on being introduced to men of so questionable a character; and had I been on private business, I should have turned to depart, and told the governor that if he thought proper to assoicate with such questionable characters, I should beg leave to be excused; but coming as we did on public business, we could not, of course, consult our private feelings.

We then stated to the governor that, in accordance with his request, General Smith had, in response to his call, sent us to him as a committee of conference; that we were acquainted with most of the circumstances that had transpired in and about Nauvoo lately, and were prepared to give him all information; that, moreover, we had in our possession testimony and affidavits confirmatory of what we should say, which had been forwarded to him by General Joseph Smith; that communications had been forwarded to his excellency by Messrs. Hunter, James, and others, some of which had not reached their destination, but of which we had duplicates with us. We then, in brief, related an outline of the difficulties, and the course we had pursued from the commencement of the troubles up to the present, and handing him the documents, respectfully submitted the whole.

During our conversation and explanations with the governor we were frequently rudely and impudently contradicted by the fellows he had around him, and of whom he seemed to take no notice.

He opened and read a number of the documents himself, and as he proceeded he was frequently interrupted by "that's a lie!" "that's a God damned lie!" "that's an infernal falsehood!" "that's a blasted lie!" etc.

These men evidently winced at an exposure of their acts, and thus vulgarly, impudently, and falsely repudiated them. One of their number, Mr. Mar, addressed himself several times to me while in conversation with the governor. I did not notice him until after a frequent repetition of his insolence, when I informed him that "my business at that time was with Governor Ford," whereupon I continued my conversation with his excellency. During the conversation, the governor expressed a desire that Joseph Smith, and all parties concerned in passing or executing the city law in relation to the press, had better come to Carthage; that, however repugnant it might be to our feelings, he thought it would have a tendency to allay public excitement, and prove to the people what we professed, that we wished to be governed by law. We represented to him the course we had taken in relation to this matter, and our willingness to go before another magistrate other than the municipal court; the illegal refusal of our request by the constable; our dismissal by the municipal court, a legally constituted tribunal; our subsequent trial before 'Sqire Wells at the instance of Judge Thomas, the circuit judge, and our dismissal by him; that we had fulfilled the law in every particular; that it was our enemies who were breaking the law, and, having murderous designs, were only making use of this as a pretext to get us into their power. The governor stated that the people viewed it differently, and that, notwithstanding our opinions, he would recommend that the people should be satisfied. We then remarked to him that, should Joseph Smith comply with his request, it would be extremely unsafe, in the present excited state of the country, to come without an armed force; that we had a sufficiency of men, and were competent to defend ourselves, but there might be danger of collision should our forces and those of our enemies be brought into such close proximity. He strenuously advised us not to bring our arms, and *pledged his faith as governor, and the faith of the State, that we should be protected, and that he would guarantee our perfect safety.*

We had at that time about five thousand men under arms, one thousand of whom would have been amply sufficient for our protection.

At the termination of our interview, and previous to our withdrawal, after a long conversation and the perusal of the documents which we had brought, the governor informed us that he would prepare a written communication for General Joseph Smith, which he desired us to wait for. We were kept waiting for this instrument some five or six hours.

About five o'clock in the afternoon we took our departure with not the most pleasant feelings. The associations of the governor, the spirit he manifested to compromise with these scoundrels, the length of time that he had kept us waiting, and his general deportment, together with the infernal spirit that we saw exhibited by those whom he had admitted to his counsels, made the prospect anything but promising.

We returned on horseback, and arrived at Nauvoo, I think, at about eight or nine o'clock at night accompanied by Captain Yates in command of a company of mounted men, who came for the purpose of escorting Joseph Smith and the accused in case of their complying with the governor's request, and going to Carthage. We went directly to Brother Joseph's, when Captain Yates delivered to him the governor's communication. A council was called, consisting of Joseph's brother, Hyrum, Dr. Richards, Dr. Bernhisel, myself, and one or two others.

We then gave a detail of our interview with the governor. Brother Joseph was very much dissatisfied with the governor's letter and with his general deportment, and so were the council, and it became a serious question as to the course we should pursue. Various projects were discussed, but nothing definitely decided upon for some time.

In the interim two gentlemen arrived; one of them, if not both, sons of John C. Calhoun. They had come to Nauvoo, and were very anxious for an interview with Brother Joseph.

These gentlemen detained him for some time; and, as our council was held in Dr. Bernhisel's room in the Mansion House, the doctor lay down; and as it was now between 2 and 3 o'clock in the morning, and I had had no rest on the previous night, I was fatigued, and thinking that Brother Joseph might not return,I left for home and rest.

Being very much fatigued, I slept soundly, and was somewhat surprised in the morning by Mrs. Thompson entering my room about 7 o'clock, and exclaiming in surprise, "What, you here! the brethren have crossed the river some time since."

"What brethren?" I asked.

"Brother Joseph, and Hyrum, and Brother Richards," she answered.

I immediately arose upon learning that they had crossed the river, and did not intend to go to Carthage. I called together a number of persons in whom I had confidence, and had the type, stereotype plates, and most of the valuable things removed from the printing-office, believing that, should the governor and his force come to Nauvoo, the first thing they would do would be to burn the printing-office, for I know that they would be exasperated if Brother Joseph went away. We had talked over these matters the night before, but nothing was decided upon. It was Brother Joseph's opinion that, should we leave for a time, public excitement, which was then so intense, would be allayed; that it would throw on the governor the responsibility of keeping the peace; that in the event of an outrage, the onus would rest upon the governor, who was amply prepared with troops, and could command all the forces of the State to preserve order;

and that the act of his own men would be an overwhelming proof of their seditious designs, not only to the governor, but to the world. He moreover thought that, in the east, where he intended to go, public opinion would be set right in relation to these matters, and its expression would partially influence the west, and that, after the first ebullition, things would assume a shape that would justify his return.

I made arrangements for crossing the river, and Brother Elias Smith and Joseph Cain, who were both employed in the printing-office with me, assisted all that lay in their power together with Brother Brower and several hands in the printing-office. As we could not find out the exact whereabouts of Joseph and the brethren, I crossed the river in a boat furnished by Brother Cyrus H. Wheelock and Alfred Bell; and after the removal of the things out of the printing-office, Joseph Cain brought the account-books to me, that we might make arrangements for their adjustment; and Brother Elias Smith, cousin to Brother Joseph, went to obtain money for the journey, and also to find out and report to me the location of the brethren.

As Cyrus H. Wheelock was an active, enterprising man, and in the event of not finding Brother Joseph I calculated to go to Upper Canada for the time being, and should need a companion, I said to Brother Cyrus H. Wheelock, "Can you go with me ten or fifteen hundred miles?"

He answered, "Yes."

"Can you start in half an hour?"

"Yes."

However, I told him that he had better see his family, who lived over the river, and prepare a couple of horses and the necessary equippage for the journey, and that, if we did not find Brother Joseph before, we would start at nightfall.

A laughable incident occurred on the eve of my departure. After making all the preperations I could, previous to leaving Nauvoo, and having bid adieu to my family, I went to a house adjoining the river, owned by Brother Eddy. There I disguised myself so as not to be known, and so effectually was the transformation that those who had come after me with a boat did not know me. I went down to the boat and sat in it. Brother Bell, thinking it was a stranger, watched my moves for some time very impatiently, and then said to Brother Wheelock, "I wish that old gentleman would go away; he has been pottering around the boat for some time, and I am afraid Elder Taylor will be coming." When he discovered his mistake, he was not a little amused.

I was conducted by Brother Bell to a house that was surrounded by timber on the opposite side of the river. There I spent several hours in a chamber with Brother Joseph Cain, adjusting my accounts; and I made arrangements for the stereotype plates of the Book of Mormon and Doctrine and Covenants, to be forwarded east, thinking to supply the company with subsistence money through the sale of these books in the east.

My horses were reported ready by Brother Wheelock, and funds on hand by Brother Elias Smith. In about half an hour I should have started, when Brother Elias Smith came to me with word that he had found the brethren; that they had concluded to go to Carthage, and wished me to return to Nauvoo and accompany them. I must confess that I felt a good deal disappointed at this news, but I immediately made preparations to go. Escorted by Brother Elias Smith, I and my party went to the neighborhood of Montrose, where we met Brother Joseph, Hyrum, Brother Richards and others. Dr. Bernhisel thinks that W. W. Phelps was not with Joseph and Hyrum in the morning, but that he met him, myself, Joseph and Hyrum, W. Richards and Brother Cahoon, in the afternoon, near Montrose, returning to Nauvoo.

On meeting the brethren I learned that it was not Brother Joseph's desire to return, but that he came back by request of some of the brethren, and that it coincided more with Brother Hyrum's feelings than those of Brother Joseph. In fact, after his return, Brother Hyrum expressed himself as perfectly satisfied with the course taken, and said he felt much more at ease in his mind than he did before. On our return the calculation was to throw ourselve under the immediate protection of the governor, and to trust to his word and faith for our preservation.

A message was, I believe, sent to the governor that night, stating that we should come to Carthage in the morning, the party that came along with us to escort us back, in case we returned to Carthage, having returned.

It would seem from the following remarks of General Ford that there was a design on foot, which was, that if we refused to go to Carthage at the governor's request, there should be an increased force called for by the governor, and that we should be destroyed by them. In accordance with this project, captain Yates returned with his *posse*, accompanied by the constable who held the writ.

The following is the governor's remark in relation to this affair:

"The constable and his escort returned. The constable made no effort to arrest any of them, nor would he or the guard delay their departure one minute beyond the time, to see whether an arrest could be made. Upon their return they reported that they had been informed that the accused had fled, and could not be found I immediately proposed to a council of officers to march into Nauvoo with the small force then under my command, but the officers were of the opinion that it was too small, and many of them insisted upon a further call of the militia. Upon reflection I was of the opinion that the officers were right in the estimate of our force, and the project for immediate action was abandoned.

"I was soon informed, however, of the conduct of the constable and guard, and then I was perfectly satisfied that a most base fraud had been attempted; that, in fact, it was feared that the 'Mormons' would submit, and thereby entitle themselves to the protection of the law. It was very apparent that many of the bustling, active spirits were afraid that there would be no occasion for calling out an overwhelming militia force, for marching it into Nauvoo, for probable mutiny when there, and for the extermination of the 'Mormon' race. It appeared that the constable and the escort were fully in the secret, and acted well their part to promote the conspiracy."*

In the morning Brother Joseph had an interview with the officers of the Legion, with the leading members of the city council, and with the principal men of the city. The officers were instructed to dismiss their men, but to have them in a state of readiness to be called upon in any emergency that might occur.

---

*——Ford's History of Illinois, page 333.

About half past 6 o'clock the members of the city council, the marshal, Brothers Joseph and Hyrum, and a number of others, started for Carthage, on horseback. We were instructed by Brother Joseph Smith not to take any arms, and we consequently left them behind. We called at the house of Brother Fellows on our way out. Brother Fellows lived about four miles from Carthage.

While at Brother Fellow's house, Captain Dunn, accompanied by Mr. Coolie, one of the governor's aid-de-camps, came up from Carthage *en route* for Nauvoo with a requisition from the governor for the State arms. We all returned to Nauvoo with them; the governor's request was complied with, and after taking some refreshments, we all returned to proceed to Carthage. We arrived there late in the night. A great deal of excitement prevailed on and after our arrival. The governor had received into his company all of the companies that had been in the mob; these fellows were riotous and disorderly, hallooing, yelling, and whooping about the streets like Indians, many of them intoxicated; the whole presented a scene of rowdyism and low-bred ruffianism only found among mobocrats and desperadoes, and entirely revolting to the best feelings of humanity. The governor made a speech to them to the effect that he would show Joseph and Hyrum Smith to them in the morning.

About here the companies with the governor were drawn up in line, and General Demming, I think, took Joseph by the arm and Hyrum (Arnold says that Joseph took the governor's arm), and as he passed through between the ranks, the governor leading in front, very politely introduced them as General Joseph Smith and General Hyrum Smith.*

---

*———The *Deseret News* gives the following account of Joseph and Hyrum Smith's passing through the troops in Carthage:

"Carthage, June 25th, 1844.

"Quarter past 9. The governor came and invited Joseph to walk with him through the troops. Joseph solicited a few moment's private conversation with him, which the governor refused.

"While refusing, the governor looked down at his shoes, as though he was ashamed. They then walked through the crowd, with Brigadier General Miner, R. Demming, and Dr. Richards, to General Demming's quarters. The people appeared quiet until a company of Carthage Grays flocked round the doors of General Demming in an uproarious manner, of which notice was sent to the governor. In the meantime the governor had ordered the McDonough troops

All were orderly and courteous except one company of mobocrats—the Carthage Grays—who seemed to find fault on account of too much honor being paid to the "Mormons." There was afterward a row between the companies, and they came pretty near having a fight; the more orderly not feeling disposed to endorse or submit to the rowdyism of the mobocrats. The result was that General Demming, who was very much of a gentleman, ordered the Carthage Grays, a company under the command of Captain Smith, a magistrate in Carthage, and a most violent mobocrat, under arrest. This matter, however, was shortly afterward adjusted, and the difficulty settled between them.

The mayor, aldermen, councilors, as well as the marshal of the city of Nauvoo, together with some persons who had assisted the marshal in removing the press in Nauvoo, appeared before Justice Smith, the foresaid captain and mobocrat, to again answer the charge of destroying the press; but as there was so much excitement, and as the man was an unprincipaled villain before whom we were to have our hearing, we thought it most prudent to give bail, and consequently became security for each other in $500 bonds each, to appear before the County Court at its next session. We had engaged as counsel a lawyer

---

to be drawn up in line, for Joseph and Hyrum to pass in front of them, they having requested that they might have a clear view of the General Smiths. *Joseph had a conversation with the governor for about ten minutes, when he again pledged the faith of the State that he and his friends should be protected from violence.*

"Robinson, the post-master, said, on report of martial law being proclaimed in Nauvoo, he had stopped the mail, and notified the post-master general of the state of things in Hancock County.

"From the general's quarters Joseph and Hyrum went in front of the lines, in a hollow square of a company of Carthage Grays. At seven minutes before ten they arrived in front of the lines, and passed before the whole, Joseph being on the right of General Demming and Hyrum on his left, Elders Richards, Taylor and Phelps following. Joseph and Hyrum were introduced by Governor Ford about twenty times along the line as General Joseph Smith and General Hyrum Smith, the governor walking in front on the left. The Carthage Grays refused to receive them by that introduction, and some of the officers threw up their hats, drew their swords, and said they would introduce themselves to the damned 'Mormons' in a different style. The governor mildly entreated them not to act so rudely, but their excitement increased; the governor, however, succeeded in pacifying them by making a speech, and promising them that they should have 'full satisfaction.' General Smith and party returned to their lodgings at five minutes past ten." *Deseret News, No. 35, Nov. 4, 1857, page 274.*

by the name of Wood, of Burlington, Iowa; and Reed, I think, of Madison, Iowa. After some little discussion the bonds were signed, and we were all dismissed.

Almost immediately after our dismissal, two men—Augustine Spencer and Norton—two worthless fellows, whose words would not have been taken for five cents, and the first of whom had a short time previously been before the mayor in Nauvoo for maltreating a lame brother, made affidavits that Joseph and Hyrum Smith were guilty of treason, and a writ was accordingly issued for their arrest, and the constable Bettesworth, a rough, unprincipled man, wished immediately to hurry them away to prison without any hearing. His rude, uncouth manner in the administration of what he considered the duties of his office made him exceedingly repulsive to us all. But, independent of these acts, the proceedings in this case were altogether illegal. Providing the court was sincere, which it was not, and providing these men's oaths were true, and that Joseph and Hyrum were guilty of treason, still the whole course was illegal.

The magistrate made out a mittimus, and committed them to prison without a hearing, which he had no right legally to do. The statute of Illinois expressly provides that "all men shall have a hearing before a magistrate before they shall be committed to prison;" and Mr. Robert H. Smith, the magistrate, had made out a mittimus committing them to prison contrary to law without such hearing. As I was informed of this illegal proceeding, I went immediately to the governor and informed him of it. Whether he was apprised of it before or not, I do not know; but my opinion is that he was.

I represented to him the characters of the parties who had made oath, the outrageous nature of the charge, the indignity offered to men in the position which they occupied, and declared to him that he knew very well it was a vexatious proceeding, and that the accused were not guilty of any such crime. The governor replied, he was very sorry that the thing had occurred; that he did not believe the charges, but that he thought the best thing to be done was to let the law take its course. I then reminded him that we had come out there at his instance, not to satisfy the law, which we had done before, but the prejudices of the people, in relation to the affair of the press; that at his instance we had given bonds, which we could not by law be required to do to satisfy the people, and that it was asking too much to require gentlemen in their position in life to suffer the degredation of being immured in a jail at the instance of such worthless scoundrels as those who had made this affidavit. The governor replied that it was an unpleasant affair, and looked hard; but that it was a matter over which he had no control, as it belonged to the judiciary; that he, as the executive, could not interfere with their proceedings, and that he had no doubt but that they would immediately be dismissed. I told him that we had looked to him for protection from such insults, and that I thought we had a right to do so from the solemn promises which he had made to me and to Dr. Bernhisel in relation to our coming without guard or arms; that we had relied upon his faith, and had a right to expect him to fulfill his engagements after we had placed ourselves implicitly under his care, and complied with all his requests, although extrajudicial.

He replied that he would detail a guard, if we required it, and see us protected, but that he could not interfere with the judiciary. I expressed my dissatisfaction at the course taken, and told him that, if we were to be subject to mob rule, and to be dragged, contrary to law, into prison at the instance of every infernal scoundrel whose oaths could be bought for a dram of whisky, his protection availed very little, and we had miscalculated his promises.

Seeing there was no prospect of redress from the governor, I returned to the room, and found the constable Bettesworth very urgent to hurry Brothers Joseph and Hyrum to prison, while the brethren were remonstrating with him. At the same time a great rabble was gathered in the streets and around the door, and from the rowdyism manifested I was afraid there was a design to murder the prisoners on the way to jail.

Without conferring with any person, my next feelings were to procure a guard, and, seeing a man habited as a soldier in the room, I went to him and said, "I am afraid there is a design against the lives of the Messrs. Smith; will you go immediately and bring your captain; and, if not convenient, any other captain of a company, and I will pay you well for your trouble?" He said he would, and departed forthwith, and soon returned with his captain, whose name I have forgotten, and introduced him to me. I told him of my fears, and requested him immediately to fetch his company.

He departed forthwith, and arrived at the door with them just at the time when the constable was hurrying the brethren down stairs. A number of the brethren went along, together with one or two strangers; and all of us, safely lodged in prison, remained there during the night.

At the request of Joseph Smith for an interview with the governor, he came the next morning, Thursday, June 26th, at half past 9 o'clock, accompanied by Colonel Geddes, when a lengthy conversation was entered into in relation to the existing difficulties; and after some preliminary remarks, at the governor's request, Brother Joseph gave him a general outline of the state of affairs in relation to our difficulties, the excited state of the country, the tumultuous mobocratic movements of our enemies, the precautionary measures used by himself (Joseph Smith), the acts of the city council, the destruction of the press, and the moves of the mob and ourselves up to that time.

The following report is, I believe, substantially correct:

Governor—"General Smith, I believe you have given me a general outline of the difficulties that have existed in the country in the documents forwarded to me by Dr. Bernhisel and Mr. Taylor; but, unfortunately, there seems to be a great discrepancy between your statements and those of your enemies. It is true that you are substantiated by evidence and affidavit, but for such an extraordinary excitement as that which is now in the country there must be some cause, and I attribute the last outbreak to the destruction of the *Expositor*, and to your refusal to comply with the writ issued by Esquire Morrison. The press in the United States is looked upon as the great bulwark of American freedom, and its destruction in Nauvoo was represented and looked upon as a high-handed measure, and manifests to the people a disposition on your part to suppress the liberty of speech and of the press. This, with your refusal to comply with the requisition of a writ, I conceive to be the principal cause of this difficulty; and you are moreover represented to me as turbulent, and defiant of the laws and institutions of your country."

General Smith—"Governor Ford, you, sir, as governor of this State, are aware of the persecutions that I have endured. You know well that our course has been peaceable and law-abiding for I have furnished this State ever since our settlement here with sufficient evidence of my pacific intentions, and those of the people with whom I am associated, by the endurance of every conceivable indignity and lawless outrage perpetrated upon me and upon this people since our settlement here; and you yourself know that I have kept you well posted in relation to all matters associated with the late difficulties. If you have not got some of my communications, it has not been my fault.

"Agreeably to your orders, I assembled the Nauvoo Legion for the protection of Nauvoo and the surrounding country against an armed band of marauders; and ever since they have been mustered I have almost daily communicated with you in regard to all the leading events that have transpired; and whether in the capacity of mayor of the city, or lieutenant general of the Nauvoo Legion, I have striven, according to the best of my judgement, to preserve the peace and to administer even-handed justice; but my motives are impugned, my acts are misconstructed, and I am grossly and wickedly misrepresented. I suppose I am indepted for my incarceration to the oath of a worthless man, who was arraigned before me and fined for abusing and maltreating his lame, helpless brother. That I should be charged by you, sir, who know better, of acting contrary to law, is to me a matter of surpirse. Was it the 'Mormons' or our enemies who first commenced these difficulties? You know well it was not us; and when this turbulent, outrageous people commenced their insurrectionary movements I made you accquainted with them officially, and asked your advice, and have followed strictly your counsel in every particular. Who ordered out the Nauvoo Legion? I did, under your direction. For what purpose? To suppress the insurrectionary movements. It was at your instance, sir, that I issued a proclamation calling upon the Nauvoo Legion to be in readiness at a moment's warning to guard against the incursions of mobs, and gave an order to Jonathan Dunham, acting major-general, to that effect.

"Am I, then, to be charged with the acts of others? and because lawlessness and mobocracy abound, am I, when carrying out your instructions, to be charged with not abiding law? Why is it that I must be made accountable for other men's acts? If there is trouble in the country, neither I nor my people made it; and all that we have ever done, after much endurance on our part, is to maintain and uphold the Constitution and institutions of our country, and to protect an injured, innocent, and persecuted people against misrule and mob violence.

"Concerning the destruction of the press to which you refer, men may differ somewhat in their opinions about it; but can it be supposed that after all the indignities to which they have been subjected outside, that people could suffer a set of worthless vagabonds to come into their city, and, right under their own eyes and protection, vilify and calumniate not only themselves, but the charecter of their wives and daughters, as was impudently and unblushingly done in that infamous and filthy sheet?

"There is not a city in the United States that would have suffered such an indignity for twenty-four hours. Our whole people were indignant, and loudly called upon our city authorities for a redress of their grievances, which, if not attended to, they themselves would have taken into their own hands, and have summarly punished the audacious wretches as they deserved. The principle of equal rights that has been instilled into our bosoms from our cradles as American citizens forbids us submitting to every foul indignity, and succumbing and pandering to wretches so infamous as these. But, independent of this, the course that we pursued we consider to be strictly legal; for, notwithstanding the result, we were anxious to be governed strictly by law, and therefore we convened the city council; and being desirous in our deliberations to abide by law, we summoned legal counsel to be present on the occasion. Upon investigating the matter, we found that our city charter gave us power to remove all nuisances. Furthermore, after consulting Blackstone upon what might be considered a nuisance, it appeared that that distinguished lawyer, who is considered authority, I believe, in all our courts, states among other things that 'a libelous and filthy press may be considered a nuisance, and abated as such.' Here, then, one of the most eminent English barristers, whose works are considered standard with us, declares that a libelous and filthy press may be considered a nuisance; and our own charter, given us by the Legislature of this State, gives us the power to remove nuisances; and by ordering that press to be abated as a nuisance, we conceived that we were acting strictly in accordance with law. We made that order in our corporate capacity, and the city marshal carried it out. It is possible there may have been some better way, but I must confess that I could not see it.

"In relation to the writ served upon us, we were willing to abide the consequences of our own acts, but were unwilling, in answering a writ of that kind, to submit to illegal exactions, sought to be imposed upon us under the pretense of law, when we knew they were in open violation of it. When that document was presented to me by Mr. Bettesworth, I offered, in the presence of more than twenty persons, to go to any other magistrate, either in our city, in Appanoose, or any other place where we should be safe, but we all refused to put ourselves into the power of a mob. What right had that constable to refuse our request? He had none according to law; for you know, Governor Ford, that the statute law in Illinois is, that the parties served with the writ 'shall go before him who issued it, or some other justice of the peace.' Why, then, should we be dragged to Carthage, where the law does not compel us to go? Does not this look like many others of our persecutions with which you are acquainted? and have we not a right to expect foul play? This very act was a breach of law on his part, an assumption of power that did not belong to him, and an attempt, at least, to deprive us of our legal and constitutional rights and privileges. What could we do, under the circumstances, different from what we did do? We sued for, and obtained a writ of *habeas corpus* from the municipal court, by which we were delivered from the hands of Constable Bettesworth, and brought before and acquitted by the municipal court. After our acquittal, in a conversation with Judge Thomas, although he considered the acts of the party illegal, he advised that, to satisfy the people, we had better go before another magistrate who was not in our Church. In accordance with his advice, we went before Esquire Wells, with whom you are well acquainted; both parties were present, witnesses were called on both sides, the case was fully investigated, and we were again dismissed. And what is this pretended desire to enforce law, and wherefore are these lying, base rumors put into circulation but to seek, through mob influence, under pretense of law, to make us submit to requisitons which are contrary to law and subversive of every principle of justice? And when you, sir, required us to come out here, we came, not because it was legal, but because you required it of us, and we were desirous of showing to you, and to all men, that we shrunk not from the most rigid investigation of our acts. We certainly did expect other treatment than to be immured in a jail at the instance of these men, and I think, from your plighted faith, we had a right so to expect, after disbanding our own forces, and putting ourselves entirely in your hands. And now, after having fulfilled my part, sir, as a man and an American citizen, I call upon you, Governor Ford, to deliver us from this place, and rescue us from this outrage that is sought to be practiced upon us by a set of infamous scoundrels."

Governor Ford.—"But you have placed men under arrest, detained men as prisoners, and given passes to others, some of which I have seen."

John P. Green, City Marshal.—"Perhaps I can explain. Since these difficulties have commenced, you are aware that we have been placed under very peculiar circumstances; our city has been placed under a very rigid police guard; in addition to this, frequent guards have been placed outside the city to prevent any sudden surprise, and those guards have questioned suspected or suspicious persons as to their business. To strangers, in some instances, passes have been given to prevent difficulty in passing those guards; it is some of these passes that you have seen. No person, sir, has been imprisoned without a legal cause in our city."

Governor.—"Why did you not give a more speedy answer to the posse that I sent out?"

General Smith.—"We had matters of importance to consult upon; your letter showed anything but an amiable spirit. We have suffered immensely in Missouri from mobs, in loss of property, imprisonment, and otherwise. It took some time for us to weigh duly these matters; we could not decide upon matters of such importance immediately, and your posse were too hasty in returning; we were consulting for a large people, and vast interests were at stake. We had been outrageously imposed upon, and knew not how far we could trust any one besides, a question necessarily arose, How shall we come? Your request was that we should come unarmed. It became a matter of serious importance to decide how far promises could be trusted, and how far we were safe from mob violence.'

Colonel Geddes.—"It certainly did look, from all I have heard, from the general spirit of violence and mobocracy that here prevails, that it was not safe for you to come unprotected."

Governor Ford.—"I think that sufficient time was not allowed by the posse for you to consult and get ready. They were too hasty; but I suppose they found themselves bound by their orders. I think, too, there is a great deal of truth in what you say, and your reasoning is plausible, but I must beg leave to differ from you in relation to the acts of the City Council. That Council, in my opinion, had no right to act in a legislative capacity and in that of the judiciary. They should have passed a law in relation to the matter, and then the Municipal Court, upon complaint, could have removed it; but for the City Council to take upon themselves the law-making and the execution of the law, is, in my opinion, wrong; besides, these men ought to have had a hearing before their property was destroyed; to destroy it without was an infringement on their rights; besides, it is so contrary to the feelings of American people to interfere with the press. And, furthermore, I cannot but think that it would have been more judicious for you to have gone with Mr. Bettesworth to Carthage, notwithstanding the law did not require it. Concerning your being in jail, I am sorry for that; I wish it had been otherwise. I hope you will soon be released, but I can not interfere."

Joseph Smith.—"Governor Ford, allow me, sir, to bring one thing to your mind that you seem to have overlooked. You state that you think it would have been better for us to have submitted to the requisition of Constable Bettesworth, and to have gone to Carthage. Do you not know, sir, that that writ was served at the instance of an 'anti-Mormon' mob, who had passed resolutions, and published them, to the effect that they would exterminate the 'Mormon' leaders? And are you not informed that Captain Anderson was not only threatened but had a gun fired at his boat by this said mob in Warsaw when coming up to Nauvoo, and that this very thing was made use of as a means to get us into their hands; and we could not, without taking an armed force with us, go there without, according to their published declarations, going into the jaws of death? To have taken a force with us would only have fanned the excitement, and they would have stated that we wanted to use intimidation; therefore, we thought it the most judicious to avail ourselves of the protection of law."

Governor Ford.—"I see, I see."

Joseph Smith.—"Furthermore, in relation to the press, you say that you differ from me in opinion. Be it so; the thing, after all, is only a legal difficulty, and the courts, I should judge, are competent to decide on that matter. If our act was illegal, we are willing to meet it; and although I can not see the distinction that you draw about the acts of the City Council, and what difference it could have made in point of fact, law, or justice between the City Councils acting together or separate, or how much more legal it would have been for the Municipal Court, who were a part of the City Council, to act separately instead of with the councilors, yet, if it is deemed that we did a wrong in destroying that press, we refuse not to pay for it; we are desirous to fulfill the law in every particular, and are responsible for our acts. You say that the parties ought to have had a hearing. Had it been a civil suit, this of course, would have been proper; but there was a flagrant violation of every principle of right—a nuisance; and it was abated on the same principle that any nuisance, stench, or putrefied carcass would have been removed. Our first step, therefore, was to stop the foul, noisome, filthy sheet, and then the next in our opinion would have been to have prosecuted the man for a breach of public decency. And, furthermore, again let me say, Governor Ford, I shall look to you for our protection. I believe you are talking of going to Nauvoo; if you go, sir, I wish to go along. I refuse not to answer any law, but I do not consider myself safe here."

Governor.—"I am in hopes that you will be acquitted, and if I go I will certainly take you along. I do not, however, apprehend danger. I think you are perfectly safe either here or anywhere else. I can not, however, interfere with the law. I am placed in peculiar circumstances, and seem to be blamed by all parties."

Joseph Smith.—"Governor Ford, I ask nothing but what is legal; I have a right to expect protection, at least from you; for, independent of law, you have pledged your faith and that of the State for my protection, and I wish to go to Nauvoo."

Governor.—"And you shall have protection, General Smith. I did not make this promise without consulting my officers, who all pledged their honor to its fulfillment. I do not know that I shall go to-morrow to Nauvoo, but if I do I will take you along."

At a quarter past ten o'clock the governor left.

At about half past twelve o'clock, Mr. Reed, one of Joseph's counsel, came in, apparently much elated; he stated that, upon an examination of the law, he found that the magistrate had transcended his jurisdiction, and that, having committed them without an examination, his jurisdiction ended; that he had him upon a pinhook; that he ought to have examined them before he committed them, and that, having violated the law in this particular, he had no farther power over them; for, once committed, they were out of his jurisdiction, as the power of the magistrate extended no farther than their committal, and that now they could not be brought out except at the regular session of the Circuit Court, or by a writ of *habeas corpus*; but that if Justice Smith would consent to go to Nauvoo for trial, he would compromise matters with him, and overlook this matter.

Mr. Reed farther stated that the "anti-Mormons," or mob, had concocted a scheme to get out a writ from Missouri, with a demand upon Governor Ford for the arrest of Joseph Smith, and his conveyance to Missouri, and that a man by the name of Wilson had returned from Missouri the night before the burning of the press for this purpose.

At half past two o'clock Constable Bettesworth came to the jail with a man named Simpson, professing to have some order, but he would not send up his name, and the guard would not let him pass. Dr. Bernhisel and Brother Wasson went to inform the governor and council of this. At about twenty minutes to three Dr. Bernhisel returned, and stated that he thought the governor was doing all he could. At about ten minutes to three Hyrum Kimball appeared with news from Nauvoo.

Soon after Constable Bettesworth came with an order from Esquire Smith to convey the prisoners to the court-house for trial. He was informed that the process was illegal, that they had been placed there contrary to law, and that they refused to come unless by legal process. I was informed that Justice Smith (who was also captain of the Carthage Grays) went to the governor and informed him of the matter, and that the governor replied, "You have your forces, and of course can use them." The constable certainly did return, accompanied by a guard of armed men, and by force, and under protest, hurried the prisoners to the court.

About four o'clock the case was called by Captain Robert F. Smith, J. P. The counsel for the prisoners called for subpœnas to bring witnesses. At twenty-five minutes past four he took a copy of the order to bring the prisoners from jail to trial, and afterwards he took names of witnesses.

Counsel present for the State; Higbee, Skinner, Sharp, Emmons, and Morrison. Twenty-five minutes to five the writ was returned as served, June 25th.

Many remarks were made at the court that I paid but little attention to, as I considered the whole thing illegal and a complete burlesque. Wood objected to the proceedings in toto, in consequence of its illegality, showing that the prisoners were not only illegally committed, but that, being once committed, the magistrate had no farther power over them; but as it was the same magistrate before whom he was pleading who imprisoned them contrary to law, and the same who, as captain, forced them from jail, his arguments availed but little. He then urged that the prisoners be remanded until witnesses could be had, and applied for a continuance for that purpose. Skinner suggested until twelve o'clock next day. Wood again demanded until witnesses could be obtained; that the court meet at a specified time, and that, if witnesses were not present, again adjourn, without calling the prisoners. After various remarks from Reed, Skinner, and others, the court stated that the writ was served yesterday, and that it will give until to-morrow at twelve m. to get witnesses.

We then returned to jail. Immediately after our return Dr. Bernhisel went to the governor, and obtained from him an order for us to occupy a large open room containing a bedstead. I rather think that the same room had been appropriated to the use of debtors; at any rate, there was free access to the jailer's house, and no bars or locks except such as might be on the outside door of the jail. The jailer, Mr. George W. Steghall, and his wife, manifested a disposition to make us as comfortable as they could; we ate at their table, which was well provided, and, of course, paid for it.

I do not remember the names of all who were with us that night and the next morning in jail, for several went and came; among those that we considered stationary were Stephen Markham, John S. Fullmer, Captain Dan Jones, Dr. Willard Richards, and myself. Dr. Bernhisel says that he was there from Wednesday in the afternoon until eleven o'clock next day. We were, however, visited by numerous friends, among whom were Uncle John Smith, Hyrum Kimball, Cyrus H. Wheelock, besides lawyers, as counsel. There was also a great variety of conversation, which was rather desultory than otherwise, and referred to circumstances that had transpired, our former and present grievances, the spirit of the troops around us, and the disposition of the governor; the devising for legal and other plans for deliverance, the nature of testimony required; the gathering of proper witnesses, and a variety of other topics, including our religious hopes, etc.

During one of these conversations Dr. Richards remarked: "Brother Joseph, if it is necessary that you die in this matter, and if they will take me in your stead, I will suffer for you." At another time, when conversing about deliverance, I said, "Brother Joseph, if you will permit it, and say the word, I will have you out of this prison in five hours, if the jail has to come down to do it." My idea was to go to Nauvoo, and collect a force sufficient, as I considered the whole affair a legal farce, and a flagrant outrage upon our liberty and rights. Brother Joseph refused.

Elder Cyrus H. Wheelock came in to see us, and when he was about leaving drew a small pistol, a six-shooter, from his pocket, remarking at the same time, "Would any of you like to have this?" Brother Joseph immediatly replied, "Yes, give it to me;" whereupon he took the pistol, and put it in his pantaloons pocket. The pistol was a six-shooting revolver, of Allen's patent; it belonged to me, and was one that I furnished to Brother Wheelock when he talked of going with me to the East, previous to our coming to Carthage. I have it now in my possession. Brother Wheelock went out on some errand, and was not suffered to return. The report of the governor having gone to Nauvoo without taking the prisoners along with him caused very unpleasent feelings, as we were apprised that we were left to the tender mercies of the Carthage Grays, a company strictly mobocratic, and whom we knew to be our most deadly enemies; and their captain, Esquire Smith, was a most unprincipled villain. Besides this, all the mob forces, comprising the governor's troops, were dismissed, with the exception of one or two companies, which the governor took with him to Nauvoo. The great part of the mob was liberated, the remainder was our guard.

We looked upon it not only as a breach of faith on the part of the governor, but also as an indication of a desire to insult us, if nothing more, by leaving us in the proximity of such men. The prevention of Wheelock's return was among the first of their hostile movements.

Colonel Markham then went out, and he was also prevented from returning. He was very angry at this, but the mob paid no attention to him; they drove him out of town at the point of the bayonet, and threatened to shoot him if he returned. He went, I am informed, to Nauvoo for the purpose of raising a company of men for our protection. Brother Fullmer went to Nauvoo after witnesses: it is my opinion that Brother Wheelock did also.

Some time after dinner we sent for some wine. It has been reported by some that this was taken as a sacrament. It was no such thing; our spirits were generally dull and heavy, and it was sent for to revive us. I think it was Captain Jones who went after it, but they would not suffer him to return. believe we all drank of the wine, and gave some to one or two of the prison guards. We all of us felt unusually dull and languid, with a remarkable depression of spirits. In consonance with those feelings I sang a song, that had lately been introduced into Nauvoo, entitled, "A poor wayfaring man of grief," etc.

The song is pathetic, and the tune quite plaintive, and was very much in accordance with our feelings at the time, for our spirits were all depressed, dull and gloomy, and surcharged with indefinite ominous forebodings. After a lapse of some time, Brother Hyrum requested me again to sing that song. I replied, "Brother Hyrum, I do not feel like singing;" when he remarked, "Oh, never mind; commence singing, and you will get the spirit of it." At his request I did so. Soon afterwards I was sitting at one of the front windows of the jail, when I saw a number of men, with painted faces, coming around the corner of the jail, and aiming towards the stairs. The other brethren had seen the same, for, as I went to the door, I found Brother Hyrum Smith and Dr. Richards already leaning against it. They both pressed against the door with their shoulders to prevent its being opened, as the lock and latch were comparatively useless. While in this position, the mob, who had come up stairs, and tried to open the door, probably thought it was locked, and fired a ball through the keyhole; at this Dr. Richards and Brother Hyrum leaped back from the door, with their faces towards it; almost instantly another ball passed through the panel of the door, and struck Brother Hyrum on the left side of the nose, entering his face and head. At the same instant, another ball from the outside entered his back, passing through his body and striking his watch. The ball came from the back, through the jail window, opposite the door, and must, from its range, have been fired from the Carthage Grays, who were placed there ostensibly for our protection, as the balls from the fire-arms, shot close by the jail, would have entered the ceiling, we being in the second story, and there never was a time after that when Hyrum could have received the latter wound. Immediately, when the balls struck him, he fell flat on his back, crying as he fell, "I am a dead man!" He never moved afterwards.

INTRODUCTORY.

I shall never forget the deep feeling of sympathy and regard manifested in the countenance of Brother Joseph as he drew nigh to Hyrum, and, leaning over him, exclaimed, "Oh! my poor, dear brother Hyrum!" He, however, instantly arose, and with a firm, quick step, and a determined expression of countenance, approached the door, and pulling the six-shooter left by Brother Wheelock from his pocket, opened the door slightly, and snapped the pistol six successive times; only three of the barrels, however, were discharged. I afterwards understood that two or three were wounded by these discharges, two of whom, I am informed, died. I had in my hands a large, strong hickory stick, brought there by Brother Markham, and left by him, which I had seized as soon as I saw the mob approach; and while Brother Joseph was firing the pistol, I stood close behind him. As soon as he had discharged it he stepped back, and I immediately took his place next to the door, while he occupied the one I had done while he was shooting. Brother Richards, at this time, had a knotty walking-stick in his hands belonging to me, and stood next to Brother Joseph, a little farther from the door, in an oblique direction, apparently to avoid the rake of the fire from the door. The firing of Brother Joseph made our assailants pause for a moment; very soon after, however, they pushed the door some distance open, and protruded and discharged their guns into the room, when I parried them off with my stick, giving another direction to the balls.

It certainly was a terrible scene: streams of fire as thick as my arm passed by me as these men fired, and, unarmed as we were, it looked like certain death. I remember feeling as though my time had come, but I do not know when, in any critical position, I was more calm, unruffled, energetic, and acted with more promptness and decision. It certainly was far from pleasant to be so near the muzzles of these fire-arms as they belched forth their liquid flames and deadly balls. While I was engaged in parrying the guns, Brother Joseph said, "That's right, Brother Taylor, parry them off as well as you can." These were the last words I ever heard him speak on earth.

Every moment the crowd at the door became more dense, as they were unquestionably pressed on by those in the rear ascending the stairs, until the whole entrance at the door was literally crowded with muskets and rifles, which, with the swearing, shouting, and demoniacal expressions of those outside the door and on the stairs, and the firing of the guns, mingled with their horrid oaths and excrations, made it look like Pandemonium let loose, and was, indeed, a fit representation of the horrid deed in which they were engaged.

After parrying the guns for some time, which now protruded thicker and farther into the room, and seeing no hope of escape or protection there, as we were now unarmed, it occurred to me that we might have some friends outside, and that there might be some chance fo escape in that direction, but here there seemed to be none. As I expected them every moment to rush into the room—nothing but extreme cowardice having thus far kept them out—as the tumult and pressure increased, without any other hope, I made a spring for the window which was right in front of the jail door, where the mob was standing, and also exposed to the fire of the Carthage Grays, who were stationed some ten or twelve rods off. The weather was hot, we all of us had our coats off, and the window was raised to admit air. As I reached the window, and was on the point of leaping out, I was struck by a ball from the door about midway of my thigh, which struck the bone, and flattened out almost to the size of a quarter of a dollar, and then passed on through the fleshy part to within about half an inch of the outside. I think some prominent nerve must have been severed or injured, for, as soon as the ball struck me, I fell like a bird when shot, or an ox when struck by a butcher, and lost entirely and instantaneously all power of action or locomotion. I fell upon the window-sill, and cried out, "I am shot!" Not possessing any power to move, I felt myself falling outside of the window, but immediately I fell inside, from some, at that time, unknown cause. When I struck the floor my animation seemed restored, as I have seen it sometimes in squirrels and birds after being shot. As soon as I felt the power of motion I crawled under the bed, which was in a corner of the room, not far from the window where I received my wound. While on my way and under the bed I was wounded in three other places; one ball entered a little below the left knee, and never was extracted; another entered the forepart of my left arm, a little above the wrist, and, passing down by the joint, lodged in the fleshy part of my hand, about midway, a little above the upper joint of my little finger; another struck me on the fleshy part of my left hip, and tore away the flesh as large as my hand, dashing the mangled fragments of flesh and blood against the wall.

My wounds were painful, and the sensation produced was as though a ball had passed through and down the whole length of my leg. I very well remember my reflections at the time. I had a very painful idea of becoming lame and decrepid, and being an object of pity, and I felt as though I would rather die than be placed in such circumstances.

It would seem that immediately after my attempt to leap out of the window, Joseph also did the same thing, of which circumstance I have no knowledge only from information. The first thing that I noticed was a cry that he had leaped out of the window. A cessation of firing followed, the mob rushed down stairs, and Dr. Richards went to the window. Immediately afterwards I saw the doctor going towards the jail door, and as there was an iron door at the head of the stairs adjoning our door which led into the cells for criminals, it struck me that the doctor was going in there, and I said to him, "Stop, doctor, and take me along." He proceeded to the door and opened it, and then returned and dragged me along to a small cell prepared for criminals.

Brother Richards was very much troubled, and exclaimed, "Oh! Brother Taylor, is it possible that they have killed both Brother Hyrum and Joseph? it cannot surely be, and yet I saw them shoot them;" and, elevating his hands two or three times, he exclaimed, "Oh Lord, my God, spare Thy servants!" He then said, "Brother Taylor, this is a terrible event;" and he dragged me farther into the cell, saying, "I am sorry I can not do better for you;" and, taking an old, filthy mattress, he covered me with it, and said, "That may hide you, and you may yet live to tell the tale, but I expect they will kill me in a few moments." While lying in this position I suffered the most excruciating pain.

Soon afterwards Dr. Richards came to me, informed me that the mob had precipitately fled, and at the same time confirmed my worst fears that Joseph was assuredly dead. I felt a dull, lonely, sickening sensation at the news. When I reflected that our noble chieftain, the prophet of the living God, had fallen, and that I had seen his brother in the cold embrace of death, it seemed as though there was a void or vacuum in the great field of human existence to me, and a dark gloomy chasm in the kingdom, and that we were left alone. Oh, how lonely was that feeling! How cold, barren and desolate! In the midst of difficulties he was always the first in motion; in critical positions his counsel was always sought. As our prophet he approached our God, and obtained for us His will; but now our prophet, our counselor, our general, our leader was gone, and amid the fiery ordeal that we then had to pass through, we were left alone without his aid, and as our future guide for things spiritual or temporal, and for all things pertaining to this world or the next, he had spoken for the last time on earth!

These reflections and a thousand others flashed upon my mind. I thought, Why must the good perish, and the virtuous be destroyed? Why must God's nobility, the salt of the earth, the most exalted of the human family, and the most perfect types of all excellence, fall victims to the cruel, fiendish hate of incarnate devils?

The poignancy of my grief, I presume, however, was somewhat allayed by the extreme suffering that I endured from my wounds.

Soon afterwards I was taken to the head of the stairs and laid there, where I had a full view of our beloved and now murdered brother Hyrum. There he lay as I had left him; he had not moved a limb; he lay placid and calm, a monument of greatness even in death; but his noble spirit had left its tenement, and was gone to dwell in regions more congenial to its exalted nature. Poor Hyrum! he was a great and good man, and my soul was cemented to his. If ever there was an exemplary, honest, and virtuous man, an embodiment of all that is noble in the human form, Hyrum Smith was its representative.

While I lay there a number of persons came around, among whom was a physician. The doctor, on seeing a ball lodged in my left hand, took a penknife from his pocket and made an incision in it for the purpose of extracting the ball therefrom, and having obtained a pair of carpenter's compasses, made use of them to draw or pry out the ball, alternately using the penknife and compasses. After sawing for some time with a dull penknife, and prying and pulling with the compasses, he ultimately succeeded in extracting the ball, which weighed about half an ounce. Some time afterwards he remarked to a friend of mine that I had "nerves like the devil," to stand what I did in its extraction. I really thought I had need of nerves to stand such surgical butchery, and that, whatever my nerves may be, his practice was devilish.

This company wished to remove me to Mr. Hamilton's hotel, the place where we had staid previous to our incarceration in jail. I told them, however, that I did not wish to go; I did not consider it safe. They protested that it was, and that I was safe with them; that it was a perfect outrage for men to be used as we had been; that they were my friends; that it was for my good they were counseling me, and that I could be better taken care of there than here.

I replied, "I don't know you. Who am I among? I am surrounded by assassins and murderers; witness your deeds! Don't talk to me of kindness or comfort; look at your murdered victims. Look at me! I want none of your counsel nor comfort. There may be some safety here; I can be assured of none anywhere," etc.

They G— d—— their souls to hell, made the most solemn asseverations, and swore by God and the devil, and everything else that they could think of, that they would stand by me to death and protect me. In half an hour every one of them had fled from the town.

Soon after a coroner's jury were assembled in the room over the body of Hyrum. Among the jurors was Captain Smith, of the "Carthage Grays," who had assisted in the murder, and the same justice before whom we had been tried. I learned of Francis Higbee as being in the neighborhood. On hearing his name mentioned, I immediately arose and said, "Captain Smith, you are a justice of the peace; I have heard his name mentioned; I want to swear my life against him." I was informed that word was immediately sent to him to leave the place, which he did.

Brother Richards was busy during this time attending to the coroner's inquest, and to the removal of the bodies, and making arrangements for their removal from Carthage to Nauvoo.

When he had a little leisure, he again came to me, and at his suggestion I was removed to Hamilton's tavern. I felt that he was the only friend, the only person, that I could rely upon in that town. It was with difficulty that sufficient persons could be found to carry me to the tavern; for immediately after the murder a great fear fell upon all the people, and men, women, and children fled with great precipitation, leaving nothing nor anybody in the town but two or three women and children and one or two sick persons.

It was with great difficulty that Brother Richards prevailed upon Mr. Hamilton, hotel-keeper, and his family, to stay; they would not until Brother Richards had given a solemn promise that he would see them protected, and hence I was looked upon as a hostage. Under these circumstances, notwithstanding, I believe they were hostile to the "Mormons," and were glad that the murder had taken place, though they did not actually participate in it; and, feeling that I should be a protection to them, they staid.

The whole community knew that a dreadful outrage had been perpetrated by those villains, and fearing lest the citizens of Nauvoo, as they possessed the power, might have a disposition to visit them with a terrible vengeance, they fled in the wildest confusion. And, indeed, it was with very great difficulty that the citizens of Nauvoo could be restrained. A horrid, barbarous murder had been committed, the most solemn pledge violated, and that, too, while the victims were, contrary to the requirements of the law, putting themselves into the hands of the governor to pacify a popular excitement. This outrage was enhanced by the reflection that our people were able to protect themselves against not only all the mob, but against three times their number and that of the governor's troops put together. They were also exasperated by the speech of the governor in town.

The whole events were so faithless, so dastardly, so mean, cowardly, and contemptible, without one extenuating circumstance, that it would not have been surprising if the citizens of Nauvoo had arisen *en masse*, and blotted the wretches out of existence. The citizens of Carthage knew they would have done so under such circumstances, and, judging us by themselves, they were all panic-stricken, and fled. Colonel Markham, too, after his expulsion from Carthage, had gone home, related the circumstances of his ejectment, and was using his influence to get a company to go out. Fearing that when the people heard that their prophet and patriarch had been murdered under the above circumstances they might act rashly, and knowing that, if they once got roused, like a mighty avalanche they would lay the country waste before them and take a terrible vengeance—as none of the Twelve were in Nauvoo, and no one, perhaps, with sufficient influence to control the people, Dr. Richards, after consulting me, wrote the following note, fearing that my family might be seriously affected by the news. I told him to insert that I was slightly wounded.

*Willard Richards' Note from Carthage Jail to Nauvoo.**

"Carthage jail, 8 o'clock 5 min. p. m., June 27th, 1844.

"Joseph and Hyrum are dead. Taylor wounded, not very badly. I am well. Our guard was forced, as we believe, by a band of Missourians from 100 to 200. The job was done in an instant, and the party fled towards Nauvoo instantly. This is as I believe it. The citizens here are afraid of the 'Mormons' attacking them; I promise them no. W. RICHARDS.

"N. B.—The citizens promise us protection; alarm guns have been fired.

"JOHN TAYLOR."

I remember signing my name as quickly as possible, lest the tremor of my hand should be noticed, and the fears of my family excited.

A messenger was dispatched immediately with the note, but he was intercepted by the governor, who, on hearing a cannon fired at Carthage, which was to be the signal for the murder, immediately fled with his company, and fearing that the citizens of Nauvoo, when apprised of the horrible outrage, would immediately rise and pursue, he turned back the messenger, who was George D. Grant. A second one was sent, who was treated similarly; and not until a third attempt could news be got to Nauvoo.

---

*——"Deseret News," No. 38, Nov. 25, 1857, p. 297.

Samuel H. Smith, brother to Joseph and Hyrum, was the first brother I saw after the outrage; I am not sure whether he took the news or not; he lived at the time in Plymouth, Hancock County, and was on his way to Carthage to see his brothers, when he was met by some of the troops, or rather mob, that had been dismissed by the governor, and who were on their way home. On learning that he was Joseph Smith's brother they sought to kill him, but he escaped, and fled into the woods, where he was chased for a length of time by them; but, after severe fatigue, and much danger and excitement, he succeeded in escaping, and came to Carthage. He was on horseback when he arrived, and was not only very much tired with the fatigue and excitement of the chase, but was also very much distressed in feelings on account of the death of his brothers. These things produced a fever, which laid the foundation for his death, which took place on the 30th of July. Thus another of the brothers fell a victim, although not directly, but indirectly to this infernal mob.

I lay from about five o'clock until two next morning without having my wounds dressed, as there was scarcely any help of any kind in Carthage, and Brother Richards was busy with the dead bodies, preparing them for removal. My wife Leonora started early the next day, having had some little trouble in getting a company or a physician to come with her; after considerable difficulty she succeeded in getting an escort, and Dr. Samuel Bennet came along with her. Soon after my father and mother arrived from Oquakie, near which place they had a farm at that time, and hearing of the trouble, hastened along.

General Demming, Brigadier General of the Hancock County Militia, was very much of a gentleman, and showed me every courtesy, and Colonel Jones also was very solicitous about my welfare.

I was called upon by several gentlemen of Quincy and other places, among whom was Judge Ralston, as well as by our own people, and a medical man extracted a ball from my left thigh that was giving me much pain; it lay about half an inch deep, and my thigh was considerably swollen. The doctor asked me if I would be tied during the operation; I told him no; that I could endure the cutting associated with the operation as well without, and I did so; indeed, so great was the pain I endured that the cutting was rather a relief than otherwise.

A very laughable incident occured at the time; my wife Leonora went into an adjoining room to pray for me, that I might be sustained during the operation. While on her knees at prayer, a Mrs. Bedell, an old lady of the Methodist association, entered, and, patting Mrs. Taylor on her back with her hand, said, "There's a good lady, pray for God to forgive your sins; pray that you may be converted, and the Lord may have mercy on your soul."

The scene was so ludicrous that Mrs. Taylor knew not wether to laugh or be angry. Mrs. Taylor informed me that Mr. Hamilton, the father of the Hamilton who kept the house, rejoiced at the murder, and said in company that "it was done up in the best possible style, and showed good generalship;" and she farther believed that the other branches of the family sanctioned it. These were the associates of the old lady referred to, and yet she could talk of conversion and saving souls in the midst of blood and murder: such is man and such consistency.

The ball being extracted was the one that first struck me, which I before referred to; it entered on the outside of my left thigh, about five inches from my knee, and, passing rather obliquely towards my body, had, it would seem, struck the bone, for it was flattened out nearly as thin and large as a quarter of a dollar.

The governor passed on, staying at Carthage only a few minutes, and he did not stop until he got fifty miles from Nauvoo. There had been various opinions about the complicity of the governor in the murder, some supposing that he knew all about it, and assisted or winked at its execution. It is somewhat difficult to form a correct opinion; from the facts presented it is very certain that things looked more than suspicious against him.

In the first place, he positively knew that we had broken no law.

Secondly. He knew that the mob had not only passed inflammatory resolutions, threatening extermination to the

"Mormons," but that they had acutually assembled armed mobs and commenced hostilities against us.

Thirdly. He took those very mobs that had been arrayed against us, and enrolled them as his troops, thus legalizing their acts.

Fourthly. He disbanded the Nauvoo Legion, which had never violated law, and disarmed them, and had about his person in the shape of militia known mobocrats and violators of the law.

Fifthly. He requested us to come to Carthage without arms, promising protection, and then refused to interfere in delivering us from prison, although Joseph and Hyrum were put there contrary to law.

Sixthly. Although he refused to interfere in our behalf, yet, when Captain Smith went to him and informed him that the persons refused to come out, he told him that he had a command and knew what to do, thus sanctioning the use of force in the violation of law when opposed to us, whereas he would not for us interpose his executive authority to free us from being incarcerated contrary to law, although he was fully informed of all the facts of the case, as we kept him posted in the affairs all the time.

Seventhly. He left the prisoners in Carthage jail contrary to his plighted faith.

Eighthly. Before he went he dismissed all the troops that could be relied upon, as well as many of the mob, and left us in charge of the "Carthage Grays," a company that he knew were mobocratic, our most bitter enemies, and who had passed resolutions to exterminate us, and who had been placed under guard by General Demming only the day before.

Ninthly. He was informed of the intended murder, both before he left and while on the road, by several different parties.

Tenthly. When the cannon was fiered in Carthage, signifying that the deed was done, he immediately took up his line of march and fled. How did he know that this signal portended their death if he was not in the secret? It may be said some of the party told him. How could he believe what the party said about the gun signal if he could not believe the testimony of several individuals who told him in positive terms about the contemplated murder?

He has, I believe, stated that he left the "Carthage Grays" there because he considered that, as their town was contigous to ours, and as the responsibility of our safety rested solely upon them, they would not dare suffer any indignity to befall us. This very admission shows that he did really expect danger; and then he knew that these people had published to the world that they would exterminate us, and his leaving us in their hands and taking of their responsibilities was like leaving a lamb in charge of a wolf, and trusting to its humanity and honor for its safe-keeping.

It is said, again that he would not have gone to Nauvoo, and thus placed himself in the hands of the "Mormons," if he had anticipated any such event, as he would be exposed to their wrath. To this it may be answered that the "Mormons" did not know their signals, while he did; and they were also known in Warsaw, as well as in other places; and as soon as the gun was fired, a merchant of Warsaw jumped upon his horse and rode directly to Quincy, and reported "Joseph and Hyrum killed, and those who were with them in jail." He reported farther that "they were attempting to break jail, and were all killed by the guard." This was their story; it was anticipated to kill all, and the gun was to be the signal that the deed was accomplished. This was known in Warsaw. The governor also knew it and fled; and he could really be in no danger in Nauvoo, for the "Mormons" did not know it, and he had plenty of time to escape, which he did.

It is said that he made all his officers promise solemnly that they would help him to protect the Smiths; this may or may not be. At any rate, some of these same officers helped to murder them.

The strongest argument in the governor's favor, and one that would bear more weight with us than all the rest put together, would be that he could not believe them capable of such atrocity; and, thinking that their talk and threatenings were a mere ebullition of feeling, a kind of braggadocio, and that there was enough of good moral feeling to control the more violent passions, he trusted to their faith. There is, indeed, a degree of plausibility about this, but when we put it in juxtaposition to the amount of evidence that he was in possession of it weighs very little. He had nothing to inspire confidence in them, and everything to make him mistrust them. Besides, why his broken faith? why his disregard of what was told him by several parties? Again, if he knew not the plan, how did he understand the signal? Why so oblivious to everything pertaining to the "Mormon" interest, and so alive and interested about the mobocrats? At any rate, be this as it may, he stands responsible for their blood, and it is dripping on his garments. If it had not been for his promises of protection, they would have protected themselves; it was plighted faith that led them to the slaughter; and, to make the best of it, it was a breach of that faith and a non-fulfillment of that promise, after repeated warning, that led to their death.

Having said so much, I must leave the governor with my readers and with his God. Justice, I conceive, demanded this much, and truth could not be told with less; as I have said before, my opinion is that the governor would not have planned this murder, but he had not sufficient energy to resist popular opinion, even if that opinion led to blood and death.

It was rumored that a strong political party, numbering in its ranks many of the prominent men of the nation, were engaged in a plot for the overthrow of Joseph Smith, and that the governor was of this party, and Sharp, Williams, Captain Smith, and others, were his accomplices, but whether this was the case or not I do not know. It is very certain that a strong political feeling existed against Joseph Smith, and I have reason to believe that his letters to Henry Clay were made use of by political parties opposed to Mr. Clay, and were the means of that statesman's defeat. Yet, if such a combination as the one referred to existed, I am not apprised of it.

While I lay at Carthage, previous to Mrs. Taylor's arrival, a pretty good sort of a man, who was lame of a leg, waited upon me, and sat up at night with me; afterwards Mrs. Taylor, mother and others waited upon me.

Many friends called upon me, among whom were Richard Ballantyne, Elizabeth Taylor, several of the Perkins family, and a number of the brethren from Macedonia and La Harpe. Besides these, many strangers from Quincy, some of whom expressed indignant feelings against the mob and sympathy for myself. Brother Alexander Williams called upon me, who suspected that they had some designs in keeping me there, and stated that he had, at a given point in some woods, fifty men, and that if I would say the word he would raise other fifty, and fetch me out of there. I thanked him, but told him I thought there was no need. However, it would seem that I was in some danger; for Colonel Jones, before referred to, when absent from me, left two loaded pistols on the table in case of an attack, and some time afterwards, when I had recovered and was publishing the affair, a lawyer, Mr. Backman, stated that he had prevented a man by the name of Jackson, before referred to, from ascending the stairs, who was coming with a design to murder me, and that now he was sorry he had not let him do the deed.

There were others also, of whom I heard, that said I ought to be killed, and they would do it, but that it was too damned cowardly to shoot a wounded man; and thus, by the chivalry of murderers, I was prevented from being a second time mutilated or killed. Many of the mob, came around and treated me with apparent respect, and the officers and people generally looked upon me as a hostage, and feared that my removal would be the signal for the rising of the "Mormons."

I do not remember the time that I staid at Carthage, but I think three or four days after the murder, when Brother Marks with a carriage, Brother James Allred with a wagon, Dr. Ells, and a number of others on horseback, came for the purpose of taking me to Nauvoo. I was very weak at the time, occasioned by the loss of blood and the great discharge of my wounds, so when my wife asked me if I could talk I could barely whisper no. Quite a discussion arose as to the propriety of my removal, the physicians and people of Carthage protesting that it would be my death, while my friends were anxious for my removal if possible.

I suppose the former were actuated by the above-named desire to keep me. Colonel Jones was, I believe, sincere; he had acted as a friend all the time, and he told Mrs. Taylor she ought to persuade me not to go, for he did not believe I had strength enough to reach Nauvoo. It was finally agreed, however, that I should go; but as it was thought that I could not stand riding in a wagon or carriage, they prepared a litter for me; I was carried down stairs and put upon it. A number of men assisted to carry me, some of whom had been engaged in the mob. As soon as I got down stairs, I felt much better and strengthened, so that I could talk; I suppose the effect of the fresh air.

When we had got near the outside of the town I remembered some woods that we had to go through, and telling a person near to call for Dr. Ells, who was riding a very good horse, I said, "Doctor, I perceive that the people are getting fatigued with carrying me; a number of "Mormons" live about two or three miles from here, near our route; will you ride to their settlement as quick as possible, and have them come and meet us?" He started off on a gallop immediately. My object in this was to obtain protection in case of an attack, rather than to obtain help to carry me.

Very soon after the men from Carthage made one excuse after another, until they had all left, and I felt glad to get rid of them. I found that the tramping of those carrying me produced violent pain, and a sleigh was produced and attached to the hind end of Brother James Allred's wagon, a bed placed upon it, and I propped up on the bed. Mrs. Taylor rode with me, applying ice and ice-water to my wounds. As the sleigh was dragged over the grass on the prairie, which was quite tall, it moved very easily and gave me very little pain.

When I got within five or six miles of Nauvoo the brethren commenced to meet me from the city, and they increased in number as we drew nearer, until there was a very large company of people of all ages and both sexes, principally, however, men.

For some time there had been almost incessant rain, so that in many low places on the prairie it was from one to three feet deep in water, and at such places the brethren whom we met took hold of the sleigh, lifted it, and carried it over the water; and when we arrived in the neighborhood of the city, where the roads were excessively muddy and bad, the brethren tore down the fences, and we passed through the fields.

Never shall I forget the difference of feeling that I experienced between the place that I had left and the one that I had now arrived at. I had left a lot of reckless, bloodthirsty murderers, and had come to the City of the Saints, the people of the living God; friends of truth and righteousness, thousands of whom stood there with warm, true hearts to offer their friendship and services, and to welcome my return. It is true it was a painful scene, and brought sorrowful rememberance to mind, but to me it caused a thrill of joy to find myself once more in the bosom of my friends, and to meet with the cordial welcome of true, honest hearts. What was very remarkable, I found myself very much better after my arrival at Nauvoo than I was when I started on my journey, although I had traveled eighteen miles.

The next day, as some change was wanting, I told Mrs. Taylor that if she could send to Dr. Richards, he had my purse and watch, and they would find money in my purse.

Previous to the doctor leaving Carthage, I told him that he had better take my purse and watch, for I was afraid the people would steal them. The doctor had taken my pantaloons' pocket, and put the watch in it with the purse, cut off the pocket, and tied a string around the top; it was in this position when brought home. My family, however, were not a little startled to find that my watch had been struck with a ball. I sent for my vest, and, upon examination, it was found that there was a cut as if with a knife, in the vest pocket which had contained my watch. In the pocket the fragments of the glass were found literally ground to powder. It then occurred to me that a ball had stuck me at the time I felt myself falling out of the window, and that it was this force that threw me inside. I had often remarked to Mrs. Taylor the singular fact of finding myself inside the room, when I felt a moment before after being shot, that I was falling out, and I never could account for it until then; but here the thing was fully elucidated, and was rendered plain to my mind. I was indeed falling out, when some villain aimed at my heart. The ball struck my watch, and forced me back; if I had fallen out I should assuredly have been killed, if not by the fall, by those around, and this ball, intended to dispatch me, was turned by an overruling Providence into a messenger of mercy, and saved my life. I shall never forget the feelings of gratitude that I then experienced towards my heavenly Father; the whole scene was vividly portrayed before me, and my heart melted before the Lord. I felt that the Lord had preserved me by a special act of mercy; that my time had not yet come, and that I had still a work to perform upon the earth.

(Signed),   JOHN TAYLOR.

THE MORMONS.

A DISCOURSE DELIVERED BEFORE THE HISTORICAL SOCIETY OF PENNSYLVANIA, MARCH 26, 1850.

BY THOMAS L. KANE.

A few years ago, ascending the Upper Mississippi in the autumn, when its waters were low, I was compelled to travel by land past the regions of the rapids. My road lay through the half-breed track, a fine section of Iowa, which the unsettled state of its land titles had appropriated as a sanctuary for coiners, horse-thieves, and other outlaws. I had left my steamer at Keokuk, at the foot of the Lower Fall, to hire a carriage, and to contend for some fragments of a dirty meal with the swarming flies, the only scavengers of the locality.

From this place to where the deep water of the river returns, my eye wearied to see everywhere sordid, vagabond and idle settlers; and a country marred, without being improved, by their careless hands. I was descending the last hill-side upon my journey, when a landscape in delightful contrast broke upon my view. Half encircled by a bend of the river, a beautiful city lay glittering in the fresh morning sun; its bright new dwellings, set in cool, green gardens, ranging up around a stately dome-shaped hill, which was crowned by a noble marble edifice, whose high tapering spire was radiant with white and gold. The city appeared to cover several miles; and beyond it, in the back-ground, there rolled off a fair country, chequered by the careful lines of fruitful husbandry. The unmistakable marks of industry, enterprise, and educated wealth everywhere, made the scene one of singular and most striking beauty. It was a natural impulse to visit this inviting region. I procured a skiff, and, rowing across the river, landed at the chief wharf of the city. No one met me there. I looked and saw no one. I could hear no one move; though the quiet everywhere was such that I heard the flies buzz, and the watter-ripples break against the shadows of the beach. I walked through the solitary streets. The town lay as in a dream, under some deadening spell of loneliness, from which I almost feared to wake it; for plainly it had not slept long. There was no grass growing up in the paved ways; rains had not entirely washed away the prints of dusty footsteps.

Yet I went about unchecked. I went into empty workshops, rope-walks and smithies. The spinner's wheel was idle, the carpenter had gone from his work-bench and shavings, his unfinished sash and casing. Fresh bark was in the tanner's vat, and the fresh-chopped lightwood stood piled against the baker's oven. The blacksmith's shop was cold, but his coal heap and ladling pool and crooked water-horn were all there, as if he had just gone off for a holiday. No work-people anywhere looked to know my errand.

If I went into the gardens, clinking the wicket-latch loudly after me, to pull the marigolds, heartsease, and lady-slippers, and draw a drink with the water-sodden well-bucket and its noisy chain: or, knocking off with my stick the tall, heavy-headed dahlias and sun-flowers, hunted over the beds for cucumbers and love-apples—no one called out to me from any opened window, or dog sprang forward to bark an alarm.

I could have supposed the people hidden in the houses, but the doors were unfastened; and when, at last, I timidly entered them, I found dead ashes white upon the hearths, and had to tread a-tiptoe, as if walking down the aisle of a country church, to avoid arousing irreverent echoes from the naked floors. On the outskirts of the town was the city grave-yard but there was no record of plague there, nor did it anywise differ much from other Protestant American cemeteries. Some of the mounds were not long sodded; some of the stones were newly set, their dates recent, and their black inscriptions glossy in the mason's hardly-dried lettering ink. Beyond the grave-yard, out in the fields, I saw, in one spot hard by where the fruited boughs of a young orchard had been roughly torn down, the still smouldering embers of a barbecue fire, that had been constructed of rails from the fencing around it. It was the latest sign of life there. Fields upon fields of heavy-headed yellow grain lay rotting ungathered upon the ground No one was at hand to take in their rich harvest.

As far as the eye could reach, they stretched away—they, sleeping too, in the hazy air of autumn. Only two portions of the city seemed to suggest the import of this mysterious solitude. On the eastern suburb, the houses looking out upon the country showed, by their splintered wood-work and walls battered to the foundation, that they had lately been the marks of a destructive cannonade. And in and around the splendid Temple, which had been the chief object of my admiration, armed men were barracked, surrounded by their stacks of musketry, and pieces of heavy ordnance. These challenged me to render an account of myself, and why I had the temerity to cross the water without a written permit from a leader of their band.

Though these men were generally more or less under the influence of ardent spirits, after I had explained myself as a passing stranger, they seemed anxious to gain my good opinion. They told the story of the dead city; that had been a notable manufacturing and commercial mart, sheltering over 20,000 persons; that they had waged war with its inhabitants for several years, and had finally been successful only a few days before my visit, in an action fought in front of the ruined suburb; after which, they had driven them forth at the point of the sword. The defense, they said, had been obstinate, but gave way on the third day's bombardment. They boasted greatly of their prowess, especially in this battle, as they called it; but I discovered they were not of one mind as to certain of the exploits that had distinguished it, one of which, as I remember, was, that they had slain a father and his son, a boy of fifteen, not long residents of the fated city, whom they admitted to have borne a character without reproach.

They also conducted me inside the massive sculptured walls of the curious temple, in which they said the banished inhabitants were accustomed to celebrate the mystic rites of an unhallowed worship. They particularly pointed out to me certain features of the building, which, having been the peculiar objects of a former superstitious regard, they had, as a matter of duty, sedulously defiled and defaced. The reputed sites of certain shrines they had thus particularly noticed; and various sheltered chambers, in one of which was a deep well, constructed, they believed, with a dreadful design. Beside these they led me to see a large and deep-chiselled marble vase or basin, supported upon twelve oxen, also of marble, and of the size of life, of which they told some romantic stories. They said the deluded persons, most of whom were emigrants from a great distance, believed their Deity countenanced their reception here of a baptism of regeneration, as proxies for whomsoever they held in warm affection in the countries from which they had come. That here parents "went into the water" for their lost children, children for their parents, widows for their spouses, and young persons for their lovers; that thus the great vase came to be for them associated with all dear and distant memories, and was therefore the object, of all others in the building, to which they attached the greatest degree of idolatrous affection. On this account, the victors had so diligently desecrated it, as to render the apartment in which it was contained too noisome to abide in.

They permitted me also to ascend into the steeple, to see where it had been lightning-struck the Sabbath before; and to look out, east and south, on wasted farms like those I had seen near the city, extending till they were lost in the distance. Here, in the face of pure day, close to the scar of the divine wrath left by the thunderbolt, were fragments of food, cruses of liquor, and broken drinking vessels, with a bass drum and a steamboat signal bell, of which I afterwards learned the use with pain.

It was after nightfall, when I was ready to cross the river on my return. The wind had freshened since the sunset, and, the water beating roughly into my little boat, I headed higher up the stream than the point I had left in the morning, and landed where a faint glimmering light invited me to steer.

Here, among the dock and rushes, sheltered only by the darkness, without roof beween them and the sky, I came upon a crowd of several hundred human creatures, whom my movements roused from uneasy slumber upon the ground.

Passing these on my way to the light, I found it came from a tallow candle, in a paper funnel shade, such as is used by street venders of apples and peanuts, and which, flaring and guttering away in the bleak air of the water, shone flickeringly on the emaciated features of a man in the last stage of a bilious, remittent fever. They had done their best for him. Over his head was something like a tent, made of a sheet or two, and he rested on a but partially ripped open old straw mattress, with a hair sofa cushion under his head for a pillow. His gaping jaw and glazing eye told how short a time he would monopolize these luxuries; though a seemingly bewildered and excited person, who might have been his wife seemed to find hope in occasionally forcing him to swallow awkwardly measured sips of the tepid river water, from a burned and battered bitter-smelling tin coffee-pot. Those who knew better had furnished the apothecary he needed; a toothless old bald-head, whose manner had the repulsive dullness of a man familiar with death scenes. He, so long as I remained, mumbled in his patient's ear a monotonous and melancholy prayer, between the pauses of which I heard the hiccup and sobbing of two little girls who were sitting upon a piece of drift-wood outside.

Dreadful, indeed, was the suffering of these forsaken beings; bowed and cramped by cold and sunburn, alternating as each weary day and night dragged on, they were, almost all of them, the crippled victims of disease. They were there because they had no homes, nor hospital, nor poor-house, nor friends to offer them any. They could not satisfy the feeble cravings of their sick; they had not bread to quiet the fractious hunger-cries of their children. Mothers and babes, daughters and grand-parents, all of them alike, were bivouacked in tatters, wanting even covering to comfort those whom the sick shivers of fever were searching to the marrow.

These were Mormons, famishing in Lee County, Iowa, in the fourth week of the month of September, in the year of our Lord 1846. The city—it was Nauvoo, Illinois. The Mormons were the owners of that city, and the smiling country around. And those who had stopped their ploughs, who had silenced their hammers, their axes, their shuttles, and their workshop wheels; those who had put out their fires' who had eaten their food, spoiled their orchards, and trampled under foot their thousands of acres of unharvested bread; these were the keepers of their dwellings, the carousers in their temple, whose drunken riot insulted the ears of their dying.

I think it was as I turned from the wretched night watch, of which I have spoken, that I first listened to the sounds of revel of a party of the guard within the city. Above the distant hum of the voices of many, occasionally rose distinct the loud oath-tainted exclamation, and the falsely intonated scrap of vulgar song; but lest this requiem should go unheeded, every now and then, when their boisterous orgies strove to attain a sort of ecstatic climax, a cruel spirit of insulting frolic carried some of them up into a high belfry of the temple steeple, and there, with the wicked childishness of inebriates, they whooped and shrieked, and beat the drum that I had seen, and rang in charivaric unison their loud-tongued steam-boat bell.

They were, all told, not more than six hundred and forty persons who were thus lying on the river flats. But the Mormons in Nauvoo and its dependencies had been numbered the year before at over twenty thousand. Where were they? They had last been seen, carrying in mournful trains, their sick and wounded, halt and blind, to disappear behind the western horizon, pursuing the phantom of another home. Hardly anything else was known of them: and people asked with curiosity, "What had been their fate—what their fortunes?"

I purpose making these questions the subject of my Lecture. Since the expulsion of the Mormons, to the present date, I have been intimately conversant with the details of their history. But I shall invite your attention most particulary to an account of what happened to them during their first year in the wilderness; because at this time more than any other, being lost to public view, they were the subjects of fable and misconception. Happily it was during this period I myself moved with them; and earned at a dear price, as some among you are aware, my right to speak with authority of them and their character, their trials, achievements, and intentions.

The party encountered by me at the river shore were the last of the Mormons that left the city. They had all of them engaged the year before, that they would vacate their homes, and seek some other place of refuge. It had been the condition of a truce between them and their assailants; and as an earnest of their good faith, the chief elders, and some others of obnoxious standing, with their families, were to set out for the west in the spring of 1846. It had been stipulated in return that the rest of the Mormons might remain behind in the peaceful enjoyment of their Illinois abode, until their leaders, with their exploring party, could with all diligence select for them a new place of settlement beyond the Rocky Mountains, in California, or elsewhere, and until they had opportunity to dispose, to the best advantage, of the property which they were then to leave.

Some renewed symptoms of hostile feeling had, however, determined the pioneer party to begin their work before spring. It was, of course, anticipated that this would be a perilous service; but it was regarded as a matter of self-denying duty. The ardor and emulation of many, particularly the young and the devout, were stimulated by the difficulties it involved; and the ranks of the party were therefore filled up with volunteers from among the most effective and responsible members of the sect. They began their march in mid winter; and by the beginning of February, nearly all of them were on the road, many of their wagons having crossed the Mississippi on the ice.

Under the most favoring circumstances, an expedition of this sort, undertaken at such a season of the year, could scarcely fail to be disastous.* But the pioneer company had to set out in haste, and were very imperfectly supplied with necessaries. The cold was intense. They moved in the teeth of keen-edged north-west winds, such as sweep down the Iowa peninsula from the ice-bound regions of the timber-shaded Slave Lake and Lake of the Woods: on the bald prairie there, nothing above the dead grass breaks their free course over the hard rolled hills. Even along the the scattered water courses, where they broke the thick ice to give their cattle drink, the annual autumn fires had left little wood of value. The party, therefore, often wanted for good camp fires, the first

---

* —— Nine children were born the first night the women camped out. "Sugar Creek," February 5.

luxury of all travelers; but to men insufficiently furnished with tents, and other appliances of shelter, almost an essential to life. After days of fatigue, their nights were often passed in restless efforts to save themselves from freezing. Their stock of food also proved inadequate; and as their systems became impoverished, their suffering from cold increased.

Sickened with catarrhal affections, manacled by the dreadfully acute fetters of rheumatisms, some contrived for awhile to get over the shortening day's march, and drag along some others. But the sign of an impaired circulation soon began to show itself in the liability of all to be dreadfully frost-bitten. The hardiest and strongest became helplessly crippled. About the same time the strength of their beasts of draught began to fail. The small supply of provender they could carry with them had given out. The winter-bleached prairie straw proved devoid of nourishment; and they could only keep them from starving by seeking for the *browse*, as it is called, or green bark and tender buds and branches of the cottonwood, and other stinted growths of the hollows.

To return to Nauvoo was apparently the only escape; but this would have been to give occasion for fresh mistrust, and so to bring new trouble to those they had left there behind them. They resolved at least to hold their ground, and to advance as they might, were it only limping through the deep snows a few small miles a day. They found a sort of comfort in comparing themselves to the exiles of Siberia;* and sought cheerfulness in earnest prayings for the spring—longed for as morning by the tossing sick.

The spring came at last. It overtook them in the Sac and Fox country, still on the naked prairie, not yet half way over the trail they were following between the Mississippi and Missouri rivers. But it brought its own share of troubles with it. The months with which it opened proved nearly as trying as the worst of winter.

The snow, and sleet, and rain which fell, as it appeared to them, without intermission, made the road over the rich prai-

---

* ——"One of the company having a copy of Mdme Cottin's "Elizabeth," it was so sought after that some read it from the wagons by moonlight. They were materially sustained, too, by the practice of psalmody, "keeping up the songs of Zion, and passing along Doxologies from front to rear when the breath froze on their eyelashes."

ric soil as impassable as one vast bog of heavy black mud. Sometimes they would fasten the horses and oxen of four or five wagons to one, and attempt to get ahead in this way, taking turns; but at the close of a hard day of toil for themselves and their cattle, they would find themselves a quarter or half a mile from the place they left in the morning. The heavy rains raised all the water courses: the most trifling streams were impassible. Wood fit for bridging was often not to be had, and in such cases the only resource was to halt for the freshets to subside; a matter, in the case of the headwaters of the Chariton for instance, of over three weeks' delay.

These were dreary waitings upon Providence. The most spirited and steady murmured most at their forced inactivity. And even the women, whose heroic spirits had been proof against the lowest thermometric fall, confessed their tempers fluctuated with the ceaseless variations of the barometer. They complained, too, that the health of their children suffered more. It was the fact, that the open winds of March and April brought with them more mortal sickness than the sharpest freezing weather.

The frequent burials made the hardiest sicken. On the soldier's march it is matter of dicipline, that after the rattle of musketry over his comrade's grave he shall tramp it to the music of some careless tune in a lively quick step. But, in the Mormon camp, the companion who lay ill and gave up the ghost in view of all, all saw he lay stretched a corpse, and all attend to his last resting-place. It was a sorrow then, too, of itself, to simple-hearted people, the deficient pomps of their imperfect style of funeral. The general hopefulness of human —including Mormon— nature, was well illustrated by the fact, that the most provident were found unfurnished with undertaker's articles; so that bereaved affection was driven to melancholy makeshifts.

The best expedient generally was to cut down a log of some eight or nine feet long, and slitting it longitudinally, strip off its dark bark in two half cylinders. These, placed around the body of the deceased, and bound firmly together with withes made of the alburnum, formed a rough sort of tubular cofin, which surviving relatives and friends, with a little show of black crape, could follow with its enclosure to the hole, or bit of ditch dug to receive it in the wet ground of the prairie. They grieved to lower it down so poorly clad, and in such an unheeded grave. It was hard—was it right?—thus hurriedly to plunge it in one of the undistinguishable waves of the great land sea, and leave it behind them there, under the cold north rain, abandoned, to be forgotten. They had no tombstones, nor could they find a rock to pile the monumental cairn. So when they had filled up the grave, and over it prayed a miserere prayer, and tried to sing a hopeful psalm, their last office was to seek out landmarks, or call in the surveyor to help them determine the bearings of valley bends, headlands, or forks and angles of constant streams, by which its position should in the future be remembered and recognized. The name of the beloved person, his age, the date of his death, and these marks were all registered with care. His party was then ready to move on. Such graves mark all the line of the first years of Mormon travel— dispiriting milestones to failing stragglers in the rear.

It is an error to estimate largely the number of Mormons dead of starvation, strictly speaking. Want developed disease, and made them sink under fatigue, and maladies that would otherwise have proved trifling. But only those died of it outright who fell in out-of-the-way places that the hand of brotherhood could not reach. Among the rest no such thing as plenty was known, while any went an hungered. If but a part of a group was supplied with provision, the only result was that the whole went on the half or quarter ration, according to the sufficiency that there was among them; and this so ungrudgingly and contentedly, that, till some crisis of trial to their strength, they were themselves unaware that their health was sinking, and their vital force impaired.

Hale young men gave up their own provided food and shelter to the old and helpless, and walked their way back to parts of the frontier States, chiefly Missouri and Iowa, where they were not recognized, and hired themselves out for wages, to purchase more. Others were sent there to exchange for meal and flour, or wheat and corn, the table and bed furniture, and other last resources of personal property which a few had still retained.

In a kindred spirit of fraternal forecast, others laid out great farms in the wilds, and planted in them the grain saved for their own bread, that there might be harvests for those who should follow them. Two of these in the Sac and Fox country, and beyond it, (Garden Grove and Mount Pisgah), included within their fences about two miles of land apiece, carefully planted in grain, with a hamlet of comfortable log cabins in the neighborhood of each.

Through all this the pioneers found redeeming comfort in the thought that their own suffering was the price of immunity to their friends at home. But the arrival of spring proved this a delusion. Before the warm weather had made the earth dry enough for easy travel, messengers came in from Nauvoo to overtake the party, with fear, exaggerated tales of outrage, and to urge the chief men to hurry back to the city, that they might give counsel and assistance there. The enemy had only waited till the emigrants were supposed to be gone on their road too far to return to interfere with them, and then renewed their aggressions.

The Mormons outside Nauvoo were indeed hard pressed; but inside the city they maintained themselves very well for two or three months longer.

Strange to say, the chief part of this respite was devoted to completing the structure of their quaintly-devised but beautiful temple. Since the dispersion of Jewry, probably, history affords us no parallel to the attachment of the Mormons for this edifice. Every architectural element, every most fantastic emblem it embodied, was associated, for them, with some cherished feature of their religion. Its erection had been enjoined upon them as a most sacred duty. They were proud of the honor it conferred upon their city, when it grew up in its splendor to become the chief object of the admiration of strangers upon the Upper Mississippi. Besides they had built it as a labor of love; they could count up to half a million the value of their tithings and free-will offerings laid upon it. Hardly a Mormon woman had not given up to it some trinket or pin-money; the poorest Mormon man had at least served the tenth part of his year on its walls; and the coarsest artizan could turn to it with something of the ennobling attachment of an artist for his fair creation. Therefore, though their enemies drove on them ruthlessly, they succeeded in parrying the last sword-thrust, till they had completed even the gilding of the angel and trumpet on the summit of its lofty spire. As a closing work, they placed on the entablature of the front, like a baptismal mark on the forehead,

THE HOUSE OF THE LORD.
Built by the Church of Jesus Christ of Latter-day Saints.
HOLINESS TO THE LORD!

Then at high noon, under the bright sunshine of May, the next only after its completion, they consecrated it to divine service. There was a carefully studied ceremonial for the occasion. It was said the high Elders of the sect traveled furtively from the camp of Israel in the wilderness, and, throwing off ingenious disguises, appeared in their own robes of holy office, to give it splendor.

For that one day the temple stood resplendent in all its typical glories of sun, moon, and stars, and other abounding figured and lettered signs, hieroglyphs, and symbols: but that day only! The sacred rites of consecration ended, the work of removing the *sacro sancta* proceeded with the rapidity of magic. It went on through the night; and when the morning of the next day dawned, all the ornaments and furniture, everything that could provoke a sneer had been carried off; and except some fixtures that would not bear removal, the building was dismantled to the bear walls.

It was this day saw the departure of the last Elders, and the largest band that moved in one company together. The people of Iowa have told me, that from morning to night they passed westward like an endless procession. They did not seem greatly out of heart, they said, but at the top of every hill, before they disappeared, were to be seen looking back, like banished Moors, on their abandoned homes, and the far-seen temple and its glittering spire.

After this consecration, which was construed to indicate an insincerity on the part of the Mormons as to their stipulated departure, or at least a hope of return, their foes set upon them with renewed bitterness. As many fled as were at all prepared; but by the very fact of their so decreasing the already diminished forces of the city's defenders, they encouraged the enemy to greater boldness. It soon became apparent that nothing short of an immediate emigration could save the remnant.

From this time onward the energies of those already on the road were engrossed by the duty of providing for the fugitives who came crowding in after them. At a last general meeting of the sect in Nauvoo, there had been passed an unanimous resolve that they would sustain one another, whatever their circumstances, upon the march; and this, though made in view of no such appalling exigency, they now with one accord set themselves together to carry out.

Here begins the touching period of Mormon history; on which, but that it is for me a hackneyed subject, I should be glad to dwell, were it only for the proof it has afforded of the strictly material value to communities of an active common faith, and its happy illustrations of the power of the spirit of Christian fraternity to relieve the deepest of human suffering. I may assume that it has already fully claimed the public sympathy.

Delayed thus by their own wants, and by their exertions to provide for the wants of others, it was not till the month of June that the advance of the emigrant companies arrived at the Missouri.

This body, I remember, I had to join there, ascending the river for the purpose from Fort Leavenworth, which was at that time our frontier post. The Fort was the interesting rendezvous of the Army of the West, and the head quarters of its gallant chief, Stephen F. Kearney, whose guest and friend I account it my honor to have been. Many as were the reports daily received at the garrison from all portions of the Indian Territory, it was a significant fact, how little authentic intelligence was to be obtained concerning the Mormons. Even the regions in which they were to be sought after, was a question not attempted to be designated with accuracy, except by what are very well called in the West "Mormon stories," none of which bore any sifting. One of these averred, that a party of Mormons, in spangled crimson robes of office, headed by one in black velvet and silver, had been teaching a Jewish pow-wow to the medicine men of the Sauks and Foxes. Another averred that they were going about in buffalo robe short frocks, imitative of the costume of Saint John, preaching baptism and the instance of the kingdom of heaven among the Iowas. To believe one report, ammunition and whisky had been received by Indian braves at the hands of an Elder with a flowing white beard, who spoke Indian, he alleged, because he had the gift of tongues—this, as far north as the country of the Yankton Sioux. According to another yet, which professed to be derived officially from at least one Indian sub-agent, the Mormons had distributed the scarlet uniforms of H. B. M's servants among the Pottawatamies, and had carried into their country twelve pieces of brass cannon, which were counted by a traveler as they were rafted across the East Fork of Grand river, one of the northern tributaries of the Missouri. The narrators of these pleasant stories were at variance as to the position of the Mormons by a couple of hundred leagues; but they harmonized in the warning, that to seek certain of the leading camps, would be to meet the treatment of a spy.

Almost at the outset of my journey from Fort Leavenworth, while yet upon the edge of the Indian border, I had the good fortune to fall in with a couple of thin-necked sallow persons, in patchwork pantaloons, conducting northward wagon loads of Indian corn, which they had obtained, according to their own account, in barter from a squatter for some silver spoons, and a feather bed. Their character was disclosed by their eager request of a bite from my wallet; in default of which, after a somewhat superfluous scriptural grace, they made an imperfect lunch before me off the softer of their corn ears eating the grains as horses do from the cob. I took their advice to follow up the Missouri; somewhere not far from which, in the Pottowatamic country, they were sure I would encounter one of their advancing companies.

I had bad weather on the road. Excessive heats, varied only by repeated drenching thunder squalls, knocked up my horse, my only traveling companion, and otherwise added to the ordinary hardships of a kind of life, to which I was as yet little accustomed. I suffered a sense of discomfort, therefore, amounting to physicial nostalgia, and was, in fact, wearied to death of the staring silence of the prairie, before I came upon the objects of my search.

They were collected a little distance above the Pottawatamie Agency. The hills of the "High Prairie" crowding in upon the river at this point, and overhanging it, appear of an unusual and commanding elevation. They are called the Council Bluffs; a name given them with another meaning, but well illustrated by the picturesque congress of their high and mighty summits. To the south of them, a rich alluvial flat of considerable width follows down the Missouri, some eight miles, to where it is lost from view at a turn, which forms the site of an Indian town of Point aux Poules. Across the river from this spot the hills recur again, but are skirted at their base by as much low ground as suffices for a landing.

This landing, and the large flat or bottom on the east side of the river, were crowded with covered carts and wagons; and each one of the Council Bluff hills opposite, was crowned with its own great camp, gay with bright white canvas, and alive, with busy stir of swarming occupants. In the clear blue morning air the smoke steamed up from more than a thousand cooking fires. Countless roads and by-paths checkered all manner of geometric figures on the hill sides. Herd boys were dozing upon the slopes; sheep and horses, cows and oxen, were feeding around them, and other herds in the luxuriant meadow of the then swollen river. From a single point I counted four thousand head of cattle in view at one time. As I approached it seemed to me the children there were to prove still more numerous. Along a little creek I had to cross were women in greater force than blanchisseuses upon the Seine, washing and rinsing all manner of white muslins, red flannels, and particolored calicoes, and hanging them to bleach upon a greater area of grass and bushes than we can display in all our Washington Square.

Hastening by these, I saluted a group of noisy boys, whose purely vernacular cries had for me an invincible home-savoring attraction. It was one of them, a bright-faced lad, who, hurrying on his jacket and trowsers, fresh from bathing in the creek, first assured me I was at my right destination. He was a mere child; but he told me of his own accord where I had best go and seek my welcome, and took my horse's bridle to help me pass a morass, the bridge over which he alleged to be unsafe.

INTRODUCTORY. 79

There was something joyous for me in my rambles about this vast body of pilgrims. I could range the wild country wherever I listed, under safeguard of their moving host. Not only in the main camps was all stir and life, but in every direction, it seemed to me I could follow "Mormon roads," and find them beaten hard, and even dusty, by the tread and wear of the cattle and vehicles of emigrants laboring over them. By day, I would overtake and pass, one after another, what amounted to an army train of them; and at night, if I encamped at the places where the timber and running water were found together, I was almost sure to be within call of some camp or other, or at least within sight of its watch-fires. Wherever I was compelled to tarry, I was certain to find shelter and hospitality, scant, indeed, but never stinted, and always honest and kind. After a recent unavoidable association with the border inhabitants of Western Missouri and Iowa, the vile scum which our own society, to apply the words of an admirable gentleman and eminent divine,* "like the great ocean washes upon its frontier shores," I can scarcely describe the gratification I felt in associating again with persons who were almost all of Eastern American origin—persons of refined and cleanly habits and decent language, and observing their peculiar and interesting mode of life; while every day seemed to bring with it its own special incident, fruitful in the illustration of habits and character.

It was during the period of which I have just spoken, that the Mormon battalion of 520 men was recruited and marched for the Pacific Coast.

At the commencement of the Mexican war, the President considered it desirable to march a body of reliable infantry to Caliornia at as early a period as practicable, and the known hardihood and habits of dicipline of the Mormons, were supposed peculiarly to fit them for this service. As California was supposed also to be their ultimate destination, the long march might cost them less than other citizens. They were accordingly invited to furnish a battalion of volunteers early in the month of July.

The call could hardly have been more inconveniently timed. The young, and those who could best have been

---
*———Reverend Dr. Morton, of Philadelphia.

spared, were then away from the main body, either with pioneer companies in the van, or, their faith unannounced, seeking work and food about the north-western settlements, to support them till the return of the season for commencing emigration. The force was therefore to be recruited from among the fathers of families, and others whose presence it was most desirable to retain.

There were some, too, who could not view the invitation without jealousy. They had twice been persuaded by (State) government authorities in Illinois and Missouri, to give up their arms on some special appeals to their patriotic confidence, and had then been left to the malice of their enemies. And now they were asked, in the midst of an Indian country, to surrender over five hundred of their best men for a war-march of thousands of miles to California, without the hope of return till after the conquest of that country. Could they view such a proposition with favor?

But the feeling of the country triumphed. The Union had never wronged them. "You shall have your battalion at once, if it has to be a class of Elders," said one, himself a ruling Elder. A central "mass meeting" for council, some harangues at the more remotely scattered camps, an American flag brought out from the store-house of things rescued, and hoisted to a tree mast—and, in three days, the force was reported mustered, organized, and ready to march.

There was no sentimental affectation at their leave-taking. The afternoon before was appropriated to a farewell ball; and a more merry dancing rout I have never seen, though the company went without refreshments, and their ball-room was of the most primitive. It was the custom, whenever the larger camps rested for a few days together, to make great arbors, or boweries, as they called them, of poles, and brush, and wattling, as places of shelter for their meetings of devotion or conference. In one of these, where the ground had been trodden firm and hard by the worshipers of the popular Father Taylor's precinct, was gathered now the mirth and beauty of the Mormon Israel.

If anything told the Mormons had been bred to other lives, it was the appearance of the women, as they assembled here. Before their flight, they had sold their watches and trinkets as the most available resource for raising ready money; and, hence, like their partners, who wore waistcoats cut with useless watch pockets, they, although their ears were pierced and bore the loop-marks of rejected pendants, were without ear-rings, finger-rings, chains, or brooches. Except such ornaments, however, they lacked nothing most becoming the attire of decorous maidens. The neatly darned white stocking, and clean, bright petticoat, the artistically clear-starched collar and chemisette, the something faded, only because too well washed, lawn or gingham gown, that fitted modishly to the waist of the pretty wearer—these, if any of them spoke of poverty, spoke of a poverty that had known its better days.

With the rest, attended the Elders of the Church within call, including nearly all the chiefs of the High Council, with their wives and children. They, the gravest and most trouble-worn, seemed the most anxious of any to be the first to throw off the burden of heavy thoughts. Their leading off the dancing in a great double cotillion, was the signal bade the festivity commence. To the canto of debonair violins, the cheer of horns, the jingle of sleigh bells, and the jovial snoring of the tambourine, they did dance! None of your minuets or other mortuary processions of gentles in etiquette, tight shoes, and pinching gloves, but the spirited and scientific displays of our venerated and merry grandparents, who were not above following the fiddle to the Fox-chase Inn, or Gardens of Gray's Ferry. French fours, Copenhagen jigs, Virginia reels, and the like forgotten figures executed with the spirit of people too happy to be slow, or bashful, or constrained. Light hearts, lithe figures, and light feet, had it their own way from an early hour till after the sun had dipped behind the sharp sky-line of the Omaha hills. Silence was then called, and a well cultivated mezzo-soprano voice, belonging to a young lady with fair face and dark eyes, gave with quartette accompaniment a little song, the notes of which I have been unsuccessful in repeated efforts to obtain since—a version of the text, touching to all earthly wanderers:

"By the rivers of Babylon we sat down and wept."
"We wept when we remembered Zion."

There was danger of some expression of feeling when the song was over, for it had begun to draw tears! but breaking the quiet with his hard voice, an Elder asked the blessing of heaven on all who, with purity of heart and brotherhood of spirit had mingled in that society, and then all dispersed, hastening to cover from the falling dews. All, I remember, but some splendid Indians, who, in cardinal scarlet blankets and feathered leggings, had been making foreground figures for the dancing rings, like those in Mr. West's picture of our Philadelphia treaty, and staring their inability to comprehend the wonderful performances. These loitered to the last, as if unwilling to seek their abject homes.

Well as I knew the peculiar fondness of the Mormons for music, their orchestra in service on this occasion astonished me by its numbers and fine drill. The story was, that an eloquent Mormon missionary had converted its members in a body at an English town, a stronghold of the sect, and that they took up their trumpets, trombones, drums, and hautboys together, and followed him to America.

When the refuges from Nauvoo were hastening to part with their table ware, jewelery, and almost every other fragment of metal wealth they possessed that was not iron, they had never thought of giving up the instruments of this favorite band. And when the battalion was enlisted, though high inducements were offered some of the performers to accompany it, they all refused. Their fortunes were with the camp of the tabernacle. They had led the farewell service in the Nauvoo temple. Their office now was to guide the monster choruses and Sunday hymns; and like the trumpets of silver, made of a whole piece, "for the calling of the assembly, and for the journeying of the camps," to knoll the people into church. Some of their wind instruments, indeed, were uncommonly full and pure-toned, and in that clear, dry air could be heard to a great dsitance. It had the strangest effect in the world, to listen to their sweet music winding over the uninhabited country. Something in the style of a Moravian death-tune blown at day-break, but altogether unique. It might be when you were hunting a ford over the great Platte, the dreariest of all wild rivers, perplexed among the far-reaching sand bars, and curlew shallows of its shifting bed—the wind rising would bring you the first faint thought of a melody; and as you listened borne down upon the gust that swept past you a cloud of the dry sifted sands, you recognized it—perhaps a home-loved theme of Henry Proch or Mendelssohn. Mendelssohn Bartholdy, away there in the Indian marches!

The battalion gone, the host again moved on. The tents which had gathered on the hill summits, like white birds hesitating to venture on the long flight over the river, were struck one after another, and the dwellers in them, and their wagons and their cattle, hastened down to cross at a ferry in the valley, which they made ply night and day. A little beyond the landing they formed their companies, and made their preparations for the last and longest stage of their journey. It was a more serious matter to cross the mountains then than now, that the thirst of our people for the gold of California has made the region between them and their desire such literal trodden ground.

Thanks to this wonderful movement. I may dismiss an effort to describe the incidents of emigrant life upon the Plains, presuming that you have been made more than familiar with them already, by the many repeated descriptions of which they have been the subject. The desert march, the ford, the quicksand, the Indian battle, the bison chase, the prairie fire—the adventures of the Mormons comprised every variety of these varieties; but I could not hope to invest them with the interest of novelty. The character of their every-day life, its routine and conduct, alone offered any exclusive or marked pecularity. Their romantic devotional observances, and their admirable concert of purpose and action, met the eye at once. After these, the stranger was most struck, perhaps, by the strict order of march, the unconfused closing up to meet attack, the skillful securing of the cattle upon the halt, the system with which the watches were set at night to guard them and the lines of *corral*—with other similar circumstances indicative of the maintenance of a high state of discipline. Every ten of their wagons was under the care of a captain. This captain of ten, as they termed him, obeyed a captain of fifty; who, in turn, obeyed his captain of a hundred, or directly a member of what they called the high council of the Church. All these were responsible and determined men, approved of by the people for their courage, discretion, and experience. So well recognized were the results of this organization, that bands of hostile Indians have passed by comparatively small parties of Mormons, to attack much larger, tbu less compact, bodies of other emigrants.

The most striking feature, however, of the Mormon emigration was undoutedly their information of the tabernacle camps and temporary stakes or settlements, which renewed in the sleeping solitudes, everywhere along their road, the cheering signs of intelligent and hopeful life.

I will make this remark plainer by describing to you one of these camps, with the daily routine of its inhabitants. I select at random, for my purpose, a large camp upon the delta between the Nebraska and Missouri, in the territory disputed between the Omaha and Otto and Missouri Indians. It remained pitched here for nearly two months, during which period I resided in it.

It was situated near the Petit Papillon, or Little Butterfly river, and upon some finely rounded hills that encircle a favorite cool spring. On each of these a square was marked out; and the wagons as they arrived took their positions along its four sides in double rows, so as to leave a roomy street or passage way between them. The tents were disposed also in rows, at intervals between the wagons. The cattle were folded in high-fenced yards outside. The quadrangle inside was left vacant for the sake of ventilation, and the streets, covered in with leafy arbor work, and kept scrupulously clean, formed a shaded cloister walk. This was the place of exercise for slowly recovering invalids, the day-home of the infants, and the evening promenade of all.

From the first formation of the camp all its inhabitants were constantly and laboriously occupied. Many of them were highly educated mechanics and seemed only to need a day's anticipated rest to engage at the forge, loom, or turning lathe, upon some needed *chore* of work. A Mormon gunsmith is the inventor of the excellent repeating rifle, that loads by slides instead of cylinders; and one of the neatest finished fire-arms I have ever seen was of this kind, wrought from scraps of old iron, and inlaid with the silver of a couple of half-dollars, under a hot July sun, in a spot where the average height of the grass was above the workman's shoulders. I have seen a cobbler, after the halt of his party on the march, hunting along the river bank for a lapstone in the twilight, that he might finish a famous boot sole by the camp fire; and I have had a piece of cloth, the wool of which was sheared, dyed and spun and woven, during a progress of over three hundred miles.

Their more interesting occupations, however, were those growing out of their peculiar circumstances and position. The chiefs were seldom without some curious affair on hand to settle with the restless Indians; while the immense labor and responsibility of the conduct of their unwieldy moving army, and the commissariat of its hundreds of famishing poor, also devolved upon them. They had good men they called Bishops, whose special office it was to look up the cases of extremest suffering; and their relief parties were out night and day to scour over every trail.

At this time, say two months before the final expulsion from Nauvoo, there were already, along three hundred miles of the road between the city and our Papillon camp, over two thousand emigrating wagons, besides a large number of nondescript turn-outs, the motley make shifts of poverty; from the unsuitably-heavy cart, that lumbered on mysteriously, with its sick driver hidden under its counterpane cover, to the crazy, two-wheeled trundle, such as our own poor employ for the conveyance of the slop-barrels; this pulled along, it may be, by a little dry dugged heifer, and rigged up only to drag some such light weight as a baby, a sack of meal, or a pack of clothes and bedding.

Some of them were in distress from losses upon the way A strong trait of the Mormons was their kindness to their brute dependents, and particularly to their beasts of draught. They gave them the holiday of the Sabbath whenever it came round: I believe they would have washed them with old wine, after the example of the emigrant Carthagenians, had they had any. Still, in the slave-coast heats under which the animals had to move, they sometimes foundered. Sometimes, too, they strayed off in the night, or were mired in morasses; or oftener were stolen by Indians, who found market covert for such plunder among the horse-thief whites of the frontier. But the great mass of these pilgrims of the desert was made up of poor folks, who had fled in destitution from Nauvoo, and been refused a resting place by the people of Iowa.

It is difficult fully to understand the state of helplessness in which some of these would arrive, after accomplishing a journey of such extent, under circumstances of so much privation and peril. The fact was, they seemed to believe that all their trouble would be at an end if they could only come up with their comrades at the Great Camp. For this they calculated their resources, among which their power of endurance was by much the largest and most reliable item, and they were not disappointed if they arrived with these utterly exhausted.

I remember a single instance of this at the Papillon camp.

It was that of a joyous-hearted, clever, fellow, whose songs and fiddle tunes were the life and delight of Nauvoo in its merry days. I forget his story, and how exactly it fell about, that after a Mormon's full peck of troubles, he started after us with his wife and little ones, from some "lying down place" in Indian country, where he had contended with an attack of a serious malady. He was just convalescent, and the fatigue of marching on foot again with a child on his back, speedily brought on a relapse. But his anxiety to reach a place where he could expect to meet friends with shelter and food, was such that he only pressed on the harder. Probably for more than a week of the dog-star weather, he labored on under a high fever, walking every day till he was entirely exhausted. His limbs failed him then; but his courage holding out, he got into his covered cart, on top of its freight of baggage, and made them drive him on, while he lay down. They could hardly believe how ill he was, he talked on so cheerfully—"I'm nothing on earth ailing, but home-sick: I'm cured the very minute I get to camp and see the brethren."

Not being able thus to watch his course, he lost his way and had to regain it through a wretched tract of low meadow prairie, where there were no trees to break the noon, nor water but what was ague-sweet or brackish. By the time he got back to the trail of the high prairie, he was, in his own phrase, "pretty far gone!" Yet he was resolute in his purpose as ever, and to a party he fell in with, avowed his intention to be cured at the camp, and nowhere else! He even jested with them, comparing his jolting couch to a summer cot in a whitewashed cockloft. "But I'll make them take me down," he said, "and give me a dip in the river when I get there. All I care for is to see the brethren."

His determined bearing rallied the spirit of his traveling household, and they kept on their way till he was within a few hours' journey of the camp. He entered on his last day's journey with the energy of increased hope.

I remember that day well. For in the evening I mounted a tired horse to go a short errand, and in mere pity had to turn back before I had walked him a couple of hundred yards. Nothing seemed to draw life from the languid air but the clouds of gnats and stinging midges; and long after sundown it was so hot that the sheep lay on their stomachs panting, and the cattle strove to lap wind like hard fagged hunting dogs. In camp, I had spent the day in watching the invalids, and the rest hunting the shade under the wagon bodies, and veering about them like the shadows round the sundial. I know I thought myself wretched enough to be of their company.

Poor Merryman had all that heat to bear, with the mere pretense of an awning to screen out the sun from his close muslin cockloft.

He did not fail till somewhere hard upon noon. He then began to grow restless, to know accurately the distance traveled. He made them give him water, too, much more frequently; and when they stopped for this purpose, asked a number of obscure questions. A little after this he discovered himself that a film had come over his eyes. He confessed that this was discouraging; but said with stubborn resignation, that if denied to *see* the brethren, he still should *hear* the sound of their voices.

After this, which was when he was hardly three miles from our camp, he lay very quiet, as if husbanding his strength; but when he had made, as is thought, a full mile further, being interrogated by the woman that was driving, whether she should stop, he answered her, as she avers, "No, no! go on!"

The anecdote ends badly. They brought him in dead, I think about five o'clock of the afternoon. He had on his clean clothes, as he had dressed himself in the morning, looking forward to his arrival.

Beside the common duty of guiding and assisting these unfortunates, the companies in the van united in providing the highway for the entire body of emigrants. The Mormons have laid out for themselves a road through the Indian Territory, over four hundred leagues in length, with substantial, well-built bridges, fit for the passage of heavy artillery, over all the streams, except a few great rivers where they have established permanent ferries. The nearest unfinished bridging to the Papillon camp was that of the Corne a Cerf, or Elk Horn, a tributary of the Platte, distant, may be, a couple of hours' march. Here, in what seemed to be an incredibly short space of time, there rose the seven great piers and abutments of a bridge, such as might challenge honors for the entire public-spirited population of Lower Virginia. The party detailed to the task worked in the broiling sun, in water beyond depth, and up to their necks, as if engaged in the perpetration of some pointed and delightful practical joke. The chief sport lay in floating along with the logs, cut from the overhanging timber up the stream, guiding them till they reached their destination, and then plunging them under water in the precise spot where they were to be secured. This, the laughing engineers would execute with the agility of happy diving ducks.

Our nearest ferry was that over the Missouri. Nearly opposite the Pull Point, or Point aux Poules, a trading post of the American Fur Company, and village of the Pottawatamies, they had gained a favorable crossing, by making a deep cut for the road through the steep right bank. And here, without intermission, their flat-bottomed scows plied, crowded with the wagons, and cows, and sheep, and children, and furniture of the emigrants, who, in waiting their turn, made the woods around smoke with their crowding camp fires. But no such good fortune as a gratuitous passage awaited the heavy cattle, of whom, with the others, no less than 30,000 were at this time on their way westward: these were made to earn it by swimming.

A heavy freshet had at this time swollen the river to a width, as I should judge, of something like a mile and a half, and dashed past, its fierce current, rushing, gurgling and eddying, as if thrown from a mill race, or *scriptural* fountain of the deep. Its aspect did not invite the oxen to their duty, and the labor was to force them to it. They were gathered in little troops on the shore, and driven forward till they lost their footing. As they turned their heads to return, they encountered the combined opposition of a clamorous crowd of bystanders, vieing with each other in the pungent administration of inhospitable affront. Then rose their hub-hub: their geeing, and wooing, and hawing; their yelling, and yelping, and screaming; their hooting and hissing and pelting. The rearmost steers would hesitate to brave such a rebuff; halting, they would impede the return of the outermost; they all would waver: wavering for a moment, the current would sweep them together downward. At this juncture a fearless youngster, climbing upon some brave bull in the front rank, would urge him boldly forth into the stream: the rest then surely followed; a few moments saw them struggling in mid current; a few more, and they were safely landed on the opposite shore. The driver's was the sought-after post of honor here; and sometimes, when repeated failures have urged them to emulation, I have seen the youths, in stepping from back to back of the struggling monsters, or swimming in among their battling hoofs, display feats of address and hardihood, that would have made Franconi's or the Madrid bull-ring vibrate with bravos of applause. But in the hours after hours that I have watched this sport at the ferry side, I never heard an oath or the language of quarrel, or knew it provoke the least sign of ill feeling.

After the sorrowful word was given out to halt, and make preparation for winter, a chief labor became the making of hay; and with every day-dawn brigades of mowers would take up the march to their positions in chosen meadows—a prettier sight than a charge of cavalry—as they laid their swaths, whole companies of scythes abreast. Before this time the manliest as well as the most general daily labor, was the herding of the cattle; the only wealth of the Mormons, and more and more cherished by them with the increasing pastoral character of their lives. A camp could not be pitched in any spot without soon exhausting the freshness of the pasture around it, and it became an ever recurring task to guide the cattle, in unbroken droves, to the nearest place where it was still fresh and fattening. Sometimes it was necessary to go farther, to distant ranges which were known as feeding grounds of the buffalo. About these there was sure to prowl parties of thievish Indians; and each drove therefore had its escort of mounted men and boys, who learned self-reliance and heroism while on night-guard alone among the silent hills. But generally the cattle were driven from the camp at the dawn of the morning, and brought back, thousands together, in the evening, to be picketed in the great corral or enclosure, where beeves, bulls, cows and oxen, with the horses, mules, hogs, calves, sheep and human beings, could all look together upon the red watch-fires, with the feeling of security when aroused by the Indian stampede, or the howlings of the prairie wolves at moonrise.

When they set about building their winter houses, too, the Mormons went into quite considerable timbering operations, and performed desperate feats of carpentry. They did not come ornamental gentlemen or raw apprentices, to extemporize new versions of Robinson Crusoe. It was a comfort to notice the readiness with which they turned their hands to woodcraft; some of them, though I believe these had generally been bred carpenters, wheelwrights, or more particularly boat-builders, quite out-doing the most notable *voyageurs* in the use of the ax. One of these would fell a tree, strip off its bark, cut and split up the trunk in piles of plank, scantling, or shingles; make posts, pins, and pales—everything wanted almost of the branches; and treat his toil, from first to last, with more sportive flourish than a school-boy whittling his shingle.

Inside the camp the chief labors were assigned to the women. From the moment, when after the halt, the lines had been laid, the spring wells dug out, and the ovens and fireplaces built, though the men still assumed to set the gaurds and enforce the regulations of police, the empire of the tented town was with the better sex. They were the chief comforters of the severest sufferers, the kind nurses who gave them, in their sickness, those dear attentions, with which pauperism is hardly poor, and which the greatest wealth often fails to buy. And they were a nation of wonderful managers. They could hardly be called housewives in etymological strictness, but it was plain they had once been such, and most distinguished ones. Their art availed them in their changed affairs. With almost their entire culinary material limited to the milk of their cows, some store of meal or flour and a very few condiments, they brought their thousand and one receipts into play with a success that outdid for their families the miracle of the Hebrew widow's cruse. They learned to make butter on a march by the dashing of the wagon, and so nicely to caculate the working of barm in the jolting heats, that, as soon after the halt as an oven could be dug in the hill-side and heated, their well-kneaded loaf was ready for baking, and produced good leavened bread for supper. I have no doubt the appetizing zest their humble lore succeeded in imparting to diet which was both simple and meagre, availed materially for the health as well as the comfort of the people.

But the first duty of the Mormon women was, through all change of place and fortune, to keep alive the altar fire of home. Whatever their manifold labors for the day, it was their effort to complete them against the sacred hour of evening fall. For by that time all the out-workers, scouts, ferrymen or bridgemen, roadmakers, herdsmen, or hay-makers, had finished their tasks and come in to their rest. And before the last smoke of the supper-fire curled up, reddening in the glow of the sunset, a hundred chimes of cattle bells announced their looked-for approach across the open hills; and the women went out to meet them at the camp gates, and with their children in their laps sat by them at the cherished family meal, and talked over the events of the well-spent day.

But every day closed as every day began, with an invocation of the divine favor; without which, indeed, no Mormon seemed to dare to lay him down to rest. With the first shining of the stars, laughter and loud talking hushed, the neighbor went his way, you heard the last hymn sung, and then the thousand-voiced murmur of prayer was heard, like babbling water falling down the hills.

There was no austerity, however about the religion of Mormonism. Their fasting and penance, it is no jest to say, was altogether involuntary. They made no merit of that. They kept the Sabbath with considerable strictness: they were too close copyists of the wanderers of Israel in other respects not to have learned like them the value of this most admirable of the Egypto-Mosaic institutions. But the rest of the week, their religion was independent of ritual observance.

They had the sort of strong-stomached faith that is still found embalmed in sheltered spots of Catholic Italy and Spain, with the spirit of the believing or dark ages. It was altogether too strongly felt to be dependent on intellectual ingenuity or careful caution of the ridiculous. It mixed itself up fearlessly with the common transactions of their every-day life, and only to give them liveliness and color.

If any passages of life bear better than others a double interpretation, they are the adventures of travel and of the field. What old persons call discomforts and discouraging mishaps, are the very elements to the young and sanguine of what they are willing to term "fun." The Mormons took the young and hopeful side. They could make sport and frolic of their trials, and often turn right sharp suffering into right round laughter against themselves. I certainly heard more jests and "Joe Millers" while in this Papillon camp than I am likely to hear in all the remainder of my days.

This, too, was at a time of serious affliction. Beside the ordinary suffering from insufficient food and shelter, distressing and mortal sickness, exacerbated, if nor originated, by these causes, was generally prevalent.

In the camp nearest us on the West, which was that of the bridging party near the Corne, the number of its inhabitants being small enough to invite computation, I found as early as the 31st of July, that 37 per cent. of its inhabitants were down with the fever, and a sort of strange scorbutic disease, frequently fatal, which they named the Black Canker. The camps to the east of us, which were all on the eastern side of the Missouri, were yet worse fated.

The climate of the entire upper "Misery Bottom," as they term it, is, during a considerable part of summer and autumn, singularly pestiferous. Its rich soil, which is, to a depth far beyond the reach of the plow, as fat as the earth of a kitchen garden, or compost heap, is annually the force-bed of a vegetation as rank as that of the tropics. To render its fatal fertility the greater, it is everywhere freely watered by springs, and creeks, and larger streams, that flow into it from both sides. In the season of drouth, when the sun enters Virgo, these dry down till they run impure as open sewers, exposing to the day foul broad flats, mere quagmires of black dirt, stretching along for miles, unvaried, except by the limbs of half-buried carrion tree trunks, or by occasional yellow pools of what the children call frog spawn; all together steaming up thick vapors redolent of the savor of death.

The same is the habit of the great river. In the beginning of August, its shores hardly could contain the millions of forest logs, and tens of billions of gallons of turbid water, that came rushing down together from its mountain head-gates. But before the month was out, the freshet had all passed by; the river diminished one-half, threaded feebly southward through the center of the valley, and the mud of its channel, baked and creased, made a wide tile pavement between the choking crowd of reeds, and sedgy grasses, and wet stalked weeds, and growths of marsh meadow flowers, the garden homes, at this tainted season, of venom-crazy snakes, and the fresher ooze by the water's edge, which stank in the sun like a naked muscle shoal.

Then the plague raged. I have no means of ascertaining the mortality of the Indians who inhabited the bottom. In 1845, the year previous, which was not more unhealthy, they lost one-ninth of their number in about two months. The Mormons were scourged severely. The exceeding mortality among some of them, was, no doubt, in the main, attributable to the low state to which their systems had been brought by long continued endurance of want and hardship. It is to be remembered, also, that they were the first turners up of the prairie sod, and that this of itself made them liable to the sickness of new countries. It was where their agricultural operations had been most considerable, and in situations on the left bank of the river, where the prevalent south-west winds wafted to them the miasmata of its shores, that disease was most rife.*

In some of these the fever prevailed to such an extent that hardly any escaped it. They let their cows go unmilked, they wanted for voices to raise the psalm of Sundays. The few who were able to keep their feet, went about among the tents and wagons with food and water, like nurses through the wards of an infirmary. Here at one time the digging got

---

*——It is certain that there is no sickness among the present inhabitants of this region comparable to that of 1846.

behind hand: burials were slow; and you might see women sit in the open tents keeping the flies off their dead children, sometimes after decomposition had set in.

In our own camp, for a part of August and September things wore an unpleasant aspect enough.* Its situation was one much praised for its comparative salubrity; but, perhaps, on this account, the number of cases of fever among us was increased by the hurrying arrival, from other localities, of parties in whom the virus leaven of disease was fermented by forced travel.

But I am excused sufficiently the attempt to get up for your entertainment here any circumstantial picture of horrors, by the fact, that at the most interesting season, I was incapaciated for nice observation by an attack of fever—mine was what they call the congestive—that it required the utmost use of all my faculties to recover from. I still kept my tent in the camp line; but, for as much as a month, had very small notion of what went on among my neighbors. I recollect overhearing a lamentation over some dear baby, that its mother no doubt thought the destroying angel should have been specially instructed to spare. I wish, too, for my own sake, I could forget how imperfectly one day I mourned the decease of a poor Saint, who, by clamor, rendered his vicinity troublesome. He, no doubt, endured great pain; for he groaned shockingly till death came to his relief. He interfered with my own hard-gained slumbers, and—I was glad when death did relieve him.

Before my attack, I was fond of conversing with an amiable old man, I think English born, who, having then recently buried his only daughter and grandson, used to be seen sitting out before his tent resting his sorrowful forehead on his hands, joined over a smooth white oak staff. I missed him when I got about again; probably he had been my mourning neighbor.

So, too, having been much exercised in my dreams at this time, by the vision of dismal processions, such as might have

---

*——This camp was moved by the beginning of October to winter quarters on the river, where, also, there was considerable sickness before the cold weather. I am furnished with something over six hundred as the number of burials in the grave yard there.

been formed by the union in line of all the forlornest and ugliest of the struggling fugitives from Nauvoo, I happen to recall as I write, that I had some knowledge somewhere of one of our new-comers, for whom the nightmare revived and repeated without intermission the torment of his trying journey. As he lay feeding life with long drawn breaths, he muttered: "Where's next water? Team—give out! Hot, hot—God, it's hot. Stop the wagon—stop the wagon—stop, stop the wagon!" They woke him—to his own content—but I believe returning sleep ever renewed his distressing visions, till the sounder slumber came on from which no earthly hand or voice could rouse him; into which I hope he did not carry them.

In a half dreamy way, I remember, or I think I remember, a crowd of phantoms like these. I recall but one fact, however, going far in proof of a considerable mortality. Earlier in the season, while going westward, with the intention of passing the Rocky Mountains that summer, I had opened, with the assistance of Mormon spades and shovels, a large mound on a commanding elevation, the tomb of a warrior of the ancient race; and, continuing on my way, had left a deep trench excavated entirely through it. Returning, fever-struck, to the Papillon camp, I found it planted close by this spot. It was just forming as I arrived; the first wagon, if I mistake not, having but a day or two before halted into place. My first airing upon my convalescence took me to the mound, which, probably to save digging, had been re-adapted to its original purpose. In this brief interval they had filled the trench with bodies, and furrowed the ground with graves around it, like the plowing of a field.

The lengthened sojourn of the Mormons in this insalubrious region, was imposed upon them by circumstances which I must now advert to.

Though the season was late, when they first crossed the Missouri, some of them moved forward with great hopefulness, full of the notion of viewing and choosing their new homes that year. But the van had only reached Grand Island and the Pawnee villages, when they were overtaken by more ill news from Nauvoo. Before the summer closed, their enemies set upon the last remnant of those who were left behind in Illinois. They were a few lingerers, who could not be persuaded but there might yet be time for them to gather up their worldly goods before removing, some weakly mothers and their infants, a few delicate young girls, and many cripples and bereaved and sick people. These had remained under shelter, according to the Mormon statement at least, by virtue of an express covenant in their behalf. If there was such a covenant it was broken. A vindictive war was waged upon them, from which the weakest fled in scattered parties leaving the rest to make a reluctant and almost ludicrously-unavailing defense, till the 17th day of September, when one thousand six hundred and twenty-five troops entered Nauvoo, and drove all forth who had not retreated before that time.

Like the wounded birds of a flock fired into toward nightfall, they came straggling on with faltering steps, many of them without bag or baggage, beast or barrow,* all asking shelter or burial, and forcing a fresh repartition of the already divided rations of their friends. It was plain now, that every energy must be taxed to prevent the entire expedition from perishing. Further emigration for the time was out of the question, and the whole people prepared themselves for encountering another winter on the prairie.

Happily for the main body, they found themselves at this juncture among Indians who were amicably disposed. The lands on both sides of the Missouri, in particular, were owned by the Pottawatamies and Omahas, two tribes whom unjust treatment by our United States, had the effect of rendering most auspiciously hospitable to strangers whom they regarded as persecuted like themselves.

The Pottawatamies on the eastern side, are a nation from whom the United States bought, some years ago. a number of hundred thousand acres of the finest lands they have ever brought into market. Whatever the bargain was, the sellers were not content with it; the people saying their leaders were cheated, made drunk, bribed, and all manner of naughty

---

*——I knew an orphan boy, for instance, who came on by himself at this time afoot, starting with no other provision than his trowser's pocket full of biscuit, given him from a steamboat on the Mississippi.

things besides. No doubt this was quite as much of a libel on the fair fame of this particular Indian treaty, as such stories generally are; for the land to which the tribe was removed in pursuance of it, was admirably adapted to enforce habits of civilized thrift. It was smooth prairie, wanting in timber, and of course in game; and the humane and philanthropic might rejoice therefore that necessity would soon indoctrinate its inhabitants into the practice of agriculture. An impracticable few, who may have thought these advantages more than compensated by the insalubrity of their allotted resting place, fled to the extreme wilds, where they could find deer, and woods, and rocks, and running water, and where, I believe, they are roaming to this day. The remainder being what the political vocabulary designates on such occasions as "friendly Indians," were driven—marched is the word—galley slaves are marched thus to Barcelona and Toulon—marched from the Mississippi to the Missouri, and planted there. Discontented and unhappy, they had hardly begun to form an attachment for this new soil, when they were persuaded to exchange it for their present *fever patch* upon the Kaw or Kansas river. They were under this second sentence of transportation when the Mormons arrived among them.

They were pleased with the Mormons. They would have been pleased with any whites who would not cheat them, nor sell them whisky, nor whip them for their poor gipsey habits, nor bear themselves indecently towards their women, many of whom among the Pottawatamies, especially those of nearly unmixed French descent, are singularly comely, and some of them educated. But all Indians have something like a sentiment of reverence for the insane, and admire those who sacrifice, without apparent motive, their worldly welfare to the triumph of an idea. They understood the meaning of what they call a great vow, and think it the duty of the right-minded to lighten the votary's penance under it. To this feeling they united the sympathy of fellow sufferers for those who could talk to them of their own Illinois, and tell the story how from it they also had been ruthlessly expelled.

Their hospitality was sincere, almost delicate. Fanny Le Clerc, the spoiled child of the great brave, Pied Riche, interpreter of the nation, would have the pale face Miss

Devine learn duets with her to the guitar; and the daughter of substantial Joseph La Framboise, the interpreter of the United States—she died of the fever that summer—welcomed all the nicest young Mormon Kitties and Lizzies, and Jennies, and Susans, to a coffee feast at her father's house, which was probably the best cabin in the river village. They made the Mormons at home, there and elsewhere. Upon all their lands they formally gave them leave to tarry just so long as should suit their own good pleasure.

The affair, of course, furnished material for a solemn council. Under the auspices of an officer of the United States, their chiefs were summoned, in the form befitting great occasions, to meet in the dirty yard of one Mr. P. A. Sarpy's log trading house, at their village. They came in grand toilet, moving in their fantastic attire with so much *aplomb* and genteel measure, that the stranger found it difficult not to believe them high-born gentlemen, attending a costumed ball. Their aristocratically-thin legs, of which they displayed fully the usual Indian proportion, aided this illusion. There is something, too, at all times very mock-Indian in the theatrical French millinery tie of the Pottawatamie turban; while it is next to impossible for a sober white man, at first sight, to believe that the red, green, black, blue, and yellow cosmetics, with which he sees such grave personages so variously dotted, diapered, cancelled, and arabesqued, are worn by them in any mood but one of the deepest and most desperate quizzing. From the time of their first squat upon the ground, to the final breaking up of the council circle, they sustained their characters with equal self-possession and address.

I will not take it upon myself to describe their order of ceremonies; indeed, I ought not, since I have never been able to view the habits and customs of our aborigines in any other light than that of a reluctant and sorrowful subject of jest. Besides, in this instance, the displays of pow wow and eloquence were both probably moderated by the conduct of the entire transaction on temperance principles. I therefore content myself with observing, generally that the proceedings were such as every way became the grandeur of the parties interested, and the magnitude of the interests involved. When the red men had indulged to satiety in tobacco smoke from their peace pipes, and what they love still better, their peculiar metaphoric rodomontade, which, beginning with celestial bodies, and coursing downwards over the grandest sublunary objects, always managed to alight at last on their Grandfather Polk, and the tenderness for him of his affectionate colored children; all the solemn funny fellows present, who played the part of chiefs, signed formal articles of convention with their unpronounceable names.

The renowned chief, Pied Riche—he was surnamed Le Clerc on account of his remarkable scholarship—then arose, and said:

"My Mormon Brethren,

"The Pottawatamie came, sad and tired, into this unhealthy Missouri Bottom, not many years back, when he was taken from his beautiful country beyond the Mississippi, which had abundant game and timber, and clear water everywhere. Now you are driven away, the same, from your lodges and lands there, and the graves of your people. So we have both suffered. We must help one another, and the Great Spirit will help us both. You are now free to cut and use all the wood you may wish. You can make all your improvements, and live on any part of our actual land not occupied by us. Because one suffers and does not deserve it, is no reason he shall suffer always, I say. We may live to see all right yet. However, if we do not, our children will.—*Bon jour.*"

And thus ended the pageant. I give this speech as a morsel of real Indian. It was recited to me after the treaty by the Pottawatamie orator in French, which language he spoke with elegance. *Bon jour* is the French, Indian and English hail and farewell of the Pottawatamies.

The other entertainers of the Mormons at this time, the Omahas, or Mahaws, are one of the minor tribes of the Grand Prairie. Their great father, the United States, has found it convenient to protect so remote a dependency against the overpowering league of the Dahcotahs or Sioux, and has judged it dangerous at the same time to allow them to protect themselves by entering into a confederation with others. Under the pressure of this paternal embarrassment and restraint, it has therefore happened, most naturally, that this tribe, once a powerful and valued ally of ours, has been reduced to a band of little more than a hundred families, and these, a few years more will entirely extinguish. When I was among them, they were so ill-fed that their protruding high check bones gave them the air of a tribe of consumptives. The buffalo had left them, and no good ranges lay within several hundred miles reach. Hardly any other game found cover on their land. What little there was, they were short of ammunition to kill. Their annuity from the United States was trifling. They made next to nothing at thieving. They had planted some corn in their awkward Indian fashion, but through fear of ambush dared not venture out to harvest it. A chief resource for them, the winter previous, had been the spoliation of their neighbors, the prairie field-mice.

These interesting little people, more industrious and thrifty than the Mahaws, garner up in the neat little cellars of their under-ground homes, the small seeds or beans of the wood pea vine, which are black and hard, but quite nutritious. Gathering them one by one, a single mouse will thus collect as much as half a pint, which, before the cold weather sets in, he piles away in a dry and frost-proof excavation, cleverly thatched and covered in. The Omaha animal, who, like enough may have idled during all the season the mouse was amassing his toilsome treasure, finds this subterranean granary to give out a certain peculiar cavernous vibration, when briskly tapped upon above the ground. He wanders about, therefore, striking with a wand in hopeful spots; and as soon as he hears the hollow sound he knows, unearths the little retired capitalist along with his winter's hope. Mouse wakes up from his nap to starve, and Mahaw swallows several relishing mouthfuls.

But the mouse has his avenger in the powerful Sioux, who wages against his wretched red brother an almost bootless, but exterminating warfare. He robs him of his poor human peltry. One of my friends was offered for sale a Sioux scalp of Omaha, "with grey hair nearly as long as a white horse's tail."

The pauper Omahas were ready to solicit as a favor the residence of white protectors among them. The Mormons harvested and stored away for them their crops of maize; with all their own poverty they spared them food enough besides, from time to time, to save them from absolutely starving; and their entrenched camp to the north of Omaha villages, served as a sort of breakwater between them and the destroying rush of the Sioux.

This was the head quarters of the Mormon Camps of Israel. The miles of rich prairie, enclosed and sowed with the grain they could contrive to spare, and the houses, stacks, and cattle shelters, had the seeming of an entire county, with its people and improvements transplanted there unbroken. On a pretty plateau, overlooking the river, they built more than seven hundred houses in a single town, neatly laid out with highways and byways, and fortified with breast-work, stockade, and block-houses. It had too, its place of worship, "Tabernacle of the Congregation," and various large workshops, and mills and factories provided with water power.

They had no camp or settlement of equal size in the Pottawatamie country. There was less to apprehend here from Indian invasion; and the people scattered themselves, therefore, along the rivers and streams, and in the timber groves, wherever they found inviting localities for farming operations. In this way many of them acquired what have since proved to be valuable pre-emption rights.

Upon the Pottawatamie lands, scattered through the border regions of Missouri and Iowa, in the Sac and Fox country, a few among the Iowas, among the Poncas in a great company upon the banks of the *L'Eau qui Coule*, or Running Water river, and at the Omaha winter quarters, the Mormons sustained themselves through the heavy winter of 1846-1847. It was the severest of their trials. And if I aimed at rhetorical effect, I would be bound to offer you a minute narrative of its progress, as a sort of climax to my history. But I have, I think, given you enough of the Mormons' sorrows. We are all of us content to sympathize with a certain extent of suffering; but very few can bear the recurring yet scarcely varied narrative of another's distress without something of impatience. The world is full of griefs, and we cannot afford to expend too large a share of our charity, or even our commiseration in a single quarter.

This winter was the turning point of the Mormon fortunes. Those who lived through it were spared to witness the gradual return of better times. And they now liken it to the passing of a dreary night, since which they have watched the coming of a steadily brightening day.

Before the grass growth of 1847, a body of one hundred and forty-three picked men, with seventy wagons, drawn by their best horses, left the Omaha quarters, under the command of the members of the High Council, who had wintered there. They carried with them little but seed and farming implements, their aim being to plant spring crops at their ultimate destination. They relied on their rifles to give them food, but rarely left their road in search of game. They made long daily marches, and moved with as much rapidity as possible.

Against the season, when ordinary emigration passes the Missouri, they were already through the South Pass; and a couple of short days' travel beyond it, entered upon the more arduous portion of their journey. It lay in earnest through the Rocky Mountains. They turned Fremont's Peak, Long's Peak, the Twins, and other king summits, but had to force their way over other mountains of the rugged Utah range, sometimes following the stony bed of torrents, the head waters of some of the mightiest rivers of our continent, and sometimes literally cutting their road through heavy and ragged timber. They arrived at the grand basin of the Great Salt Lake, much exhausted, but without losing a man, and in time to plant for a partial autumn harvest.

Another party started after these pioneers, from the Omaha winter quarters, in the summer. They had 566 wagons, and carried large quantities of grain, which they were able to put in the ground before it froze.

The same season also these were joined by a part of the Battalion and other members of the Church, who came eastward from California and the Sandwich Islands. Together, they fortified themselves strongly with sun-brick walls and block-houses, and living safely through the winter, were able to tend crops that yielded ample provision for the ensuing year.

In 1848, nearly all the remaining members of the Church left the Missouri country in a succession of powerful bands, invigorated and enriched by their abundant harvests there; and that year saw fully established their commonwealth of the New Covenant, the future STATE OF DESERET.

INTRODUCTORY.

I may not undertake to describe to you in a single lecture the geography of Deseret, and its great basin. Were I to consider the face of the country, its military position, or its climate and its natural productions, each head, I am confident, would claim more time than you have now to spare me. For Deseret is emphatically a new country; new in its own characteristic features, newer still in its bringing together within its limits the most inconsistent peculiarities of other countries. I cannot aptly compare it to any. Descend from the mountains where you have the scenery and climate of Switzerland, to seek the sky of your choice among the [many climates of Italy, and you may find, welling out of the same hills, the freezing springs of Mexico, and the hot springs of Iceland, both together coursing their way to the salt sea of Palestine in the plain below. The pages of Malte Brun provide me with a less truthful parallel to it than those which describe the happy valley of Rasselas or the continent of Balnibarbi.

Let me then press on with my history, during the few minutes that remain for me.

Only two events have occurred to menace seriously the establishment at Deseret; the first threatened to destroy its crops, the other to break it up altogether.

The shores of the Salt Lake are infested by a sort of insect pest which claims a vile resemblance to the locust of the Syrian Dead Sea. Wingless, dumpy, black, swollen-headed, with bulging eyes, in cases like goggles, mounted upon legs of steel wire and clock spring, and with a general personal appearance that justified the Mormons in comparing him to a cross of the spider on the buffalo, the Deseret cricket comes down from the mountains at a certain season of the year, in voracious and desolating myriads. It was just at this season, that the first crops of the new settlers were in the full glory of their youthful green. The assailants could not be repulsed. The Mormons, after their fashion, prayed and fought, and fought and prayed, but to no purpose. The "Black Philistines" mowed their way, even with the ground, leaving it as if touched with an acid or burnt by fire.

But an unlooked for ally came to the rescue. Vast armies of bright birds, before strangers to the valley, hastened across the lake from some unknown quarter, and gorged themselves upon the well-fatted enemy. They were snow white, with little head and clear dark eyes, and little feet, and long wings, that arched in flight "like an angel's." At first the Mormons thought they were new enemies to plague them; but when they found them hostile only to the locusts, they were careful not to molest them in their friendly office, and to this end declared a heavy fine against all who should kill or annoy them with fire-arms. The gulls soon grew to be tame as the poultry, and the delighted little children learned to call them their pigeons. They disappeared every evening beyond the lake; but returning with sunrise, continued their welcome visitings till the crickets were all exterminated.

This curious incident recurred the following year, with this variation, that in 1849 the gulls came earlier and saved the wheat crops from all harm whatever.

A severer trial than the visit of the cricket-locusts threatened Deseret in the discovery of the gold of California. It was due to a party of the Mormon Battalion recruited on the Missouri, who on their way home found employment at New Helvetia. They were digging a mill race there, and threw up the gold dust with their shovels. You all know the crazy fever that broke out as soon as this was announced. It infected every one through California. Where the gold was discovered, at Sutter's and around, the standing grain was left uncut; whites, Indians, and mustees, all set them to gathering gold, every other labor forsaken, as if the first comers could rob the casket of all it contained. The disbanded soldiers came to the Valley; they showed their poor companions pieces of the yellow treasure they had gained; and the cry was raised, "To California—To the Gold of Ophir our brethren have discovered! To California!"

Some of you have perhaps come across the half-ironic instruction of the heads of the Church to the faithful outside the Valley:—"THE TRUE USE OF GOLD is for paving streets, covering houses, and making culinary dishes; and, when the Saints shall have preached the gospel, raised grain, and built up cities enough, the Lord will open up the way for a supply of gold to the perfect satisfaction of His people. Until then let them not be over anxious, for the treasures of the earth are in the Lord's storehouse, and He will open the doors thereof when and where he pleases."—*II General Epistle*, 14.

The enlightened virtue of their rulers saved the people and the fortunes of Deseret. A few only went away—and they were asked in kindness never to return. The rest remained to be healthy and happy, to "raise grain and build up cities."

The history of the Mormons has ever since been the unbroken record of the most wonderful prosperity. It has looked as though the elements of fortune, obedient to a law of natural re-action, were struggling to compensate to them their undue share of suffering. They may be pardoned for deeming it miraculous. But, in truth, the economist accounts for all, who explains to us the speedy recuperation of cities, laid in ruin by flood, fire, and earthquake. During its years of trial, Mormon labor has subsisted on insufficient capital, and under many trials: but it has subsisted, and survives them now, as intelligent and powerful as ever it was at Nauvoo, with this difference, that it has in the meantime been educated to habits of unmatched thrift, energy and endurance, and has been transplanted to a situation where it is in every respect more productive. Moreover, during all the period of their journey, while some have gained by practice in handicraft, and the experience of repeated essays at their various halting-places, the minds of all have been busy framing designs and planning the improvements they have since found opportunity to execute.

* * * * * * * * * *

I have gone over the work I assigned myself when I accepted your Committee's invitation, as fully as I could do without trespassing too largely upon your courteous patience. But I should do wrong to conclude my lecture without declaring, in succinct and definite terms, the opinions I have formed and entertain of the Mormon people. The libels of which they have been made the subject, make this a simple act of justice. Perhaps, too, my opinion, even with those who know me as you do, will better answer its end following after the narrative I have given.

I have spoken to you of a people, whose industry had made them rich, and gathered around them all the comforts and not a few of the luxuries, of refined life, expelled by lawless force into the wilderness; seeking an untried home far away from the scenes which their previous life had endeared to them; moving onward, destitute, hunger-sickened, and sinking with disease; bearing along with them their wives and children, the aged, and the poor, and the decrepid; renewing daily on their march the offices of devotion, the ties of family, and friendship, and charity; sharing necessities and braving dangers together; cheerful in the midst of want and trial, and persevering until they triumphed. I have told, or tried to tell, you of men who, when menaced by famine, and in the midst of pestilence, with every energy taxed by the urgency of the hour, were building roads and bridges, laying out villages, and planting corn-fields, for the stranger who might come after them, their kinsman only by a common humanity, and peradventure a common suffering—of men who have renewed their prosperity in the homes they have founded in the desert and who, in their new-built city, walled around by mountains like a fortress, are extending pious hospitalities to the destitute emigrants from our frontier lines—of men who, far removed from the restraints of law, obeyed it from choice, or found in the recesses of their religion something not inconsistent with human laws, but far more controlling; and who are now soliciting from the government of the United States, not indemnity— for the appeal would be hopeless, and they know it—not protection, for they now have no need of it—but that identity of political institutions, and that community of laws with the rest of us, which was confessedly their birthright when they were driven beyond our borders.

I said I would give you the opinion I formed of the Mormons: you may deduce it for yourselves from these facts. But I will add that I have not yet heard the single charge against them as a community—against their habitual purity of life, their integrity of dealing, their toleration of religious differences in opinion, their regard for the laws, or their devotion to the constitutional government under which we live— that I do not, from my own observation, or the testimony of others, know to be unfounded." * * * *

THE MORMOM BATTALION, AND FIRST WAGON ROAD OVER THE GREAT AMERICAN DESERT.

BY MISS ELIZA R. SNOW.

When "Mormon" trains were journeying thro'
To Winter Quarters, from Nauvoo,
Five hundred men were called to go
To settle claims with Mexico—
To fight for that same Government
From which, as fugitives we went.
What were their families to do—
Their children, wives, and mothers too,
When fathers, husbands, sons were gone?
Mothers drove teams, and camps moved on.

And on the brave Battalion went,
With Colonel Allen who was sent
As officer of Government.
The noble Colonel Allen knew
His "Mormon boys" were brave and true,
And he was proud of his command,
As he led forth his "Mormon Band."
He sickened, died, and they were left
Of a loved leader, soon bereft!
And his successors proved to be
The embodiment of cruelty,
Lieutenant Smith the tyrant, led
The Cohort on, in Allen's stead,
To Santa Fe, where Colonel Cooke,
The charge of the Battalion, took.

'Twas well the vision of the way,
Was closed before them on the day
They started out from Santa Fe.
'Tis said no infantry till then,
E'er suffered equal to those men.
Their beeves were famished and their store
Was nigh exhausted long before
They neared the great Pacific shore.
Teams e'en fell dead upon the road,
While soldiers helped to draw the load!
"Twas cruel, stern necessity
That prompted such severity;
For General Kearney in command
Of army in the western land,
Expressly ordered Colonel Cooke,
The man who failure could not brook,
To open up a wagon-road
Where wheels, till then, had never trod;
And Colonel Cooke was in command
Across that desert waste and sand:
He, with a staunch and iron will,
The general's orders to fulfill,
Must every nerve and sinew strain
The expedition's points to gain.
Tho' stern, and e'en at times morose,
Strict sense of justice marked his course.
He, as his predecessors, knew
The "Mormon" men were firm and true.

They found road-making worse by far
Than all the horrors of the war:
Tried by the way—when they got thro'
They'd very little more to do:
The opposing party, panic struck,
Dare not compete with "Mormon" pluck,
And off in all directions fled—
No charge was fired—no blood was shed.

Our God who rules in worlds of light,

If need, His purpose to fulfill,
He moves the nations at His will—
The destinies of men o'errules,
And uses whom He will as tools.
The wise can see and understand,
While fools ignore His guiding hand.

Ere the Battalion started out
Upon that most important route,
'Twas thus predicted by the tongue
Of the Apostle, Brigham Young,
"*If to your God and country true,
You'll have no fighting there to do.*"

Was General Kearney satisfied?
Yes, more—for he with martial pride
Said, "O'er the Alps Napoleon went,
But *these men cross'd a continent.*"

And thus, with God Almighty's aid
The conquest and the road were made,
By which a threatning storm was staved,
And lo! the Saints of God were saved.

MORMON BATTALION HISTORY.

BY D. TYLER.

CHAPTER I.

From a perusal of the foregoing chapters, the reader will be somewhat acquainted with the condition of the Latter-day Saints previous to and at the time of the mustering of the Mormon Battalion; and indeed, with some subsequent events also, which are anticipated in the address of General Kane. However, that the circumstances connected with the raising of the Battalion may be fully understood, some further explanation should be given.

From the time the Saints first consented to leave Nauvoo in order to secure freedom from persecution, rumors and speculations were rife as to their probable destination. It was confidently asserted by many persons in authority that the Government would interfere to prevent them, if they attempted to journey west of the Rocky Mountains. Governor Ford, in writing to Sheriff Backenstos as early as Dec. 29, 1845, expressed the belief that the Government would prevent their removal, as they would be likely to "join the British." Soon afterwards Amos Kendall, ex-Postmaster General, who claimed to be familiar with the plans of the President and Cabinet, also informed Elder Samuel Brannan that such was the intention. They were to be prevented upon the plea that it was contrary to law for an armed force from the United States to invade the dominion of another government. Of course, the Saints did not propose to go as a hostile force, but as peaceable citizens, seeking a home. They had, however, suffered so much in the past without cause, that this new threat was regarded with apprehension. Conciliatary letters were therefore written from Nauvoo to Hon. Stephen A. Douglas and several other members of Congress to secure their influence in opposition to such a measure. Efforts were also made by the authorities of the Church to obtain Government patronage while journeying westward with a view to securing protection from persecution as well a means of subsistence.

Oregon at that time was in possession of the United States, and President Polk had recommended to Congress that stockade forts be built along the overland route to that distant part, as a protection to emigrants. In anticipation of a law being passed to this effect, the Saints endeavored to secure the work of building the forts. They knew they could do the work as well and as cheap as any others, as they expected to travel some distance in that direction. Besides, the means to be earned by such work would greatly aid in supporting them; and the fact of their being in the employ of the Government might serve as a guaranty of their good faith.

In alluding to this, in a circular issued by the High Council, at Nauvoo, Jan. 20, 1846, it was stated that, "Should hostilities arise between the Government of the United States and any other power, in relation to the right of possessing the territory of Oregon we are on hand to sustain the United States government to that country. It is geographically ours; and of right no foreign power should hold dominion there; and if our services are required to prevent it, those services will be cheerfully rendered according to our ability."

President Young also wrote to Elder J. C. Little who was presiding over the Saints in the New England States on the 26th of Jan., 1846, as follows: "If our Government should offer facilities for emigrating to the western coast, embrace those facilities if possible. As a wise and faithful man, take every honorable advantage of the times you can. Be thou a savior and a dileverer of the people, and let virtue integrity and truth be your motto—salvation and glory the prize for which you contend."

On receipt of this letter, Elder Little obtained letters of introduction to Vice President Dallas, Hon. George Bancroft,

Secretary of the Navy, and other officials at Washington, and soon afterwards proceeded to the seat of government. He obtained an interview with President Polk, and also called upon Hon. Amos Kendall, ex-Postmaster General, who promised to take an interest in his case and see the President about it.

Two days subsequently he was informed by Mr. Kendall that the President designed to take possession of California by the aid of the "Mormons," who would receive orders to push through, take the country and fortify it in the name of the United States.

To execute his design Elder Little was to go forthwith to the camps and raise one thousand picked men to make a dash into and take possession of the country as before stated. They were to have their own officers except the commander, who was to be an appointee of the President. Another thousand were to be sent by way of Cape Horn in a U. S. transport, for the same service.

This was the plan which the President laid before the Cabinet.

Elder Little remained at Washington several days, awaiting definite instructions in regard to the matter, and in the meantime addressed an appeal to the President, setting forth some of the grievances of the Saints, alluding to their intention to journey westward and testifying to their loyalty.

Afterwards Elder Little had another interview with the President, which lasted about three hours. The President informed him that he had read the petition with interest, and that his people should be protected as good citizens, which he believed them to be.

Before leaving, however, the Elder learned, by a subsequent interview, that the design of the President had been changed, and that only five hundred men would be called for. He also learned that the President had instructed the Secretary of War to make out dispatches to Colonel Kearney, commander of the Army of the West, relative to the contemplated Mormon Battalion.

The foregoing will perhaps be sufficient to give the reader a general idea as to how the plan of raising the Battalion was at first conceived.

I now give Colonel Kearney's order to Captain Allen.

"HEAD QUARTERS, ARMY OF THE WEST,
"FORT LEAVENWORTH,
"June 19, 1846.

"SIR:

"It is understood that there is a large body of Mormons who are desirous of emigrating to California, for the purpose of settling in that country, and I have, therefore, to direct that you will proceed to their camps and endeavor to raise from among them four or five companies of volunteers to join me in my expedition to that country, each company to consist of any number between seventy-three and one hundred and nine; the officers of each company will be a captain, first-lieutenant and second lieutenant, who will be elected by the privates and subject to your approval, and the captains then to appoint the non-commissioned officers, also subject to your approval. The companies, upon being thus organized, will be mustered by you into the service of the United States, and from that day will commence to receive the pay, rations and other allowances given to the other infantry volunteers, each according to his rank. You will, upon mustering into service the fourth company, be considered as having the rank, pay and emoluments of a lieutenant-colonel of infantry, and are authorized to appoint an adjutant, sergeant-major and quartermaster-sergeant for the battalion.

"The companies, after being organized, will be marched to this post, where they will be armed and prepared for the field, after which they will, under your command, follow on my trail in the direction of Santa Fe, and where you will receive further orders from me.

"You will, upon organizing the companies, require provisions, wagons, horses, mules, etc. You must purchase everything that is necessary, and give the necessary drafts upon the quartermaster and commissary departments at this post, which drafts will be paid upon presentation.

"You will have the Mormons distinctly to understand that I wish to have them as volunteers for twelve months; that they will be marched to California, receiving pay and allowances during the above time, and at its expiration they will be discharged, and allowed to retain, as their private property, the guns and accoutrements furnished to them at this post.

"Each company will be allowed four women as laundresses, who will travel with the company, receiving rations and other allowances given to the laundresses of our army.

"With the foregoing conditions, which are hereby pledged to the Mormons, and which will be faithfully kept by me and other officers in behalf of the government of the United States, I cannot doubt but that you will, in a few days, be able to raise five hundred young and efficient men for this expedition.

"Very respectfully, your obedient servant,
"To CAPTAIN JAMES ALLEN,   (Signed) S. F. KEARNEY,
 "First Reg. Dragoons,   Colonel of First Dragoons.
 "Fort Leavenworth."

Acting upon this order, Captain Allen proceeded to Mount Pisgah, one of the camps of the Saints, and explained the object of his visit by issuing the following:

CIRCULAR TO THE MORMONS.

"I have come among you, instructed by Colonel S. F. Kearney, of the U. S. Army, now commanding the Army of the West, to visit the Mormon camps, and to accept the service, for twelve months, of four or five companies of Mormon men who may be willing to serve their country for that period in our present war with Mexico; this force to unite with the Army of the West at Santa Fe, and be marched thence to California, where they will be discharged.

"They will receive pay and rations, and other allowances, such as volunteers or regular soldiers receive, from the day they shall be mustered into the service, and will be entitled to all comforts and benefits of regular soldiers of the army, and when discharged, as contemplated, at California, they will be given, gratis, their arms and accoutrements, with which they will be fully equipped at Fort Leavenworth. This is offered to the Mormon people now.

"This gives an opportunity of sending a portion of their young and intelligent men to the ultimate destination of their whole people, and entirely at the expense of the United States, and this advanced party can thus pave the way and look out the land for their brethren to come after them. Those of the Mormons who are desirous of serving their country, on the conditions here enumerated, are requested to meet me without delay at their principal camp at Council Bluffs, whither I am now going to consult with their principal men, and to receive and organize the force contemplated to be raised.

"I will receive all healthy, able-bodied men of from eighteen to forty-five years of age.

"J. ALLEN, Captain 1st Dragoons.

"*Camp of the Mormons, at Mount Pisgah,*
"*one hundred and thirty-eight miles east*
"*of Council Bluffs, June 26, 1846.*

"NOTE.—I hope to complete the organization of this battalion in six days after my reaching Council Bluffs, or within nine days from this time."

A meeting of the High Council of Mount Pisgah was called, before which the foregoing circular was read, but the only thing the council felt authorized to do was to treat the government agent with courtesy and respect, and give him a letter of introduction to President Brigham Young and other authorities at Council Bluffs, which they did.

Elder Wilford Woodruff, of the quorum of the Twelve Apostles, who was at the time in Mount Pisgah, dispatched a special messenger to inform President Young of the arrival of Captain Allen, and the object of his mission.

On the 1st of July, Captain Allen having arrived at Council Bluffs, a council, composed of President Brigham Young, Heber C. Kimball, Willard Richards, Orson Hyde, Orson Pratt, George A. Smith and Levi Richards, was called. Before this council, Captain Allen made known his errand.

It may well be imagined that many of the Saints hesitated about responding to this call. It was not from lack of courage either. The danger of such an expedition would never have caused them to shrink or falter; but they had been deceived so many times by those who held authority in the nation that they looked upon this new requisition with distrust.

The Saints were in peculiar circumstances. They were

scattered all the way from Nauvoo to Council Bluffs, and even west of there, for some had crossed the Missouri. They were destitute, having been forced to part with nearly every available thing to procure bredstuffs. The poor and sick and helpless who had been left in Nauvoo were looking to those in the advance camps to help them, and many of the latter were under promise to do so. They had hostile Indians in advance of them, and still more hostile Missouri and Illinois mobocrats in their rear. Responding to the call would prevent the pioneer company, which for several days previous had been making preparations to start, from pushing forward to the mountains that year. How were their families to exist in that wilderness when winter came on? How would the helpless women and children do if the fathers and brothers, upon whom they had depended for support and protection, were taken away? These were questions that were bound to arise.

Assistance in emigrating with their families westward, would have been hailed with joy. Work of any kind and at any price, on the route of their proposed journey, by which they could earn a subsistence, would have been considered a God-send. But joining the army and leaving their families in such a condition was repugnant to their feelings. Such a thing had never been thought of, much less asked for, by the Saints. The assertion which has been made by their enemies: that they desired and solicited the privilege of joning the army to go against Mexico, leaving their wives and children homeless and destitute wanderers on the banks of the Missouri, is a base libel on the character of the Saints. They were loyal citizens, but they never expected such a sacrifice would be required of them to prove their loyalty to the government. Though Captain Allen represented the call as an act of benovelence on the part of the government, and assured the Saints that here were hundreds of thousands of volunteers in the States ready to enlist, it is doubtful whether he would have got one of the Saints to join him if it had been left to his own influence. Indeed, it is said that he admitted afterwards that he could not have blamed the people if they had refused to respond. He would not have enlisted under such circumstances himself, even to save the government.

The condition of the people as Captain Allen passed their camps and the kind treatment he everywhere met, including that of the High Council at Mount Pisgah, had touched a tender chord in the brave officer's manly heart. His manner was pleasing, and he gained the good will of the people quite readily; but it required something else than his influence to raise the Mormon Battalion.

On receiving the call, President Young and those associated with him in council decided almost instantly that the Battalion should be raised. There is much, however, to prove that they did not regard it simply as an invitation which they could accept or decline with impunity. President Young said, "we want to conform to the *requisition* made upon us, and we will do nothing else till we have accomplished this thing. If we want the privilege of going where we can worship God according to the dictates of our consciences, we must raise the Battalion."

President Geo. Q. Cannon, writing upon this subject, says, "Captain Allen did not inform the people—for the reason, probably, that he knew nothing about it—what the design was in case the Battalion was not raised. The secret history of the transaction is, as President Young was afterwards informed on the best of authority, that Thomas H. Benton, United States Senator from the State of Missouri, got a pledge from President Polk, that if the Mormons did not raise the Battalion of five hundred, he might have the privilege of raising volunteers in the upper counties of Missouri, to fall upon them and use them up."

To say the least of it, it was a very severe test of their loyalty. President Young "asked the people to make a distinction between this action of the general government, in calling upon them for volunteers, and their former oppressions in Missouri and Illinois," and with a full sense of the sacrifice required, the people responded.

Presidents Brigham Young, Heber C. Kimball and Willard Richards rode back to Mount Pisgah, visiting all the intermediate camps by the way, as recruiting sergeants, and sent epistles to Garden Grove and Nauvoo explaining what was required, and urging an immediate response. At the same time others were busy in the vicinity of Council Bluffs, raising all the volunteers they could.

President Young encouraged the men by assuring them that their families should be cared for, that they should fare as well as his did, and that he would see that they were helped along. He also predicted that not one of those who might enlist would fall by the hands of the nation's foe, that their only fighting would be with wild beasts; that there would not be as many bullets whistle around their ears as did around Dr. Willard Richards' in Carthage jail, etc.

These predictions were repeated in President Young's farewell address to the command at Council Bluffs. The sequel will show, improbable as it naturally looked at the time and during the travels of the Battalion, that these predictions were literally fulfilled.

On the 16th day of July, 1846, four companies of over four hundred men, all told, and part of the fifth, were mustered into the service of the United States, at Council Bluffs, Iowa Territory. Our pay and rations dated from this period. The fifth company was soon afterwards filled.

The following are the names of officers and men, also families accompanying the command, as far as they have been obtained:

LIST OF NAMES IN THE MORMON BATTALION.

COMPANY A.

OFFICERS.

Jefferson Hunt, *Captain.*
George W. Oman, 1st. *Lieutenant.*
Lorenzo Clark, 2nd. *Lieut.*
William W. Willis, 3rd *Lieut.*
  (1st *Sergeant at Muster In*)
James Ferguson, *Sergt. Major.*
Phinehas R. Wright, (1st *Sergeant Private at M. O.*)
Ebenezer Brown, 2nd *Sergt.*
Reddick N. Allred, 3rd *Sergt.*

Alexander McCord, 4th *Sergt.*
Gilbert Hunt, 1st. *Corporal.*
Lafayette N. Frost, 2nd *Corp.*
Thomas Weir, 3rd *Corp.* (*Private at M. O.*)
William S. Muir, 4th *Corp.* (*Private at M. I.; 1st. Sergeant at M. O.*)
Elisha Everett *Musician.*
Joseph W. Richards   "
  (Died at Pueblo.)

PRIVATES.

1. Allen Rufus C.
2. Allred James R.
3. Allred James T. S.
4. Allred Reuben W.
5. Allen Albern
6. Brown John
7. Butterfield Jacob K.
8. Bailey James
17. Bryant John S.
18. Curtis Josiah
19. Cox Henderson
20. Chase Hiram B.
21. Calkins Alva C.
22. Casper William W.
23. Calkins James W.
24. Calkins Sylvanus
25. Calkins Edwin R.
26. Colman George
27. Clark Joseph
28. Clark Riley G.
29. Decker Zechariah B.
30. Dobson Joseph
31. Dodson Eli
32. Earl James C.
33. Egbert Robert C.
34. Fairbanks Henry
35. Frederick David
36. Glines James H. (Q. M. Sergeant at M. I., Private at M. O.)
37. Garner David
38. Gordon Gilman
39. Goodwin Andrew
40. Hulett Schuyler
41. Holden Elijah E.
42. Hampton James (died at camp on Rio Grand)
43. Hawkins Benjamin
44. Hickenlooper William F.
45. Hunt Martial
46. Hewett Eli B.
47. Hudson Wilford
48. Hoyt Timothy S.
49. Hoyt Henry P.
50. Ivy Richard A.
51. Jackson Charles A.
52. Johnson Henry
53. Kelley William
9. Brunson Clinton D.
10. Brass Benjamin
11. Blanchard Mervin S.
12. Beckstead Gordon S.
13. Beckstead Orin M.
14. Bickmore Gilbert
15. Brown William W.
16. Bevan James
54. Kelley Nicholas
55. Kibley James
56. Lemon James W.
57. Lake Barnabas
58. Moss David
59. Maxwell Maxie
60. Mayfield Benjamin F.
61. Naile Conrad
62. Oyler Melcher
63. Packard Henry, (M. O. as Corporal.)
64. Persons Ebenezer
65. Roe Cariatat C.
66. Ritter John
67. Steele George E.
68. Steele Isaiah C.
69. Sessions Richard
70. Shepherd Lafayette, (M. O. as Corporal.)
71. Swartout Hamilton
72. Sexton George S.
73. Sessions John
74. Sessions William B.
75. Taylor Joseph
76. Thompson John
77. Vrandenburg Adna
78. Weaver Miles
79. Wriston John P.
80. Wriston Isaac N.
81. Weaver Franklin
82. Wilson Alfred G.
83. Wheeler Merrill W.
84. White Samuel S. (Samuel F. in original)
85. Webb Charles Y.
86. Winn Dennis
87. Woodworth Lysander
88. White Joseph
89. Willey Jeremiah

COMPANY B.

OFFICERS.

Jesse D. Hunter, *Captain*
Elam Luddington, 1st *Lieut.*
Ruel Barrus, 2nd *Lieut.*
Philemon C. Merrill, 3d *Lieut.*
William Coray, 1st *Orderly Sergeant*
William Hyde, 2nd *Orderly Sergeant*

David P. Rainey, 1st *Corp.*
Thomas Dunn, 2nd *Corp.*
John D. Chase, 3rd *Corp.*
William Hunter, *Musician*
George W. Taggart,
Albert Smith, 3rd *Orderly Sergeant*

PRIVATES.

 1 Allen George
 2 Allen Elijah
 3 Alexander Horace
 4 Allen Franklin
 5 Bush Richard
 6 Bird William
 7 Bingham Thomas
 8 Bingham Erastus
 9 Billings Orson
 10 Bigler Henry W.
 11 Boley Samuel (died on Missouri river)
 12 Borrowman John
 13 Brackenberry Benj. B.
 14 Brown Francis
 15 Bliss Robert S.
 16 Bybee John
 17 Clark George S.
 18 Colton Philander
 19 Cheney Zacheus
 20 Callahan Thomas W.
 21 Church Haden W.
 22 Camp J. G.
 23 Carter P. J.
 24 Curtis Dorr P.
 25 Carter Richard
 26 Dayton William J.
 27 Dutcher Thomas P.
 28 Dalton Henry S.
 29 Dunham Albert
 30 Evans Israel
 31 Evans William
 32 Eastman Marcus N.
 33 Freeman Elijah
 34 Follett William A.
 35 Fife Peter
 36 Green Ephraim
 37 Garner William A.
 38 Garner Phillip
 39 Hawk Nathan
 40 Huntsman Isaiah
 41 Hoffheins Jacob
 42 Hanks Ephraim R.
 43 Hawk William
 44 Hinkley Arza E. (Ezra on original)
 45 Hunter Edward
 46 Haskell George
 47 Harris Silas
 48 Jones David H.
 49 Keyser Guy M.
 50 King John M.
 51 Kirk Thomas
 52 Lawson John
 53 Morris Thomas
 54 McCarty Nelson
 55 Mount Hiram B.
 56 Martin Jesse B.
 57 Murdock John
 58 Murdock Price
 59 Myers Samuel
 60 Miles Samuel
 61 Noler Christian
 62 Owens Robert
 63 Pearson Ephraim
 64 Persons Harmon
 65 Prouse William
 66 Park James, 1st
 67 Park James, 2nd
 68 Richards Peter F.
 69 Rogers Samuel H.
 70 Study David

LIST OF NAMES.

71 Smith Azariah
72 Stevens Lyman
73 Stoddard Rufus
74 Simmons William A.
75 Sly James C.
76 Steers Andrew J.
77 Stillman Dexter
78 Workman Andrew J.
79 Walker William
80 Willis Ira

81 Workman Oliver G.
82 Willis W. S. S.
83 Watts John
84 Whitney Francis T.
85 Wright Charles
86 Wilcox Edward
87 Wilcox Henry
88 Wheeler John L.
89 Winters Jacob
90 Zabriskie Jerome

COMPANY C.

OFFICERS.

James Brown, *Captain*
George W. Rosecrans, *1st Lieutenant*
Samuel Thompson, *2nd Lieut.*
Robert Clift, (*promoted from Ord. Sergt. to 3rd Lieut.*)
Orson B. Adams, *1st Sergt. at M. I., 2nd Sergt. at M. O.*
Elijah Elmer, *2nd Sergt. at M. I., 1st Sergt. at M. O.*
Joel J Terrill, *3rd Sergt. (Private at M. O.)*

David Wilkin, *4th Sergt.; (Private at M. O.)*
Jabez Nowlin, *1st Corporal; (Private at M. O.)*
Alexander Brown, *2nd Corp.*
Edward Martin, *3rd Corp.; (2nd Sergt. at M. O.)*
Daniel Tyler, *4th Corp., (3rd Sergt. at M. O.)*
Richard D. Sprague, *Musician*
Russell G. Brownell, *(Corporal at M. O.)*

PRIVATES.

1 Adair Wesley
2 Boyle Henry G. (Henry B. Miller on original)
3 Burt William
4 Barney Walter
5 Babcock Lorenzo
6 Brown Jesse J.
7 Bailey Addison
8 Bailey Jefferson
9 Beckstead William E.
10 Brimhall John
11 Blackburn Abner
12 Bybee Henry G.
13 Clift James
14 Covil John Q. A.
15 Condit Jeptha

16 Carpenter Isaac
17 Carpenter William H.
18 Calvert John
19 Catlin George W.
20 Donald Neal
21 Dunn James
22 Dalton Harry
23 Dalton Edward
24 Durphy Francillo
25 Dodge Augustus E.
26 Forbush Lorin
27 Fellows Hiram W.
28 Fife John
29 Fifield Levi
30 Gould John C.
31 Gould Samuel

32 Gibson Thomas
33 Green John
34 Hatch Meltiah *Meltial*
35 Hatch Orin
36 Holt William
37 Harmon Ebenezer
38 Harmon Lorenzo F.
39 Holdaway Shadrach
40 Hendrickson James
41 Hancock Charles G.
42 Hancock George W.
43 Ivie Thomas C.
44 Johnston William J.
45 Johnston Jesse W.
46 Johnson Jarvis
47 Layton Christopher
48 Larson Thurston
49 Landers Ebenezer
50 Lewis Samuel
51 Myler James
52 McCullough Levi H.
53 Morey Harley
54 Maggard Benjamin
55 Mowrey John T.
56 Mead Orlando F.
57 More Calvin W.
58 Olmstead Hiram
59 Perkins David
60 Perkins John
61 Pickup George

62 Peck Thorit, (Corp. at M. O.)
63 Peck Isaac
64 Pulsipher David
65 Persons Judson A.
66 Richie Benjamin
67 Rust William W.
68 Richmond Benjamin
69 Reynolds William
70 Riser John Jacob
71 Smith Milton
72 Smith Richard D.
73 Shupe James
74 Shupe Andrew J.
75 Shipley Joseph
76 Squires William (Corp. at M.-O.)
77 Shumway Aurora
78 Thompson James Lewis
79 Thomas Nathan T.
80 Thomas Elijah
81 Tuttle Elanson
82 Truman Jacob M.
83 Tindell Solomon
84 Wade Edward
85 Wade Moses
86 Wood William
87 White John B.
88 Wilcox Matthew
89 Welsh Madison
90 Wheeler Henry

COMPANY D.

OFFICERS.

Nelson Higgins, *Capt.*
George P. Dykes, 1st *Lieut.*
Sylvester Hulett 2nd *Lieut.*
Cyrus C. Canfield, 3rd *Lieut.*
Nathaniel V. Jones, 1st *Sergt.* (*Private at M. O.*)
Thomas Williams, 2nd *Sergt.*
Luther T. Tuttle, 3rd *Sergt.*
Alpheus P. Haws, 4th *Sergt.*

Arnold Stephens, 1st *Corp.*
John Buchanan, 2nd *Corp.*
William Coon, 3rd *Corp.*
Lewis Lane, 4th *Corp.* (*Private at M. O.*)
Willard Smith, *Musician*
Henry W. Jackson, (Henry J. on original) *Musician*

LIST OF NAMES.

PRIVATES.

1. Abbott Joshua
2. Averett Luthan
3. Brown James 1st
4. Brown James S.
5. Badlam Samuel
6. Button Montgomery
7. Brizee Henry W.
8. Boyd George W.
9. Boyd William
10. Barger William
11. Compton Allen
12. Cole James
13. Casto William
14. Casto James
15. Curtis Foster
16. Clawson John
17. Cox Amos
18. Collins Robert H.
19. Chase Abner
20. Davis Sterling
21. Davis Eleazer
22. Davis James
23. Douglass Ralph
24. Douglass James
25. Fleether Philander
26. Frazier Thomas L.
27. Fatoute Ezra
28. Forsgreen John
29. Finlay Thomas
30. Gilbert John
31. Gifford William W.
32. Gribble William W.
33. Hoagland Lucas
34. Henry Daniel
35. Hirons James
36. Huntington Dimick B.
37. Hendricks Wm.
38. Holmes Jonathan H
39. Higgins Alfred
40. Hunsaker Abraham, (1st Sergt. at M. O.)
41. Jacobs Sanford, (Corp. at M. O.)
42. Kenny Loren Edward
43. Lamb Lisbon
44. Laughlin David S.
45. Maxwell William
46. Meeseek Peter J.
47. Meacham Erastus
48. Bingham Erastus
49. Merrill Ferdinand
50. McArthur Henry
51. Oakley James
52. Owen James
53. Peck Edwin M.
54. Perrin Charles
55. Pettegrew James P.
56. Rollins John
57. Rawson Daniel R.
58. Roberts Benjamin
59. Runyan Levi
60. Rowe William
61. Richmond William
62. Robinson William
63. Raymond Almon P.
64. Smith John G.
65. Stephens Alexander
66. Spencer William W.
67. Stewart Benjamin
68. Stewart James
69. Stewart Robert Boyd
70. Sargent Abel M.
71. Savage Levi
72. Stillman Clark
73. Swarthout Nathan
74. Sharp Albert
75. Sharp Norman
76. Shelton Sebert C.
77. Sanderson Henry W.
78. Steele John
79. Thompson Henry
80. Thompson Miles
81. Tanner Myron
82. Twitchel Anciel
83. Tubbs William
84. Treat Thomas W.
85. Hayward Thomas
86. Tippets John
87. Walker Edwin
88. Woodward Francis
89. Whiting Almon
90. Whiting Edmond

COMPANY E.

OFFICERS.

Daniel C. Davis, *Captain.*
James Pace, 1*st. Lieut.*
Andrew Lytle, 2*nd. Lieut.*
Samuel L. Gully, 3*rd Lieut.*
Samuel L. Brown, 1*st Sergt.*
Richard Brazier, 2*nd Sergt.*
Ebenezer Hanks, 3*rd Sergt.*
Daniel Browett, 4*th Sergt.*
James A. Scott, *Corp.* (died at Pueblo)
Levi W. Hancock, *Musician.*
Jesse Earl, "

PRIVATES.

1 Allen John, (drummed out of service; non-"Mormon")
2 Allen George
3 Bentley John
4 Beers William
5 Brown Daniel
6 Buckley Newman
7 Bunker Edward
8 Caldwell Matthew
9 Campbell Samuel
10 Campbell Jonathan
11 Cazier James
12 Cazier John
13 Clark Samuel
14 Clark Albert
15 Chapin Samuel
16 Cox John
17 Cummings George
18 Day Abraham
19 Dyke Simon
20 Dennett Daniel Q.
21 Earl Jacob
22 Ewell Wm.
23 Ewell Martin F.
24 Earl Justice C.
25 Findlay John
26 Follett William T.
27 Glazier Luther W.
28 Harmon Oliver N.
29 Harris Robert
30 Harrison Isaac
31 Hart James S.
32 Harrison Israel
34 Hickmot John
35 Hopkins Charles A
36 Hoskins Henry
37 Howell T. C. D.
38 Howell William
39 Jacobs Bailey
40 Judd Hiram
41 Judd Zadock Knapp
42 Jimmerson Charles
43 Knapp Albert
44 Kelley George
45 Karren Thomas
46 Lance William
47 McLelland Wm.
48 Miller Daniel
49 McBride Haslam
50 Miller Miles
51 Park Wm. A.
52 Pettegrew David
53 Pixton Robert
54 Phelps Alva (died on the Arkansas)
55 Porter Sanford
56 Pugmire Jonathan, jun.
57 Rollins ——
58 Richardson Thomas
59 Richards L.
60 Roberts Levi
61 Sanders Richard T.
62 Scott Leonard M.
63 Scott James R.
64 Skein Joseph
65 Spidle John
66 Slater Richard

68 Smith Lot
69 Smith David
70 Smith Elisha
71 Smith John
72 St. John Stephen M.
73 Stevens Roswell
74 Standage Henry

75 Strong William
76 Tanner Albert
77 West Benj.
78 Wilson George
79 Woolsey Thomas
80 Williams James V.
81 Whitworth Wm.

SERVANTS TO OFFICERS.

The following names have been sent me as having served as servants to officers in the Mormon Battalion, and as they were mostly too young to be received as soldiers, are entitled to much praise for their youthful patriotism and bravery. There may have been a few others not reported:

Zemira Palmer, to Col. James Allen until his death; to Dr. George B. Sanderson from Ft. Leavenworth to Santa Fe, thence to Lieut. Lorenzo Clark until the corps was discharged. William Byron Pace, to Lieut. James Pace. Wilson D. Pace, to Lieut. Andrew Lytle. N. D. Higins, to Captain Nelson Higgins. Charles Edwin Colten, to Adjutant P. C. Merrill. James Mowrey, to Lieuts. George Rosecrans, Samuel Thompson and Robert Clift. Elisha Smith, to Capt. Daniel C. Davis.

LIST OF FAMILIES WHO ACCOMPANIED THE BATTALION.

Mrs. Celia Hunt, wife of senior Captain Jefferson Hunt; sons: Hyrum, John, Joseph, Parley; daughters: Jane, Harriet, Mary; second wife, Matilda; in the family, Peter Nease, Ellen Nease, John Bosco and wife, Jane. Mrs. Hunter, wife of Captain Jesse D. Hunter, of Company B., died at San Diego, left an infant and perhaps other children. Mrs. Mary Brown, wife of Captain James Brown, of Company C.; son: David Black, and some children by first wife. Mrs. Captain Nelson Higgins, of Company D.; sons: Alpheus, Don Carlos; daughters: Druzilla, Almira (married John Chase at Pueblo), and one child born at Pueblo. Mrs. Susan, wife of Captain Daniel C. Davis, of Company E; son: Daniel C. Davis, Jr. Mrs. Fanny

Mariah, wife of Dimick B. Huntington; sons: Clark Allen, Lot; daughters: Martha, Zina, Betsey Prescinda (born at Pueblo). Mrs. Malinda, wife of Milton Kelley; Malinda Catherine (born at Pueblo, now wife of Benj. L. Alexander). Mrs. Elizabeth, wife of Sergt. Sebert C. Shelton; sons: Jackson Mayfield, John Mayfield; daughters: Sarah Mayfield, Caroline Shelton, Mariah Shelton. Mrs. Eunice, wife of James P. Brown; sons: Robert, Newman, John (born while traveling between Pueblo and Salt Lake Valley); daughters: Sarah Jane and Mary Ann. Mrs. Norman Sharp; daughter born at Pueblo. Miss Caroline Sargent. Mrs. Montgomery Button; sons: James, Jutson, Charles; daughter: Louiza. Mrs. Albina, wife of Thomas S. Williams; son: Ephraim; daughters: Caroline, Phebe, (the latter born at Pueblo.) Mrs. Jane Hanks, wife of Sergt. Ebenezer Hanks. Mrs. Phebe, wife of Sergt. Ebenezer Brown. Mrs. Sophia, wife of William Tubbs. Mrs. Catherine, wife of John Steele; daughter: Mary; also Young Elizabeth (born twelve days after arriving in Salt Lake Valley). Mrs. Susan, wife of Sergt. Orson B. Adams. Mrs. Mary Ann, wife of John Hyrons. Mrs. Emeline, wife of John Hess. Mrs. Rebecca, wife of Elisha Smith. Mrs. Isabella, wife of David Wilkin. Mrs. J. T. S. Allred. Mrs. Reuben Allred. Mrs. Sarah Shupe, wife of Andrew Jackson Shupe. Mrs. Coray, wife of Sergt. Coray. Mrs. Ruth Abbott. Mrs. Harriet Brown, wife of Daniel Brown. Mrs. Sarah, wife of Nicholas Kelley; son: Parley. Mrs. Agnes, wife of Sergt. Edward L. Brown. Mrs. Caroline, wife of John Sessions.

There may have been a few others, not reported, as all are collected from memory.

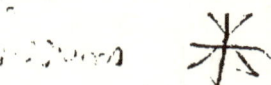

CHAPTER II.

First Orders Issued—Condition of Families and Feeling of Soldiers—Instructions of Church Authorities—A pathetic Story by a Soldier's Wife.

The following orders were read immediately after the first four companies and part of the fifth were mustered into service:

"Head Quarters, Mormon Battalion,
Council Bluffs, Iowa,
July 16, 1846.

(Order No. 1.)

"In virtue of authority given me by the Col. commanding the army of the west, I hereby assume the command of the Mormon Battalion, raised at this place for the service of the United States. Therefore, companies now organized will be held in readiness to march at the shortest notice, and as soon as the fifth company be filled all will be ready for movement.

J. Allen, Lt. Col. U. S. A., Commanding."

(Order No. 2.)

"The following appointments are made in the Battalion:

"First lieutenant, George P. Dykes, to be Adjutant; private, James H. Glines, to be Sergeant Major; private, Sebert C. Shelton, of Company A, to be Quartermaster Sergeant. They will be respected and obeyed accordingly.

J. Allen, Lt. Col. U. S. A., Commanding."

"Head Quarters, Mormon Battalion,
Council Bluffs,
July 16, 1846.

(Order No. 3.)

"William L. McIntyre, of the Mormon people, is hereby appointed assistant surgeon to the Mormon Battalion of volunteers of the United States, and under my command. He will be obeyed and respected accordingly, and will be entitled to the pay and emoluments as an assistant surgeon in the United States Army.

J. ALLEN, Lt. Col. U. S. A., Commanding."

To show the feelings of the members of the Batallion, as well as the condition of their families, I will here quote from the journal of the late Sergeant Wlliam Hyde, which may be taken as a sample of many:

"A few had tents or temporary cabins. We were mustered into the service of the United States, on 16th of July, 1846, and marched to the Missouri river, a distance of eight miles, to purchase blankets and other necessary articles for the campaign, the price of the same to be deducted from our first draft on government.

"The thoughts of leaving my family at this critical time are indescribable. They were far from the land of their nativity, situated upon a lonely prairie with no dwelling but a wagon, the scorching sun beating upon them, with the prospect of the cold winds of December finding them in the same bleak, dreary place.

My family consisted of a wife and two small children, who were left in company with an aged father and mother and a brother. The most of the Battalion left families, some in care of the Church and some in the care of relatives, with some in their own care. When we were to meet with them again, God only knew. Nevertheless, we did not feel to murmur."

Sergeant Hyde further says: "On Saturday, the 18th of July, 1846, President B. Young, H. C. Kimball, P. P. Pratt, W. Richards, John Taylor and Wilford Woodruff met in private council with the commissioned and non-commissioned officers, on the bank of the Missouri river, and there gave us their last charge and blessing, with a firm promise that, on condition of faithfulness on our part, our lives should be spared, our expedition should result in great good and our names should be held in honorable remembrance to all generations. They instructed the officers to be as fathers to the privates, to remember their prayers, to see that the name of the Deity was revered, and that virtue and cleanliness were strictly observed. They also instructed us to treat all men with kindness and never to take that which did not belong to us, even from our worst enemies, not even in time of war if we could possibly prevent it; and in case we should come in contact with our enemies and be successful, we should treat prisoners with kindness and never take life when it could be avoided."

The foregoing instructions from the leaders of the Latter-day Saints, given in a private council, are a complete refutation of the oft trumped-up charge that they teach honesty, virtue and forbearance in public, and the reverse in private. They are in accord with the teachings of the Prophet Joseph Smith and other leading men with whom the author has been acquainted almost half a century.

The following synopsis of a painfully interesting letter from the pen of Sister Margaret Bridges, formerly wife of Alva Phelps, whose death will be noticed in the proper place, is, by no means, descriptive of an isolated case of suffering:

"FILLMORE CITY,
"April 30, 1878.

"*Brother Tyler:*

"DEAR SIR:—In complying with your request to give a sketch of the circumstances attending the enlistment of my former husband, Alva Phelps, in the Mormon Battalion, I find, on referring to my memory, that my sketch must necessarily be brief, as at that time I was suffering from a severe illness, leaving events only of the most sorrowful nature to be impressed with any degree of vividness upon my recollection.

"We were traveling when the call came for him to leave us. It was midnight when we were awakened from our slumbers with the painful news that we were to be left homeless, without a protector. I was very ill at the time, my children all small, my babe also extremely sick; but the call was pressing; there was no time for any provision to be made for wife or children; no time for tears; regret was unavailing. He started in the morning. I watched him from my wagon-bed till his loved form was lost in the distance; it was my last sight of him.

"Two months from the day of his enlistment, the sad news of my bereavement arrived. This blow entirely prostrated me. But I had just embarked upon my sea of troubles; winter found me bed-ridden, destitute, in a wretched hovel which was built upon a hill-side; the season was one of constant rain; the situation of the hovel and its openness, gave free access to piercing winds, and water flowed over the dirt floor, converting it into mud two or three inches deep; no wood but what my little ones picked up around the fences, so green it filled the room with smoke; the rain dropping and wetting the bed which I was powerless to leave; no relative to cheer or comfort me, a stranger away from all who ever loved me; my neighbors could do but little, their own troubles and destitution engrossing their time; my little daughter of seven my only help; no eye to witness my sufferings but the pitying one of God—He did not desert me.

"Spring brought some alleviation from my sufferings, yet one pan of meal was my all, my earthly store of provisions. I found sale for the leaders of my team. The long, dreary winter had passed, and, although it was many months before health and comparative comfort were my portion, still I thank the Lord this was the darkest part of my life.

"The incidents immediately connected with my husband's death I believe you are better acquainted with than I am, so for me to give an account of his sad fate, would be both unnecessary and painful. If, in this short epistle, you can find any item of information, I shall be happy in forwarding it to you. Thanking you for the interest you are taking in our dear departed and the respect you manifest for our honored dead, I am, sincerely yours, in the bonds of the everlasting gospel.

"MARGARET BRIDGES,

"(Formerly MARGARET PHELPS.)"

The motive that prompted our government to ask of a body of outraged, banished exiles, more than two hundred times their proper quota of men, according to the ratio required of the several States in the Union, has already been explained.

Our best men, and even children, in some instances had been inhumanly massacred, and women had been shot and brutally outraged. We had appealed to the various officials, from the justice of the peace to the President and Congress, in vain, for redress of our wrongs, getting the only satisfaction of—"Gentlemen, your cause is just, but we can do nothing for you," one of the potent reasons assigned being that if they attempted to give us our rights according to their oaths, our enemies would not vote for them at the next election.

CHAPTER III.

Money Subscribed by the Soldiers for their Families and Poor Friends—First Death on the Journey—Out of Flour—A Prejudiced Missourian—Regrets of Mobocrats—Hurricane—Arrival at Fort Leavenworth—Anecdote of Colonel C.—Dr. Sanderson appointed Surgeon—Haste to get Muskets—Character of Missouri Volunteers—More Money Subscribed by the Soldiers—Superior Intelligence and Obedience.

PREVIOUS to taking up the line of march, on the 20th of July, the men of each company subscribed liberally of their wages to be sent back for the support of their families and to aid in gathering the poor from Nauvoo.

A rain storm prevailed during the forenoon of the following day and in the afternoon we traveled about four miles through sand and mud. Elder Jesse C. Little spent that night with us, and the next day, at the request of the officers, he delivered a short and encouraging address to the command while formed in a hollow square. He spoke in high terms of the integrity and energy of Brother Samuel Boley, who was dangerously ill. The invalid was very kindly nursed and doctored by our assistant surgeon, Dr. Wm. L. McIntyre. The 5th company, having been previously filled up and organized, overtook the command on Mosquito creek.

On the morning of the 23rd, we had to perform the painful duty of burying brother Samuel Boley, who died between the hours of 12 and 1 o'clock the previous night. This was the first death that occurred in our ranks. He was wrapped in his blanket and buried in a rough lumber coffin, which was the best we could get.

On the succeeding day we crossed the Nishnabotany River at Hunsaker's, Ferry, and camped near Lindon, Missouri. The weather being excessively warm, Colonel Allen was in favor of moderate marches; but Adjutant Dykes, being himself a great walker, and having the advantage of a horse to ride, urged long marches. *Colonel Allen consented to this, presuming, probably, that the men wished it. They, however, desired only reasonable, healthful marches. Thus many began to fail at almost the beginning of a journey of over two thousand miles. Several parties, about this time, were taken sick, among whom was the author, and were healed by anointing with oil and the laying on of hands, and went on their way rejoicing.

Sergeants Wm. Hyde and Wm Coray, finding the long marches in the broiling sun too hard for them, each purchased an Indian pony from an old settler, paying twenty-five dollars apiece for them.

On the evening of the 25th, the command being out of flour, and there being none in the vicinity to purchase, many retired to bed fasting, while others made the best supper they could on parched corn; yet all seemed to be in excellent spirits in the expectation of soon having full rations. No flour, however, was obtained for two days afterwards, during which time a distance of thirty-eight miles was traveled in the heat and dust, and that too while many of the men were sick. When we had crossed the Nodaway River and camped at the town of Oregon, a Missourian, probably a mobocrat of the old type, whose name we regret, does not appear, who had been hired to deliver a load of flour, stopped at some distance from our camp and refused to deliver it to the Quartermaster and take his receipt, because he was a Mormon. He would deliver it to no one but the Colonel. That noble officer, however, was highly insulted, and ordered him to deliver the flour immediately upon pain of being arrested and put under guard.

Delivery was made immediately.

"Good for the Colonel!" and "God bless the Colonel!" were repeated from one end of the camp to the other.

Passing on from the Nodaway river, we found the country poor and broken, the road bad and the inhabitants very miserable. A great many of the settlers in this part of the country, were old mobocrats, as several of them admitted,

They said that they had been misled by false rumors, and very much regretted having persecuted the Saints. They would have been glad to take their old "Mormon" neighbors back. They had not prospered since the Saints were banished from the State, and the men they then hired to labor for them accomplished only about one half the amount of work in a day that the "Mormons" did.

On the 29th, we passed St. Joseph, then a town of some importance, in good order, keeping time to the tune of "The Girl I left Behind Me," and camped one mile outside of the town. While here Luke Johnson, formerly one of the Twelve Apostles, but at that time out of the Church, met Sergeant Wm. Hyde and informed him that the Missourians were perfectly astonished at the course the "Mormons" were taking. The Missourians had supposed, when they heard of the President's requisition, that the Saints would only spurn it. But when they saw the Battalion march through with civility and in good order, they were really dumbfounded.

On the 30th, we passed through Bloomington and camped on a small creek, where, about 9 o'clock p. m., the wind commenced to blow a gale and continued until the trees fell in all directions around the camp.

The men were aroused from their slumbers, and hurried out of their rude brush shelters or "wigwams," looking every moment for the trees in camp to fall. About eighty smouldering fires were revived by the gale, while the howling of the wind, the crashing of the trees as they fell around us, the vivid lightning and the roar of thunder made the scene one of terror. Yet the fact that not one tree fell in our camp proved that God was with us. Our teams were in a field covered with deadened timber, which fell thick around the animals, but the only harm done was the killing of one ox. The owner of the field afterwards remarked that it was a marvel that they were not all killed. He had been quite alarmed lest his house, which was in the vicinity should blow down.

The following day we passed through the thriving town of Weston, keeping time to music, the same as at St. Joseph, to the admiration and astonishment of the inhabitants. They said none but Mormons, under such forbidding circumstances, would have enlisted. They frankly admitted that they would not have thought of such a thing. Some of them said "the call is a disgrace and a shame to the Government." The generality of the citizens of this town were honorable, upright people, and have always been opposed to any spirit of persecution.

From Weston we marched to the ferry on the Missouri river, opposite Fort Leavenworth, and were nearly five hours in crossing and making our way to the garrison. We found companies of Missouri volunteers there. We received our tents the same day; these added much to our comfort, but, as every rose has its thorn, so with our movable houses; the hot sun beating upon them "made it warm for us" in the middle of the day, though we were very comfortable compared with our previous condition. We camped on the public square of the Fort.

Henry W. Bigler was shaking terribly with the ague at the time we camped.

Our tents, being new, and pitched in military order, presented a grand appearance, and the merry songs which resounded through the camp made all feel like "casting dull care away."

Between Council Bluffs and Fort Leavenworth the following laughable occurrence took place:

In the Battalion was a man whom we will call C., who had, by some means, procured a peculiar kind of hat belonging to an officer's uniform of the Nauvoo Legion. This lone hat was the only article of uniform in the Battalion, except that worn by the colonel. Our friend C. was the "speckled bird" of the flock. Naturally enough his messmates teased him, and by others many rich and perhaps some cutting jokes were passed at his expense. C., being somewhat eccentric in his way, concluded he had rather "too much of a good thing," and dropped out of the ranks, as some supposed, to desert and return to the Bluffs. This opinion was strengthened by his long absence.

Finally "Joe," who is now a resident of Utah, an acquaintance of C., overtook the command on the way to Fort Leavenworth, and gave the following account of the missing man, whom he had passed on the road, and who he thought would be in camp that night.

A Missouri farmer, learning that "Joe" belonged to the Mormon community, informed him that he had had the honor of having his colonel to dine with him, and represented him as being a fine appearing man and a gentleman. On receiving a description of the colonel's person and dress, "Joe" concluded that it could have been no other than our eccentric friend, C. An hour or two after "Joe's" arrival, but not until the story of the fine dinner had been pretty well circulated through our camp, in came the missing man, C. No sooner did he enter the lines than one of the boys swung his hat, crying out at the top of his voice, "Three cheers for Colonel C.," which, we believe, were several times repeated, accompanied with loud hurrahs throughout the camp. Col. Allen, who was lying on the ground in his tent, hearing the noise, sprang to his feet and hastily inquired what was the cause of it. On being informed, instead of being angry and ordering him under arrest, as many a stiff-collared fourth corporal would have done, the noble, high-minded commander settled himself down again and laughed and shook his sides until he almost wept. To this day there are many members of the Battalion to whom our friend is known only as Colonel C.

I trust my genial friend, for whom I entertain a high regard, will pardon me for taking away a portion of the monotony of our narrative at his expense.

The distance from Council Bluffs to Fort Leavenworth is in round numbers two hundred miles, directly down the Missouri river.

On the day of our arrival at the garrison we received the following:

(ORDER No. 4.)

"HEAD QUARTERS, MORMON BATTALION,
FORT LEAVENWORTH,
August 1, 1846.

"Dr. George B. Sanderson, of Platte County, Missouri, is hereby appointed a surgeon in the United States Army, to serve with the Mormon Battalion of volunteers. This appointment is subject to the approval of the President of the United States.

Surgeon Sanderson will, on his acceptance of this appointment, make his proper requisition on the medical officer of this post for such medical supplies as he may deem necessary for the service of five hundred men for six months, or the march of these men to California.

J. ALLEN, Lt. Col., Commanding."

On the 3rd of August, companies A, B and C drew their arms, which consisted of U. S. flint-lock muskets, with a few cap-lock yaugers for sharpshooting and hunting purposes. The usual accoutrements were also drawn, as well as camp equipage and provisions, the want of which had been seriously felt on the way.

Quite a crowd gathered around the arsenal before it was opened, each seeming desirous to get the first gun issued. Col. Allen accompanied the officer who was to issue the arms, and, seeing the crowd around the door, in his good-natured, humorous way, said, "Stand back, boys; don't be in a hurry to get your muskets; you will want to throw the d——d things away before you get to California."

On the 4th, companies D and E drew their arms, accoutrements, etc.

Volunteers from different parts of the country arrived at the garrison daily, to get their outfits. Many of them were rough, desperate-looking characters. Quarreling and fighting were not unusual among those from Upper Missouri. While we remained at the Fort, one of the Missouri volunteers, from Platte Co., struck a comrade with a hatchet, inflicting a dangerous, perhaps mortal, wound.

On the 5th we drew forty-two dollars each, as clothing money for the year. Most of the money was sent back by Elder P. P. Pratt and others for the support of the families of the soldiers, and for the gathering of the poor from Nauvoo. There was also a donation to aid Elders P. P. Pratt, O. Hyde and John Taylor, of the quorum of the Twelve Apostles, in pursuing their mission to England, and to assist Elder J. C. Little to go upon his mission to the Eastern States. The paymaster was much surprised to see every man able to sign his own name to the pay roll, as, according to a reliable journal in my possession, only about one in three of the Missouri volunteers, who drew their pay previously, could put his signature to that document.

The members of the Mormon Battalion, too, were not only more intelligent than their fellows, but they were more submissive and obedient to their commanding officers. Col. Allen was heard to say, in conversation with a prominent officer of the garrison, that he "had not been under the necessity of giving the word of command the second time. The men, though unacquainted with military tactics, were willing to obey orders." While at the garrison a company election was held, resulting in the election of one 3rd Lieutenant, one 4th Lieutenant and one 4th Corporal for each company.

Private John R. Murdock, of company B, (now President of the Beaver stake of Zion and member of the Utah Legislature) while endeavoring to train a six-mule team was run over by the wagon while the hind wheels were locked, and seriously hurt.

CHAPTER IV.

Departure of Elders on Missions—Sickness—Start from Fort Leavenworth—Henry Standage lost—News of Col. Kane's Sickness—A Severe Storm—Feast of Honey—Ancient Ruins—Sanford Porter Healed in Answer to Prayer—Wagon Overturned in a Creek—Colonel Allen's Death—Death of Jane and John Bosco.

On the 8th of Aug. Elders Orson Hyde, John Taylor and J. C. Little took leave of the Battalion at Fort Leavenworth and proceeded on their missions.

The first Sunday spent by the Battalion at Fort Leavenworth was observed by holding religious service. Elder Geo. P. Dykes preached a kind of military and gospel sermon, which was his usual style on such occasions.

The weather at this time was extremely warm, the thermometer indicating 101° in the shade and 135° in the sun. Some of those who had taken sick on the road were much improved, but a number of new cases of sickness from ague and fever were developed while in garrison. Sergeant Wm. Hyde was among the number. Jonathan Pugmire, Jr., of company E, (recently Bishop's Agent of Bear Lake Stake of Zion, and lately deceased) was also taken seriously ill with fever. In writing of this, under date of April 25, 1878, he said: "At Leavenworth I was detailed to do blacksmithing, that being my trade. Having no conveniences of a shop, I had to work out of doors, under the scorching heat of an August sun, the rays of which, reflected from a bed of limestone, made the heat almost unbearable. Just as I finished the last wheel and gave the last stroke of the hammer, I fell to the ground in a raging fever, and had to be carried to my tent. For my services as blacksmith up to date I have not received a cent. I still feel the effects more or less of the sickness thus contracted. I had to be hauled a considerable portion of the way to Santa Fe, and the fever being intense, I suffered severely for want of water."

This case is a sample of many, so far as fevers and suffering for want of water are concerned, as our water was generally carried in canteens and flagons, hanging from straps over the shoulders of the men. Col. Allen was taken seriously ill after our arrival at Fort Leavenworth, and as there seemed to be no improvement in his case while we remained there, he instructed the senior Captain, Jefferson Hunt, to advance with the command while he would remain there to recruit and complete the business pertaining to outfitting the Battalion.

On the 12th, companies A., B. and C, took up the line of march for Santa Fe, and traveled that day five miles, finding only poor water and but little of it, which made it very bad for the sick, several of whom had raging fevers. One of company B's wagons also broke down.

On the 3rd, Henry Standage traveled ahead of his company, and was not heard from until the following day, when he was overtaken, to the infinite joy and relief of himself and friends, as he had been without either food or blankets for almost two days and much anxiety had been caused by his absence.

On the 14th, companies D and E left Leavenworth for Santa Fe, and the same day news was received, by express, through Brother Joseph Matthews, from the Twelve at Council Bluffs, to the effect that Col. Thomas L. Kane was lying at the point of death. We also learned from Brother Matthews that the main body of the Church had crossed the Missouri River, at

Sarpee's Point, and traveled up the west side some fifteen or twenty miles, where they had established Winter Quarters.

On the 15th the advance companies crossed the Kansas or Kaw river, which, at the ferry, was about three hundred yards in width. We were ferried over in flat boats by some half-civilized Delaware and Shawnee Indians who were living there and cultivating the soil. In the evening we reached Spring Creek, where we found more than a dozen springs within twenty yards of each other. We remained at this point two days, during which time a heavy shower of rain fell and we learned that although our tents did us considerable good, they were not as substantial as shingle-roofed houses. The rain spattered through and ran under them, and we were pretty thoroughly drenched. While here, Robert S. Bliss found a bee-tree containing twenty or more pounds of nice honey, which made him and his immediate friends an excellent repast.

It was intended to remain longer at Spring Creek, but our beef cattle became so troublesome to the crops of the Indians, that the command advanced about four miles, to Stone Coal Creek. Here we were overtaken by companies D and E. After our encampment, a furious hurricane, accompanied by rain, hail, vivid lightning and peals of thunder, like the constant roar of heavy artillery, met us from the west. Before it reached us we beheld in the distance a heavy dark cloud illumined only by the vivid lightning, while our ears were saluted with continuous rolling thunder and the sweeping of the wind. When the storm reached us only five or six out of over one hundred tents were left standing, and it took six men to each tent to hold it. Three wagons were upset, two of which were heavy government baggage wagons; the other, a light two-horse carriage, was slightly injured. Sergeant Wm. Coray's carriage was driven before the wind about ten rods. The ground was descending to the east. Mrs. Coray was in the carriage when it started, but she preferred exposure to the storm to risking the dangers of being driven in the carriage before the wind, and sprang to the ground, and with womanly dignity and courage took the driving rain and the pelting hail. The author, being unable to stand and brace against the strength of the gale, was driven some twelve or fifteen rods to a patch of willows flattened by the wind like lodged grain, nearly to the ground. He fell to his face, held to the willows with his right hand, and placed his left arm over his head, at the same time pulling the willows over the back of his head to shield it from the pelting hail. His hat, like many others, was blown away at the commencement of the storm. There were many sick in our camp, among whom were Mrs. Celia Hunt, wife of Senior Captain Jefferson Hunt, and her twin babes, who were taken with chills and fever before leaving Fort Leavenworth. They were very sick. The matron lady happened to be in her wagon, while her husband held the babes in the tent, which blew down. With much difficulty the Captain kept the little ones from drowning and suffocating. As everything was wet they were forced to sleep in their wet clothes. Strange to say, with all the exposure, neither the good lady nor her "dear angels," as she termed her babes, had any more chills and fever. My recollection is that others, also, were cured by this wonderful shower bath. The storm lasted about twenty minutes.

Colonel Sterling Price and his command of cavalry, who left the garrison two days in advance of us, were encamped at Stone Coal Creek, when we arrived there. During the storm his animals were scattered in all directions, and several days were spent in searching before they could be recovered. The result was a portion of Price's cavalry did not overtake the Battalion until after we arrived at Santa Fe.

The day after the storm we rested and dried our clothes. During the afternoon the Battalion was called together and was addressed by Captain Hunt, Corporal Daniel Tyler, Musician Levi W. Hancock and Sergeant Wm. Hyde respectively. An excellent spirit prevailed, and all seemed to appreciate the remarks. Three persons were also baptized for their health and one for the remission of sins.

R. S. Bliss, the Nimrod of the Battalion, here found another bee-tree, and provided another treat for himself and friends.

While at this place two pieces of artillery, a blacksmith forge and six or eight wagons loaded with ammunition for Kearney's Brigade, passed us.

On the 21st Adjutant Dykes arrived from the garrison, and brought word that Col. Allen was still very sick. Many prayers ascended to God for his recovery. He was universally beloved by the command. Our hospital wagon also arrived.

On the 22nd the Battalion left Stone Coal Creek, or, as it was called, by the command, "Hurricane Point," and had traveled but a short distance when we came to a small stream which was very difficult to cross. Long ropes were fastened to the wagons on each side, with ten to fifteen men to each rope to aid the teams in crossing. All were over about noon. After traversing a fine prairie of rich bottom land, we camped at night at Allen's Grove. The sick were much improved in health.

During our next day's travel we passed an old stone wall, some five feet thick. Ruins of an ancient city were also plainly visible, showing that the country must have been inhabited sometime long ages past by a civilized people. Sanford Porter, of company E, was taken sick while traveling this day, and fell behind the command. He suffered so intensely that he thought he must die; but while alone he summoned all his faith and called upon the Lord in fervent prayer, asking that his life might be spared if there was any further work for him to do. In an instant all pain left him and he was as vigorous and healthful as he ever had been in his life.

On the 24th we traveled over a district of country, which, if cultivated, would make excellent farms. Parties who had worked in the precious metals, also, thought they saw strong indications of lead ore along our route. We nooned at Schwitzer's Creek, and at night camped on Beaver Creek.

On the 25th, three yoke of oxen being lost, John G. Smith and others remained and hunted for, but did not find them. The command moved on and while nooning the camp was visited by a number of Kaw Indians, who afterwards followed us some distance. During the afternoon we met Bro. McKenzie, who had been to Bent's Fort as Indian interpreter to General S. F. Kearney. Several letters were sent back by him to anxious friends.

On the following day, while crossing a creek, one of company C's wagons was upset in the stream, containing six or seven sick men and a number of women. The water was several feet deep, and the banks high. The men who were on the banks jumped into the stream and pulled the inmates from the wagon. All of them were completely immersed and some were strangling as they were unable to get their heads above water. Among those who assisted in clearing the wagon was the author of this narrative. Being overheated from traveling, as well as exhausted by his efforts to rescue the parties from a watery grave and to turn the wagon right side up, he contracted a severe cold and fever which resulted in chronic catarrh and other afflictions, from which he still suffers.

The lost oxen were recovered and Sergeant Shelton overtook the command and brought the painful news of the death of our highly esteemed and much loved Colonel, James Allen, who departed this life at 6 o'clock a. m. of the 23rd day of August, 1846.

On the 28th some Santa Fe traders brought and delivered to us Sergeant Hyde's pony, which he had lost several days previously, in consequence of which he had, while still in very poor health, been compelled to walk about seventy miles.

The same day an aged English lady by the name of Jane Bosco, who was traveling in company with Captain Hunt, died, and her husband, John Bosco—not a soldier—died before daylight the next morning. Thus they gained an oft-repeated wish, that neither should be left to mourn the loss of the other. They were very highly respected. They were buried in one grave, and a dry substantial stone wall was built around and over the tomb, under the supervision of Elisha Averett, to mark their last resting place and to shield their bodies from the wolves. The covering was of good but unpolished flat rock.

On the 29th, Adjutant Dykes preached the funeral sermon of the lamented Colonel, James Allen. Senior Captain Jefferson Hunt also made some very appropriate remarks on the occasion. We also learned of a row in a camp of Missouri volunteers not far distant from ours, in which one soldier shot and mortally wounded another.

CHAPTER V.

Question of a New Commander—Captain Hunt Elected—Arrival of Smith and Sanderson—Council of Officers—Smith Elected to take Command—Smith's Inhuman Treatment of the Sick—Repulsed by Sergeant Williams—The Sick Object to take Drugs—Sergeant Jones Protests Against their Being Forced to—Dykes' Perfidy—Letter from President Young—The "old Iron Spoon"—A Fiendish Doctor.

After learning of the death of Colonel Allen, the question naturally arose as to who should succeed him as our commander. On this and other points, the late Lieutenant Wesley W. Willis, has, in substance, the following: "On receipt of this intelligence, the officers held a council, and agreed that Captain Hunt should assume the command of the Battalion, which decision was unanimously sustained by the men. At the same time the officers wrote a letter to the President of the United States, informing him of the death of Colonel Allen, and praying him to appoint Captain Hunt to the command. This letter was forwarded to Independence, Mo., by Sergeant Ebenezer Brown, of company A.

We continued our march under the orders of Captain Hunt to Council Grove. Here, on learning that Lieutenant Smith was on the way, intending to take command, the officers appointed a committee of two, viz., Jesse D. Hunter, Captain of company B, and Adjutant George P. Dykes, to examine the law and ascertain to whom the right of command belonged and report accordingly to the council. Captain Hunter reported in favor of Captain Hunt, but Lieutenant Dykes reported against him, being of the opinion that inasmuch as we were enlisted by a United States officer, the right of command belonged to an officer of the regular army.

While here, Lieutenant Smith, Major Walker, Dr. George B. Sanderson, and others, came to us, bringing a letter to Captain Hunt from Major Horton, of Fort Leavenworth, informing him that the Government property in possession of the Battalion was not receipted for, and advising us to submit to the command of Lieutenant Smith and he would forward receipts for the same, as it might save us considerable trouble.

This caused another council to be convened to hear what these gentlemen had to say. The council was addressed by Major Walker and Lieutenant Smith, both of whom advised that Major Horton's suggestion be acceded to. Captain Hunt stated boldly and emphatically that it was his right to assume command, and that he had no fears of the responsibility of leading the Battalion; and then left it with the council to say who should command. It was moved by Captain Higgins and seconded by Captain Davis, that Smith should take command. The motion was carried, all voting for it except three, viz: Lieutenants Lorenzo Clark, Samuel Gully and Wesley W. Willis."

When the command was given to Lieutenant Smith, the soldiers were not consulted. This caused an ill-feeling between them and the officers that many hold to this day. The appointment of Smith, even before his character was known, caused a greater gloom throughout the command than the death of Colonel Allen had.

On the morning of the 31st of August, we struck tents at 7 a. m., under the command of Lieutenant Smith, and marched that day to Diamond Springs, at which place we were mustered and inspected by our new commander.

The following day we reached Lost Springs so called from being a kind of lonesome place, destitute of timber. Our food had been cooked the previous day, as we had been apprised of the situation at Lost Springs, and we followed the Arab style, of digging narrow trenches in which we burned weeds, to heat water for our tea and coffee.

On the 2nd of September we camped at Cottonwood Creek, in the Comanche Indian country. These Indians were very hostile at that time.

Lieutenant Smith, at this point, pulled several of the sick out of the wagons because they had neglected to report themselves to Dr. Sanderson. When he learned that some of them did not design being drugged, he used some horrid oaths and threats. Sergeant Thomas S. Williams, who had purchased a team to haul a portion of our knapsacks, had some of the sick in his wagon. Smith approached the wagon with the intention of hauling the sick out, when the Sergeant ordered him to stop. At this Smith became furious and drew his sword and threatened to run Williams through if he attempted to allow any more sick to ride in the wagon without his permission. Williams braced himself, grasped the small end of his loaded whip and told him if he dared to make one move to strike he would level him to the ground; that the team and wagon were his private property and he would haul whom he pleased. He further told him that these men were his brethren, that they did not believe in taking drugs and that he would never leave one lying sick on the ground while they could crowd into the wagon, or so long as his team could pull them.

Smith slunk away and inquired who that man was, and was told that it was Sergeant Williams. He next went to some officers and had some talk with them, which resulted in a suggestion to "Tom"—as the Sergeant was familiarly called—to meet with all the officers at night and to "treat" them, beginning with the Colonel, which he did.

Thus, with a single drink of whisky, the wound was healed without any apology from either side. It was noticeable ever after, however, that when they passed each other, Sergeant Williams was recognized and saluted in a respectful manner.

About this time Sergeant N. V. Jones went in a respectful manner to Colonel Smith and informed him that the soldiers were loyal; that it was not out of any disrespect to him or Dr. Sanderson that the sick declined to take the Doctor's medicine; but that they had religious scruples against taking mineral medicine.

The Colonel replied that he did not know anything about our religion, and that he did not wish to force men against their religious convictions. He then turned to Adjutant Dykes and asked him if Jones' statement was true, and the Adjutant replied that there were no such religious scruples, and that the Church authorities themselves took such medicine.

This made matters worse for the sick, if such a thing were possible, than they were before. The humane, patriotic Sergeant did his duty manfully, but his good offices in behalf of his comrades in arms were turned to evil by one who might have saved them much persecution, sorrow and, in some cases, perhaps, even death. Ever after this an ill-feeling was perceptible between the Adjutant and Sergeant Jones.

That the position taken by Sergeant Jones was correct, the following letter, which was subsequently received, will amply prove:

"CAMP OF ISRAEL, OMAHA NATION, CUTLER'S PARK,
August 19, 1846.

To Captain Jefferson Hunt and the Captains, Officers, and Soldiers of the Mormon Battalion:—

We have the opportunity of sending to Fort Leavenworth, this morning, by Dr. Reed, a package of twenty-five letters, which we improve, with this word of counsel to you all: If you are sick, live by faith, and let surgeon's medicine alone if you want to live, using only such herbs and mild food as are at your disposal. If you give heed to this counsel, you will prosper; but if not, we cannot be responsible for the consequences. A hint to the wise is sufficient.

In behalf of the Council,

BRIGHAM YOUNG, President.
W. Richards, Clerk."

About this time, quite a number of the Battalion took sick with the chills and fever, and were administered to by Dr. Sanderson out of an old iron spoon. After this it was customary every morning for the sick to be marched to the tune of "Jim along Joe" to the Doctor's quarters, and take their portion from that same old iron spoon. It was believed by many that this spoon had been thrown away by some soldier at the garrison and picked up by the Doctor, thinking a new one would either be too expensive or too good for the "Mormons" to use in taking their medicine. It may, however, have descended from the Doctor's ancestors and been preserved by him as a precious heirloom.

So determined was Dr. Sanderson that the men should take his calomel and arsenic (these being all, or nearly all, the medicines he used except a decoction of bayberry bark and camomile flowers, as strengthening bitters to the convalescent), that he threatened with an oath, to cut the throat of any man who would administer any medicine without his orders.

Dr. McIntyre, a good botanic physician, had been appointed assistant surgeon by Colonel Allen on the day of our enlistment; yet under pain of this threat he must not administer one herb to his afflicted friends and brethren unless ordered so to do by the mineral quack who was his superior in office.

Every morning at sick call, those who were unable to travel reported themselves to the Surgeon, not only to receive his medicine but his wicked cursing also.

It would have been difficult to select the same number of American citizens from any other community who would have submitted to the tyranny and abuse that the Battalion did from Smith and Sanderson. Nor would we have done so on any consideration other than as servants to our God and patriots to our country.

CHAPTER VI.

A Faithful Sentinel Arrests the Colonel—The Colonel Frightened—Buffalo Meat—Military Law Read—Difficult Crossing—The Author Sick—Dread of the Doctor's Poisonous Drugs—Begs to be Left to Die—News of the Capture of Santa Fe—Dosed with Calomel—Disobey the Doctor and Recover—Doctor Claims Credit for the Cure—Camomile Tea—Who Used the Brandy—Pace's Account of Colonel Allen's Death, etc.

Soon after Smith took command, while going the grand rounds alone, to see that the sentinels were doing their duty, he was halted by Thomas C. D. Howell, a sentinel on guard. The Colonel, by mistake, gave the wrong countersign, and Howell held him as a prisoner until the arrival of the relief guard, when he turned him over to the Corporal. The Colonel was not only very wrathy, but it may also be presumed that he was a little frightened, for he afterwards remarked to another officer, that the man who took him prisoner "would just as leave kill a man as look at him."

Those who are acquainted with the peaceable character of Brother Howell will be able to appreciate the effect of his firmness upon the Colonel, for there was generally nothing blood-thirsty indicated in his looks or manner.

It appeared that the Colonel had without knowing it given the password of the previous night, but would not be convinced of his mistake until the Adjutant pointed out the proper countersign in his own handwriting. Smith never forgave Howell. Posterity, however, will commend the sentinel for his integrity.

On the 5th we saw a few buffalo, the first that most of us had ever seen. Several carcasses of these animals that had been killed by Missouri Volunteers lay by the wayside, no portion of them having been used except the tongues. We thought of the scripture—"Woe unto those who take life and waste flesh when they have no need."

On the following day we not only saw plenty of buffalo, but one of the soldiers killed one. We thought the meat very good. It was, however, like most of the male "sentinels," rather tough. We learned in time to select for our eating younger and more tender animals, instead of shooting the oldest, which were generally found singly, at some distance from the herd.

On the 7th of September we were ordered on parade at 5 p. m., and had the military law read to us for the first time, the object being that we might be better posted in regard to campaign duties.

On the evening of the 8th we encamped on a stream known as Pawnee Fork, the crossing of which was very difficult, and occupied some time. Each wagon had to be let down the bank with ropes, while on the opposite bank from twenty to thirty men with ropes aided the teams in pulling the wagons up. The water was muddy, very much like that of the Missouri river.

The following day we encountered a heavy rain storm, and found no timber to cook our suppers with. As a rather poor substitute, we used wet buffalo-chips.

The author, having been attacked by fever several days previous, found himself growing rapidly worse. The teamsters feared trouble with the Doctor if they allowed him to ride in the wagons unless he was on the sick report, and as he preferred the mercy of the savages to the cruelty and wicked abuse of Dr. Sanderson, with his poisonous drugs, he lay down upon the ground and begged his messmates to leave him, and report him dead and buried. His comrades reported him to Lieutenant Rosecrans, who was in command of Company C., in the absence of Captain Brown, who was sick, and that officer directed them to put him in a wagon and report him to be entered on the sick list. This was just as the command was about breaking camp.

Soon after an express from Santa Fe brought us the glad news of the surrender of that place to General S. F. Kearney, without resistance. An order from the General directed the Battalion to leave the road and not go by way of Bent's Fort, whence we had been ordered by Colonel Allen, but march direct to Santa Fe, which, of course, we proceeded to do, although the most of our provisions, etc., and two pieces of artillery, were in advance of us towards the former place, where we understood our lamented Colonel, James Allen, designed us to winter, in case we were too late to cross the mountains that fall.

In the evening two comrades led the author to the quarters of the indolent Doctor, who never visited a wagon to see the sick while they could move one limb before the other, with a man under each arm to bear the weight of the body. The doctor first demanded to know the sick man's name; next, what ailed him; then, how long he had been sick; next, why he had not come before, and, last, but not least, if he did not know that fevers did not cure themselves. This was in response to the explanation from the sick man that he had hoped to get over his affliction without troubling the doctor.

Instead of doing up his calomel powders in papers as he had previously done, to allow the soldiers to take them at their quarters, the doctor brought out the "rusty old spoon" previously referred to, mixed the powders in molasses and ordered them taken in his presence. He had learned that his medicine was not generally taken, as a number of the men had been thoughtless enough to strew it along the road where he saw it.

The sick man was compelled either to take the medicine quietly, have it forced down him, or be left to perish on the plains; of course, on reflection, he chose the former.

About noon on the 11th, we reached the Arkansas river. This stream, at the point where we crossed it, was about a quarter of a mile wide and was filled with sand from bank to bank, with here and there a small stream of brackish water coursing down a narrow channel. The first rivulet being some distance from the eastern shore of the river, the men dug holes about two or three feet deep in the sand, thereby obtaining a sufficiency of water for all needful purposes. The afternoon was a general time of washing. Having considerable fever the writer drank an incredible amount of water in the afternoon and evening, although the doctor had forbidden him drinking any cold water for two days at least after taking his medicine, saying that if he did, the result would be death. The water had the desired effect, that of breaking up the fever, and it caused a greater degree of perspiration than he ever experienced before or afterwards, and left him very weak.

On the morning of the 12th two men again took him to sick call. On arriving, the Doctor said, with an oath, "Tyler, your fever is broke. I had no idea of being able to break it so soon."

The writer did not inform him that he had disobeyed his orders, but left him to imagine that he had wrought a wonderful cure. He has ever since believed, however, that the water, under Divine Providence, was the cause of preserving his life instead of taking it away, as the Doctor predicted that it would. He did not give him any more strong medicine at that time, but at the regular evening and morning call, he marched to the tune of "Jim along Joe" and took as much as the old iron spoon would hold of the decoction of bayberry bark and camomile flowers; for that is what it really was, without a drop of the brandy the Government furnished for mixing medicines with; that we understood was drank by the Doctor and Smith and their immediate associates, including their negro servants, who sometimes got rather tipsy. In the latter case, of course, the plea was they had stolen it; and to pass it off, they got a little "cussing."

Here Lieutenant James Pace, of company E, overtook the command. The following is a condensation of a report kindly furnished by him to the author:

"I left the command at Hurricane Point, Aug. 21st 1846, by permission of Captain D. C. Davis, and returned to Fort Leavenworth, to learn the condition of Colonel Allen. I arrived at the fort on the 22nd and learned that the Colonel

was not expected to live many hours. At the request of
Lieutenant Gully, I remained through the day watching over
the Colonel. At evening he was removed to his old quarters.
Lieutenant Gully and myself followed in the procession. We
remained with him through the night. His niece, a fine
young lady of sixteen or eighteen years of age, gave her
special attention to him during the night. She was the only
relative I heard of as being present, and her name I have not
on my record. The Colonel died at six o'clock a. m., Aug. 23rd,
1846, at Fort Leavenworth, Kansas. At the announcement of
the Colonel's death, Lieutenant Smith and Dr. Sanderson were
for pushing Quartermaster Gully out forthwith to join the
Battalion. The requisition was warmly repulsed by Gully,
who informed them finally that he was not under their command, nor would he remove until it suited him. At this
pressing moment Major Horton, commander of the post, sent
by his orderly, requesting Lieutenant Gully and myself to come
to his quarters. He desired to know the whereabouts of the
Battalion, also if every necessary requisition was filled and
completed; which Quartermaster Gully promptly answerd in
the affirmative. Lieutenant Smith and Dr. Sanderson followed
us up to hear what Major Horton would say to us. After the
necessary inquiries, and being informed of Smith's and
Sanderson's arrogant assumptions, he said we now had a perfect
right to elect our own Colonel, and that no one had any right
to assume the command. He also stated that he had written
a letter to that effect to Captain Hunt, and that he would send
an express forthwith to Gereral Kearney and inform him of
our situation. He also added that we were a separate corps,
from all other soldiers in the service. He then suggested that
one of us should return to Council Bluffs and inform our
President of our situation, and return to the command as soon
as possible. It was decided that I should go, as Lieutenant
Gully, as quartermaster, had charge of our entire outfit.
Lieutenant Smith and Dr. Sanderson, on hearing what the
Major said to us, changed their tactics, and in very smooth,
language, and with much sophistry, asked me to do them the
favor of taking a letter from each of them to President Young,
which I did. Their object was to solicit the President's
influence for Smith to take command as Colonel, and Sander-

son to be the surgeon of the Battalion. I also took a letter from Lieutenant Gully, asking the President's counsel in regard to our future action. I took my leave about noon of Aug. 23d, being well fitted out with a good horse and other things necessary, by order of Major Horton, and arrived at the camp of the Saints at Cutler's Creek, west side of the Missouri, about 18 miles above Sarpee's Point, Aug. 26th, at 10, a. m. I took only a few letters, as the command was about forty-five miles in the advance, and knew nothing of my intended return. I delivered what letters I had. I then sat in council, answering questions, and receiving special counsel for the Battalion. Howard Egan and John D. Lee accompanied me on my return. On reaching Fort Leavenworth, I was received by Maj. Horton as a gentleman and an officer. He deemed it unsafe for so small a party to travel alone. I insisted on following up the Battalion, to which he finally consented, at the same time charging me to keep with one train until I was sure I could reach another the same night. He fitted me out with a fresh horse and all the grain our carriage could haul, with three packages of letters for different commands. We left the garrison on the 6th of September, and, I think, overtook the Battalion on the 11th, at the crossing of the Arkansas river.

CHAPTER VI.

Correspondence Between Sanderson and Smith and President Young—The True Version of How the New Commander should have been Selected,

The following are the letters referred to by Lieutenant Pace, with their replies:

Fort Leavenworth,
August 27, 1846.

Mr. Brigham Young and Others,
  Council Bluffs,

    Gentlemen:—I have the painful task to perform of informing you of the death of our friend, Lt. Col. Allen, of the Mormon Battalion. He died this morning about six o'clock, after a confinement, of about ten days, to his bed. He died of congestive fever; was indisposed for many days previous to taking to his bed. Your people have lost a devoted friend and good officer. I am in hopes, in fact I have no fears, nor you need not entertain any, your people will be taken care of. The most perfect harmony has prevailed among themselves since their arrival at this post, and every one speaks to their praise. Lt. Smith, of U. S, A. will go out with them until they overtake Gen. Kearney, who will take them under his special care. I am going out myself as Surgeon to the Battalion. I was appointed by Col. Allen on the 1st inst., and everything that I have in my power shall be extended to them for their comfort. Please to give kindest regards to Col. Kane, and had it been in my power I should have visited him during his illness. I have just learned he is much better.

  I have the honor to be your obedient servant,

Geo. B. Sanderson,
Surgeon M. B.

FORT LEAVENWORTH, August, 23, 1846.

President Brigham Young:

SIR:—It is with the deepest regret that I have to inform you of the death of Lieutenant Colonel James Allen, late commander of the Mormon Battalion. The command left this post last week, and is now encamped about forty miles from here. The particulars of the lamented and universal favorite, Colonel Allen, will be communicated to you by Lieutenant James Pace, the bearer of this note. If it is the wish of your people that I should take charge of the Battalion, and conduct it to General Kearney, I will do it with pleasure and feel proud of the command.

I have in my possession most, if not all, the papers that relate to the movements of this Battalion, and will use my best endeavors to see all orders and promises heretofore given, carried into execution.

I am, sir, very respectfully,
Your obt. servant,
A. J. SMITH,
1st Lt. 1st Dragoons.

CAMP OF ISRAEL, OMAHA NATION.
Aug, 27, 1846

Sir,

Your letter of the 22nd inst, to Mr, Young and others has just arrived, and while we mourn the loss of a gentleman, and noble officer with our friends in the Battalion, and his brother officers of the army, we are consoled with the assurance you have made that our brethren have won the praise of their country, by their harmony and good order, and we doubt not your services to the Battalion will be duly appreciated. Your regards have been presented to Col. Kane, who is convalescent, and thinks he shall be able to ride out in a few days.

Most respectfully,
In behalf of the Council,
Brigham Young, President.
Willard Richards, Clerk.

To Geo. B. Sanderson,
Surgeon, Mormon Battalion.

CAMP OF ISRAEL, OMAHA NATION,
August 27, 1846.

SIR,

Your letter of the 23rd inst., to President Young, announcing the death of Lt. Col. Allen, was received this day, and we feel to sympathize with you and our friends of the Battalion in this deep affliction.

You kindly offered to take the charge of the Battalion and conduct it safely to Gen. Kearney. We have not the pleasure of a personal acquaintance, and consequently can have no personal objections to you; but, sir, on the subject of command we can only say, Col. Allen settled that matter at the organization of the Battalion; therefore, we must leave that point to the proper authorities, be the result what it may. Any assistance you may render the Battalion while moving will be duly acknowledged by a grateful people.

Most respectfully, Sir,
Yours in behalf of the Council.
BRIGHAM YOUNG, President.
WILLARD RICHARDS, Clerk

A. J. Smith, 1st Lt. 1st Dragoons,
U, S, Army of the West.

The following letter explains itself:

"CAMP OF ISRAEL, OMAHA NATION,
August, 27, 1846.

Samuel Gulley, Quartermaster, and the "Mormon Battalion."

BELOVED BROTHER,—Your letters of the 21st and 23rd inst., per Lieutenant Pace, we received, and feel to mourn the loss we have sustained in the death of Lieutenant Colonel Allen, who, we believe, as a gentleman and officer, had the affections of all his acquaintances. To such dispensations of Providence, we must submit, and pray our Heavenly Father to guide your steps, and move in all your councils.

You will all doubtless recollect that Colonel Allen repeatedly stated to us and the Battalion that there would be no officer in the Battalion, except himself, only from among our people; that if he fell in battle, or was sick, or disabled by any means, the command would devolve on the ranking officer, which would be the Captain of Company A, and B, and so on, according to *letter*. Consequently the command must devolve on Captain Jefferson Hunt, whose duty we suppose to be to take the Battalion to Bent's Fort, or wherever he has received marching orders for, and there wait further orders from General Kearney, notifying him by express of Colonel Allen's decease at the earliest date.

From the great confidence we had in Colonel Allen's assurance of the order of making officers in command, and the confidence we have in General Kearney and the officers of the United States, that they will faithfully perform, according to the pledges made by Colonel Allen as an officer on the part of the Government, we consider there is no reasonable chance for a question on the future command of the Battalion, and as to expediency, we know of none worthy of consideration. But should General Kearney propose any other course, we presume the Battalion would not feel disposed to act upon it until they had notified the General of the pledges they had received from the Government through Colonel Allen, and received his answer, and we know of no law that could require the brethren to act contrary to those pledges, or under any circumstance contrary to their wish. We trust there is not a man in the Battalion who would let pass the first opportunity of procuring the rules and regulations of tactics of the United States army and making himself master of the same before the close of the year.

For the Council,
BRIGHAM YOUNG, President.
W. Richards, Clerk.

This letter was not received until Smith was in command, hence too late to be acted upon. A little postponement by the officers until Lieutenant Pace's return, which was daily looked for, would have been satisfactory to all, and Captain Hunt, who had been duly elected would have continued in command with the rank of Lieutenant Colonel.

CHAPTER VIII.

Novel way of Catching Fish—Wagon Upset, and Man Injured—Overtake Price's Regiment—Character of Price and his Men—Higgins' Detachment Sent to Pueblo—Dissatisfaction—Alva Phelps Drugged to Death—Curious Phenomenon—Suffer from Thirst—Forced-Marches—Men Salivated.

While at the crossing of the Arkansas, many fish were caught by the soldiers by spearing them in the shallow water with swords and bayonets.

After reaching the Arkansas, we traveled up the river about one hundred miles, and then crossed it at a point where the road branched, one road leading up the river to Bent's Fort and the other to Santa Fe. While journeying up the river one of the wagons upset, somewhat injuring Francis Whitney. After crossing the river we overtook five companies of Colonel Sterling Price's regiment from western Missouri. We found them a profane, wicked and vulgar set of men. Price will be remembered as the commander of a portion of the mob militia at Far West in 1838, when a few officers and about seventeen ministers of different denominations sat as a court martial and condemned Joseph Smith and others to be shot on the public square in view of their families.

At this point, Captain Higgins, with a guard of ten men, was detailed to take a number of the families that accompanied the Battalion, to Pueblo, a Mexican town located farther up the Arkansas, to winter.

Many of the Battalion were dissatisfied with this move, as President Young had counseled the officers not to allow the Battalion to be divided on any account. Colonel Allen had also promised President Young that they should not be divided. Lieutenants Pace and Gully strenuously opposed the separation of the families from the Battalion, as well as any deviation from the pledges of Colonel Allen, and requested that a council be called and letters from the Twelve Apostles read; but Adjutant Dykes objected, saying there was no time for calling councils, and that President Young did not know our circumstances. The families, therefore, were forced to leave us on the 16th of September, notwithstanding the fears and protests of their relatives and friends, and take up their line of march for Pueblo, in care of Captain Higgins and the soldiers, whose names, according to the best information at hand are as follows: Corporal Gilbert Hunt, Dimick B. Huntington, Montgomery Button, John H. Tippets, Milton Kelley, Nicholas Kelley, Norman Sharp, James Brown, Harley Morey, Thomas Woolsey and S. C. Shelton. When the detachment left, the command made preparations to march on, but after the teams were hitched up and all were ready to start, the marching order was countermanded to give the officers time to make out their monthly report.

While we remained at that point Alva Phelps, of company E, died, a martyr to his country and religion. It is understood that he begged Dr. Sanderson not to give him any strong medicine, as he needed only a little rest and then would return to duty; but the Doctor prepared his dose and ordered him to take it, which he declined doing, whereupon the Doctor, with some horrid oaths, forced it down him with the old rusty spoon. A few hours later he died, and the general feeling was that the Doctor had killed him. Many boldly expressed the opinion that it was a case of premeditated murder. When we consider the many murderous threats previously made, this conclusion is by no means far-fetched. Brother Phelps was buried on the south side of the Arkansas river, in a grave only about four feet deep, its shallowness being due to the fact that the water was very near the surface of the soil. He was the husband of Margaret Phelps (now Margaret Bridges) and father of the two little children mentioned in her very touching letter published previously in this work.

On the evening of Brother Phelps' death, what appeared to be a star was noticed in the east as dancing in the air. It continued to move both north and south, up and down; it was directly in the course we had traveled. It attracted considerable attention while it remained in sight, and finally disappeared below the eastern horizon.

The following day we traveled twenty-five miles across a dreary desert and suffered intensely from excessive heat and want of water. Our teams also shared in the suffering. There was a mirage, which was very deceptive to the sight. It had the appearnce at times of a fog continually rising from stagnant pools and at other times of lakes of water in plain view. This mirage moved along as we traveled and stopped when we halted, thus keeping the same distance from us. What an aggravation to a person almost dying for the want of water! We passed one lone pond full of insects of all sizes and shapes. Out of this pond we drove several thousand Buffalo.

Even when the water was not roiled it was discolored and had a most disgusting appearance. The animals, doubtless, rendered it more noisome than it otherwise would have been by gathering in it to defend themselves from the flies. Our readers will perhaps imagine that we were now more disappointed than before. On the contrary, kind friends, no luxury was ever more thankfully received. The few whose canteens and flagons were not exhausted, of course did not use it, but, bad as it was, it was very welcome to the most of us.

The following day we continued on across the dry, parched desert, without finding any water, except a pond similar to that first mentioned, and which was hailed with joy and considered a great blessing. That night we again made a "dry camp," but started at 4 o'clock the next morning and traveled 10 miles to Cimmeron Springs before breakfast.

Whether Colonel Smith had had no experience in traveling with teams, or whether he desired to use up the teams and leave the Battalion on the plains helpless, does not appear. It is true, however, that, for the last two hundred miles, where there had been but little feed, he had shown no wisdom or care in preserving either man or beast; but on the contrary, no matter whether our drives were to be long or short, he had driven on forced marches, on which account many, in fact nearly all, of the teams as well as men, failed very fast. Probably he relied too much on the judgment of his Adjutant.

On the 20th we traveled ten miles, and encamped before the sink of Cimmeron Creek, where we obtained brackish water by digging holes in the sand. Our only fuel for ten days had been buffalo chips, and in some places they were very scarce, having been mostly used by troops in advance of us. At night the commissioned officers, with David Pettegrew, known as Father Pettegrew, and Levi W. Hancock, our spiritual advisers, met in council, with Egan, Lee, Pace and others, when our condition was freely discussed, but nothing was or perhaps could be done to ameliorate it.

On the 21st we traveled eighteen miles and camped again on the Cimmeron, and had to dig in the sand in the bed of the river for water for both man and beast. The country over which we had passed through the day was rough and sandy.

Samuel H. Rogers' journal of this date has the following: "Last night I stood horse-guard. When I went to report myself to the Adjutant I found the five orderlies and the Colonel talking about the sick. It appears that the Colonel and Surgeon are determined to kill us, first by force marches to make us sick, then by compelling us to take calomel or to walk and do duty."

We continued along the same stream the following day. Both men and teams failed fast, many completely giving out from exhaustion and sickness. The author and many others were badly salivated. We camped at night at a bold spring.

About this time I appealed to Captains Hunt and Brown, separately, calling attention to the mal-practice of Sanderson, referring to the fact that new cases of severe salivation were of daily occurrence. I requested them to inform the Colonel that this mineral practice was contrary to our religious faith. Captain Hunt replied that he had informed him that it was "rather against our religious faith," and that his reply was, that he knew nothing about our religious faith. On my insisting that HE SHOULD BE MADE TO KNOW, the Captain replied: "Brother Tyler, you would raise a mutiny." I answered: "There would be no mutiny; the Battalion would sustain you to a man." He replied to the effect that he could do nothing, and the subject was dropped. I felt that I had only discharged a plain duty.

CHAPTER IX.

Rations Reduced—Bones of Mules Found—Ancient Ruins—The Officers and Healthy Men Push on for Santa Fe—Sick Left to Follow Without a Doctor—Style of Milking Spanish Goats—Arrival at Santa Fe—Partiality shown the Battalion by General Doniphan—Glimpse at Missouri Persecutions.

To add to the hardships of the men they were reduced to two-thirds rations, and, through drinking brackish water, many were attacked with summer complaint. Many of the feeble ones also suffered severely from cold and rain while on guard at night, as they preferred to bear their portion of camp duties while they could possibly do so, rather than make their condition known and have to take the doctor's drugs and abuse.

On the 24th we found the bones of about one hundred mules which died in a cold storm about a year previously. The storm consisted of snow and hail. A human skull was found among the bones. Dr. Sanderson believed it to be the skull of an Indian. The animals belonged to a company of "fur traders." We learned the particulars from an emigrant returning to the east, who informed us that it was with difficulty that the white men who owned the animals had escaped with their lives. It was the most severe storm, so far as we could learn, that had ever occurred in that region.

The two mountain peaks known as the Rabbit's Ears, and which serve as a guide to travelers, were in sight on our route.

A company of traders going south of Santa Fe camped with us that night. Buffalo chips, which had been our only fuel since leaving the Arkansas river, were very scarce.

On the 25th we marched twenty miles, over a rough and mountainous road and camped at Gold Spring, the first good water for several days; we also had a view of the first timber seen for nine days, there having been no shrubbery, even, along the whole distance traversed in that time.

On the 26th we saw a number of deer, elk, and antelope. We reached Cedar Springs at night, at which place we found cedar, spruce, and cottonwood timber.

On the 27th we marched over rough sand hills and encamped by a pond of stagnant water. There were a few buffalo chips, which were soon gathered, when some who had none of this kind of fuel, traveled two miles to timber and brought wood on their shoulders. A few antelope added to our short rations were quite a treat. The monotony of the barren plains in our rear was considerably relieved by the view of numerous mountain peaks in front, the first many of us ever saw, including the Rabbit's Ears.

Sergeant William Hyde incidentally remarks here: "Our encampments generally inclose from four to six acres of ground."

During the next day our route for a considerable distance was over hills and high ridges. A number of antelope were killed and some bears and wild turkeys were seen, but no buffalo were visible, as we were quite out of the country over which they ranged.

On the 29th we passed the "Rabbits Ears" about noon. The teams and men were continually failing on account of a lack of feed, water and judgment on the part of our commander. The following day we passed Rock Creek. On account of finding no feed for our animals, we traveled until about 9 o'clock at night, and were on the move again the next morning at day break.

About noon on the 1st of October we passed within half a mile of the walls of an ancient structure situated on the north side of the road. There were two solid walls about four feet apart running parallel nearly due north and south. The total length of these walls was about one hundred and ninety feet; for one hundred and thirty feet they were intact. The rock was laid in cement, which had become solid as the rock itself.

Whether these had been partition walls of a castle or some large building, or a part of a fortification, it would be difficult to determine. It was evident that the whole face of the country had undergone a change. There were numerous canals or channels where large streams had once run, probably for irrigating, but which were then quite dry, and to all appearance had not been used for generations.

We reached Red River on the 2nd of October and on the 3rd camped by a large spring, the outlet of which formed a small creek. Here a council of officers was called. The commander informed the council that he had received orders from General Kearney that unless the command reached Santa Fe by the 10th we would be discharged. He suggested selecting fifty able-bodied men from each company, taking the best teams and traveling on a double forced march, leaving the sick with the weak teams to follow as best they could.

This proposition was carried, being opposed only by Lieutenants James Pace, Andrew Lytle, Samuel Gulley and, we think, Lieutenant W. W. Willis, with invited guests, Levi W. Hancock, David Pettegrew, Sergeant Wm. Hyde and others. Their opposition was on the ground that Colonel Allen had pledged himself that the Battalion should not be divided.

Accordingly, the Battalion was divided, the able-bodied soldiers and most of the commissioned officers, including Colonel Smith and Dr. Sanderson, making their way with all possible haste to Santa Fe, leaving the sick and feeble men and the worn out teams to follow as best they could.

The fact of Dr. Sanderson leaving the sick behind while he proceeded on with those who were healthy, is a fair indication of the interest he took in attending to the duties of his office. But the sick did not complain on that score. The sorrow which they felt at the loss of friends through having the Battalion divided, was in a great measure compensated by the relief they experienced at being rid of the Doctor's drugs and cursing for a few days. There was a noticeable improvement, too, in most of those who were sick after the Doctor left, so that when they arrived in Santa Fe many of them were convalescent.

After the division of the command, no unnecessary time was spent on the road even by those who brought up the rear. They were anxious to reach Santa Fe as early as possible, lest their friends of the advance division should be attached to some other corps and they be left to serve under their old religious persecutor, of Missouri memory, Colonel Sterling Price.

The feed and water, too, became better as we advanced, and we were able to force our jaded animals a little farther in a day than we had previously done. We passed a number of Mexican towns, and were visited by many of the inhabitants, who offered to sell us bread and cakes. The houses in these towns were generally small and squatty. They were built of adobies, or unburnt brick, of a very large size. The roofs, which were mostly flat, were covered with clay. The streets were narrow and irregular. The fields were unfenced, and the method of farming pursued was of the most primitive style. The people generally were a cross between the Spaniards and Indians.

While passing through the village of San Miguel, we saw for the first time Spanish sheep and goats, and were amused at watching the process of milking the latter. It was generally done by boys, who sat at the rear of the animals, and the milk pail caught frequent droppings of nanny-berries, which were carefully skimmed out with the fingers. Possibly, this may in some degree account for the extreme richness of the goat's milk cheese.

The first division of the Battalion arrived at Santa Fe on the evening of October 9th, 1846. On their approach, General Doniphan, the commander of the post, ordered a salute of one hundred guns to be fired from the roofs of houses, in honor of the Mormon Battalion. The second division arrived on the 12th of October.

When Colonel Sterling Price with his cavalry command which left Fort Leavenworth two or three days ahead of us, arrived at Santa Fe, he was received without any public demonstration, and when he learned of the salute which had been fired in honor of the "Mormons," he was greatly chagrinned and enraged.

This same General Doniphan, who had been an eminent lawyer of Clay County, Missouri, was present, when Joseph Smith and others were tried by a court-martial of the mob at Far West, in 1838. When the prisoners were sentenced upon that occasion to be shot in presence of their families, General Doniphan denounced the decision as "cold-blooded murder," and swore that neither he nor the regiment which he commanded should witness the execution. He was not only an officer in the militia, but he was the only lawyer of prominence who was present on that occasion, and his influence was such that by his firm and spirited action the decision of the court-martial was changed and the prisoners were turned over to the custody of the civil authorities of the State.

When the Battalion arrived at Santa Fe, General Doniphan was pleased to find a number of old acquaintances and friends among the soldiers, whom he knew to be honorable, upright and loyal men, and it was probably the memory of the wrongs which they had suffered from the Missouri mobocrats which prevented him from extending any courtesies to Colonel Price and his disgraceful command on their arrival.

CHAPTER X.

Captain Higgins' Detachment—Norman Sharp Accidentally Shot—Left to be Doctored by an Indian, and Dies—Colonel Cooke Takes Command of the Battalion—His Orders.

We will leave the main army for a season and return to the Arkansas river and follow Captain Higgins' detatchment to Pueblo, their winter quarters. This detatchment left the Battalion at the last crossing of the Arkansas river on the 16th of September.

Our narrative will necessarily be very brief, having received no journal and but a few items by letter and verbally from members of the party.

After four days' travel up the river, private Norman Sharp accidentally shot himself in the arm. He was so badly wounded it was deemed advisable to send him back a few miles to a friendly Indian village for treatment. The medicine man appeared very friendly and seemed almost certain he could cure him in a very few days. His treatment, however, was against his recovery. A warm fire was kept up day and night for about three days, when mortification set in and he died a stranger in a strange land. Mrs. Sharp and her sister, about ten years old, and Thomas Woolsey remained with him and did all their circumstances would permit for his recovery but to no avail. Woolsey and a squaw buried him. Peace to the remains of the faithful martyr until the resurrection morn, when he will be crowned with eternal life. Mrs. Sharp, the now bereaved widow with a sorrowful heart, her young sister and Wolsey, soon overtook the detatchment, which had stopped to set wagon tires.

We have nothing more of importance until the arrival of the company at their destination; hence we will return to Santa Fe and accompany Captain James Brown, with a detatchment of the sick to the same point.

Immediately after the arrival of the Battalion at Santa Fe, Colonel Cooke, who was there awaiting our arrival, assumed command, having been appointed to do so by General Kearney, who left Santa Fe some time previously. He greeted us with the following:

(Orders No. 7.)
    HEAD QUARTERS MORMON BATTALION,
       SANTA FE,
         October 13, 1846.

By virtue of my appointment, as Lieutenant Colonel of the Battalion of Volunteers, by the General commanding the Army of the West, and pursuant to his instructions contained in Order No. 33, of the 2nd of October, I hereby assume the command of that Battalion now encamped in this city.

First Lieutenant A. J. Smith, 1st dragoons, will receive actg. A. C. L., from Captain Grier, 1st dragoons, A. A. C. L., eight hundred dollars of specie funds belonging to the subsistence department.

Brevet Second Lieutenant George Stoneman, 1st dragoons, will perform the duties of Assistant Quartermaster on the expedition to Upper California. He will give the proper receipts for transportation, etc., not issued to the Captains of companies.

    (Signed.)   P. ST. GEORGE COOK.
      Lieutenant Colonel Commanding.

(Orders No. 8.)
    "HEAD QUARTERS MORMON BATTALION,
      SANTA FE, October 15, 1846.

Agreeable to instructions from the Colonel commanding, Capt. Jas. Brown will take the command of the men reported by the assistant Surgeon as incapable, from sickness and debility, of undertaking the present march to California. The Lieutenant Colonel, commanding, deems that the laundresses on this march will be accompanied by much suffering and would be a great encumbrance to the expedition; and as nearly all are desirous of accompanying the detachment of invalids which will winter near the source of the Arkansas river, it is ordered that all be attached to Captain Brown's party. The detachment will consist of Captain James Brown, three Sergeants, two Corporals, and sixteen privates of company C; First Lieutenant E. Luddington and ten privates of company B; one Sergeant and Corporal and twenty eight privates of company D; and one Sergeant and ten privates of company E, and four Laundresses from each company. Captain Brown will without delay require the necessary transportation and draw rations for twenty-one days. Captain Brown will march on the 17th inst. He will be furnished with a descriptive list of the detachment. He will take with him and give receipts for a full proportion of camp equipments.

(2) The commanding officer calls the particular attention of company commanders to the necessity of reducing the baggage as much as possible; transportation is deficient. The road most practicable is of deep sand and how soon we shall have to abandon the wagons it is impossible now to ascertain. Skillets and ovens cannot be taken, and but one camp kettle to a mess, of not less than ten men.

(3) Company commanders will make their requisitions on the Assistant Quarter Master, Captain W. M. D. McKissock, for mules and wagons, provision bags, pack saddles complete, and such other articles as are necessary for the outfit.

By order of

LIEUT. COL. COOKE.

(Orders No. 9.)
"HEAD QUARTERS MORMON BATTALION,
SANTA FE, October 15, 1846.

(1) Sergeant Major J. H. Glines having been reported incapable of performing the march to California, he is assigned

to company A, and will be borne on the rolls of that company accordingly.

(2) Sergeant James Ferguson, of company A, is appointed Sergeant Major of the Battalion. He will be obeyed and respected accordingly.

By order

LIEUT. COL. COOKE.
(Signed)　GEORGE P. DYKES, Adjutant.

(Orders No. 10.)

Sergeant J. J. Terry and D. Wilkin and Corporal J. Nowlan, of company C, preferring to acoompany the detachment for Fort Pueblo, are hereby reduced to the rank.

(2) On recommendation of their company commander, Corporals Edward Martin and Daniel Tyler are promoted to the rank of Sergeant, and privates R. G. Brownell, Wm. Squires and John Fife are appointed Corporals, all in company C. They will be obeyed and respected accordingly.

By order

LIEUT. COL. COOKE.
(Signed)　G. P. DYKES, Adjutant.

CHAPTER XI.

Detachment sent to Pueblo from Santa Fe—Death of Milton Smith—Death of Joseph W. Richards—Tributes from his Comrades, and Sister Hunt.

The names of the officers and men who went from Santa Fe to Pueblo to winter, under command of Captain James Brown, are as follows, so far as known:

COMPANY A.

Joseph W. Richards, *Musisian* (died)
1 Allred James T. S.
2 Allred Reuben W.
3 Blanchard Marvin S.
4 Calkins James W.
5 Garner David
6 Glines James H.
7 Hulett Schuyler
8 Holden Elijah E.
9 Jackson Charles A.
10 Lake Barnabas
11 Oyler Melcher
12 Roe Caratat C.
13 Sessions John
14 Wriston John P.

COMPANY B.

Elam Luddington, 1st. *Lieut.*
John D. Chase, 3d. *Corp.*
1 Allen Franklin
2 Bingham Erastus
3 Bird William
4 Garner Philip
5 Persons Harmon D.
6 Stephens Lyman
7 Stillman Dexter
8 Walker William
9 Wright Charles

COMPANY C.

Orson B. Adams, 1st. *Sergt.**
Alexander Brown, 2nd. *Corp.*
1 Brown Jesse J.
2 Beckstead William E.
3 Carpenter William H.
4 Carpenter Isaac
5 Calvert John
6 Durphy Francillo
7 Gould Samuel
8 Gould John C.
9 Johnson Jarvis
10 Larson Thurston
11 Nowlin Jabez (*Corp. at M. I., Private at M. O.*)
12 Persons Judson A.
13 Smith Richard
14 Smith Milton (died)
15 Shupe Andrew J.
16 Shupe James
17 Terrill Joel J.
18 Tindell Solomon
19 Wilkin David (*Corp. at M. I., Private at M. O.*)
20 Perkins David
21 Perkins John

*——Reported erroneously on former roll as 2nd Sergt.

COMPANY D.

Thomas S. Williams 2nd Sergt.
Arnold Stephens 1st. Corp.
1 Abbott Joshua
2 Averett Jonathan
3 Casto William
4 Chase Abner (died)
5 Davis James
6 Douglass Ralph
7 Gifford William R.
8 Hirons James
9 Kenney Lorin E.
10 Lamb Lisbon
11 Laughlin David S.
12 Meeseek Peter J.
13 Oakley James
14 Rowe William
15 Steele John
16 Sargent Abel M.
17 Gribble William
18 Roberts Benjamin
19 Sanderson Henry W.
20 Sharp Albert
21 Stillman Clark
22 Smith John G.
23 Tanner Myron
24 Whiting Almon
25 Whiting Edmund

COMPANY E.

Ebenezer Hanks 3d. Sergt.
1 Clark Samuel
2 Cummings George
3 Glazier Luther W.
4 Hess John W.
5 Hopkins Charles
6 Karren Thomas
7 Miller Daniel
8 Park William A.
9 Pugmire Jonathan, jr.
10 Stevens Roswell
11 Jacobs Bailey

I believe the detachment took up its line of march on the 18th instead of the 17th, as directed in the order of Colonel Cooke; so says John G. Smith, one of the party, who kept a daily journal.

Few incidents occurred on the journey from Santa Fe to Pueblo outside of the ordinary routine of travel. Very good time was made in traveling, considering the miserable plight of the teams and the feeble condition of most of the men. The third day after starting several yoke of fresh oxen were obtained, which proved a great benefit to the detachment.

On the night of the 27th Milton Smith died and the next day received as good a burial as his friends could give him on the prairie.

Owing to the weak condition of the teams, the sick were obliged to walk when ascending steep hills and where the roads were unusually bad, which was a great hardship to them.

On the 9th of November, when the detachment had reached the Arkansas river, Captain James Brown, and others, left the command and proceeded on to Bent's Fort, to secure sixty days' provisions, and the following day the detachment crossed the river and traveled on towards Pueblo.

The detachment arrived within four miles of Pueblo on the 15th of November, where a halt was made to allow time for the officers to make the necessary arrangements for the winter quarters.

On the 17th the Arkansas river was crossed, Pueblo entered and a camping place selected near the quarters of Captain Higgins' detachment and a company of Saints from Mississippi, who had stopped there to winter.

The greeting which occurred between comrades and old friends, husbands and wives, parents and children, when the two detachments met, was quite touching. A thrill of joy ran through the camp which none but those living martyrs can fully comprehend.

It was immediately agreed that 15 rooms, fourteen feet square, should be erected for the winter quarters, and the men who were able to chop were dispatched to the woods to procure timbers for the houses, with the understanding that the first rooms finished should be allotted to the sick. The work of erecting the houses was pushed with all possible rapidity, but before they were finished sufficiently to shelter the sick from the piercing winds and cold mountain storms, some had already succumbed. Among the number, was Joseph Wm. Richards, a very estimable young man, who died on the 24th of November. Of his death, C. C. Roe, a comrade, writing to Apostle Franklin D. Richards, brother to the deceased, says:

"The Battalion left Point Pool, on the Missouri river, on the 24th day of July, 1846, and marched to Fort Leavenworth on foot, without tents or shelter of any kind, sleeping on the ground, which was sometimes saturated with rain and heavy dews. Some rain storms fell upon us while thus sleeping under the open canopy of the heavens. At Fort Leavenworth Joseph Wm. Richards took sick, doubtless from exposure on the road. When the command left the garrison he remained in the hospital unable to be moved. By kind treatment and medical aid he was soon able to be forwarded, and overtook us at Council Grove. From this time his health fluctuated. When the Battalion was divided by order of Lieutenant A. J. Smith, and the stronger portion put on a forced march to be in Santa Fè in time to cross the mountains to California the same fall, he, being stronger than usual, was selected as one of them. When I arrived with the invalids I found Joseph again prostrated, so far at least that he was considered unfit to attempt to cross the mountains and deserts to California. As my health increased his seemed to fail, and as we had been very much attached from the beginning, he placed himself entirely in my care. On the sad night of his departure, while I was endeavoring, at his request, to render him some assistance, after grasping me with a hug which almost took my breath, he gradually sank down and in a few moments expired in my arms without a struggle or a groan, but quietly passed away like a child going to sleep."

Apostle Franklin D. Richards, writing of his brother's death, says: "When the call for the Battalion was made known to us, the massacred body of one of my brothers, George S. Richards, lay buried in the well, with about fifteen others, at Haun's Mill, in Caldwell County, Missouri; another, Joseph William Richards, born in Richmond, Berkshire County, Massachusetts, May 25, 1829, died at Fort Pueblo, *enroute* from Council Bluffs, Iowa, to California, in November, 1846. Brother Samuel and myself were in England, on our first mission."

James Ferguson, himself Sergeant Major of the Battalion, in a lecture delivered before an assembly of Elders, including the Presidency of the European Mission, in Liverpool, England, November 7, 1855, speaks thus of Brother Richards' enlistment, travels, virtues and the patriotism of his aged and feeble mother:

"Exposed to enemies who lurked in every grove, President Young visited the various camps, nor ceased his exertions till the last muster roll was filled. But few knew the sacrifice it cost. There was one scene that was particularly touching. An aged mother to whom the call of the government and the wish of the President were made known came forward. She had five sons—one was murdered and now lay buried deep and unavenged in the tragic well in Missouri. Two were in a foreign land, preaching the faith for which their brother's blood was shed; one was still too young to administer, but needed care and comfort; the other was a young man, the sentinel and protector of her tottering steps. Even in her aged heart, withered and broken as it was, the love of country burned deep and strong. She yielded up her son and never saw him more. I knew him well. We marched side by side. He had been worn down by the bitterness and exposure of many persecutions. But Joseph Richards was noble, generous and brave, and never complained."

Sister Celia Hunt, who often took him nourishment and said comforting words to him, giving him the last food he ever ate, a few hours before his death, speaks of him as among the most noble young men she ever knew. He never complained of his lot.

We will now leave these two detachments, for the present, and return to Santa Fe, and follow the main army again.

CHAPTER XII.

Colonel Cooke's Statement of the Condition of the Battalion—Paid in Checks that could not be Cashed—Send them to Council Bluffs—Reason for Lieutenant Gully's Resignation—Condition of Animals—Strict Discipline of Colonel Cooke—An Officer the first to be Punished.

Of the condition and fitness of the Battalion to pursue their journey across the great American Desert, Colonel P. St. George Cooke, our new commander, very properly and truthfully remarks: "Everything conspired to discourage the extraordinary undertaking of marching this Battalion eleven hundred miles, for the much greater part through an unknown wilderness, without road or trail, and with a wagon train.

"It was enlisted too much by families: some were too old, some feeble, and some too young; it was embarrassed by many women; it was undisciplined; it was much worn by traveling on foot, and marching from Nauvoo, Illinois; their clothing was very scant; there was no money to pay them, or clothing to issue; their mules were utterly broken down; the quartermaster department was without funds, and its credit bad; and animals were scarce. Those procured were very inferior, and were deteriorating every hour for lack of forage or grazing. So every preparation must be pushed—hurried. A small party with families (Captain Higgins' company, already mentioned) had been sent from Arkansas crossing up the river, to winter at a small settlement close to the mountains, called Pueblo. The Battalion was now inspected, and eighty-six men, found inefficient, were ordered, under two officers, with nearly all the women, to go to the same point; five wives of officers were reluctantly allowed to accompany the march, but furnished their own transportation.

"By special arrangement and consent, the Battalion was paid in checks—not very available at Santa Fe.

"With every effort, the quartermaster could only undertake to furnish rations for sixty days; and, in fact, full rations of only flour, sugar, coffee and salt; salt pork only for thirty days, and soap for twenty. To venture without pack-saddles would be grossly imprudent and so that burden was added."

Redick N. Allred, Quartermaster Sergeant, of company A, made the purchases here mentioned.

I will here add, in relation to Colonel Cooke's assertion that the Battalion "was much worn by traveling on foot and marching from Nauvoo, Illinois," that while his statement is strictly correct, it was much worse "worn" by the foolish and unnecessary forced marches of Lieutenants Smith and Dykes, which utterly broke down both men and beasts, and was the prime cause of the greater part of the sickness and probably of many deaths.

I am satisfied that any other set of men but Latter-day Saints would have mutinied rather than submit to the oppressions and abuse thus heaped upon them.

About noon, October 19th, we took leave of John D. Lee and Howard Egan, who started with our checks for Council Bluffs, being accompanied by Lieutenant Samuel L. Gulley, ex-quartermaster of the Battalion, and Roswell Stevens.

The stand Lieutenant Gully took against Lieutenants Smith and Dykes and Dr. Sanderson, at Fort Leavenworth, and subsequently, had created such a prejudice among the non-Mormon officers that it was thought best for him to resign and return home. He had, however, established his character as a brave, noble-minded and undeviating friend to the Battalion, in whose memory the very name of Samuel L. Gully is associated with all the noble characteristics that grace a model officer. He would have sacrificed his life rather than be untrue to his friends.

With a hearty shake of the hand and "God bless you, Brother Gully, and give you a safe journey to the bosom of your family and the church," we bade him adieu and never saw him after. He returned with the parties mentioned, and died the next year in crossing the plains *en route* for Salt Lake. Peace to his ashes.

Simultaneously with the departure of these men, the Battalion broke camp at Santa Fe and traveled six miles to Aqua Frio, the nearest point for grazing.

Under date of November 19th, the commander adds: "I have brought road tools and have *determined* to take through my wagons; but the experiment is not a fair one, as the mules are nearly broken down at the outset. The only good ones, about twenty, which I bought near Albuquerque, were taken for the express for Fremont's mail—the General's order requiring "the twenty-one best in Santa Fe."

It is but justice to the Colonel and the command to state here that, with few exceptions, the mule and ox teams used from Santa Fe to California were the same worn-out and broken down animals that we had driven all the way from Council Bluffs and Fort Leavenworth; indeed, some of them had been driven all the way from Nauvoo the same season.

On the 20th of November, after we had traveled past every place where it would be possible to purchase provisions for a considerable length of time, to the surprise of the command the rations were reduced, as will be seen by the following:

(Orders No. 11.)

"HEAD QUARTERS MORMON BATTALION,
"SANTA FE.

"Until further orders, three-fourths pound of flour, also three-fourths rations sugar and coffee will be issued. Beef one and a half pounds will be issued for a day's ration. The commanders of companies will select a non-commissioned officer from each company. He will be reported on daily duty, whose duty it will be to issue rations and superintend the loading of the wagons and the care of the mules. They will have immediate command of the teamsters and assistants. Commanders of companies will be held strictly responsible that the issue of rations is made carefully as now ordered. The welfare and safety of the Battalion may depend on it.

(2) "Hereafter, no muskets or knapsacks will be carried in a public wagon or on a public mule without orders or express permission of the commanding officer, and no one will leave his company a quarter of a mile without permission, and no musket will be fired in camp. The officer of the day will attend to the execution of these regulations and confine under guard any one who disobeys them. At reveille all will turn out under arms. The company commanders will order turns of guard or confine those who fail. After roll call the ranks will be opened and an officer will pass down each rank and see that all are fully armed and equipped. Immediately after roll call, breakfast will be disposed of and everything packed in the wagons by a sufficient number of each mess under the acting Quartermaster Sergeants of the company, as provided for in the order. All this will be done without waiting for signals or the loss of a moment. The teams will be hitched up as the teamsters get their breakfast. Morning reports will be handed in to the Adjutant ten minutes after. Every teamster must have one or more buckets or camp kettles with which to water his team. The teams will not stop to water unless ordered by the commanding officers, as everything depends on our animals. I call all the officers and the Quartermaster Sergeants of companies and the teamsters and the assistants to do the best for them possible. The order will be read twice at the head of each company by its commanders.

"By order of

        LIEUT. COL. COOKE.
  (Signed) G. P. DYKES, Adjutant."

The foregoing order was strictly observed. The officers and soldiers were brought to the letter of the law. The discipline enforced was quite as strict as that of the regular army. There was one feature about Colonel Cooke's discipline which differed materially from that of Colonel Smith. His theory was that officers should obey first, and set the example to the men. The first breach of the regulations was by an officer, and it was promptly punished.

Captain Jesse D. Hunter, of company B, was put under arrest on the morning of the 21st of October and made to march in the rear of his company during the day, for remaining over night in Santa Fe without the knowledge or consent of the commanding officer. By this move the Battalion learned that if their new commander was strict in his discipline, he was impartial, as officers would be held to the same accountability as soldiers. Smith's policy was just the reverse of this, for while privates were punished by him for the merest trifles, officers could go where and do what they pleased, without any notice being taken of them.

I cannot forego the temptation to allude to a couple of incidents showing the contrast between the Battalion of "Mormons" and a portion of Price's regiment of Missouri volunteers. Some of the latter were doubtless among those who aided, under this same Colonel Price, in driving the Saints from Missouri. I further quote from Cooke's "Conquest of New Mexico and California:"

"At the last moment I learned that nineteen beeves and fourteen mules were missing. * * I was, of course, without mounted men to send after the missing cattle. I sent the officer of the day, and every member of the old guard in pursuit, in four parties, * * but this consumed an hour. They were all recovered."

Under date of the 23rd, he says: "Passed the camp of a Major and three companies of Price's regiment, who left Santa Fe, four days before the Battalion; the Major said that after a day's march it took him two or three to collect the animals."

CHAPTER XIII.

Mexicans too much Prejudiced to sell us Supplies—Mexican Costumes—Sergeant Elmer Reduced to the Ranks—Navajo Raids on the Mexicans—Hardships of our Journey—Animals Devoured Wholly, Except Bones and Hair—Men Have to Pull the Wagons—A Song.

On the 22nd, the Assistant Quartermaster vainly endeavored to obtain fresh mules and oxen from some small Mexican towns that we passed. The prejudice of the natives was so strong against the Government of the United States, that they would render no assistance beyond selling a little feed and perishable vegetables. On the 23rd, however, he succeeded in exchanging thirty of our worthless mules for half the number of fresh, though, as a rule, small mules, the stock owned by the Mexicans being rather diminutive. The Colonel also purchased eight mules from officers of Captain Burgwin's command. He also exchanged about as many more for better ones, and obtained ten yoke of oxen.

Two of our poorest heavy wagons were also exchanged for lighter and better ones. The hand of an all-wise providence was certainly in these things, as, without something of the kind, we must inevitably have been left without means of conveyance, on the great desert, in an enemy's country, surrounded by the most ferocious savages.

On the 24th we passed another town of Mexicans or "Greasers," as those of mixed blood are frequently termed. Many of the men were as nude as when born, except a breech-clout, or, as Colonel Cooke has it, "center-clothing," tied around the loins.

On the 25th we received the following:
(Order No. 12.)

"The oxen may be unyoked every evening on reaching camp and be herded with the beef cattle, by the Sergeant, one Corporal and twelve of the guard. The officer of the day will select a separate position for this part of his guard. At or before the first call for reveille the Quartermaster Sergeant and teamsters will turn out and change the mules to fresh grass.

When there is corn it must be fed at the pickets, where the mules will be so far apart that they cannot reach each other. Breakfast and packing up must go on without loss of time after reveille; and at trumpet signal, and not before, must the mules and oxen be harnessed, yoked and hitched up. The mules must be taken far out at first when not herded, and not brought in nearer; another trumpet signal, will be sounded every evening for taking them to water. The Quartermaster will equalize the teams with the new purchase and assign the six extra mules to each company command. The company commanders will relieve the flagging mules with these from day to day. The guard must hereafter be kept more strictly at their post. When the guard is stationed, death is the punishment awarded by law to a sentinel who sleeps on his post in time of war, which now exists.

(2) Sergeant E. Elmer, of company C, is hereby reduced to the ranks for neglecting, this morning, to form his company while reveille was beating and for telling his Colonel that he did so because he could not see to call the roll."

"By order of

LIEUT. COL. COOKE.

(Signed.)   G P. DYKES, Abjutant."

Although the reason assigned by Sergeant Elijah Elmer for being about one or possibly two minutes late in forming the company at reveille, was, that he could not see to call the roll, the facts were, however, as I understood them, that he stopped to lace or tie his shoes, but did not wish to make this excuse to his commander.

The author was selected to perform the duties of orderly until further instructed.

Sergeant Elmer, like Pharaoh's butler, was subsequently restored to his office, and retained the respect and friendship of all his acquaintances up to the time of his death, which occurred quite recently at Panguitch, in Iron County, Utah.

Quartermaster Stoneman, who was a gentleman in all that the word implies, used every effort to obtain a larger supply of good animals before leaving the last Spanish-Indian settlements. He was several times highly insulted by Mexicans, who contemptuously refused to trade with him. He could hardly seem to realize that he was endeavoring to deal with a whipped, though as yet unconquered foe.

As we passed Captain Burgwin's command we learned that he had received a letter from the American traders below, stating that General Armijo was marching up to seize their property, and asking protection. General Armijo was soon after captured and put in irons.

On the 26th, we passed several Mexican villages. The Assistant Quartermaster crossed the river to purchase pack-saddles, blankets and mules. He declined, however, to pay the unreasonable prices demanded. Otero, of whom he thought to make the purchase, had had about five or six thousand sheep driven off the previous evening by Indians, and two shepherds were killed. He rode the entire night endeavoring to hire men to pursue the Indians, but without success, so far as we were able to learn. In one of the towns we passed through, 6,600 sheep were reported stolen and two shepherds killed; thus over 12,000 sheep were stolen and four men killed in one day within a few miles of our encampment.

Our course now lay down the Rio Del Norte. We found the roads extremely sandy in many places, and the men while carrying blankets, knapsacks, cartridge boxes (each containing thirty-six rounds of ammunition), and muskets on their backs, and living on short rations, had to pull at long ropes to aid the teams. The deep sand alone, without any load, was enough to wear out both man and beast. Upon one occasion, several wild geese were killed by some of the hunters, which proved a treat to them and their immediate comrades or messmates. Once in awhile, also, as we passed the Mexican villages, those who had money or anything to trade found opportunities for purchasing Spanish grapes. These, however, were exceptional cases, as most of the men were without money, that which they had drawn at Fort Leavenworth having been sent back to their families, and the payment made at Santa Fe having been in checks that were not negotiable in that region. The men were ready to eat anything that would furnish them any nourishment, the rations issued to them being insufficient to satisfy the cravings of hunger. When we left Santa Fe we supposed the few fat cattle taken along were intended for beef, but we were soon undeceived upon that point. When one of them was slaughtered the second day out, the Colonel gave positive orders that no more of them should be killed, as they must be used as work animals, and only such killed for beef as were unable from sheer weakness and exhaustion to work. From that time on it was the custom to kill the work animals as they gave out and issue the carcasses as rations. Nor was any portion of the animal thrown away that could possibly be utilized for food. Even to the hides, tripe and entrails, all were eagerly devoured, and that, too, in many cases without water to wash them in. The marrow bones were considered a luxury, and were issued in turns to the various messes.

On the 27th, we encountered cold rain in the valley of the Rio Del Norte. Heavy snow also fell upon the mountains.

The storm had one good effect, though, it made the road much better by settling the sand, but at best we could say with Levi W. Hancock's song:

"How hard, to starve and wear us out,
Upon this sandy desert route!"

Canals for irrigating purposes were found all along the banks of the river. Some of them several miles in length. They conveyed water to the farms, or as they were called in that country, ranchos. There being little or no rain during the growing season the water was made to flow over the ground until it was sufficiently saturated, and then shut off until needed again for the same purpose. The inhabitants of that region were generally of the lower class, and had but little respect for chastity.

On the 30th we had to leave the river for a time and have twenty men to each wagon with long ropes to help the teams pull the wagons over the sand hills. The commander perched himself on one of the hills, like a hawk on a fence post, sending down his orders with the sharpness of—well, to the Battalion, it is enough to say—Colonel Cooke.

The following is the song by Levi W. Hancock to which reference was made previously:

THE DESERT ROUTE.

While here, beneath a sultry sky,
Our famished mules and cattle die;
Scarce aught but skin and bones remain
To feed poor soldiers on the plain.

CHORUS.

How hard, to starve and wear us out,
Upon this sandy, desert route.

We sometimes now for lack of bread,
Are less than quarter rations fed,
And soon expect, for all of meat,
Naught less than broke-down mules, to eat.

Now, half-starved oxen, over-drilled,
Too weak to draw, for beef are killed;
And gnawing hunger prompting men
To eat small entrails and the skin.

Sometimes we quarter for the day,
While men are sent ten miles away
On our back track, to place in store
An ox, given out the day before.

And when an ox is like to die,
The whole camp halts, and we lay by:
The greedy wolves and buzzards stay,
Expecting rations for the day.

Our hardships reach their rough extremes,
When valiant men are roped with teams,
Hour after hour, and day by day,
To wear our strength and lives away.

A SONG.

The teams can hardly drag their loads
Along the hilly, sandy roads,
While trav'ling near the Rio Grande,
O'er hills and dales of heated sand.

We see some twenty men, or more,
With empty stomachs, and foot-sore,
Bound to one wagon, plodding on
Thro' sand, beneath a burning sun.

A Doctor which the Government
Has furnished, proves a punishment!
At his rude call of "Jim Along Joe,"
The sick and halt, to him must go.

Both night and morn, this call is heard;
Our indignation then is stirr'd,
And we sincerely wish in hell,
His arsenic and calomel.

To take it, if we're not inclined,
We're threatened, "You'll be left behind:"
When bored with threats profanely rough,
We swallow down the poisonous stuff.

Some stand the journey well, and some
Are by the hardships overcome;
And thus the "Mormons" are worn out
Upon this long and weary route.

CHAPTER XIV.

Lieutenant Dykes resigns his Adjutancy—Dinner of Sheep's Lights—Mexican Spurs—Mexican Woman Stolen by the Navajoes—Hampton Reported Well by Dr. Sanderson, and Dies a Few Hours Afterwards—Another Reduction in Rations—Rumors of Intended Revolt—Two Men Punished Through the Meanness of Dykes—Sergeant Elmer Restored to Office—Discouraging Reports of Guides—Condition of Teams.

Up to the 1st of November Lieutenant Dykes, of Company D, had acted in the capacity of Adjutant to the Battalion, while Cyrus C. Canfield, the 2nd Lieutenant, had command, during the absence of Captain Nelson Higgins. Upon this date, however, Lieutenant Dykes resigned his position as Adjutant, and assumed command of the company, as will be seen by the following:

(Orders No. 13).

"In consequence of the absence of Captain Higgins and the importance that the first lieutenant of his company should command it, the resignation of his adjutancy by 1st Lieutenant George P. Dykes is hereby accepted and he will assume the command of the company, giving reciepts to Lieutenant Hulett for its public property. First Lieutenant Dykes has the thanks of his commanding officer for his faithful performance of his duties while adjutant of the Battalion.

Second Lieutenant Merrill is hereby appointed Adjutant of the Battalion. He will be obeyed and respected accordingly.

(Signed.) P. St. GEORGE COOKE,
LIEUT. Col. COMMANDING."

This change gave general satisfaction to the Battalion with the exception of Company D.

Many, after leaving Santa Fe, contracted severe colds, from which they suffered for some time, but as we advanced the effects gradually wore off. We found the judgment of

Colonel Cooke in traveling much better than that of Smith, in fact, it was first-class. He never crowded the men unnecessarily, but as we advanced the roads grew so much worse that both men and teams failed fast, and our only hope of success lay in our faith in God and on pulling at the ropes.

On the 2nd of November a number of teams gave out and several wagons were sent back to Santa Fe, empty. The same day about 300 miserably poor Spanish sheep were brought to the camp for food. Such as could travel were subsequently dealt out as rations and those that gave out by the way, when discovered, were killed and eaten by the worn-out straggling soldiers, who were unable to keep pace with the main body. On one occasion the author, being behind all, seeing a smoke a little way from the road side, went to it and found that parties who were a little in advance of him had butchered one of these stragglers and consumed every thing but the lights. Of these he made a sumptuous dinner by roasting them on the coals and eating without water. His thoughts at partaking of this repast are still vividly impressed upon the author's mind. He had frequently heard it said in his childhood that if a person ate sheep's light's he would be sure to go blind. Although the story came to his mind it didn't have much weight with him upon that occasion. The craving for food was so strong that he readily made up his mind to eat the lights and take his chances.

While traveling on the 2nd we met the guides engaged by General Kearney, and sent out ahead of the Battalion to explore the country, who reported to us that it would take at least ninety days to reach the Pacific coast, and gave very discouraging accounts of the route.

The same day we saw a number of Mexicans, mounted, with spurs ten to twelve inches long and rowels one to two inches long. These were a source of wonder to us, being the first of the kind we had ever seen.

While passing a ranch a few days previously, Colonel Cooke had been appealed to by a Mexican senora for protection as she feared the Navajoes, who had already stolen her husband's stock, would return and take her prisoner. Colonel Cooke wrote a letter to Captain Burgwin, who was in charge of a detatchment of General Kearney's brigade, not far distant, asking him to render her what aid he could. The news which we subsequently received proved that the woman's fears were well grounded. The Navajoes took her prisoner and stole the remainder of her stock. Captain Greer's company, which was in advance of Captain Burgwin's, pursued the Indians and recaptured the cattle and sheep, but were repulsed by the Indians and failed to recover the woman.

On the morning of the 3rd, Brother James Hampton who had been on the sick list a few days was reported by Dr. Sanderson as ready for duty, but so far from being well, he died about 2 o'clock in the afternoon of the same day. He was a faithful soldier and worthy Latter-day Saint. When it was learned that he was dying, a halt of about twenty minutes was made, and after his death he was placed in a wagon and carried to our next camping place, where he was buried, a lone stranger in a strange land, but, as we shall soon see, he was not destined to long occupy the grave alone.

The same day we received the following:

(Orders No. 14.)

"The commanding officer feels it his duty, on the report of his principal guide, for the safety of the Battalion, to make further reduction of its rations. Hereafter ten ounces of pork will be issued as the rations, and nine ounces of flour. Fresh meat will be issued at a pound and a half.

"By order of LIEUT. COL. COOKE, Commanding,

"P. C. MERRILL, Adjt."

On the 4th, after passing through a country which was very rough and broken, and over a road which was almost impassable, we encamped near some ancient ruins. Here we were overtaken by Thomas Woolsey, one of Captain Higgins' detachment, who went to Pueblo from the crossing of the Arkansas. He brought us the first information we received of the accidental shooting and subsequent death of Norman Sharp, which has already been mentioned.

About the same time a rumor reached us of a movement which was said to be on foot among the Mexicans in the region through which we were traveling, to revolt against the American rule, and we also learned of a similar intention on the part of the Mexicans at Santa Fe. Should such a thing have occurred at that period our situation would have been extremely perilous, as we were not over four hundred strong, and surrounded by hostile Indians as well as Mexicans, who had the advantage of an acquaintance with the country, while we were strangers there, with nothing to depend upon this side of heaven but our muskets. Our guides were fearful and quite downcast at learning the news, but our commander took the matter very coolly and maintained an air of indifference.

While traveling that day, two weary soldiers were tied behind an ox wagon and obliged to march in that position through wind and dust, for neglecting to get up and salute Lieutenant Dykes while on the grand rounds of the camp the previous night, to visit the guards stationed at different points. They had just been relieved from standing guard for two hours and lain down to take their rest, of which, it is scarcely necessary to inform the reader, they stood in much need, when the officer of the guard, seeing Dykes approaching, gave the usual order, "Turn out the guard! Officer of the day!" As the two men failed to "turn out," Dykes considered it a great indignity, and reported it accordingly to Colonel Cooke, who ordered the humiliating and disagreeable punishment already described.

Referring to this matter, Sergeant William Hyde, among other things, says: "It was plainly manifest that Lieutenant Dykes sought to gain favor of and please the wicked rather than favor his brethren." Every Battalion man will endorse the Sergeant's statement. Lieutenant Dykes afterwards became so notorious for his officious and captious manner, that the Battalion accorded to him the title of "the accuser of the brethren."

On the 6th of November, we arrived at the place where General Kearney had left his wagons, and from which point he had proceeded with pack-animals.

It may be as well to explain here, that General Kearney, having learned while he was at Santa Fe that the Mexicans in California had surrendered to Commodore Stockton, resolved to push on through as hastily as possible and assume control of the country as governor and commander-in-chief of California, in accordance with his commission from the President of the United States, received previous to starting upon the campaign. He accordingly disbanded most of his soldiers at Santa Fe, and, with one hundred picked men, set out for the coast some time previous to our arrival at that post. Previous to starting, however, he gave orders for Colonel Cooke to follow on with the Mormon Battalion, and open a wagon road to the coast.

The prospect before us from this point was anything but encouraging. Besides what we had previously endured from hunger and having to help our worn-out animals pull the overloaded wagons, we now had before us the additional task of having to construct a wagon road over a wild, desert and unexplored country, where wagons had never been before.

On the 7th, a little relief was afforded some of the men by the killing of a black-tailed deer. It was a rich treat to those who got a taste of it.

On the 8th, we received the following:

(Orders No. 15.)

(1) "On the recommendation of the company commander, private E. Elmer, of Company C., is appointed 1st Sergeant of the same company.

(2) "Quartermaster Sergeant Shelton of the Battalion, having failed to join it, agreeable to the order of acting Lieutenant Colonel A. J. Smith, is hereby reduced to the ranks. He is assigned to Company D., by

"Lieut. Col. Cooke,
"P. C. Merrill, Adjutant."

The forepart of this order simply restored Sergeant Elmer to his former position. It is understood that it was not the intention of the Colonel to do this simple act of justice, but as the military regulations provided that non-commissioned officers should be appointed on the recommendation of their respective company commanders, he could not well do otherwise, as in this case Lieutenant Rosecrans, commander in the absence of Captain Brown, who was on detached service, very properly declined to recommend any other.

On the evening of the 8th, four pilots who had been sent forward by Colonel Cooke several days previously, to explore a route, returned and reported that the country was of such a nature that they considered it impossible to get through with wagons. The Colonel, however, was inexorable. He had started out to make a wagon road across the great American desert, and he was determined not to abandon the enterprise.

During the same day we encountered the first mezquit brush that we had seen. It is a thorny shrub, bearing a slight resemblance to the honey locust.

On the 9th, Colonel Cooke estimated that during the last six days previous we had only traveled forty miles, and yet our travel had been attended with a great deal of exertion, as the country was sandy and broken. Colonel Cooke, writing of the condition of the animals at this time, says: "The guides say that most of the mules could not be driven loose to California. I have carefully examined them, and found that whole teams seemed ready to break down. Twenty-two men are on sick report. Quite a number have been transported in wagons."

CHAPTER XV.

Lieutenant Willis Sent Back with the Sick—Only Five Days' Rations for a Journey of 300 Miles—Ox Mired and Killed—Oxen Providentially Provided—Death of Elijah Freeman and Richard Carter—Wagons Exchanged for Pack Animals—Sickness of Men—Left on the Way—A Severe Journey—Snow Four Feet Deep—Arrival at Pueblo—Condition of Men—Gilbert Hunt Sent Back for the Sick—Sad Death of Coleman.

On the 10th, it was decided that a detachment of fifty-five sick men, under command of Lieutenant W. W. Willis, be sent back to Pueblo, by way of Santa Fe, to winter. The Colonel ordered that they be furnished with twenty-six days' rations, allowing ten ounces of flour per day—eighteen ounces being the usual soldier's ration. It appears though, that through some mistake, probably an oversight in loading the wagon, this amount was not taken.

Following are the names of those who accompanied Lieutenant Willis:

COMPANY A.

1 Bevan James
2 Calkins Alva
3 Curtis Josiah
4 Carl James C.
5 Frederick David

6 Hewett Eli B.
7 Maxwell Max
8 Wriston Isaac N.
9 Woodworth Lysander

COMPANY B.

1 Bybee John
2 Bingham Thomas
3 Camp James
4 Church Hayden W.

5 Clark George S.
6 Eastman Marcus
7 Hinkley Arza E.

COMPANY C.

1 Blackburn Abner
2 Brimhall John
3 Babcock Lorenzo
4 Burt William
5 Dunn James
6 Johnston Jesse

7 Rust William W.
8 Richmond Benjamin
9 Shipley Joseph
10 Squires William, *Corp.*
11 Thomas Nathan
12 Welsh Madison

COMPANY D.

1 Badlam Samuel
2 Compton Allen
3 Higgins Alfred
4 Hoagland Lucas
5 Mecham Erastus D.
6 Stuart James

7 Stuart Benjamin
8 Tubbs William R.
9 Tippetts John H.
10 Thomas Haywood
11 Dalton Edward
12 Dalton Harry

COMPANY E.

1 Brazier Richard *Sergt.*
2 Burns Thomas R.
3 Brown Daniel
4 Cazier John
5 Cazier James

6 McLelland William (or McClellan)
7 Richardson Thomas
8 Wilson George
9 Skeen Joseph
10 Woolsey Thomas

Lieutenant Willis, writing from memory of the incidents of the Battalion, says:

"Active preparations now commenced to carry into effect the Colonel's orders, and by 4 o'clock of the same day we had collected of invalids fifty-six, one big government wagon, four yoke of poor cattle, five days' rations and two dressed sheep, as food for the sick. Our loading for the one wagon consisted of the clothing, blankets, cooking utensils, tents and tent poles, muskets, equipage, and provisions, and all invalids who were unable to walk. With some difficulty I obtained a spade or two and a shovel, but was provided with no medicines or other necessaries for the sick except the mutton before referred to, and only five days' rations, to travel near three hundred miles.

"Thus armed and equipped we commenced our lonesome march, retracing our steps to Santa Fe. We marched the same day about two miles and were visited by Captain Hunt and others at night, who spoke words of comfort to us and blessed us, administering the Church ordinance to the sick, and bidding us God speed. They left us the next day.

"We resumed our march, camping in the evening near some springs. One yoke of our oxen got mired in the mud. We took off the yoke when one got out. The other we undertook to pull out with a rope and unfortunately broke his neck. Our team was now too weak for our load. In the night Brother John Green died, and we buried him by the side of Brother James Hampton.

"What to do for a team we did not know. This was a dark time, and many were the earnest petitions that went up to our God and Father for Divine aid.

"The next morning we found with our oxen a pair of splendid young steers, which was really cheering to us. We looked upon it as one of the providences of our Father in heaven. Thus provided for, we pursued our march. We traveled two days without further accident.

"During the night of the 25th of November, Elijah Freeman was taken very ill. We hauled him next day in our wagon and could distinctly hear his groans to the head of our little column. We lay by next day for his benefit. It was very cold and snowy. Next day we resumed our march, but were forced to stop the wagon for our afflicted comrade to die. After his death we resumed our march until the usual time of camping when we buried the corpse. Richard Carter also died the same night and we buried him by the side of Brother Freeman. Their graves are four miles south of Secora, on the Rio Grande.

"We continued our march to Albuquerque, where we presented our orders for assistance to Captain Burgwin, of Kearney's brigade. He gave me five dollars, cash, and the privilege of exchanging our heavy wagon for a lighter one. I had fuel and everything to buy, and spent $66.00 of my own private money before reaching Santa Fe, which was, as near as I can recollect, about the 25th of November.

"On my arrival at that place, General Price, commander of the post, ordered me to Pueblo, on the Arkansas River. He also ordered Quartermaster McKissock to furnish us with the necessary provisions, mules, etc. I obtained from the Quartermaster ten mules and pack-saddles, ropes and other fixtures necessary for packing. With this outfit we had to perform a journey of about three hundred miles, over the mountains, and in the winter.

"Packing was new business to us, and at first we were quite awkward. This was about the 5th of December. The first day we marched about ten miles. Here we gave Brother Brazier, who was too sick to travel, a mule, and left Thomas Burns to wait upon him and follow, when he got able, to a Mr. Turley's, where I designed leaving those who were unable to cross the mountains.

"The next day we traveled about twenty miles and camped on a beautiful stream of water where we had to leave one broke-down mule. The day after, we marched about fifteen miles, and camped in a Spanish town. Here Alva Calkins, at his own request, remained to await the arrival of Brothers Brazier and Burns. About ten inches of snow fell that day, and the next day it snowed until about noon, after which we marched ten or twelve miles and hired quarters of a Spaniard. Here the men bought bread, onions, pork, etc., from their own private means. Brother William Coleman was seized with an unnatural appetite, and ate to excess. In the night we were all awakened by his groans. Dr. Rust gave him a little tincture of lobelia, the only medicine in camp, which gave him partial relief.

"Continuing our journey, we traveled within about ten miles of Turley's, Brother Coleman riding on a mule with the aid of two men to help him on and off. The next morning, started early for Mr. Turley's to make arrangements for the sick. I left my saddle mule for the sick man, with strict instructions to have him brought to that place. On my arrival I made the necessary arrangements, and about noon the company arrived, but to my surprise and regret without Brother Coleman. They said he refused to come. Mr. Turley, on hearing me express my regret and dissatisfaction at his being left, proffered to send his team and carriage to go back next day and bring him in, which offer I accepted, and agreed to pay him for his trouble. I left quite a number of sick with Mr. Turley, paying him out of my own private funds for their rations and quarters, and then traveled about ten miles. At night, strong fears were entertained that the snow was so deep we could not cross the mountains and some resolved not to attempt it, accusing me of rashness. I called the company together and stated the fact to them that I was unauthorized to draw rations except for the journey and other necessaries unless for the sick, and that I was expending my own private money. I also stated that I should carry out my instructions and march to Pueblo to winter, if I had to go alone. I then called for a show of right hands of all who would accompany me. All voted but one, and he fell in afterwards and begged pardon for his opposition.

"We continued our march from day to day, traveling through snow from two to four feet deep, with continued cold, piercing wind. The third day, about noon, we reached the summit of the mountain. Before reaching the top, however, I had to detail a rear guard of the most able-bodied men, to aid and encourage those who began to lag, and felt unable to proceed farther, whilst with others I marched at the head of the column to break the road through enormous snow banks. It was with the greatest exertion that we succeeded, and some were severely frost-bitten. When we got through the banks, to our inexpressible joy, we saw the valley of the Arkansas below, where the ground was bare. The drooping spirits of the men revived, and they soon descended to the plain below, where they were comparatively comfortable. From here the command had good weather and pleasant traveling to Pueblo, their destination for the remainder of the winter.

"We arrived on the 24th of December, and found the detachments of Captains Brown and Higgins as well as could be expected, and enjoying themselves with some comfortable quarters."

John G. Smith, of Captain Brown's detachment, gives December 20th as the day upon which the first portion of Willis' detachment arrived at Pueblo, instead of the 24th, as stated in the narrative of Lieutenant Willis. It is likely that Brother Smith's date is the correct one; as he kept a daily journal and was very accurate in regard to dates. He states that the men in Willis' command were haggard and emaciated on their arrival, from the sickness, hunger and fatigue which they had endured.

Lieutenant Willis got Gilbert, son of Captain Jefferson Hunt, who had accompanied the families to this point, to go back to Mr. Turley's and bring up the sick he had left there. They started on the 27th, and the same day the Lieutenant started for Bent's Fort, a distance of seventy-five miles. He arrived on the 2nd and was very kindly received by Captain Enos, commander of the post and acting Quartermaster, who furnished sixty days' rations for the company and transportation to Pueblo with ox teams. On Lieutenant Willis' return, the detachment went to work, preparing their quarters, each mess to build a log cabin.

About the middle of January Corporal Gilbert Hunt and company returned with all the sick except Brother Coleman. Mr. Turley forwarded the Lieutenant a letter by Corporal Hunt to the effect that he sent his carriage as agreed upon, but on arriving at the place where Brother Coleman was left, he was not there. The Spaniard reported that after the company had left, in spite of entreaties to the contrary, Brother Coleman, followed on after the company, and it was supposed, after traveling a short distance, he expired, as he was afterwards found dead, by the road-side not far distant.

CHAPTER XVI.

Detachments of Brown and Higgins—Death of Milton Kelley—Houses Completed—Death of Two Children, also John Perkins, Brother Scott, Arnold Stevens and M. S. Blanchard—Rumors of a Revolt—Visit to Soda Fountain—Description of the Place—Game Killed—Pay Received, also Orders to March to California.

Few incidents of importance had occurred with the detachments of Captains Brown and Higgins up to this time since their arrival at Pueblo. One death occurred on the 4th of November, that of Milton Kelley, which was supposed to have been caused by taking cold while upon a hunting expedition. He was a noble and brave soldier, and previous to enlisting in the Battalion had fought in the Blackhawk war. He was also a kind husband, a good neighbor, an excellent traveling companion and a faithful Latter-day Saint. He had been married several years, but had no issue. Soon after his death, however, his wife was delivered of a fine daughter, which was named Malinda Catherine Kelley, and who is now the wife of Benjamin L. Alexander.

Most of the houses built by the detachments were so far completed as to be occupied by the 5th of December. Though only rude cabins, they found them much better than tents to live in. The valley in which they were located was well adapted for winter quarters. What snow fell soon melted, and there was good grazing for their animals. True, they had occasional wind storms, when the dust would be blown through the crevices of their houses, covering their food and everything else, but though unpleasant and annoying, this was so slight an evil, compared with what they had previously suffered from, that they felt to bear it without complaining.

The men and families, too, were tolerably well supplied with food, so that none need suffer from hunger. An occasional hunting expedition would result in securing a supply of venison, which furnished a very acceptable change of diet. Most of the sick were also very much improved since getting rid of the drugs of the inhuman doctor. A few cases of sickness, however, still lingered on.

"On the 1st of January, 1847, the twin son of Captain Jefferson Hunt, by his wife Celia, died. The same day Mrs. Fanny Huntington, wife of Dimick B. Huntington, gave birth to a child which also died a few hours afterwards. Both the little innocents were buried in one grave.

"On the 15th of January, nine wagons, loaded with sixty days' rations, for the command, arrived from Bent's Fort, and the convalescent soldiers and their families were thereby enabled to experience the contrast between short food and hard labor and full rations and no labor.

"On the 19th, John Perkins, a fine young man, died, after a lingering illness, and was buried the following day.

"About this time the command commenced the practice of squad drills, in which the men became very proficient.

"Owing to rumors being freely circulated to the effect that the Mexicans and Indians intended to attack Pueblo, preparations for defense were made, and Captain Brown also called upon the old settlers for assistance, which they promised to render. The people of Bent's Fort were also alarmed, lest the enemy might make a sudden raid upon them. Communication with Santa Fe had been cut off.

"On the 5th of February another death occurred, that of a Brother Scott, a promising young man, after a short but severe illness, from winter fever and liver complaint. He was buried with the honors of war.

"On the evening of the 28th, Corporal Arnold Stevens died and was buried the next day, with military honors; and on the 10th of April M. S. Blanchard also departed this life, after a lingering illness. The great number of deaths that occurred among that portion of the Battalion who wintered at Pueblo were doubtless due, mainly, to diseases contracted through the exposure and hardships of the journey and the murderous drugging which they had received from Dr. Sanderson, though the unhealthfulness of Pueblo may partly account for them, as some claim. As many of the Missouri volunteers who were also stationed at Pueblo for the winter, died, it is probable that climatic influences may have been one cause.

Captain Brown, having returned from Santa Fe on the 9th, with only a part of the pay due the men, set out again for that post on the 1st of May, for the purpose of trying to obtain the balance.

On the 2nd of May, John G. Smith and others, with one wagon and three yoke of oxen, started for Soda Fountain, where they arrived two days later. One of the springs at this place is described by Brother Smith as being four feet in diameter. The ground surrounding it is somewhat elevated, except at the outlet, and a kind of shelly incrustation abounds on the margins of the water. Another spring, about the same size, is said to boil up quite strongly and the water is impregnated with soda to such an extent that it is unexcelled for raising bread. A hanging rock, resembling saleratus, probably formed from the little rill that runs from the spring, projects over the creek; it is about six feet thick, thirty feet wide and forty long. There is another small spring, in the vicinity which is only about one foot in diameter, and boils up slowly, passing off in a little rivulet. These springs and their surroundings would be an excellent study for scientists. To see soda or saleratus streaming from the earth, all ready for use, without the aid of man, and that, too, of the best and purest quality, is certainly marvelous. This is one of those facts that are stranger than fiction.

As spring advanced the hunters were quite successful in killing the Rocky Mountain or black-tailed deer, which abounded in the mountains in that region. They do not differ materially from other deer, except that they are larger and darker in winter than those found east of the Rocky Mountains. When fat, their meat has a fine flavor and is preferable to the more eastern species. In fact, this rule holds good with most mountain game, and even domestic animals.

On the 18th of May, Captains Brown and Higgins and others, returned from Santa Fe with the soldiers' money and orders to march to California.

The wagons were loaded, and the command took up the line of march and crossed the Arkansas River on the 24th of May, 1847, at noon.

CHAPTER XVII.

Journey Commenced—Meeting with A. M. Lyman and Others from Council Bluffs—Emotions at Meeting—A Perilous and Severe Journey by Tippetts and Woolsey—Arrival of the Detachment at Fort Laramie—Follow the Pioneer Trail—Arrival in Salt Lake Valley—Disbanded.

On the 26th the company laid by, waiting for the provision wagons from Bent's Fort, and the following day Captain Higgins went back to Pueblo for the loose cattle.

On the 29th travel was resumed towards California by way of Fort Laramie, on the Platte river. The Platte river was reached on the 3rd of June, and from that time the course of travel lay down the stream.

On the 5th the South Fork of the Platte river was crossed, and owing to the great depth of the water, the wagon boxes had to be raised and blocks of wood put under them to keep the loading dry.

On the afternoon of the 11th of June, while on Pole Creek, to the great joy of the detachments, they were met by Elder Amasa M. Lyman of the Quorum of the Twelve Apostles, who was accompanied by Brothers Thomas Woolsey, Roswell Stevens and John H. Tippetts, from Winter Quarters, bringing letters from the families and friends of the soldiers, as well as counsel from President Brigham Young; also news of the travels and probable destination of the Church.

Kind reader, if you can fancy yourself banished from civilization, ostracized, your Government failing to redress your wrongs; your best friends and leading citizens murdered in cold blood, when held as prisoners, under the plighted faith of your State for their protection; yourselves and families fleeing before ruthless mobs during one of the coldest winters ever known in the Western States; many sick, and all short of provisions, living to a considerable extent on short rations of parched corn or corn meal. Imagine that no luxuries or palatable food for the sick were to be had except a quantity of quails sent by Divine Providence into your camp, nay more, into your tents and seeking to conceal themselves under the very bedding where your sick wife or child or even your aged father lay (and him perhaps a revolutionary soldier who had fought many a hard battle to gain his and your liberty,) and perhaps under the couch of that mother who had given you life and cared for your tender years, whose emaciated face and sinking and tottering limbs you had fondly hoped to make happy and comfortable in her declining years. Then picture your beloved wife and little ones, not now in the cold February storms, but in an almost tropical July sun, without house or home, perhaps living in a tent and perhaps only a mere wagon with one yoke of oxen, and in an Indian country. Fancy the penalty of returning to civilization to be death, of remaining on the Indian lands of Nebraska to be incurring the displeasure of and threatened ejectment by Government officials. Then suppose you had petitioned every officer, from the justice of the peace to the chief executive of the nation, to redress your wrongs, and that the only satisfaction given was, "*Your cause is just, but I can do nothing for you.*" Suppose your patriotism had induced you to leave—not home, being without a home to leave—but your family, in an Indian country, without food, and, at the call of your country, had enlisted to aid in the suppression of the common enemy, and served for months without news from your family. Then suppose some portions of your family, and for aught you knew every member, had succumbed either to the inclemency of the weather, starvation or the tomahawk!

If you can imagine all of these facts as your own experience, you may have a faint idea of the feelings and emotions of this loyal band of soldiers.

This picture, so far from being overdrawn, is but a faint synopsis of the existing facts. But we will leave the painful past and explain how John H. Tippetts and Thomas Woolsey, two members of the detachments that wintered at Pueblo, happened to be at Winter Quarters when Elder Amasa M. Lyman left there, as it has been stated that they accompanied him to meet the detachments, and yet no mention was previously made of their having left the Battalion.

On the 23rd day of December, 1846, these fearless soldiers left Pueblo, on the head waters of the Arkansas River, alone and without a guide, to take money to their families and friends, whom they had not heard from since John D. Lee and Howard Egan overtook the Battalion as previously noted.

"The second day they passed Pike's Peak. When they awoke in the morning they found themselves ensconced under about six inches of snow. The fourth night they camped on Cherry Creek, near where Denver City now stands. On arriving at the South Fork of the Platte river, they followed down it, passing an old deserted Indian village. A severe east wind arose, which forced them to take shelter under the bank of the river during the night, where they slept on the ice. Brother Tippetts avers that the weather was so cold that six inches of the tail of one of the mules was frozen. Another day's travel took them to where they could get wood. Here they remained for three days, owing to the severity of the weather. They killed a buffalo, which gave them a supply of meat. After one day's travel from this point, one of the men went for water and was driven back by a buffalo sentinel. They followed the river down to Grand Island, where some Pawnee Indians took them prisoners and detained them one day and night.

They crossed the river below the island on the ice, then continued eastward to the Elk Horn River. Here they packed sand in their blankets to keep the mules from slipping on the ice, which was rather thin and weak, but they succeeded in crossing in safety.

The same day they were stopped by a band of Omaha Indians. Among them was a white man. Brother Tippetts asked him if he could speak English. He answered "Yes." Then he exclaimed, "For God's sake, tell us where we are!" They found themselves within sixteen miles of Winter Quarters, where they arrived at dark, on the 15th of February, 1847, at the house of President Brigham Young, where a picnic party was gathered. Being invited, they freely partook of the supper, which was to them a great treat, as they had been three days without food. Brother Tippetts had previously dreamed of partaking of just such a feast. They were out fifty-two days, traveling like Abraham, not knowing whither they went.

"After the meeting with Brother Lyman and the friends who accompanied him, the journey was resumed, and on the 13th of June, while resting, during the afternoon, the detachment was addressed by Apostle Amasa M. Lyman, who imparted such instructions as he had received from President Young and the quorum of the Twelve, for the Battalion, prominently among which was an exhortation to live as Saints and followers of Jesus Christ, and forsake all of their sins and evil deeds.

It was then supposed the detachment would have to march to California to be discharged.

On the night of the 16th, the command camped within one mile of Fort Laramie, about five hundred and forty miles west of Council Bluffs, where they were mustered into service eleven months before.

President Young, with a company of pioneers, making their way westward, had passed Laramie twelve days previously, and with a view to overtaking them, the command made an early start on the morning of the 17th and followed up their trail.

The road was bad, almost impassable in places, so that travel was necessarily slow and tedious; but they gradually gained on the Pioneers, whose journeyings they occasionally learned of by finding a post set up at a camping place, with writing on it, showing when the Pioneers had passed there.

On arriving at the ferry on the Platte, the command learned that the Pioneers were one day's travel in advance. Finding a blacksmith working at this point, a halt was made for one day, in order to get animals shod. Many emigrants on their way to Oregon or California were crossing the ferry, and among them many of the old enemies of the Saints, the Missouri mobocrats. All the way from this point to where the pioneer trail branched off from the Oregon route, many emigrants were seen making their way to the western coast by the northern route.

Nothing of importance occurred during the remainder of the journey to Salt Lake Valley. The command failed to overtake the Pioneers, but arrived on July 27, 1847, three days after the company of Pioneers entered the valley. Here they were formally disbanded, without having to proceed on to California as expected.

CHAPTER XVIII.

Travels of the Main Army—Two Wagons Left—Antics of Oxen on being Packed—Muskets Used for Tent Poles—First Indian Wigwams—Ancient Earthenware and Glass—Leave the Rio Grande—Ancient Gold Mine—Goats Killed—Table Land—Road Turns to Mexican Settlements—Council Decides to go that Way—Prayers for the Colonel's Mind to be Changed—A Scare—Prayer Answered—Men March Ahead of Teams to Break the Road—Charboneaux Kills his Mule.

Our narrtive left the main army of the Battalion on the Rio Grande del Norte, on the 10th of November, to follow the travels of the detachments. Let us now return to that point, and follow the fortunes of the army journeying under command of Colonel Cooke.

Having parted with Lieutenant Willis and his detachment, with many prayers and much anxiety for their safety, but with a strong desire to meet them all again, we naturally turned our attention to the task before us; and no very promising picture did it present. However, our trust was in our Father in Heaven, and the promises made to us by His servants previous to our enlistment, and the sequel will show that the trust was not in vain.

Deeming it impracticable to take all of the wagons farther, Colonel Cooke issued an order requiring the acting assistant quartermaster to leave there the two remaining ox wagons, the teams for them being absolutely necessary for the further march of the Battalion. The commanders of companies were also required to reduce their number of tents to one for nine instead of six men, and for all the upright poles and the extra camp kettles to be left there.

We did some packing that same day of both oxen and mules. The former created much merriment, and took away for the moment some of the monotony of our surroundings. It was certainly very laughable to witness the antics of our frightened bullocks, which scarcely knew which end they stood upon, nor we either for that matter, for as some of the boys had it, "they kicked up before and reared up behind;" they bellowed and snorted, pawed and plowed the ground with their horns, whirling and jumping in every direction. Even our very sedate commander for once had his nature overcome sufficiently to get off the following: "Thirty-six mules were lightly packed, besides oxen; some of which performed antics that were irresistibly ludicrous (owing to the crupper perhaps), such as jumping high from the ground in quick-step time [he might have said *double*-quick time] turning round the while—a perfect jig."

On the 11th, we marched about fifteen miles, and while Charboneaux, one of the guides, had gone some miles ahead in search of water for camp, Colonel Cooke, seeing a patch of willows and cane grass, rode into it and followed down the bottom for near a mile, where he found water and grass plentiful. We camped on the bluff.

Here, for the first time, we tried our commander's new invention of using our muskets for tent poles. This was done simply by setting the breeches of the guns on the ground, one in front and another in the rear of the tent, with bayonets off; in the muzzle of each a peg large enough to fill it was inserted, the upper end of which entered the ridge pole, the same as the iron peg in our former poles. The backs of the tents were opened and a gore inserted, which gave them a rather low pyramidal shape, and made them more roomy; but I must be excused from going into extacies over the external beauties of our camp, under this new arrangement. The hight of our tents was reduced about six inches.

We saw, the same day, for the first time during our journey, some Indian wigwams, although we were traveling through a country where Indians were numerous. Their hostility to the whites led them to keep their families secluded.

We also found a large amount of ancient pottery-ware, which lay in broken fragments over the ground. Some of it was glazed and flowered. There were also some pieces of glass.

According to the estimate of the commanding officer, eight days' rations had been saved to the Battalion by the return of Lieutenant Willis' detachment. This estimate did not include the twenty-two, out of the twenty-seven days' rations, for the detachment of fifty-six men overlooked and not sent as ordered, and for the want of which they so severely suffered.

While traveling on the 13th, we received directions from our guides to turn off to the right; so we took final leave of the Rio Grande del Norte and traveled in a south-westerly direction, camping the following night near a natural reservoir in the rocks in a deep ravine. This well was about thirteen feet in diameter and probably a hundred feet deep. The route which we were now taking was perfectly new to the guides even, as they had never traveled in this direction.

During our next day's travel, we found the ruins of an ancient building, about thirty-six feet square, and containing five rooms.

The 15th of November being Sunday, we concluded to lay by on the bank of a small stream. An old white ox which had seen at least a dozen summers, and which we had driven all the way from Fort Leavenworth, having given out the day before a few miles back, was brought into camp, butchered and issued as rations. He was a mere skeleton, and his small amount of remaining flesh was more like a sickly jelly than real meat. In consequence of this incident we named the valley in which we were encamped "White Ox Valley," and the little rivulet "White Ox Creek."

The day was stormy, snow and rain falling alternately. Some of the hunters went about five miles from the camp, up a ravine, and found an old deserted vineyard, with some good grapes still hanging on the vines, upon which they feasted.

Passing around the base of a mountain on the 16th to a narrow canyon, we found a marshy water hole, which was given the name of "Cooke's Spring" a name which it still bears. Here, again, we found much broken earthen ware scattered all over the ground. By whom it had been made or why it was scattered so extensively, could only be conjectured.

The next day we passed through the gap in the mountains, and came to a place where mining, for precious metals, had evidently been carried on at some time in the distant past. There were at least thirty holes cut in the solid rock, from ten to fourteen inches deep, and from six to ten inches in diameter, evidently for the purpose of catching and retaining water when showers occurred. Here we also found, for the first time, California partridges or quail. These birds do not differ much in size from those of the Eastern and Middle States, but are of a bluish color, with oblong bodies, and beautiful top-knots. They are swift runners. They are common in some parts of Utah.

A new variety of oak was also found here, which has since received the name of *quercus emoryi*; also a new and very beautiful variety of oose, or Spanish bayonet, some of the leaves of which were a yard long, with edges resembling saw-teeth and stalks running up the center from fifteen to eighteen feet high.

One of our guides here killed two goats which must have strayed from some passing herd or been stolen and then lost by some Indians, as both were ear marked.

On the 18th, we marched north-west eighteen miles and camped on a stream of clear water, which, however, like most of the creeks in this country, sank in the sand a short distance below. This place is known as the Mimbres. For beauty of landscape, this part of the country can scarcely be excelled. It is what is known as "table land." There are flats of thousands of acres of good soil, but with no timber or rocks of any note, extending several miles each way. When you leave one of these tables or flats, it is only to ascend or descend, as the case may be, to another. Elevated to the highest of these, no matter which way you cast your eye, a most beautiful, grassy plain attracts your vision, stretching out as far as you can discern. But alas! as "every rose has its thorn," this "paradise found" has drawbacks so serious that it cannot be inhabited. There are no seasonable rains to moisten the earth nor sufficient water with which to irrigate it.

On the 17th, we struck the copper mine road leading from the mine to Yanos. Along this we marched eighteen miles over a gradually ascending prairie to Ojo de Vaca, or Cow Springs.

On the 20th, we laid by, and the guides, having been twelve miles ahead, and being able to see from there much farther without being able to discover any indication of water, returned disheartened, declaring that they did not think any more would be found short of the Gila river, a distance of about one hundred miles. As David Crockett would define it, the Colonel was "dumbfounded." To turn back was starvation and chagrin; to go forward seemed rashness; and to follow the road to Yanos and thence to other Mexican settlements was, at best (if we escaped the enemy, which we were not likely to do), to fall in under General Wool, and find ourselves in Old Mexico, instead of California, at the end of the war or the term of our enlistment, on the 16th of July following.

The commander called his staff and the captains of companies together in council. The decision was to follow the road, which was said, by the guides, to lead in a south-westerly direction, through settlements where food and fresh teams could be obtained.

A gloom was cast over the entire command. All of our hopes, conversation and songs, since we had to leave Nauvoo were centered on California; somewhere on that broad domain we expected to join our families and friends.

In this critical moment, brother David Pettegrew, better known as Father Pettegrew, owing to his silver locks and fatherly counsels, and Brother Levi W. Hancock, went from tent to tent, and in a low tone of voice counseled the men to "pray to the Lord to change the Colonel's mind." Then they invited a few to accompany them to a secret place where they could offer up their petitions and not be seen by those in camp. That night over three hundred fervent prayers ascended to the throne of grace for that one favor.

While we remained at this place an amusing incident occurred, which reflected rather badly on the courage of one of the men. One of the guides ascended a hill not far from our camp and raised a signal smoke, in hopes of attracting some Mexicans, and learning from them something concerning the country over which we proposed to travel, and negotiating, if possible, for provisions and animals. The smoke had the desired effect; it attracted a number of Mexicans. It happened, however, that one of our men was in the vicinity of this hill gathering fuel, and seeing the Mexicans approaching, without knowing what their purpose was, he dropped his wood and ran into camp terribly excited, creating considerable merriment among his comrades at his expense. But, although the guides talked with the Mexicans, and some of the latter even came to the camp and stayed all night, no information of importance could be obtained from them, nor could any purchases be made.

On the morning of the 21st, the command resumed its journey marching in a southern direction for about two miles, when it was found that the road began to bear south-east instead of south-west, as stated by the guides. The Colonel looked in the direction of the road, then to the south-west, then west, saying, "I don't want to get under General Wool, and lose my trip to California." He arose in his saddle and ordered a halt. He then said with firmness: "This is not my course. I was ordered to California; and," he added with an oath, "I will go there or die in the attempt!" Then, turning to the bugler, he said, "Blow the right."

At this juncture, Father Pettegrew involuntarily exclaimed, "God bless the Colonel!" The Colonel's head turned and his keen, penetrating eyes glanced around to discern whence the voice came, and then his grave, stern face for once softened and showed signs of satisfaction.

The next day we traveled about eighteen miles and camped without water. Here it was decided and ordered that the men walk in double file in front of the wagons, just far enough apart to make trails for the wheels, and that at the end of an hour's march the leading companies and teams halt and allow the others to precede them and take their turn at breaking the road. This gave all an equal share of the burden. This plan was followed subsequently in traveling over all the heavy, sandy road until we reached the coast. It was much like tramping snow—very hard on the men, especially those who took the lead, as we had no road or trail to follow.

Here, also, Charboneaux, one of the guides, came into camp, packing his saddle and pistols on his back. He said he got off to let his mule graze, when the animal kicked him, ran off and would not be caught; hence he shot him down to save his saddle and pistols, as he claimed, from falling into the hands of the Apache Indians.

CHAPTER XIX.

Author's Birthday—Severe Suffering from Thirst——Mirage—Reach Water—John R. Murdock Sick—Henry G. Boyle Healed in Answer to Prayer—Bear Killed—Crossing the Mountains—Wagons Lowered With Ropes—Dykes Almost Shot While Playing the Spy—Wild Cattle—Killing a Wild Bull—Return of John Allen—His Adventures.

The 23rd was the thirtieth anniversary of the author's birth, and this is how it was celebrated: The command started early, and after about twelve miles' travel came to a hole or crevice in a rock at the point of a mountain, where there was, perhaps, water enough to give each man a half pint. As the Colonel and staff rode up to it, the former remarked to the latter in a rather low tone, "The men can do without water better than the animals." He cast a look behind and seemed disappointed at my being so near. His mule with his staff and their mules, drained the spring. The author waited a few moments for a little to seep in and obtained, perhaps, a quarter of a gill of muddy water. In the meantime, others came up, some casting a wistful look into the hole and passing on, while others stopped and dipped with spoons what they could get. In writing on this point, our sympathizing commander says: "In the mountain ridge the water was found, mentioned by Spaniards last night, who thought there would be enough for the men a drink. It was soon gone [of course it was!] and the poor fellows were waiting for it to leak from the rocks, and dipping it with spoons! There was nothing to do but toil on over the ridge." Six miles beyond, a guide was met with the news of water three leagues (nine miles) further on. While crossing this valley, before meeting the guide, the commander, remarked to some of the men that he had marched with a [knapsack on his back, but his sufferings were nothing like theirs, and he feared theirs would be worse before they got through to California.

CASE OF HEALING IN ANSWER TO PRAYER. 209

Here something resembling the deceptive mirage described before in this work, was constantly before us, seeming to keep the same distance off; sometimes it looked like a river, at others like a sea or lake.

After dark, we reached what seemed to be the bottom of a lake or pond, which was dry and solid, and the wagons rolled on it with perfect ease. Colonel Cooke very properly says: "It appeared in the obscurity (of twilight) something between smooth marble and a great sheet of ice; wagons moved with traces unstretched, and made no track." We followed it only about two or three miles, when, to our great joy, water was found in some swamp holes on its western shore. Here the front rank arrived about 8 o'clock that evening; the rear, about 7 o'clock the next day, having made an arduous and continuous march of about twenty-four hours, and having been without water for about forty-eight hours.

About thirty years previous a terrible treachery and cowardly slaughter of Apache Indians, by one Johnson, who still lived in Sonora, took place here, for the purpose of obtaining scalps, for which the Governor was offering $50 each.

This clay flat is about thirty miles long, and is called by the Mexicans Las Playas. Here John R. Murdock, who drove the Colonel's baggage wagon, was taken sick, and was unable to drive for a week or more. This was his only sickness on the route. He drove a team from Leavenworth to California.

We did not travel the following day, owing to so many teams and men being exhausted from the previous two days' and nights' march.

Our quartermaster purchased some five mules of visiting Mexicans. Here, also, Henry G. Boyle was taken violently sick, through drinking too much water on his arrival when he was very warm and thirsty. It being his turn to go on guard, he had no alternative but to go or report himself on sick list. He chose the latter, and Sanderson, the doctor, gave him the usual dose—calomel—which, however, he did not swallow, but consigned it to the flames. The writer and another Elder or two were called upon to anoint him with oil and lay hands upon him, and before night he was well.

Here pioneers were sent forward to work a road over the backbone of the Rocky Mountains. The down grade was found to be much more difficult than the ascent. The descent, for over a half mile, was at an angle of about forty-five degrees.

On the 25th, Charboneaux, the guide, who was a little ahead of the command, ascended one of the mountains and was confronted by three grizzly bears. He showed great presence of mind and bravery. A second or third shot leveled the most ferocious one. He escaped the others by climbing upon a rock, when they soon retreated in good order. The meat of the one killed was put in the wagons and eaten for supper.

On the 28th we reached the backbone of North America—the summit of the Rocky Mountains. Here we found plenty of deer, bear, antelope and small game. Several of the men went into the Sugar Loaf Mountains for the purpose of hunting. They got lost in their rambles, but all found their way back to camp the following day except John Allen, a worthless fellow, who attached himself to the Church at Fort Leavenworth that he might join the Battalion and obtain passage and protection to California. It was thought by some that he had deserted.

On the 29th, preparations were made for descending the mountain to the valley below. Most all of the animals were packed and sent down the mountain a distance of about six miles, into the valley, where a guard was left in charge of the baggage while the men and animals returned. The next day this process was repeated, and then the work of taking the wagons down was commenced.

The Colonel and his staff, on arriving at the summit of the mountain, estimated that it would require from five to ten days to descend, but it was accomplished in two days. Long ropes were attached to the wagons, upon which the men pulled, and in this manner the wagons were all lowered. One of them, by some accident, got loose, and ran down with such force that it became badly damaged, and was abandoned as worthless. One or two others were slightly injured, but were soon repaired.

During the three days that we were encamped on the ridge the weather was extremely cold and disagreeable, but when we arrived in the valley, which was perhaps three quarters of a mile lower in altitude, it was warm and pleasant.

of December we resumed our journey, traveling
on. While encamped that night, Lieutenant
kes, who was officer of the day, attempted to play
y, in order, as was supposed, to find some cause
against the men. His fault-finding disposition
m his life in this instance. He sneaked around,
line and was stealthily making his way to where
stacked, when he was discovered by the senti-
Ienry G. Boyle (now a highly respected resident
ho, supposing him to be an enemy, cocked and
in and was on the point of pulling the trigger
gnized Dykes. Had he not at that moment dis-
it was, a half ounce ball and ten or twelve buck-
ave ended the sneaking business so far as Lieu-
was concerned. Brother Boyle says to this day
 shudder when he thinks of how narrowly he
g the man, although no blame could have been
m had he fired before recognizing him.
he west of the dividing ridge, we found that all
 ran westward instead of eastward, as previously.
ras most beautiful, with mountain precipices and
hapes and sizes heaped upon each other. The
d vegetable, sometimes roasted by Indians for
nd there, as well as the Spanish bayonet, ever-
ottonwoods and sycamores, the leaves of which
inted by frost. Everything there, even to the
brilliant shade or tint of some kind.
, we reached the ruins of the rancho, San Bernar-
ring and dwelling had been surrounded by a
bastions (adobe, if my memory serves me right),
re now much dilapidated. The country seemed
nezquit flats or tables.
ild cattle were found here. They were of Mexi-
ving been brought here by a Mexican, who was
 the Apache Indians and forced to leave his stock
of the guides killed a wild bull and was found
eat on our arrival. A few hunters were imme-
out, and more went out on their own responsi-
thor among the latter. Every now and then a
past him, having been routed by the hunters.

After following one and another, in the hope of getting a shot, he discovered one standing under a lone tree, at a distance of perhaps half a mile. He crouched and sneaked along from bunch to bunch of the Mezquit until one half the distance was made, when the crack of a musket and a rather sharp screech or lowing of the animal proved that another hunter had found his quiet resting place. His thigh bone was broken. Another shot succeeded in bringing him to the ground. By this time I had approached within a few rods, when the well-known voice of Walter Barney, one of my messmates, directed me to stop until he fired again. I insisted, however, on going up and cutting the animal's throat to save the waste of ammunition; but as he claimed that there might be danger of the animal rising and goring me, I picked up a rock about the size of a man's fist and threw it a distance of, perhaps, ten feet, against the horn of the animal. Quick as thought he bounded to his feet, and, with a wild, shrill bellow, hobbled after me on three legs. I fired and he fell again, only to arise and pursue his intended victim with the more fury. I was below him on a hill-side; as he neared me I dodged him, and while he was turning round gained a few feet up the hill. My comrade fired again, and the animal once more fell to the ground. This time a bullet from my musket, a little below the curl in the pate, ended the battle. Six bullet holes, all in fatal places, showed that these cattle could endure as much lead as a buffalo. He had a very large body, with horns about two yards from tip to tip, and he was round and fat. We soon found a way to strip a piece of his hide off, by which we got some meat, and Barney started for camp.

It was now after sunset. We had wandered some four miles from camp, and I, having been sickly from the day before we reached the Arkansas river, was completely exhausted and unable to return; hence, it was agreed that I should remain, and, after dark, keep up a light, in order that my comrades might come with pack-animals and take me and the best part of the meat of the huge animal to camp. I had but little fear of other wild beasts or Indians, although the country abounded with both. I made my supper mainly from the roasted melt or spleen of the animal. My comrade, with others, returned with mules about 10 p. m. We took what meat the mules could pack, I mounted the one with the lightest load, and reached camp about 12 o'clock, some time having been occupied in dressing the beef.

This same evening, John Allen, the desperado and hunter, who was supposed to have deserted, came into camp, having been absent five days. He was minus his gun, coat, vest, shoes and butcher knife, which he said were taken from him by Apache Indians. They made signs to him to take off his shirt, also; but the weather was cold, and he felt that if they did not kill him he must soon perish, hence he bared his breast and signified that he would prefer them to shoot him. They then let him go.

He finally struck our trail, and finding Captain Jesse D. Hunter's dead horse, gnawed through his posterior like a wolf and got his first meal since leaving the command. He had killed a turkey, but the sound of his gun betrayed him to the Indians, who took it from him. The poor fellow had even picked up the hoofs of dead animals and gnawed off the most tender portions and eaten them.

He was, for once, humbled, and much of his disagreeable, wicked, profane and quarrelsome nature seemed for a time to have left him.

Cooke sets him down as "the only member of the Battalion not a Mormon."

CHAPTER XX.

The Apache Indians—Jerking Beef—Loading of Guns and Firing at [Game Prohibited—Order Disregarded—Author Sick—Calomel and Arsenic as Medicine—Death of Elisha Smith—Howling of the Wolves—A Song.

The commander expected to obtain some fresh animals of the Indians at the rancho, San Bernardino, but was disappointed.

We rested one-and-a-half days at this place, and the hunters brought in five days' allowance of wild beef, which was issued as rations. Wild cattle abounded in that region. It is asserted that 80,000 head were driven to this rancho before it was abandoned.

Colonel Cooke mentions the Apaches as being "poor, dirty Indians." They may be such, but those who visited our camp were, in my view, not as bad as represented. For a downtrodden race, they had quite an intelligent, dignified look, and were certainly much more cleanly and tidy in appearance than the Iowas, Poncas, Pottawatomies or Omahas.

We jerked beef until about 2 p. m., when we were ordered to take up the line of march. This order gave much dissatisfaction, as another day or even the remainder of this day and night, would have enabled us to dry much more meat without increasing the weight of our loads. Besides, the commander promised to lay in enough when we reached the wild cattle to do us through to California. As it was, considerable fresh beef had to be left on the ground.

Before breaking camp, the following orders were issued.

"HEAD QUARTERS MORMON BATTALION,
CAMP AT SAN BERNARDINO,

"Rations for six days have been wasted since leaving Santa Fe. Of the present allowance there is enough, allowing for no wastage or accident.

"Commanders of companies hereafter will give no permission to leave the column of march or the camp, and muskets will not be fired at game. The Battalion will be in readiness to march at one o'clock.

"By order

LIEUT. COL. COOKE.

(Signed) P. C. MERRILL, Adjutant."

A verbal order was also issued at this place to have no loaded guns in the command.

This last order concerning the firing at game, although doubtless well-meant, gave much dissatisfaction, and was disregarded; not on account of our short rations so much as the fact that we were about to go among thousands of wild cattle, ten-fold more dangerous than the buffalo. The Colonel thought that if the cattle were wounded there would be more danger of serious consequences, while the soldiers took the view that to stand and tamely suffer themselves to be gored to death was a cruel and unjust requirement. This was the only order not strictly obeyed.

On the 5th we traveled about twelve miles, crossing some low mountains. Many wild cattle were seen, amounting to hundreds, if not thousands. Several were killed, and the most of the carcasses left. In some cases, the best cuts were saved.

The next day we made twelve miles, cutting our way, a part of the distance, through mezquit brush. A cold rain and some snow fell. During that day's journey the author was quite sick, but avoided making known his condition by hiding in the tall grass until the command had all passed by, and then slowly and painfully making his way to camp. He had not forgotten, nor, indeed, entirely recovered, from the effects of his previous drugging and dreaded having to take another dose of Dr. Sanderson's calomel or arsenic. The fact that the doctor's calomel had given out and arsenic was substituted, was no secret. Sanderson openly stated the fact long before we reached California.

Our camp, that night, was in a grove of ash, oak and black walnut. We called the stream Ash Creek, because that was the predominating timber.

While encamped here, Elisha Smith, not an enlisted soldier, but hired by Captain Davis as teamster, or servant, died, and the large wolves, probably scenting the corpse, made the night hideous with their howls. Their grum voices almost rent the air only a few feet from our camp.

He was buried in the wilderness, alone, and, like the others, without a coffin, or a slab, to mark his last resting place. Brush and billets of wood were piled upon his grave and there burned to conceal his remains from the Indians and wolves.

His wife had gone with one of the detachments to winter at Pueblo, hence she was not with him during his last, short illness and death. She subsequently married Thomas Burns, who claimed to be a descendant of the Scottish Bard, Robert Burns.

The following song, by Levi W. Hancock, is in memory of Mr. Smith's death and burial:

DEATH AND THE WOLVES.

BY LEVI W. HANCOCK.

The Battalion encamped
  By the side of a grove,
Where the pure waters flowed
  From the mountains above.
Our brave hunters came in
  From the chase of wild bulls—
All around 'rose the din
  Of the howling of wolves.

When the guards were all placed
  On their outposts around,
The low hills and broad wastes
  Were alive with the sound,
Though the cold wind blew high
  Down the huge mountain shelves,
All was rife with the cry
  Of the ravenous wolves.

DEATH AND THE WOLVES.

Thus we watched the last breath
  Of the teamster, who lay
In the cold grasp of death,
  As his life wore away.
In deep anguish he moan'd
  As if mocking his pain,
When the dying man groan'd
  The wolves howl'd a refrain.

For it seem'd the wolves knew
  There was death in our camp,
As their tones louder grew,
  And more hurried their tramp.
While the dead lay within,
  With our grief to the full,
O, how horrid a din
  Was the howl of the wolves!

Then we dug a deep grave,
  And we buried him there—
All alone by the grove—
  Not a stone to tell where!
But we piled brush and wood
  And burnt over his grave,
For a cheat, to delude
  Both the savage and wolf.

'Twas a sad, doleful night!
  We by sunrise, next day,
When the drums and the fifes
  Had performed *reveille*—
When the teams were brought nigh,
  And our baggage arranged,
One and all, bid *Good bye*,
  To the grave and the wolves.

CHAPTER XXI.

Wild Horses—Game Plentiful—Wild Cattle Congregate on our Route—A Battle with them—Losses on Both Sides—One man Thrown Ten Feet in the Air—Wonderful Tenacity of Life in the Wild Bulls—Coolness and Bravery of Corporal Frost—A Song on the Bull Fight.

From Ash Creek we marched seventeen miles north-west and encamped without wood or water, except a little fine brush. Wild horses were first seen here.

Starting at sunrise on the morning of the 9th, we traveled to San Pedro Creek, a distance of ten miles, where we nooned. We then crossed over and marched six miles down the stream, where we encamped.

The grass here looked as though it was of no more strength than dry straw, but the wild cattle and horses fattened on it, and it proved to be the best feed we had found for some time.

The bottom land in that region seemed pretty good, but we saw but little timber. Bear, deer and antelope, as well as wild cattle, were tolerably plentiful, especially the latter.

Continuing our journey down the San Pedro, we encamped on the night of the 11th in a canyon. A kind of cane grass grew in this region, from four to six feet high, being very profuse and luxuriant in the bottom near the stream. The soldiers, who went out in advance of the command, passed along the bluffs on each side of the stream and came upon hundreds of wild cattle, which, startled at their approach, rushed down into the bottom for shelter. The animals, congregated on the line of our route, on hearing the rumblings of our approaching wagons, were startled, and some ran off in afright. Others, however, to gratify their curiosity, perhaps, marched towards us, as if bent upon finding out who dared to intrude upon their quiet retreat. Their terribly beautiful forms and majestic appearance were quite impressive.

A FIGHT WITH WILD BULLS.

Contrary to the orders of the Colonel, as previously noticed, every man had his musket loaded, and a battle followed. In the open ground, where the cattle could see us from a distance, they would run away, but when near us, whether wounded or not, they were the assaulting party. Hence, the roar of musketry was heard from one end of the line to the other. One small lead mule in a team was thrown on the horns of a bull over its mate on the near side, and the near mule, now on the off side and next to the bull, was gored until he had to be left with entrails hanging a foot below his body. One or two pack-mules were also killed. The end-gates of one or two wagons were stove in, and the sick, who were riding in them, were of course frightened. Some of the men climbed upon the wheels of the wagons and poured a deadly fire into the enemy's ranks. Some threw themselves down and allowed the beasts to run over them; others fired and dodged behind mezquit brush to re-load their guns, while the beasts kept them dodging to keep out of the way. Others, still, climbed up in small trees, there being now and then one available.

Brother Amos Cox was thrown about ten feet into the air, while a gore from three to four inches in length and about two or three in depth was cut in the inside of his thigh near its junction with the body. Sanderson sewed up the wound. Cox was an invalid for a long time, but finally recovered, so far, at least, that the Surgeon reported him able for duty; but he complained bitterly that injustice was done him, and I do not think his complaint was without cause. I saw him in Pottawatomie County, Iowa, a year afterwards, and he still felt the effects of his injury.

Albert Smith, quartermaster sergeant of company B., was run over by a wounded bull, and, I understand, had three of his ribs partially severed from the back bone. He suffered severely for several weeks, but declined going on sick report to avoid Dr. Sanderson's cure-all, calomel and arsenic.

Major Clowd, our paymaster, had one of his pack mules killed. Dr. William Spencer, assistant surgeon's steward, shot six balls into one bull, and was pursued by him, rising and falling at intervals, until the last and fatal shot, which took effect near the curl of the pate, was fired. The wounds were as follows: Two bullets through the lights, two through the heart and two in the pate. The Doctor carried the heart two or three days, exhibiting it to all who desired to see it, and relating the particulars of his remarkable adventure. The author saw the heart and heard the painfully interesting narrative of his informant's hair-breath escape from death or severe injury. Of course, either of the shots would eventually have proved fatal, but this incident showed how severely the animals might be wounded and still live long enough to fight and kill or injure human beings.

Colonel Cooke, in his writings, refers to this circumstance, and acknowledges to having seen the heart.

Another incident the commander relates thus: "I was very near Corporal Frost, when an immense coal-black bull came charging upon us, a hundred yards distant. Frost aimed his musket, a flint-lock, very deliberately, and only fired when the beast was within six paces; it fell headlong almost at our feet."

To show the cool deliberation of Corporal Frost, eye-witnesses add the following: The Corporal was on foot, while, of course, the Colonel and staff were mounted. On the first appearance of the bull, the Colonel, with his usual firm manner of speech, ordered the Corporal to load his gun, supposing, of course, that he had observed the previous order of prohibition. To this command he paid no attention. Thinking him either stupefied or, again quoting Davey Crockett, 'dumbfounded," with much warmth and a foul epithet he, next ordered him to run, but this mandate was as little heeded as the other. Doubtless Cooke thought one man's "ignorance with some stubbornness" was about to receive a terrible retribution, but when he saw the monster lifeless at his feet, through the well-directed aim of the brave and fearless Corporal, how changed must have been his feelings! The Corporal, who might have fled and concealed himself from danger, stood firm at the risk of his own life to protect his brave though austere commander, not even resenting or seeming to notice the abrupt manner in which he was ordered to run, thus showing not only a brave but generous and forgiving heart. Colonel Cooke gave Corporal Frost the credit of being "one of the bravest men he ever saw."

Lieutenant Stoneman, quartermaster of subsistance, in an attempt to fire a fifteen-shooter rifle at one of these bulls, by some accident, burst his gun and seriously injured the thumb of his right hand. One bull was shot and fell near where one of the butchers, Robert Harris, stood, who ran to cut the bullock's throat, when, quick as thought, the animal bounded to his feet, caught the butcher's cap on his horn and ran off, the butcher shouting, "Stop you thief; I'll have some beef," and pursued him about seventy-five yards when the animal again fell and the fatal knife quickly ended all disputes.

The number of bulls killed is not known, but it is probably not less than twenty. Henry Standage and Sanford Porter, who fell behind on account of trying to catch some salmon trout, which, it was said, abounded in the river, on entering our trail, saw nine lying in one place. After stopping and roasting what choice cuts they wanted, they followed on and overtook the command. Probably twice as many or more were fatally wounded; thus making the number about sixty. This is considered a very low estimate; one writer says eighty-one were killed outright.

The following song was composed on this event:

THE BULL FIGHT ON THE SAN PEDRO.

BY LEVI W. HANCOCK.

Under command of Colonel Cooke,
When passing down San Pedro's brook,
Where cane-grass, growing rank and high,
Was waving as the breeze pass'd by:

There, as we gain'd ascending ground,
Out from the grass, with fearful bound,
A wild, ferocious bull appear'd,
And challeng'd fight, with horns uprear'd.

"Stop, stop!" said one, "just see that brute!"
"Hold!" was responded, "let me shoot."
He flashed, but failed to fire the gun—
Both stood their ground, and would not run.

The man exclaimed, "I want some meat,
I think that bull will do to eat;"
And saying thus, again he shot
And fell'd the creature on the spot:

It soon arose to run away,
And then the guns began to play;
All hands at work—amid the roar,
The bull was dropp'd to rise no more.

But lo! it did not end the fight—
A furious herd rushed into sight,
And then the bulls and men around,
Seemed all resolved to stand their ground.

In nature's pasture, all unfenc'd,
A dreadful battle was commenc'd;
We knew we must ourselves defend,
And each, to others, aid extend.

The bulls with madden'd fury raged—
The men a skillful warfare waged;
Tho' some, from danger, had to flee
And hide or clamber up a tree.

A bull at one man made a pass,
Who hid himself amid the grass,
And breathless lay until the brute
Pass'd him and took another shoot.

The bulls rushed on like unicorns,
And gored the mules with piercing horns,
As if the battle ground to gain,
When men and mules should all be slain.

With brutal strength and iron will,
Poised on his horns with master skill,
A bull, one mule o'er mule did throw,
Then made the latter's entrails flow.

One bull was shot and when he fell,
A butcher ran his blood to spill,
The bull threw up his horns and caught
The butcher's cap, upon the spot.

"Give up my cap!" exclaimed the man,
And chased the bull, as on he ran:
The butcher beat, and with his knife
Cut the bull's throat and closed his life.

O. Cox, from one bull's horns was thrown
Ten feet in air: when he came down,
A gaping flesh-wound met his eye—
The vicious beast had gored his thigh.

The Colonel and his staff were there,
Mounted, and witnessing the war:
A bull, one hundred yards away,
Eyed Colonel Cooke as easy prey.

But Corp'ral Frost stood bravely by,
And watch'd the bull with steady eye;
The brute approach'd near and more near,
But Frost betray'd no sign of fear.

The Colonel ordered him to run—
Unmov'd he stood with loaded gun;
The bull came up with daring tread,
When near his feet, Frost shot him dead.

Whatever cause, we did not know,
But something prompted them to go;
When all at once in frantic fright,
The bulls ran bellowing out of sight.

And when the fearful fight was o'er,
And sound of muskets heard no more,
At least a score of bulls were found,
And two mules dead upon the ground.

CHAPTER XXII.

Decide to March Through Tucson—Guide held at Tucson as Prisoner—Mexican Soldiers Arrested and held as Hostages until Foster is Released—Mexicans Refuse to Surrender—Prepare for an Engagement—Mexican Soldiers Desert the Town—We March Through—Kindness of Citizens—Public Wheat Taken for Mule Feed—Primitive Mills—An Alarm—An Excited Officer—Letter to the Governor of Sonora.

We followed down the river on the 12th and 13th, and found the roads were more rough as we passed near the base of the mountains extending towards the Gila River. Our course was nearly north.

Leroux and other guides returned from an exploration of the table land to the west, where, at twenty miles distant, they had found water on a trail leading to Tucson.

They found a party of Apache Indians and some Mexicans distilling mezcal into whiskey, and learned of a garison of two hundred Mexican soldiers being stationed at Tucson.

Leroux, to get off, had to invent the following story, and Foster, the interpreter, had thought proper to go to Tuscon to give it more probability.

He said: "Tell the commander at Tucson that an army of Americans are *en route* to California; that the front guard is about three hundred and sixty men, and if it stops to drill it will be to give time for the main army to come up. He may judge of the strength of the main army by the guard."

It was also to be understood, if Foster did not return by a stated time, that he was a prisoner at Tucson; hence the following order, which is referred to but not given in Cooke's work, was issued:

"HEAD QUARTERS MORMON BATTALION,
"CAMP ON THE SAN PEDRO,
"December 13th, 1846.

"Thus far on our course we have followed the guides furnished us by the General (Kearny). These guides now point to Tucson, a garrisoned town, as our road, and assert that any other course is a hundred miles out of the way and over a trackless wilderness of mountains, rivers and hills. We will march, then, to Tucson. We came not to make war on Sonora, and less still to destroy an important outpost of defense against Indians; but we will take the straight road before us and overcome all resistance. But shall I remind you that the American soldier ever shows justice and kindness to the unarmed and unresisting? The property of individuals you will hold sacred. The people of Sonora are not our enemies.

"By order of

"LIEUT. COL. COOKE,
"(Signed)   P. C. MERRILL, Adjutant."

On the 14th, the Battalion ascended the bluff and traveled up hill mainly for eight or nine miles, when it struck a trail leading to Tucson. The commander selected fifty men with whom he pushed forward. Passing the front guard, he soon reached water, where he found four or five Mexican soldiers cutting grass. Their arms and saddles were on their horses near by, easily accessible to our little troupe; but they had no wish to molest them. The Mexicans paid but little attention to our men.

The Colonel learned from a Mexican sergeant that a rumor of a large force of American soldiers had reached the town and great excitement prevailed.

Of course, the Colonel, who was possessed of generalship as well as discipline, took no pains to disabuse their minds, and thus expose our little army to unnecessary peril.

Indians who had seen us in the distance had largely overestimated our numbers, and this served to impress the people of Sonora with the truth of the statement made by the guides.

The Colonel also learned from the Mexican sergeant that the commander of the garrison had orders from the governor not to allow an armed force to pass through the town without resistance. A message was, therfore, sent to the commander by this same sergeant that the people need not be alarmed, as we were their friends, we would do them no harm but would simply purchase some supplies and pass on.

. The next day we traveled about twelve miles, passing a distillery and camped without water. The Battalion marched in front of the wagons to protect the provisions.

Here a new species of cactus proved very troublesome. It was jointed, and when an animal rubbed against the thorns, it would break loose at the joints, and sections, some three inches long, more or less, would stick fast to the animals. The same variety is found in Southern Utah.

A corporal, son of Comaduran, commander of the post, and three soldiers were met but showed no signs of fear until Colonel Cooke ordered them arrested, when they seemed terribly frightened. On arriving at camp, the corporal was questioned by our commander as to Foster. He said (which proved to be the fact) that Foster was under guard, but had been earnestly requested to come with them and refused. He feigned indignation at being arrested, lest the Mexicans should suspect our weakness as to our numbers, and get reinforcements and fight us. As he anticipated, his conduct inspired them with terror.

One of the prisoners was released and sent to the garrison with two of the guides, one of whom took a note to the commander of the post demanding Foster's release, and stating that the other three were held as hostages.

About midnight, Foster was brought to camp by two officers, one of whom was authorized "to make a special armistice."

Colonel Cooke sent a proposition to the commander that he deliver up a few arms as a guarant of surrender and that the inhabitants of Tucson would not fight against the United States, unles they were exchanged as prisoners of war. The Mexican prisoners were also released.

Our camp at this time was about sixteen miles from the fort. The following day, when a few miles from town, a cavalry man met us with a note from Captain Comaduran, declining the proposition for a surrender.

We were now ordered to load our muskets and be ready for an engagement; but we had not traveled far before two other Mexicans met us, stating that the soldiers had fled and forced most of the inhabitants to leave the town. They had also taken two brass pieces of artillery with them.

About a dozen well-armed men, probably soldiers in citizen's dress, met and accompanied the Battalion to the town.

Before passing through the gate, a halt was ordered, when Colonel Cooke made a short speech. He stated that the soldiers and citizens had fled, leaving their property behind and in our power; that we had not come to make war on Sonora, and that there must not be any interference with the private property of the citizens.

We then marched through the town, where a few aged men and women, as well as some children, brought us water and other little tokens of respect.

The author remembers, with much gratitude, the silver-haired Mexican, of perhaps more than three score years and ten, who, when signs of thirst were given, ran to the brook as fast as his tottering limbs could carry him, dipped up his water, and, almost out of breath, but with cheerful countenance, delivered the refreshing and much needed draught. He has doubtless, long since, been gathered to his fathers; if so, peace to his ashes. Surely, "I was athirst, and he gave me drink." We made no halt in the village which had contained 400 or 500 inhabitants, all of whom, with the exception of one hundred, had fled, but traveled down the stream about a half mile and camped.

The Colonel, with a few others, then went back to the town. At first, some of the women were much frightened, but, on receiving only marked kindness, from both officers and soldiers, their excitement was allayed, and they showed strong signs of gratitude. Both the persons and property of the citizens were held sacred. A quantity of public wheat, however, was found (perhaps about 2,000 bushels) stored there, of which our commander ordered taken to camp, what he thought the teams could haul, for feeding the animals.

The starving soldiers boiled some of this wheat, and ate it, and, as a consequence, many suffered with diarrhœa.

The grinding of grain here was done by what Americans generally term "corn-crackers," with which most of the families were provided. A small species of the donkey was the motive power. The mills were on the same plan as hand-mills; a circuit of the donkey making one revolution of the upper mill-stone. This, however, being so far ahead of the method pursued by the surrounding native tribes, who ground all of their seeds and grain by hand, on flat rocks, hollowed out a little for the purpose, was doubtless considered an important improvement. On arriving at Tucson, the Battalion had been some time without salt, and only about three bushels could be obtained there.

On the 17th, the Colonel and staff, with other officers and men to the number of about fifty, passed up the creek about five miles above Tucson towards a village where they had seen a large church from the hills which we had passed over. They, however, returned before reaching the village, as they found the route so covered with mezquit brush, as to afford the Mexicans an excellent ambush, if disposed to make an attack.

As our passage through Tucson was on Sunday, it was rumored that the inhabitants, being Catholics, had marched to the little village higher up the stream before our arrival and held mass, that the commander could report to the Governor, as an excuse for allowing us to pass without resistance, against orders, that we surprised the town while they were at worship.

Some of our soldiers purchased a little unbolted flour of the Mexicans at Tucson, which most of them afterwards carried on their backs as they traveled, to avoid disobeying orders, while others concealed theirs in the wagons unknown to the Colonel. Quinces and semi-tropical fruits were also purchased here, as well as beans, corn, etc.

On the night of the 17th, a picket guard was placed some distance above Tucson, with instructions that if more than a certain number of Mexicans passed in or out of the town (a dozen or twenty, I think), to fire an alarm and run into camp. About midnight, signal guns were fired by the pickets, Alburn Allen and Rufus C. Allen, his son, who saw more men passing than the Colonel's order allowed. They also ran to camp, as directed, and notified the officer of the day, Lieutenant George Oman, who was considerably excited, and called for the music, saying: "Beat that drum, beat that drum—if you can't beat that drum, beat that fife." He also ordered every man into line. Lights were raised by replenishing the camp-fires and the music played a lively air. Each company formed in a separate column.

At this point, which was, perhaps, reached in less time than it has taken to write the incidents, Colonel Cooke appeared on the scene, and with a stern voice ordered: *"Cease that music! Dust those lights!"* and then formed his line of battle, placing the companies alternately on either side of the road. It happened to be the author's turn to take charge of the camp guard. The light was dusted by the men throwing sand upon it with their hands. A line was formed from left to right in single file, each man being stationed about ten feet or more from his left-hand comrade, thus extending about one hundred feet. The Sergeant's idea was, in case of an attack, not to have his commander complain, as a certain officer did in the Blackhawk war, when six bullet holes were found in one of the chiefs, that "it was a great waste of ammunition," but that each soldier should have an opportunity to pick his man. Another reason for taking this course was that his own men might be less exposed to the enemy's fire.

After half an hour or more had elapsed, the Sergeant Major passed out from camp about fifty yards, towards where the guard was stationed, and shouted "Where is the guard?" The Sergeant ordered him to advance and give the countersign, which was done. He was surprised to find the guard about 100 yards from camp, and ordered it nearer by, then directed the Sergeant to place his men at intervals around the command. About this time the Colonel sent Lieutenant Stoneman, with ten picked men from company A, to reconnoitre and see what they could discover. They marched stealthily into the little city, but found all silent as the grave. On their way back to camp they were met by Quartermaster Sergeant Redick N. Allred, with another detachment, which had been sent to look after the welfare of the first, whose long absence had awakened some fears for their safety.

There being no discoveries made, after about one hour, or, perhaps, a little more, from the time of forming the line, the men, after being instructed to remember their places and to have their arms in easy reach, were allowed to retire. Nothing further came of the alarm.

A quotation from "Cooke's Conquest," will show that our movements had been watched and reinforcements from three other garrisons had been ordered, and were on their way to aid their Tucsonian brethren in the defense of their pueblo. How numerous the reinforcements were we are not informed, but the force, when combined, was doubtless far superior to our own. In fact, the soldiers and citizens able to bear arms, at Tucson alone would have outnumbered us, and, having a fort and walled town, with two pieces of cannon, could have resisted a force far superior to our little band of about 360, all told.

Cooke says: "Signal smokes had been observed, and it was afterwards ascertained, that at this Indian-like announcement of the approach [of the fifty men up the creek] the Mexicans [who had fled from Tucson] further retreated, and the reinforcements, which had come from the presidios of Fronteras, Santa Cruz and Tubac, marched to return to their posts."

Who shall say that the same God who sent terror into the camps of the enemies of ancient Israel, did not have an eye over the little modern Israelitish force then crossing the great desert by his Divine command through the Prophet Brigham, who had said, "There will be no fighting, except with wild beasts."

Cooke further says: "A note was written to Captain Comaduran on his return, enclosing a letter for Don Manuel Gandara, Governor of Sonora, at Ures, who was said to be very well disposed towards the United States; it is here given:

"CAMP AT TUCSON, SONORA,
Dec. 18, 1846.

Your Excellency:—The undersigned, marching in command of a Battalion of United States infantry from New Mexico to California, has found it convenient for the passage of his wagon train to cross the frontier of Sonora. Having passed within fifteen miles of Fronteras, I have found it necessary to take this presidio in my route to the Gila. Be assured I did not come as an enemy of the people whom you represent; they have received only kindness at my hands." After some further conciliatory statements he concludes: "Meanwhile, I make a wagon road from the streams of the Atlantic to the

Pacific Ocean, through the valuable plains and mountains, rich with minerals, of Sonora. This, I trust, will prove useful to the citizens of either republic, who, if not more closely, may unite in the pursuits of a highly beneficial commerce.

With sentiments of esteem and respect, I am your Excellency's most obedient servant,

P. St. G. Cooke,
Lieut. Col. of United States Forces.

To his Excellency, Sen. Don Manuel Gandara, Governor of Sonora, Ures, Sonora."

CHAPTER XXIII.

Long and Difficult March Without Water—Great Suffering—A Laughable Occurrence—The Pima Village—The Natives—News from Kearny—A Cruel Order—The Maricopa Indians—Their Honesty.

On the 18th, the command resumed its journey. At the end of seven miles, the mules were watered. This was the last water for a considerable distance, as the stream sank at that place. We traveled about three miles down the dry bed, and found the sand very heavy. Our progress, after leaving the bed of the stream, although over level clay ground, was frequently obstructed with mezquit thickets. We made camp without water at 9 p. m., having traveled twenty-four miles. The mules were tied up and fed grain.

Straggling, worn-out, famishing men came into camp at all hours of the night, and the rear guard did not reach camp until near daylight.

On the 19th, those who were able started forward on the arrival of the rear guard, while the more feeble, who had but just arrived, rested until after daylight. Water was reported at a hole between two mountains, fourteen miles distant, but on our arrival it could not be found. The report was probably an encouraging ruse of the guides.

The main portion of the road was baked clay, but in places we had sand beds to pull through. At sundown the advance of the command reached a small pool of water, enough to give the most of those present a drink by lying down to it, which was the only method allowed. Dipping was forbidden, in order that as many as possible might have a chance for a drink.

The main portion of the army, however, had no water during the entire day, save a few drops which the men managed to suck from the mud in small puddle holes found by the wayside. Nor could they cook anything except a little wheat which some managed to parch.

They traveled during the day, and especially as night set in, in a straggling, scattered condition. The men might be found all along the road in squads of two or three, without blanket, fire or tent. In the evening the Colonel gave permission to the Captains to halt their companies at discretion during the night, but only for a short time at once, as the only hope for water was by traveling on, and both men and mules could travel in the cool of the night without water better than in the day time. But in no case were the halts, during the night, to exceed six hours.

Company C was in the rear of the others, and Lieutenant Rosecrans left his men and rode on in advance and into the hills in search of water, and, fortunately, found a hole some distance from the road. He took the foremost of his command to it, then filled their canteens, mounted his mule, and, riding back to his famishing men, gave them what water he had and led them to the spring. After having drank their fill from the weak spring of water, which soon became muddy, they cooked some provisions and pursued their journey to overtake the command, which they did about 3 a. m., but not without passing many lying by the way begging for water. Some small pools had been found in one or two places, but the famishing animals had consumed or spoiled them.

The advance struck water and camped about noon on the 20th and several parties took mules and canteens and went back and relieved the suffering of their comrades, or doubtless some would have perished. The stragglers continued to arrive the whole of the afternoon.

To narrate each individual's suffering this day alone would make quite a book.

HONESTY OF THE PIMA INDIANS.

On the 21st, a march of ten miles brought us to the Gila river, where we made a halt. While here our camp was visited by from 1,500 to 2,000 Pima Indians. Although all our property was exposed in such a manner that many articles might have been easily stolen, not a thing was molested by them. Weaver, one of the guides, assured us that these Indians were so scrupulous that they had been known to follow travelers half a day to restore lost property to the owner.

A rather laughable incident occurred here. Henry W. Bigler, now a much respected citizen of St. George, but then a soldier, and "Colonel's orderly" for the day, was asked by the Colonel if his musket was loaded. The reason of the question was that the commander had given his mule some grain and another mule seemed bent on sharing it with him. Several times Cooke had driven it away and it had as often returned.

On Brother Bigler replying that his gun was not loaded, he was ordered to load it, and the Colonel added, with an oath, that he would shoot the mule, and walked into his tent.

The orderly glanced at and recognized the mule as a private animal, belonging to one of his comrades. Quick as thought he bit off the bullet, put it into his pocket, emptied the powder from the cartridge into his gun and rammed the paper on top of it.

By this time Cooke returned, took the gun, walked to within about ten feet of the mule (which stood broadside to him), leveled the piece, and, as he supposed, fired the fatal shot. On seeing the animal uninjured, however, he looked daggers at the orderly, threw the gun upon the ground, and, with another oath, said, "you didn't load that gun right," and turned on his heel and again entered his tent amid roars of laughter from teamsters and others who had witnessed the whole affair.

At this point, the Colonel sketched a map of our route from where Kearney left the Rio Grande, with the aid of no instrument but a compass. The map appears in his "Conquest of New Mexico and California," and is proven to be as accurate as could be expected. It shows this part of our journey to have been almost a semi-circle. The distance between the points is estimated to be 474 miles. The following quotation from Cooke's writings will show at least one of the national benefits of this arduous campaign:

"A new administration in which Southern interests prevailed, with the great problem of the practicability and best location of a Pacific Railroad under investigation, had the map of this wagon route before them with its continuance to the west, and perceived that it gave exactly the solution of its unknown element, that a southern route would avoid both the Rocky Mountains and Sierra Nevada, with their snows, and would meet no obstacle in this great interval. The new 'Gadsden Treaty' was the result; it was signed, December 30, 1853." Thus, while the Mormon Pioneers, under President Brigham Young and associates, were paving the way for the Union Pacific Railroad up the Platte and over the South Pass of the Rocky Mountains to San Francisco, the Mormon Battalion, under Colonel Cooke and associates, were virtually locating the prospective Southern Pacific across the great desert to San Diego.

"Mormon" enterprise is also suggesting a cross-line to connect Utah and our Northern Territories with Mexico and the Southern States. Such connection is only a matter of time.

On the 22nd, we marched ten miles and arrived at the Pima village, supposed to contain about 4,000 inhabitants. They were quite a large-sized, fine-looking race of people and very industrious and peaceable. They engaged in agriculture, and manufactured blankets and other fabrics by hand. The poison of the civilized asp is unknown among them, and our American and European cities would do well to take lessons in virtue and morality from these native tribes.

Long before we reached the village, we were met by the Indian women and children, many of whom were quite pretty and graceful, and walked generally by twos, with arms lovingly entwined around one another, presenting a picture of contentment and happiness that was very pleasing to look upon. Even our stern and matter-of-fact Colonel was not proof against their bewitching charms. In writing of them, he says:

"One little girl particularly, by a fancied resemblance, interested me much; she was so joyous that she seemed very pretty and innocent; I could not resist tying on her head, as a turban, a bright new silk handkerchief, which I happened to wear to-day; the effect was beautiful to see—a picture of happiness!"

Kindness to the natives, by military officers, as manifested in several instances by Colonel Cooke, is so rare in this age, that this circumstance may be mentioned, as one of the noteworthy events of our journey.

In this connection, it may be well to state that on the day following, the Colonel presented their chief with three ewe sheep with a fair prospect of increase; thereby encouraging their industries, in fact, inaugurating a new one—the culture of sheep and woolen manufacture.

The Colonel stopped at the chief's house a few minutes and congratulated him on having the most prosperous and happy tribe he had ever met with. He advised him, although these Indians were peaceable and never troubled their neighbors, to be prepared for any emergency that might arise, and especially to resist any outside pressure. Some of the soldiers traded buttons taken off their clothes for cakes of bread; obtaining a cake for each button; others called at a hut and were treated with stewed pumpkin. We also traded some old clothing for corn, beans, molasses, squash, etc.

On the 23rd, we left the Pima village and proceeded on fifteen miles. During the day we met three pilots who had been through to San Diego with General Kearny. They informed us that we were at least one month in advance of the General's expectations. We learned that General Kearny had been twelve days in going from the Pima village to San Diego with pack-mules, and it was thought that we would be from forty to sixty days with wagons. The news received from General Kearny was to the effect that the Mexicans had again revolted, and that the safety and conquest of California depended upon the prompt and energetic action of the General and command. The letter was written at Warner's rancho, in California.

Our march was now through rich, cultivated grounds. There seemed to be a beautiful plain of from fifteen to twenty miles in all directions.

In the evening, the Colonel, who had not prohibited private purchases, ordered that all private provisions should be left on the ground or carried by the owners, as he claimed the teams were unable to haul any more. This the men took rather hard, as they had sold clothing off their backs, indeed, one or two had even sold their last shirt to get it, and, besides, they were on less than half rations. The result of this order was that a great deal of provisions was left on the ground by the starving men.

On the night of the 23rd, and during the 24th, we camped at a village of the Maricopa Indians, who were estimated to number about ten thousand. Their head chief was named Don Jose Messio. They lived in dome-shaped houses, thatched with corn-stalks and straw, varying from about twenty to fifty feet in diameter, with arbors in front, on which lay, piled up, cotton stalks, with unopened bolls, to dry. This was probably from late crops, as the rule for picking out cotton is when the bolls open in the field. We saw domesticated animals here, the horse, mule, ox, dog and even Spanish fowls. Their implements of husbandry consisted of axes, hoes, shovels, and harrows. Plows were not seen and probably only forked sticks were used to loosen the soil, as it was loose, rich and easily worked. The natives showed no signs of fear, and did not run like the Apaches, who, at the time, were said to be hostile.

Colonel Cooke very kindly suggested to our senior officers that this vicinity would be a good place for the exiled Saints to locate. A proposition to this effect was favorably received by the Indians.

As an evidence of the honesty of the Pima and Maricopa Indians, it may be mentioned that General Kearny left some bales of goods and a number of broken down mules with the former to be called for by Colonel Cooke on his arrival, and they were promptly delivered up. Other mules that General Kearny had been forced to leave to their fate, when given out after passing the Maricopa village, were found and cared for by the Indians, and promptly and voluntarily delivered to us on our arrival there. Here, then, were two tribes of Indians, at least, who should be excepted from the rule laid down by a certain military officer, late of Fort Cameron, that "no Indian is good until buried six feet under ground."

At one of these villages a portion of the men of company E boiled and ate some of the public corn. Lieutenant Dykes reported the fact to the commander, who, in great pretended indignation, ordered the ration of beef due company E to be fed to the mules. This ironical order was actually carried out, and the beef, as I understand, was left on the ground, where the mules refused to eat it.

CAAPTER XXIV.

Cross a Bend of the Gila—Brackish Water—Difficult Traveling—Boat made of two Wagon-boxes—Provisions Shipped in it—Fears for its Safety—Boating a Failure—Cargo Left—Another Reduction in Rations—Feed on Mezquit Seeds—Arrival at the Colorado—Crossing the River—Suffering of the Men Sent Back for Flour—Wagon Stuck in the Middle of the River—Left there by the Colonel—His Statement Incorrect—Wagons Abandoned.

We spent Christmas day by marching eighteen miles from the Maricopa village, mainly up hill and over sand, and camped without water. The following day we advanced twenty-three miles and encamped near the Gila River. Our route between the Maricopa village and this point lay across a bend of the river. From our having to follow around the base of a mountain the distance was considerably greater than a direct line would have been.

We found the water quite brackish, owing to the fact that the Saline River, which is a larger stream than the Upper Gila, empties into it just below the Maricopa village. At this point our loads were lightened by a cache of three-hundred mule shoes.

Our route from this point lay down the river, over heavy sandy bottoms, in some places quicksand. It was so difficult traveling that we only made sixty miles in six days, and even then the men had to work very hard at helping the mules to pull the loads. Of course, all our beef secured in the wild bull region was exhausted, and the famished sheep and oxen that were slaughtered had so little flesh on their bones that very little could be got from them to appease our hunger or furnish us sustenance. Dr. Sanderson pronounced such flesh very unwholesome, and predicted that if we did not adopt the plan of broiling or frying it instead of boiling it, as we had been doing, we would "die off like rotten sheep." How to fry it without grease was "beyond our ken," and to broil it would be to waste so much by shrinkage and loss of juice that it would only aggravate our hunger, so we continued to boil it and drink the soup. Sometimes we would add to the soup about two spoonfuls of flour for each man. The entrails were generally utilized by hanging them over a stick and broiling and then eating them. The hide was used by cutting it up into pieces, singeing the hair off and boiling it until tender enough to eat. The tripe was also boiled. When an animal was slaughtered the entire carcass was rationed out to companies and messes; and then, again, after cooking, the meat was divided into as many lots as there were men in the mess, and allotted to the men after a somewhat original fashion. One man would be required to turn his face from the food, so as not to see it, while another would point to a lot and ask him "who shall have this?" He would name a man, and thus one after another of the men had his portion accorded to him.

As we traveled down the river, we found rocks covered with ancient hieroglyphics, including profiles of men, beasts and reptiles.

Grass in many places was very scant, and our animals fared badly. On the 1st of January, 1847, we had recourse to cutting down the cottonwood trees for our animals to browse upon. Either from eating too much of this food or from some other cause, a number of our mules and sheep died, with strong symptoms of poison.

Despairing of our teams being able to continue with such heavy loads, a rather novel plan was hit upon to convey a portion of the baggage. Colonel Cooke writing of it, says:

"I am now preparing a boat of two pontoon wagon-bodies lashed together, end to end, between two dry cottonwood logs; in this I shall put all the baggage I can risk.   *   *
I have determined to send Lieutenant Stoneman in charge; he professes to have had similar experience, and is desirous to undertake it."

This move cast a gloom over the men generally, as they took the view that with our already scanty supplies no further risk of loss ought to be taken.

This curious barge, which was loaded with twenty-five hundred pounds of provisions for the men and corn for our mules, was launched on the 1st or 2nd of January. It was expected that it would be moored or fastened near our camp every night, but trouble was experienced almost immediately after it started, in getting it over a sandbar, and after that we neither saw nor heard anything of it for several days. During this time, the command struggled along the river bank with great difficulty, and were oppressed with apprehensions concerning the boat and its valuable cargo. Fears were entertained that it had fallen into the hands of the Mexicans or Indians, or that it had foundered on a sandbar.

Finally, on the 5th, Doctor Foster, one of our guides and interpreter, brought the sad news that, owing to the many sandbars in the river, much of the provisions had been taken from the boat and left on the sandbars and on the river bank, and that the boat was moving slowly down the stream.

Men were immediately detailed to go back and aid the boat. After about three miles travel, they met it, with the crew, but the last of the provisions had been left about twenty miles further up the stream, and the main bulk about fifteen miles still farther back.

Several of the men had already fainted and fallen to the earth, through hunger and exhaustion, but now, sad to relate, another reduction in the rations of one ounce to the man was ordered. A few more such reductions and nothing would have remained.

On the 7th of January, the quartermaster ordered the remaining provisions weighed, and found that we had only four days allowance of our short rations left. That day we advanced only seven miles, owing to the pioneers having to work the road over rocky points of ridges and gullies. When we camped our mules had to swim the river to obtain feed, and then it only consisted of flag-grass and willows.

The following day we traveled over a rich alluvial bottom, where we found wild hemp growing, and reached the mouth of the Gila River. In the absence of grass, the mules were fed on the fruit or seed pods growing upon a variety of the mezquit which the men called "mescrew." For several days previously the men had also resorted to the eating of these seeds to make up for their lack of rations. They ground them in coffee mills and made cakes of the meal. It was found to be nutritious and quite palatable to the starving men, but its use had to be abandoned as it produced constipation.

On the 9th, a march of ten miles over a bottom, which in some places was heavy sand and in others miry clay, brought us to the crossing of the Colorado. Here forty men were detailed to gather the mezquit seeds, or tornia, to feed the famishing mules upon. The river was found to be quite as wide, though not so deep as the Missouri, and the water much the same color as that river.

Francisco, a Spanish guide, was sent across the stream to fire the thickets on the opposite shore, in order that the command might travel over the next day.

Here we were overtaken by some of the men who had been sent back to recover the provisions left on the Gila from the barge. They brought with them about four hundred pounds of flour, but found no pork, and the rest of the men were left to search farther for it. These men were in a pitiable plight; their clothing was torn into shreds, through having to travel and crawl through thorny brush to get to the river bank to search for the provisions. They had also suffered severely for want of food. One man reported being two days without anything to eat. The corporal "returned with a shirt."

Ferrying across the river in the pontoon wagon-boxes was commenced on the 10th and continued all night and until late the next morning.

The crossing ranged down the river, which was over half a mile wide, hence the ford was nearly a mile long, including two channels, in the middle of which it was difficult to reach the bottom with our tent poles. Planks from wagon-boxes left on the road were laid on top of the wagon-beds and a portion of the provisions placed upon them, and hauled over by the mules, which had to swim in the deepest portions of the river. Two mules were drowned while being driven across.

Quartermaster Sergeant Smith, who, as previously mentioned, was severely injured by a wild bull, was ordered by the Colonel to ford the stream, although, by virtue of his office, he had the right to ride in any wagon of his company. The water in some places was up to his neck.

After the baggage was all over, the loose animals were driven across. One hundred and thirty of our poor sheep were still alive, though, like ourselves, almost famished.

After crossing, the main army traveled about fifteen miles to a well dug by General Kearny. Company C's wagon, however, got stuck on the sand bar in the river, between the two channels, with a broken-down team. The Colonel refused to allow the other companies to wait or render any assistance, but proceeded on with them. The wagon which was stuck in the quicksand was released by the worn-out men getting into the water and aiding, as on the sandy desert. The Colonel charged that it was the inactivity of the men that kept the wagon on the bar; this charge he has wrongfully and foolishly permitted to be published in his "Conquest." Great and brave as he was, he here lost an excellent opportunity for glory and fame by not, Washington or Jackson-like, jumping into the river and putting his shoulder to the wheel, thus aiding the half-starved, worn-out men and team, the former of whom were suffering severely through his indiscretion in hazarding and losing their food by the boat disaster.

I esteem Colonel Cooke very highly, and think, perhaps, a less independent and persevering man would have failed in making the journey with wagons. I also give him much credit for the general justice he has done the Battalion in his work referred to, and sincerely regret the necessity that has prompted this defense of my injured companions in arms. The fact was, the team was broken down, and nine miles farther on the wagon had to be abandoned.

Private animals were pressed into service to aid the wagons, but even with this help, three were abandoned and the baggage was packed on the team mules.

CHAPTER XXV.

Troublesome Fires in the Brush—Discouraging Prospect—No Water—Alas, for Human Hopes—A Trying March—Great Suffering from Thirst—Meet Fresh Mules and some Beeves—Freezing at Night and Scorching by Day—Arrival at the Coriza—Happy Relief—Good Water to Drink—Novel Style of Boots.

The fire set by the guide, which seemed the only method of getting a road, annoyed us very much. In some cases the wagons were in danger of being consumed, and, in others, the mules' feet were liable to be ruined, by the live coals from the burning brush. A quantity of the mezquit fruit was gathered for the animals, by the very wise direction of our commander. There was but very little grass at our camp.

The following will show that the Colonel was not insensible of our true situation. "I was met by a man who told me there was not a drop of water" (in the well). The worst prospect for sixty miles ahead instantly arose to frighten me for the 360 nearly worn-out footmen, who confide all to me."

When he arrived at the camping place about 9 p. m., on the 11th, he found a portion of the men cleaning out and sinking the old well, while another party were digging a new one. Some mud and a little water were struck in the old well, but the quicksand ran in and not only obscured the water, but endangered the lives of the men, who were now ten feet or more below the surface. How to remedy the evil was a question. Some one suggested that the wife of one of the Captains had a wash tub, which, by boring holes in the bottom, might answer as a curbing. The Captain's team soon came up and the vessel was called for, but the good lady, who perhaps had brought it all the way from Nauvoo or even farther, could not consent, on any account, to part with it. It was, however, pressed into service, and bored, and sunk in the sand. This proved a failure. Then the bottom was ordered to be knocked out, when it worked better; some water came in, but, alas, for human hopes! the fluid soon disappeared and all seemed lost. In this emergency, Weaver, one of the guides and an old mountaineer trapper, was sent for, to ascertain the practibility of traveling sixty miles more or less down the river. He thought, with our weak teams and worn-out men, it would be next to impossible. According to Cooke's account, which is doubtless correct, he now cast one more anxious look down the old well, and, as a last but faint hope of success, ordered a fresh detail to further sink the new well, which was already more than two feet below the old one, with no better prospect. A half hour later all hearts were made glad with the tidings of water deep enough to fill our camp kettles.

Colonel Cooke says, of the news of water: "It was like a great light bursting on darkness and gloom." Further on, the anxious commander adds: "Eighteen hours of unceasing labor has been my lot to-day, with anxiety enough to turn one gray." With all this anxiety, the ever hopeful officer says: "My faith had not failed." Lieutenant Oman, with twelve picked men, was ordered to go on a forced march the next day, as far as Alamo Mocho, to dig a well or wells, that we might have water on our arrival.

On the morning of the 12th, the mules of three out of the five companies were watered from the well by 11 o'clock, when those three companies resumed the march, leaving the others to water their animals and follow on afterwards. That night a dry camp was made, and not until two o'clock next day did we reach the well, *Alamo Mocho*, where we found Lieutenant Oman and party had cleaned out the old well and dug another; but very little water had been obtained, and that of a poor quality. It did not seem to satisfy the thirst of either men or animals, and the latter had to be forced away from the well in order to get them to browse upon the scant squaw bushes. About twenty bushels of tornia, gathered by the men near the Colorado and carried along for the use of the mules, helped to keep those poor animals alive.

On the morning of the 14th, Lieutenant Stoneman and Weaver, with about twenty-five men, started early to hasten on to the next well, called the Pozo Hondo, and make preparations for the arrival of the command. Leaving two of the wagons which the famishing animals were unable to take any farther, the Battalion proceeded on and camped again without water. A portion of the way we had heavy sand, but, in other places, solid clay, so hard that neither animals nor wagons made much impression on it. In the sandy places were signs of large herds of cattle and horses, which had been driven to Sonora, to prevent them falling into the hands of the Americans. Sea-shells and salt were also found on the great clay flat, which led to the conclusion that at some time in the distant past, the Gulf of California may have extended over these parts.

On the 15th, we marched seven miles to the Pozo Hondo wells. A rainbow was visible in the morning, a sight rarely seen on these arid deserts.

On arriving at the well, one of our guides, who had been sent ahead to purchase fresh mules and beef cattle, met us with thirty-five mules, all in good condition. He had started with fifty-seven, but unfortunately the other twenty-two were lost by the way. Ten fat beeves were also brought and one was killed, which was a great treat to the men, after having little else than worn-out oxen since leaving Santa Fe. The most of the mules were wild and some got away. One broke loose from three men and made good his escape, harness and all.

The well afforded us but a little very poor water; it served, however, to save life until better could be reached. We left Pozo Hondo at about 4 p. m., and continued our march until 11 p. m., making about ten miles, when we halted until 2 a. m., of the 16th.

As usual, the night was very cold, and the half-naked men suffered for want of more and better clothing. The contrast between an almost tropical sun in the day time and a December cold atmosphere at night was very hurtful and weakening to both man and beast. The Indians call that region "the hot land"—a name which strikes the writer as being quite appropriate, as it is by far the hottest region he ever saw.

We continued our march twenty miles farther to the Cariza, a small creek known to the Battalion as the "first running water," on account of it being the first seen since leaving the Colorado river. The march of the last five days was the most trying of any we had made, on both men and animals. We here found the heaviest sand, hottest days and coldest nights, with no water and but little food. Language fails to provide adjectives strong enough to describe our situation; it must be left to the imagination of the reader to picture it.

At about noon, the best teams reached camp. The last, however, did not arrive until the next morning. There were many occasions, during our travels through the deserts, when twenty well-armed men might have nearly used up the command, in our scattered condition.

John Lawson reached camp after dark; he was riding and packing a private mule, on which was carried his clothing, blankets, gun, etc. He left the mule packed for a few minutes, and was not able to find either the animal or its loading afterwards, although a thorough search was made that night and the next morning.

At this time the men were nearly barefooted; some used, instead of shoes, rawhide wrapped around their feet, while others improvised a novel style of boots by stripping the skin from the leg of an ox. To do this, a ring was cut around the hide above and below the gambrel joint, and then the skin taken off without cutting it lengthwise. After this, the lower end was sewed up with sinews, when it was ready for the wearer, the natural crook of the hide adapting it somewhat to the shape of the foot. Others wrapped cast-off clothing around their feet, to shield them from the burning sand during the day and the cold at night.

Before we arrived at the Cariza, many of the men were so nearly used up from thirst, hunger and fatigue, that they were unable to speak until they reached the water or had it brought to them. Those who were strongest reported, when they arrived, that they had passed many lying exhausted by the way-side. Among that number was the author, who was then on sick report and in such a feeble condition that, after riding a few rods on a poor government mule, he was obliged to lay down on his back to ease the pain, which seemed to be seated in his back and loins. At one time, it was even supposed that he was dead. This supposition was strengthened by the fact that his riding mule got loose and marched into camp. It happened, however, that there were other men in the rear of him, one of whom had a mule which he placed him upon and allowed him to ride until he reached the creek at about eight o'clock in the evening.

About sixteen or more mules gave out entirely during the two last days' travel and were abandoned. During that part of our journey made in the morning, it was piercing cold. The guides got lost and we traveled a mile or more out of our way, through very heavy sand. Our fresh animals were nearly exhausted.

CHAPTER XXVI.

Heavy Roads—Last Food Eaten—Messengers from San Diego—Cheerfulness of Men—News of Battles—Cutting a Road Through a Mountain Gorge—Arrival at Warner's Rancho—A Full Meal—Cheap Beef—Hot Spring—Sleeping Under Water—Flour from the Boat Disaster—March for San Diego—Beef Diet.

On the 17th, we traveled fifteen miles over very heavy sand and encamped between two mountains. The fresh animals, after getting rested, did good work. On the score of both men and mules, Cooke very properly remarks: "That this fifteen miles of very bad road was accomplished, under the circumstances, by mules or men, is extraordinary. The men arrived here completely worn down; they staggered as they marched, as they did yesterday"—he might have added, "and many other days."

Some of the men, unable to keep up with the wagons, traveled and slept at intervals, during the night, and did not reach camp until daylight the following morning. The sheep arrived about noon on the 18th. They numbered from seventy to eighty, but were so poor that when one was slaughtered and skinned, the bones had but a very thin covering, and the scant flesh that remained contained very little nourishment. The Colonel, in writing on the day's incidents, says: "I went through their companies this morning; they were eating their last four ounces of flour; of sugar and coffe, there has been none for some weeks."

All of our government wagons had been abandoned at this time, but five. During this day, the Indian magistrate (Alcalde) of the town of San Philipi, and a companion, brought a letter to the Colonel from the Governor of San Diego, announcing the arrival of our men, who had been sent for supplies, and promising assistance. He welcomed our approach. The Governor's messengers were nearly naked, and not unlike the Apaches in appearance.

We did not advance any on the 18th, but spent the day in cleaning up our arms, and in the evening the men were paraded and inspected.

The Colonel expressed great surprise at seeing the half starved, worn-out men who, only the night previous, had staggered into camp, like so many inebriates, from sheer exhaustion and hunger, now playing the fiddle and singing merry songs.

The messengers having heard of several other battles in California, the Colonel entered into precautionary measures, as it was thought we might meet a large force of the enemy retreating towards Sonora.

Brother Henry Standage's journal, of this date, says: "We have nothing but beef and very small rations of that; I was glad, to-day, to go and pick up the pork rinds that were thrown away by the Colonel's cook, although they were in the sand." The reader can make his own comments.

On the 19th, after about three or four miles of hard travel, mainly up hill, we came to a halt; even Weaver, our regular guide, believed "we were penned up." Our indefatigable commander, however, seemed to think it was too late in the day to abandon the wagon enterprise. He very sternly told the guide if he did not find a crossing or passage through these rocks and mountain gorges, he would send men that would do it.

We had a rugged mountain ridge some two hundred or more feet high to surmount. Owing to rumors that we would probably meet an army of Californians, the Colonel ordered the baggage to the rear.

We surmounted all difficulties and succeeded in getting over the ridge inside of two hours. Other and seemingly more formidable barriers now presented themselves. Our route lay up a dry ravine, through openings in the solid rocks. Our guides, who had always traveled either north or south of this route, were as ignorant of its practicability as ourselves. As we traveled up the dry bed, the chasm became more contracted until we found ourselves in a passage at least a foot narrower than our wagons. Nearly all of our road tools, such as picks, shovels, spades, etc., had been lost in the boat disaster. The principal ones remaining were a few axes, which the pioneers were using at the time the boat was launched, a small crowbar, and perhaps a spade or two. These were brought into requisition, the commander taking an ax and assisting the pioneers. Considerable was done before the wagons arrived. One wagon was taken to pieces and carried over about an hour before sunset. The passage was hewn out and the remaining wagons got through about sundown, by unloading and lifting through all but two light ones, which were hauled by the mules.

Both men and teams were now exhausted and the water we had expected to reach early in the afternoon was at least seven or eight miles farther on. We traveled until dark and camped without water, but with good grass for the animals.

That night was very cold, and we had only a little brush for fuel.

We were on the march before sunrise on the morning of the 20th. We had a sand ridge to pull over, in the usual way, by the use of long ropes, with fifteen to twenty men to each wagon; after that we had an exceedingly rough, rocky, descending road to a little valley, then a good road to San Phillippi, a deserted Indian village, the inhabitants, probably, leaving on our approach.

The teams were turned loose to graze and two beeves killed, our only food. After a brief rest, we traveled seven miles farther over a low mountain pass and encamped for the night where there was a blessing we could appreciate—plenty of water. There was very little feed, however, for the animals. We had a drill on the way, while halting for the teams to come up.

At this point we met Charbonaux, returning from San Diego, and learned that the Governor of that place had detained Hall and Leraux, lest they might fall into the hands of the hostile Californians, who, it seemed, held a grudge against them. Orders were also received for the Battalion to march to San Diego instead of Los Angeles.

On the 21st, we traveled about ten or twelve miles to Warner's rancho. Warner's was the first house we saw in California, although we had been in that State since crossing the Colorado river. The weather was cold and cloudy, with signs of snow. The route lay over low mountains not difficult to pass. The road (then a mere trail) ran through a fine grove of large live oaks. This, with the high green grass, although the weather was rather chilly, was cheering, and we felt that we were descending into an atmosphere of spring. We crossed a mountain ridge, dividing the waters of the Colorado and the gulf from those emptying into the Pacific. Fine timber and perpetual snows crowned the mountain peaks and high ridges. We reached the rancho about 2 p. m., and encamped. The owner, Mr. Warner, understood the Californians were hard pressed by our forces, near Los Angeles, and hence we were liable to meet a large force retreating to Sonora any day. The guides, who had been sent forward for supplies on the 28th of December, were instructed by the Colonel to meet the Battalion at Warner's rancho on the 21st of January, and it is rather remarkable that they as well as the Battalion arrived on that very day. Here we had the first full meal, except at Tucson and the wild bull country, since the reduction of our rations on the Rio Del Norte This meal consisted of fresh, fat beef without salt, obtained from Mr. Warner, a native of the State of Massachusetts.

A few pancakes were purchased from Indians, but no other bread could be got. Three fat beeves were purchased (Warner reserving the hides), for about $3.50.

Cattle and horses were very cheap, the country being overrun with them; some ranchmen owned several thousand head, and there was no general market for live stock.

We remained at Warner's and rested during the 22nd, and our rations were raised to four pounds of beef per day. We had no other food nor even salt to season our meat. The weather was warm, like that of April or May in the Middle States.

A hot spring of considerable volume, and of a temperature of about 170° F., issued from some rocks on this rancho. It sent up a cloud of steam for over half a mile below its source. Near the center of this valley, stood an evergreen oak tree; its boughs reaching within five feet of the ground, and its foliage forming a circumference, according to Colonel Cooke's estimate, of two hundred and seventy feet. The hot spring branch ran around one side of this tree and a cold stream around the other.

Strange as it may appear, it was asserted, not only by Warner but by eye-witnesses of our own men, that during cold nights, the Indians (who were nearly nude) slept with their bodies in the warm stream while their heads lay upon the soddy banks. This seems another of those facts which are "stanger than fiction." There were a number of Indians here from San Luis Rey. They were friendly to the United States government, and had recently captured, brought here and killed some ten or eleven Californians. They had, however, lost thirty-eight of their own number killed by Californians and some other hostile tribe in retaliation, in Temecula Valley, who lay in ambush and took them by surprise.

These Indians begged the Colonel to allow them to accompany the Battalion, that they might bury their dead on the way and the Colonel consented. The name of their chief was Antonio. He, with ten of his men, were employed as scouts and to take charge of and drive our beef cattle.

During the night of the 22nd, the wind blew all our tents down.

On the 23rd, the commanding officer decided to march towards Los Angeles and join and assist General Kearny in capturing that place, it being the Spanish capital of California. Before leaving the rancho, the Colonel had a talk with Baupista, a prominent chief of the Cohuillos, a tribe about two thousand strong, all told, who stood aloof from all other tribes and were very independent.

The chief was firmly told that it would be folly for his tribe to interfere in any way with the Americans, as that nation would soon and forever govern California. These Indians professed friendship and did not interfere with either our persons or property.

At this point, the parties sent back for lost provisions, overtook us, with about four hundred pounds of flour—a trifle over one pound to the man. As a rule, we used about two spoonfuls per day each to thicken our soup. When asked by the commander why they did not come in sooner, the Corporal in charge promptly replied that they "dared not come in without flour."

It had rained steadily for about twenty four hours before we left Warner's, and continued through the next day and night, this being the rainy season for that country, the climate of which was similar to that of ancient Palestine. In scripture language, these would be called the "early or former rains;" while, after a dry summer, the "latter," or, as we term them, the fall rains set in, and there was much suffering from cold and being wet. Several mules died and others strayed, the fresh Indians, including Chief Antonio, soon gathered up the missing ones.

On the 25th, we received a dispatch from General Kearny, ordering the march to San Diego, as at first anticipated, to meet him there. We reached Temecula Valley that day, where we found a portion of the San Luis Rey Indians, who had gathered to bury their dead, and they mistook us and we them for Californians. Both lines were in battle array before the mistake was discovered. The Indians were much pleased to see us, and the leading men shook hands heartily with Cooke and many others.

Following a road that branches off towards San Diego, we passed through the San Luis Valley. There we found grass from two to ten inches high, and plenty of wild mustard, the foliage of which, large and fresh, made excellent greens, which proved a luxury with our only other food, beef.

We had some difficulty in crossing the San Luis River owing to the quicksand. We saw in that region many thousand head of cattle and horses, besides a large herd of donkeys, as well as wild geese, brants, ducks, pelicans, gulls, etc., by the million.

On the 26th, our rations were increased to five pounds of beef per day. If any of our readers have an idea that beef alone is substantial food, the writer would beg leave to disagree with them. In connection with bread it fills an important place as an article of diet, but when taken alone, it is not near equal to "mush and milk," nor will it satisfy hunger so long. A person living on meat alone can eat a hearty meal every hour or two without the stomach refusing to perform its duties of digestion; in fact, it will crave each meal and relish it as a sweet morsel. Five pounds of fresh beef a day, alone—don't be startled, kind reader—is a rather *small* allowance for a healthy laboring man. In fact, five pounds is only a half ration compared with what was issued to Fremont's battalion, when without other food than beef, as in that case each man "consumed an average of ten pounds a day of fat beef." Yet five pounds each (and seldom that amount) was the extent ever issued to the famishing "Mormon" soldiers, although it could be obtained in abundance for less than one cent per pound.

CHAPTER XXVII.

First View of the Pacific Ocean—Arrival at San Diego Mission—Complimentary Order from Colonel Cooke—Genearl Kearny's Entry to California—Skirmishes with Californians.

Traveling down the river, on the 27th, we arrived at San Luis Rey, a deserted Catholic mission, about noon. One mile below the mission, we ascended a bluff, when the long, long-looked for great Pacific Ocean appeared plain to our view, only about three miles distant. The joy, the cheer that filled our souls, none but worn-out pilgrims nearing a haven of rest can imagine. Prior to leaving Nauvoo, we had talked about and sung of "the great Pacific sea," and we were now upon its very borders, and its beauty far exceeded our most sanguine expectations. Our joy, however, was not unmixed with sorrow. The next thought was, where, oh where were our fathers, mothers, brothers, sisters, wives and children whom we had left in the howling wilderness, among savages, or at Nauvoo, subject to the cruelties of the mobs? Had the government we were serving ordered them off the reservation? If so, had it ordered them back, whence they came, to perish by the ruthless mobs it had failed even to rebuke, while the blood of innocence, even of children, cried to heaven for vengeance? Or, if allowed to move on, had they found a resting place where they could dwell in peace until they could raise a crop, or go, unknown, among their enemies and labor to replenish their exhausted store of provisions? We trusted in God that they were in the land of the living somewhere, and hoped we might find them on our return in or near the valley of Great Salt Lake, within the limits of California, then a Mexican State, but this was only hope. We comforted ourselves with the fact that it was the "Lord's business to provide for His Saints," and that He was "not slack concerning His promises." Amid it all, we went on our way rejoicing.

An express from General Kearny directed that we take quarters in a Catholic mission, five miles from San Diego.

As nearly all our beeves were lost on the night of the 27th, the Colonel gave orders to gather up more on the march; but as he did not direct how many were to be gathered, our Indian scouts brought to our camp, the next morning, several hundred, probably ten times as many as we had lost; this caused a good deal of merriment at their expense.

Traveling in sight of the ocean, the clear bright sunshine, with the mildness of the atmosphere, combined to increase the enjoyment of the scene before us. We no longer suffered from the monotonous hardships of the deserts and cold atmosphere of the snow-capped mountains. January there, seemed as pleasant as May in the northern States, and the wild oats, grass, mustard and other vegetable growths were as forward as we had been used to seeing them in June. The birds sang sweetly and all nature seemed to smile and join in praise to the Giver of all good; but the crowning satisfaction of all to us was that we had succeeded in making the great national highway across the American desert, nearly filled our mission, and hoped soon to join our families and the Saints, for whom, as well as our country, we were living martyrs.

Much of the soil over which we passed was very rich, and the vegetable growth exceedingly luxuriant. The water was clear and good, being mainly cold mountain streams, somewhat warmed by the brilliant rays of the sun in the middle of the day.

On the 29th of January the Battalion came in sight of the long talked-of San Diego. Our camp was located a mile below the Catholic Mission and some four or five miles from the seaport town of San Diego, where General Kearny was quartered. The Colonel rode down in the evening and reported to the General.

The buildings, of the old Catholic Mission of San Diego, were dilapidated, and only used by a few rather filthy Indians The olive, date and some ornamental trees were found in the garden of the mission.

While encamped there we learned, for the first time, our commander's real sentiments towards the Battalion. His extremely strict discipline and stern, morose appearance and acts had led to a query whether he would do us justice in any respect. Even when nearing Tucson he hardly knew whether to trust to our courage and fidelity or not. At that time, a soldier, passing, heard him ask Major Cloud whether he thought he (Cooke) could rely on these "Mormons" in case of an attack. The Major unhesitatingly replied: "The Battalion will follow where you dare to lead," which he proved very satisfactorily to be true. This distrust is not to be wondered at, when it is considered that though having no personal acquaintance with the "Mormons" previous to meeting the Battalion at Santa Fe, he was very much prejudiced against them from the reports he had heard of their character.

But after about 1,400 miles travel, during 104 days, under the painful circumstances already enumerated, his feelings had materially changed, and he, accordingly, issued the following:

"HEAD QUARTERS MORMON BATTALION,
MISSION OF SAN DIEGO,
January 30, 1847.

(Orders No. 1.)

"The Lieutenant-Colonel commanding congratulates the Battalion on their safe arrival on the shore of the Pacific Ocean and the conclusion of their march of over two thousand miles.

History may be searched in vain for an equal march of infantry. Half of it has been through a wilderness where nothing but savages and wild beasts are found, or deserts where, for want of water, there is no living creature. There, with almost hopeless labor we have dug deep wells, which the future traveler will enjoy. Without a guide who had traversed them, we have ventured into trackless table-lands where water was not found for several marches. With crowbar and pick and axe in hand, we have worked our way over mountains, which seemed to defy aught save the wild goat, and hewed a passage through a chasm of living rock more narrow than our wagons. To bring these first wagons to the Pacific, we have preserved the strength of our mules by herding them over large tracts, which you have laboriously guarded without loss. The garrison of four presidios of Sonora concentrated within the walls of Tucson, gave us no pause. We drove them out, with their artillery, but our intercourse with the citizens was unmarked by a single act of injustice. Thus, marching half naked and half fed, and living upon wild animals, we have discovered and made a road of great value to our country.

"Arrived at the first settlement of California, after a single day's rest, you cheerfully turned off from the route to this point of promised repose, to enter upon a campaign, and meet, as we supposed, the approach of an enemy; and this too, without even salt to season your sole subsistence of fresh meat.

"Lieutenants A. J. Smith and George Stoneman, of the First Dragoons, have shared and given valuable aid in all these labors.

"Thus, volunteers, you have exhibited some high and essential qualities of veterans. But much remains undone. Soon, you will turn your attention to the drill, to system and order, to forms also, which are all necessary to the soldier.

By order

    LIEUT. COLONEL P. ST. GEORGE COOKE.
    P. C. MERRILL, Adjutant."

The foregoing order (one of those simple acts of justice so rarely done to "Mormons") which was not read until February 4th, six days after it was written, was cheered heartily by the Battalion.

A few words, now, about the brave and generous General S. F. Kearney, will not be inappropriate, as, by his orders, we followed on his trail from Leavenworth to Santa Fe, and thence to San Diego, in accordance with the stipulations of our enlistment, under Captain James Allen, of company I, First Dragoons.

After taking Santa Fe, in New Mexico, the General was informed, on what he supposed good authority, that California had been subjugated to the American arms; hence he discharged, or otherwise distributed his entire brigade, except an escort of one hundred picked men to accompany him to California, and the Mormon Battalion, an independent corps, attached to his command, by orders from Washington. His escort was mainly as follows: Captain H. S. Turner, First Dragoons; Lieutenant W. H. Emory, Topographical Engineers, and Captain A. R. Johnston, First Dragoons, A. D. C.; one hundred men of the First Dragoons, commanded by Captain Ben. Moore, and Lieutenant T. C. Hammond, all mounted on mules; also two mountain howitzers, in charge of Lieutenant J. W. Davidson, First Dragoons. The baggage was packed on mules from where he left his wagons on the Rio Del Norte.

He was at first ordered to California to take possession of the same in the name of the United States and thereby become Governor and Commander-in-chief of the State, then under Mexican rule. Subsequent events will show that, although the Californians had been whipped they were not conquered, and the General and small escort had some severe battles, with serious results before reaching the coast.

The General did not learn his mistake until he reached Warner's rancho, in Lower California, on the second of December, 1846. He had run short of provisions, and avers that seven of his men ate, at a single meal, a fat, full-grown sheep. Here an Englishman by the name of Stokes, who claimed to be neutral, informed the General that Commodore Stockton had possession of San Diego and that the enemy were in possession of the country from there to Santa Barbara. As he stated he was going to San Diego next morning, Kearny gave him a letter to the Commodore.

The mules in possession of Kearny's troops being poor and jaded, he saw the necessity of securing fresh animals before engaging in battle with the enemy. On learning that there was a band of horses and mules belonging to the Mexican General, Flores, about fifteen miles distant, on the road to Los Angeles, Lieutenant Davidson and fifteen men, accompanied by Carson, were sent to capture them. They returned with their booty next day, December 3rd, at noon. But the animals, being wild, were not of much service.

The following is copied from the General's official report: "Having learned from Captain Gillespie, of the volunteers, that there was an armed party of Californians at San Pascual, three leagues distant, * * I sent Lieutenant Hammond, First Dragoons, with a few men to make a reconnoissance of them. He returned at two in the morning of the 6th inst., reporting that he had found the party in the place mentioned, and that he had been seen, though not pursued, by them. I then determined that I would march for and attack them by break of day; arrangements were accordingly made for the purpose. My aid-de-camp, Captain Johnston, First Dragoons, was assigned to the command of the advanced guard of twelve dragoons, mounted on the best horses we had; then followed about fifty dragoons and Captain Moore, mounted, with few exceptions, on the tired mules they had ridden from Santa Fe, ten hundred and fifty miles. * * As the day, December 6th, dawned, we approached the enemy at San Pascual, who were already in the saddle; Captain Johnston made a furious charge upon them with his advanced guard, and was, in a short time after, supported by the dragoons, soon after which the enemy gave way, having kept up, from the beginning, a continual fire upon us. Upon the retreat of the enemy, Captain Moore led off rapidly in pursuit, accompanied by the dragoons, mounted on horses, and followed, though slowly, by those on their tired mules.

"The enemy, well mounted and among the best horsemen in the world, after retreating about half a mile, and seeing an interval between Captain Moore, with his advance, and the dragoons coming to his support, rallied their whole force, charged with their lances, and, on account of their greatly superior numbers, but few of us in front remained untouched;

"Their number was thirty-eight, all of whom, save two, were killed or wounded. For five minutes, they held the ground from us, when, our men coming up, we again drove them, and they fled from the field not to return to it, which we occupied and encamped upon. A most melancholy duty now remains for me: it is to report the death of my aid-de-camp, Captain Johnston, who was shot dead at the commencement of the action; of Captain Moore, who was lanced just previous to the final retreat of the enemy; and of Lieutenant Hammond, also lanced, who survived but a few hours. We also had killed, two sergeants, two corporals and ten privates of the First Dragoons; one private of the volunteers, and one engaged in the topographical department. Among the wounded, are myself, (in two places), Lieutenant Warner, topographical engineer (in three places), Captain Gillespie and Captain Gibson, of the volunteers (the former in three places), one sergeant, bugler and nine privates of the dragoons; many of them receiving from two to ten lance wounds, most of them when unhorsed and incapable of resistance. The enemy proved to be a party of about one hundred and sixty Californians, under Andreas Pico, brother of the late governor.

"Our provisions were exhausted, our horses dead, and mules on their last legs; and our men now reduced to one-third their number, were ragged, worn down by fatigue, and emaciated.

"On the morning of the 7th, having made ambulances for our wounded, we proceeded on our march, when the enemy showed themselves occupying the hills in our front, which they left as we approached, till reaching San Bernardo; a party of them took possession of a hill near to it and maintained their position until attacked by our advance, who quickly drove them from it, killing and wounding five of their numbers with no loss on our part."

CHAPTER XXVIII.

Kearny's Stubborn defense on the Hill—Providential Strategem of the Enemy—Desperate Resolve—Timely Relief—Sufferings of Kearny's Men—The last Decisive Battle—Civil War Feared—Fremont's Men Refuse to Deliver Public Property—Commodore Stockton's Report to the Secretary of the Navy—Commodore Stockton refuses to Treat with Jose Ma Flores—Colonel Fremont's Assumption—Articles of Capitulation—Dispute Settled—Wisdom of Stockton and Kearny—Battalion and Dragoons the only Regularly Mustered Soldiers in California.

Kearny's troops retained the position on the hill at the expense of losing their beef cattle, which fell into the hands of the enemy.

On the 10th of December, the enemy drove a band of wild horses near the hill with a view of running them over the troops and thus routing them, but the hill being well fortified by nature on three sides, the charges did not amount to much, beyond having some of the best of their horses killed, which served Kearny's men for food and proved a fine treat to them, as they had been for several days living on their own broken-down mules which they brought from Santa Fe. One of the two messengers who had been sent by General Kearny to San Diego returned, and the other, who had been captured by the enemy, was exchanged; he claimed to have hidden papers from Commodore Stockton, in a designated tree, which papers were understood to contain Stockton's refusal to send aid; at all events, no aid came, nor were the papers ever found. That night Lieutenant Beale, of the navy, Carson and an Indian took a circuitous route to San Diego, a distance of thirty miles, which they reached in safety.

After waiting two days longer, and having but little hopes of the second dispatch being more successful than the first, the General determined to "fight it out on that line," and advance to San Diego himself; hence he ordered everything they could not take, even to the soldiers' overcoats, burned. The next morning at daybreak, one hundred sailors and eighty marines arrived, and the enemy fled. This detatchment left San Diego on the night of the 9th, concealed themselves during the daylight on the 10th, and reached the General's rendezvous during the night and distributed their food and clothing among the half-naked and emaciated braves, who had been living on mule and horse-flesh and without water for several days.

While their sufferings were not as prolonged as those of the Battalion, they were quite as acute, and when we, take into account the number killed, wounded and dying of their brave officers and men, they were even more severe. But the trouble was not all over yet. A difficulty arose between General Kearny and Colonel Fremont about the governorship.

General Kearny and Commodore Stockton had fought the last decisive battle with the Californians at Los Angeles, on the 8th and 9th of January, 1847. The enemy fled and met Fremont coming from the north, where they entered into a treaty with him, he signing himself governor, etc.

For a time, civil war seemed inevitable. Many of the enemy as well as Commodore Stockton were said to be in sympathy with Fremont, while some of his officers refused to surrender public property to Kearny's command without Fremont's order. On this subject the Commodore, in an official report to the secretary of the navy, says: "Jose Ma Flores, the commander of the insurgent forces, two or three days previous to the 8th, sent two commissioners with a flag of truce to my camp to make a 'treaty of peace.' I informed the commissioners that I could not recognize Jose Ma Flores, who had broken his parole as an honorable man, or one having any rightful authority worthy to be treated with; that he was a rebel in arms, and if I caught him I would have him shot. It seems that, not being able to negotiate with me, and having lost the battles of the 8th and 9th, they met Colonel Fremont on the 12th instant, on his way here, who, not knowing what had occurred, entered into capitulation with them, which now I send you; and, although I refused to do it myself, still I have thought it best to approve it."

The following are the "articles of capitulation made and entered into at the rancho Couenga, this 13th day of January, 1847, between P. B. Reading, Major Louis McLane, Jr., commanding third artillery; William H. Russell, ordnance officer, commissioners appointed by J. C. Fremont, United States Army, and military commandant of California, and Jose Antonio Carrillo, commandant squadron, Agustin Olivera, deputado, commissioners appointed by Don Andreas Pico, commander-in-chief of the California forces under the Mexican flag.

"*ARTICLE I.*—The commissioners on the part of the Californians, agree that their entire force shall, on presentation of themselves to Lieutenant Colonel Fremont, deliver up their artillery and public arms, and that they shall return peaceably to their homes, conforming to the laws and regulations of the United States, and not again take up arms during the war between the United States and Mexico, but will assist and aid in placing the country in a state of peace and tranquility.

"*ARTICLE II.*—The commissioners on the part of Lieutenant Colonel Fremont agree, and bind themselves on the fulfillment of the first Article by the Californians, that they shall be guaranteed protection of life and property, whether on parole or otherwise.

"*ARTICLE III.*—That until a treaty of peace be made and signed between the United States of North America and the rebublic of Mexico, no Californian, or any other Mexican citizen, shall be bound to take the oath of allegiance.

"*ARTICLE IV.*—That any Californian or citizen of Mexico desiring, is permited by this capitulation to leave the country without let or hindrance.

"*ARTICLE V.*—That by virtue of the aforesaid Articles, equal rights and privileges are vouchsafed to every citizen of California as are enjoyed by the citzens of North America.

"*ARTICLE VI.*—All officers, citizens, foreigners and others shall receive the protection guaranteed by the second Article.

"*ARTICLE VII.*—This capitulation is intended to be no bar in effecting such arrangement as may in future be in justice required by both parties.

CUIDAD DE LOS ANGELES,
January 16, 1847.

"*ADDITIONAL ARTICLE.*—That the paroles of all officers, citizens, and others of the United States and of naturalized citizens of Mexico, are by this foregoing capitulation canceled, and every condition of said paroles, from and after this date, are of no further force and effect, and all prisoners of both parties are hereby released.

"P. B. READING, Major, California Battalion.

"LOUIS MCLANE, Commander Artillery.

"WM. H. RUSSELL, Ordnance Officer.

"JOSE ANTONIO CARILLO, Command't of Squadron.

"AUGUSTIO OLLIVERA, Deputado.

"Approved, J. C. FREMONT. Lieut. Colonel, U. S. Army, and Military Commandant of California.

"ANDREAS PICO, Commander of Squadron and Chief of the National Forces of California."

Colonel Cooke thinks this treaty was not signed until after the junction of Fremont's, Kearny's and Stockton's armies at Los Angeles, on the 14th, also that Fremont knew of their presence and that they were his superiors in rank. He also thinks Commodore Stockton understood as much, although he reported differently to the government.

The dispute was finally settled at Washington by depriving Colonel Fremont of his office in the army. His subsequent appointments, however, go to show that whatever wrongs he may have committed he was not disposed to desert the old flag.

The wisdom of Commodore Stockton and General Kearny in ratifying the treaty, although made by a subordinate and mere provisional officer, is apparent from the fact that thereby the peace of the country was preserved until all national disputes were settled by the treaty of Guadeloupe Hidalgo. A counter course might have resulted in a civil war, more terrible than all of the battles fought on the coast, and especially more disastrous to the American arms. A few Dragoons and the Mormon Battalion (less than five hundred all told) were at that time the only regularly enlisted soldiers in California. Others, of course, subsequently arrived. Fremont and men had espoused the American cause, as had also the marines and sailors, but according to Cooke were not regularly mustered into the service.

Had not the matter been referred to Washington, doubtless the Californians would have taken advantage of the situation to again take possession of the country. Thus the hand of God was again visible in preventing the shedding of blood. The many hair-breadth escapes of the Battalion from death and the shedding of blood are living miracles.

CHAPTER XXIX.

Men Visit San Diego—Precautionary Measure—March to San Luis Rey—Police Detailed—Men nearly Naked—Exhorbitant Prices of Clothing—Catholic Church—Public Square about four Acres—Semi-Tropical Fruit Trees—Large Reservoir—Duties of Soldiers in Garrison—Regrets at Having to Shave—Reasons assigned—Fleas and Vermin—Only Clothing—R. N. Allred a Non-Commissioned Staff Officer—Sunday Dress Parade—The Drill Commenced—Incident of Drill—Religious Services—Seventies' Meetings—Considered Officious.

The foregoing is, perhaps, sufficient to give the reader a general idea of the situation; hence a return to the Battalion narrative is proper.

On the 31st, of January 1847, the Battalion remained in camp. Several of the men visited the port of San Diego, about five miles west of the Mission. In the evening orders were issued for a return to San Luis Rey. This was an essential precautionary measure to hold the mission as a military post, and that the Battalion might be in readiness to meet whatever emergency might arise, either in arresting Colonel Fremont or aiding to settle by force, if necessary, civil or national difficulties. At the same time they could there keep an important position between Pueblo de Los Angeles and San Diego out of the enemy's hands, in case hostilities were again resumed, which, at the time, and for some time subsequently, seemed quite probable.

Accordingly, on the 1st of February, 1837, the Battalion took up the line of march for San Luis Rey, where we arrived about noon on the 3rd.

On the 4th, about eighty men were detailed as police to clear up the square and quarters and make necessary repairs, which was done in good order, making everything look as cheerful and respectable as our dirt floors would permit. Many of the men were almost naked, without a change of underclothing to keep off dust or the worst of vermin, with which the country abounded and which even many of the *elite* of the native Californians were said to be never free from. What little clothing was in the country was in the hands of army sutlers, and held at such extravagant prices that a short time before our discharge, one of our poets, in a plaintive song, very properly says: "To buy them we are too poor," and adds, "We'll return" (to place of enlistment) "and old clothes burn." That we did so, the reader need not be told.

The public square of the mission, with a large adobe Catholic Church and a row of minor buildings forming the outside wall, contained about four acres of ground, with orange and other tropical trees in the center. The olive, pepper, orange, fig and many other varieties of semi-tropical fruit and ornamental trees grew in the garden. There was also a large reservoir, used for bathing, washing clothes and watering the garden. Two large vineyards were also connected with this mission.

On the 5th, an order was read relating to the duties of the Soldiers when in garrison, such as times of parade, cleaning arms and clothes, shaving, cutting hair, saluting officers, etc., all of which were very good in their way. The only ground for complaint this order afforded, so far as the author heard, was that some who had not shaved since leaving home preferred not to do so until they returned. They were probably desirous that their wives, who had never looked upon their beautiful visages ornamented with a foot, more or less, of what they doubtless supposed to be very comely hair, should have a chance to see the luxuriant growth before it was sacrificed. Perhaps, in some instances the rich growth proved a shield or covering to features not as inviting as might be desired, hence the dread of submitting to the tonsorial operation. But this, like all other military orders, was imperative. It prescribed that no beard be allowed to grow below the tip of the ear; hence the moustache only could be saved. The hair also must be clipped even with the tip of the ear and everything made as neat and tidy as circumstances would permit.

By the 6th of February we had finished cleaning up and repairing our quarters, which, in some respects, were not the most pleasant, as we were overrun with fleas as well as the more filthy vermin, and no person, however cleanly he aimed to be, could escape from them.

The following quotation from the diary of Henry Standage, then a member of the Battalion, will show to what a strait the men were reduced for want of clothes, and also how they managed to wash their scant apparel:

"February 6.—Went into the garden and washed my shirt and a pair of pants, which I had made out of an old wagon cover—all the clothing I had."

After arriving at San Luis Rey, the very able and worthy quartermaster sergeant of company A, Redick N. Allred, was appointed quartermaster sergeant in Colonel Cooke's non-commissioned staff, in which he remained until our final discharge.

During the first Sunday we spent in our new quarters, the Battalion was called out on dress parade. This practice was followed up nearly if not every Sunday until we were discharged.

On the 8th, Colonel Cooke and Lieutenant Stoneman commenced the squad drill with officers, which continued and extended to companies and thence to the Battalion, and lasted altogether for twenty days, when the Battalion was supposed to have learned the drill, and all the officers were considered capable of teaching it. During these exercises, many laughable circumstances occurred, besides some not so agreeable; among the latter was that of a Sergeant being reduced to the ranks for failing to learn the drill, and among the former was the case of a rather nervous lieutenant, who was placed as a sentry on whom to form a line, on change of base. He was directed not to move until the line was formed. As he was "'bout face" to the Battalion, however, as the little army moved, he turned as pivot man to correspond with what he supposed to be the intended movement. The Colonel, discovering this, ran and turned him back and held him a few moments, saying: "Now, Lieutenant ——, I will take my hands off carefully, and see if you can stand still," fitting the action to the word. No sooner were the hands fairly off than the officer again began the usual turn, when the commander left him with the remark, "No, d—d if he can." The Lieutenant must, of course, be nameless in this connection.

While we were in garrison, we made it a rule, when possible, to hold religious services on Sunday, which were frequently presided over by Captain Hunt, but sometimes by Father Pettegrew or Levi W. Hancock. As many of the men of the Battalion were members of the Seventies' quorums, Seventies' meetings were also held occasionally, when circumstances would permit. These were always presided over by Brother Hancock in his capacity as one of the First Presidency of that organization. Brother Hancock was very zealous, and did his best to influence the men to live as their religion taught under every circumstance. He was really deserving of much credit for the zeal and diligence he manifested in his missionary work among his brethren, but it was very apparent that some of the officers regarded his actions as officious, and entertained a feeling of jealousy towards him on that account. He, however, denied the imputation that he was prompted by any other than the best and purest of motives, and he retained the good feelings of the others and his influence among them, notwithstanding the prejudice that existed towards him among those few officers.

CHAPTER XXX.

Company B sent to San Diego—Change of Diet—Religious Services—Sentinel Court-martialed for Sleeping at his Post—Colonel, Dissatisfied with the Meagre Penalty, Remits the Sentence — Barrowman Accepts the Result as an Answer to Prayer—Detachment sent after Wagons—Curious Ox Yokes—Garrison Duties — Lieutenant Stoneman and Detachment sent to San Diego—Reduced to the Ranks—Unsettled Condition of Governorship—Circular from Commodore Shubrick and Proclamation from Kearny—Orders to Fremont to Disband his Forces—His Refusal.

On the 15th of February, company B was ordered to the port of San Diego to garrison that place.

Up to the 19th of February our fare continued to be about the same—fresh beef. Upon that date, however, Lieutenant Oman returned from Roubideau's, whither he had been sent five days previously, with a quantity of unbolted flour and some beans—a most agreeable change of diet. Each man immediately had ten ounces of flour and two-and-a-third gills of beans issued to him per day, and a reduction made in his ration of beef.

News reached us on the 20th that provisions for the army had been brought by Major Swords from the Sandwich Islands. The next day being Sunday, the Colonel's regular day for expeditions, a detachment started for San Diego to bring a supply to our camp. The same day, meeting was called at 11 a. m., when, by special request, Elder Daniel Tyler preached on the importance of revering the name of the Deity and avoiding sin of every kind, and of our duties to each other.

On the 26th, a supply of bolted flour, soap, sugar, coffee and candles, arrived. The same day, John Barrowman, who had been confined at the guard quarters for several days for having been caught asleep while on guard duty, was tried by court martial. The evidence went to show that the man was almost worn out, and had but just been overcome by sleep when he was discovered by the Sergeant, who felt compelled to report him to save his own credit. The sentence was therefore made as light as possible—six days' imprisonment, two hours of each of the first five days in a dark cell, and a stoppage of $3.00 of his pay.

The Colonel was indignant at this meagre penalty, and remitted it.

Three other soldiers plead guilty, before the same court, to killing an Indian's cow, and were sentenced to ten days' imprisonment and a stoppage of $2,50 of their pay to remunerate the Indian for his loss. The Indian was well satisfied with his $7.50, as cows usually sold for about two to four dollars. This last sentence was executed.

Of Barrowman's sentence, the Colonel says: "The sentence of the court in the case of Private John Barrowman is excessively lenient, and the court probably considered some mitigating circumstances which should only have been done in recommending the prisoner to mercy. That the prisoner was brought before a Battalion court martial, instead of a general court martial, whose power of inflicting punishment extended, for this crime, to the life of the criminal, was the exercise of great leniency on the part of the commanding officer, and it will not be repeated. Proceedings, therefore, in this case, are disapproved, and the sentence is remitted."

The commanding officer held the power to mitigate the sentence or annul it, but, very properly, not to increase it. The reader will perceive that the fine was remitted, not out of any sympathy for the exhausted soldier, who had been guilty of dozing on his post, but because the commander had not the power to make the penalty more severe; hence, no further cases of the kind would be intrusted to a Battalion court martial. This was the beginning, and, the author thinks, under the circumstances, very properly the end of court martials.

Brother Barrowman accepted the Colonel's action as a specific and direct answer to prayer, which was doubtless a correct conclusion.

On the 28th (Sunday of course) Lieutenant Samuel Thompson, with ten men, was detached to return to the region of the Colorado, and bring in the wagons left there.

On the 1st of March, a small company of Spaniards and Indians, probably moving to Sonora, camped near our garrison. Some had pack-animals and others ox teams; the ox yokes were straight poles lashed to the back of the oxen's horns with rawhide. The cattle were large and fat and of the same variety as the wild bulls.

The following day an Indian child, killed by the bite of a rattlesnake, was buried according to the rites of the Catholic Church, eight bells being tolled.

Our daily garrison duties were: Roll call at daylight, sick call at 7.30 a. m., breakfast call at 8.40, drill at 10 a. m. and 3 p. m., roll call at sundown, tattoo at 8.30 and taps of the drum at 9 p. m., after which lights must be out except in case of sickness. All must then be silent, and were supposed to retire for the night.

The following order explains itself:

(Orders No. 2.)

"HEAD QUARTERS U. S. FORCES,
SAN LUIS REY,
March 2, 1847.

Authentic information of the withdrawal of all naval forces from the town and harbor of San Diego having been received, Lieutenant Stoneman, with a detachment of thirty-one non-commissioned officers and privates, dismounted men of the First Dragoons, will march to-morrow morning to take the post (formerly occupied by marines and sailors) at San Diego, for the protection of the town and the depot of provisions and other public property. He will take rations for four days, and will make necessary requisitions and provision returns on Major F. Swords, Quartermaster U. S. Army and acting assistant commissary of subsistence.

By order

LIEUT. COL. COOKE,
P. C. MERRILL, Adjutant."

On the 8th, three or four non-commissioned officers were reduced to the ranks for not being experts in learning the drill. Their places were filled from the ranks.

Matters remained in the same unsettled condition in regard to who held authority from the Government of the United States to act as Governor and Commander-in-chief of California. General Kearny had gone to Monterey, and in his absence Colonel Cooke was left to act at his discretion. Writing of the condition of affairs, on the 12th of March, Colonel Cooke says:

"General Kearny is supreme—somewhere up the coast; Colonel Fremont supreme at Pueblo de los Angeles; Commodore Stockton is Commander-in-chief at San Diego; Commodore Shubrick, the same at Monterey, and I at San Luis Rey; and we are all supremely poor, the government having no money and no credit, and we hold the territory because Mexico is poorest of all."

On the 14th of March, however, Major H. S. Turner arrived at San Luis Rey, bearing documents to Colonel Cooke, announcing that Commodore Shubrick, who had arrived at Monterey on the 23rd of January, had issued a circular on the 1st of March, announcing himself as "Commander-in-chief of the naval forces" and General Kearny as "Brigadier General and Governor of California." General Kearny had also issued a proclamation as Governor; it "absolved all the inhabitants of California from any further allegiance to the Republic of Mexico," and announced that they might consider themselves as citizens of the United States, as henceforth Americans and Californians would be one people. Orders were sent at the same time by General Kearny to Lieutenant Colonel Fremont, ordering him to disband his battalion, with the understanding that those desiring it might re-enlist under Colonel Cooke. Accordingly, a courier was sent by Cooke to Fremont, to ascertain what number of men had been mustered into service, to which he received a reply signed by "Governor" Fremont through his "Secretary of State," announcing that none of his men wished to re-enter the public service. He also refused to disband his men, on the pretext that an insurrection was probable. He asked for no aid in view of the prospective insurrection, but added that his "battalion would be amply sufficient for the safety of the artillery and ordnance stores," from which it was inferred that he intended to hold possession of them.

Major Turner returned to General Kearny and reported Fremont's refusal to obey orders, but he was followed up immediately by Fremont himself, who rode post haste to Monterey, and managed to satisfy the General that he was ready to submit to his commands.

On the 15th of March, we received the following:

"(Orders No. 3.)

"(1) Captain Hunter in command of Company B, Mormon Battalion, will march this morning for San Diego. Arrived there, his company will constitute the garison for the protection of the town, and he will take charge of all the defenses of the place.

"(2) Brevet Lieutenant Stoneman, 1st dragoons, will march from San Diego with his detatchment of Company C, 1st dragoons, for this post, on the 17th inst.

"(3) 2nd Lieutenant Clift will proceed without delay to San Diego. He is appointed to receive there such ordnance as shall be turned over to him by officers of the navy. Lieutenant Clift will perform the duties of assistant commissary of subsistence, and assist the quartermaster at San Diego, and receive such subsistence and other property as will be turned over to him by Major Swords, quartermaster, U. S. A.

"P. St. George Cooke.
"Lieut. Col. Commanding."

CHAPTER XXXI.

Complaints of Short Rations—Tale-Bearing Dykes—Sergeant Jones and Corporal Lane Reduced to the Ranks—March to Los Angeles—Cooke Applies for Ordnance and Fails—Four Indians Killed — Captain Hunt's Explanation — Death of David Smith—San Luis Rey Abandoned—Petition for Discharge of Battalion Treated with Contempt by Officers—Arrival of ¦Colonel Mason—Hatred of Fremont's Men towards the Battalion—Cajon Pass Guarded.

Much dissatisfaction among the men was felt about this period in consequence of being kept on short rations of beef as well as bread, when beef was so plentiful and cheap, and some of them even became so indignant over it as to refuse to drill until their rations were increased.

Sergeant N. V. Jones and Corporal Lewis Lane, while in the presence of Lieutenant Dykes, happened to express their disgust at the stingy policy pursued by the officers in this respect, and were promptly reported by that tale-bearing official. The result was the following:

"Orders No. 25.)

"HEAD QUARTERS MORMON BATTALION,
"SAN LUIS REY, March 18th, 1847.

"(1) Sergeant N. V. Jones and Corporal Lewis Lane, of Company D, having been guilty of insubordination and conduct disgraceful to them as non-commisioned officers, they are hereby reduced to the ranks.

"(2) On the recommendation of their Captain commanding, private Abraham Hunsaker is hereby appointed a Sergeant, and private Sanford Jacobs and William Barger are appointed Corporals, all in Company D. They will be obeyed and respected accordingly.

"(3) Pursuant to S. M. D., orders No. 4, of this date, first Lieutenant Oman and Sergeant Brown and nine privates of Company A, eight privates of Comany C, Sergeant Hunsaker and five privates of Company D, and eight privates of Company E, will comprise the detachment which will remain to garrison this post. 1st Lieutenant Oman, in command, will receive such public property as will be left and pay special attention to the safety of public mules. Returns will be made immediately for three additional day's rations, including *no* salt meat. By order,

"Lieut. Col. Cooke, Commanding."

With regard to reducing Sergeant N. V. Jones and Corporal Lewis Lane to the ranks, the Sergeant says for himself, and the same is probably true of Corporal Lane: "He" (Dykes) "carried false reports to the Colonel, and through his false reports broke me of my office, which he had purposed to do from the beginning, and had boasted of it."

The reader should keep in mind the difference between finding fault with officers for real or supposed neglect of duty and finding fault with the government. The former was understood at the time to have been the sole cause of the difficulty, and there were just grounds for complaint, for the best California beef could be procured in large or small quantities for less than one cent per pound on foot; in fact, some could be had for killing and dressing, the owners retaining the hides and tallow.

As will be inferred from the Colonel's order of the 18th, providing for a few men, under Lieutenant Oman, to remain to garrison San Luis Rey, the balance of the Battalion was required to go elsewhere. The fact was, their presence was needed at the Pueblo de Los Angeles, to hold that place, which had formerly been the Mexican capital.

Accordingly, on the 19th, Companies A, C, D and E, took up the line of march for Pueblo de Los Angeles.

We traveled over broken country near the sea shore, and arrived at Pueblo de Los Angeles about noon on the 23rd. This town is near the San Gabriel River. We camped at the eastern edge of the town; the dragoons who came with us, camped in the town.

On the 24th, Colonel Cooke rode to San Gabriel Mission, about eight miles from Los Angeles, where Fremont's battalion was stationed. He found Captain Owens in command, in the absence of Fremont, and both he and the other officers there disclaimed any knowledge of orders having been received for their disbandment or of Commodore Shubrick's circular. They regarded Colonel Fremont as the highest authority in the land, and, as he had left orders on his departure for them not to turn over the ordnance to any one except on his order, Captain Owens refused to let Colonel Cooke have possession of any of the cannon.

There being no provisions to be had at Los Angeles, and the small amount brought with us from San Luis Rey being nearly exhausted, eight mule teams were dispatched for San Diego on the 25th to procure a fresh supply. Before their return, we ran entirely out of food and had to go to bed supperless one night, and fast next morning until eleven o'clock before we got anything to eat.

On the 27th, we removed our camp about one mile north of the town to a beautiful location on the river bottom.

On the 28th, Lieutenant Stoneman, with a detachment of dragoons, returned from following a party of marauding Indians, having killed four of them. These Indians had been raiding on the Californians, and had killed one or two of them.

Colonel Fremont returned to Los Angeles on the 30th, and at a meeting of the Battalion held the same day, Captain Hunt related the circumstances of his giving up the command to Lieutenant Smith, which were about as given in the earlier part of this work. He remarked in substance, that, after stating his right and willingness to take command, he submitted the decision to a council of officers, who voted him out and Smith in. This was the first time the facts had been made public. This speech removed some prejudice.

On the 1st of April, we received news of the death of David Smith, one of our brethren, at San Luis Rey. It was believed by those in attendance that his death was the result of medicine given him by Dr. Sanderson previous to the command leaving that post, as he got worse and so continued from the time of taking the medicine until death relieved him. The two last days previous to his demise, he was speechless. He died as he had lived, true to his God, his country and his religion.

On the 5th, our teams returned heavily laden with provisions, soap, candles, etc. On the next day the following order was issued:

"(Order No. 5.)

"HEAD QUARTERS, SOUTHERN MILITARY DISTRICT,
"CUIDAD DE LOS ANGELES,
"April 6th, 1847.

"The post of San Luis Rey will be discontinued until further orders. 1st Lieutenant, Oman, Mormon Battalion, will march his detachment, composing its garrison, to this city without delay. He will drive here all the public mules and bring with him other public property in his charge.

"P. ST. GEORGE COOKE,
"LIEUT. COL. Commanding."

On the 6th, a petition for the discharge of the Battalion was gotten up and signed by most of the soldiers, on the ground that peace was declared in California and their services could be dispensed with, allowing them to return and aid their outcast families.

A council of officers was called, at which the petition was read and thrown under the table, and not presented to Colonel Cooke and General Kearny, as requested. Captain Daniel C. Davis, and Lieutenants James Pace, Andrew Lytle and Samuel Thompson, favored the petition, while the majority of the commissioned officers favored a universal reenlistment with Captain Jefferson Hunt as Lieutenant Colonel.

General Kearny having sent word to his superiors in office in the east that he was anxious to be relieved of his charge in California as soon as peace was established, Colonel R. B. Mason was sent to succeed him in command; and he, being superior in rank to Fremont, was sent by Kearny to Los Angeles to enforce the discharge of Fremont's battalion and obedience to other orders.

After some difficulty, he finally succeeded in discharging Fremont's men and taking ten pieces of cannon held by them, which were immediately brought to Los Angeles and turned over to Colonel Cooke.

For some reason unknown to us, and certainly without a just cause, the men who composed Fremont's command manifested a great deal of animosity towards the Mormon Battalion. It was currently reported, and was probably true, that Fremont himself did all he could to arouse this ill-feeling, not only among his own men but also among the native population. We were assured by some of the Mexicans that he had told them the "Mormons" were cannibals, and especially fond of eating children. It seemed, too, that the story gained some credence among the natives, for their shyness about approaching near our camp for sometime was attributed by them to this cause.

After Colonel Cooke made the demand upon Fremont's men for ordnance stores, which Captain Owens refused to comply with, and especially after their subsequent discharge, their bitterness towards us seemed to increase. We frequently heard of their threatening to make a raid upon our camp and wipe us out of existence. However, they never attempted to put any such threat into execution, and it was probably as well for them that they did not, as they would have met with a warm reception. A few of the most beligerent of them sought quarrels with some of our men on meeting them in Los Angeles, but beyond this we were not molested by them.

On the 10th, Lieutenant Hulett tendered his resignation to return to his family.

Owing to the fact that the Californians were not allowed to bear arms, the following and other similar orders were issued for their protection from marauding bands of Indians:

"(Orders No. 7.)

"HEAD QUARTERS, SOUTHERN MILITARY DISTRICT,
"LOS ANGELES, April 11th, 1847.

"(1) Company C, Mormon Battalion, will march to-morrow and take post in the canyon pass of the mountains, about forty-five miles eastward of this town. Lieutenant Rosecrans, its commander, will select a spot for his camp as near to the narrowest and most defensible part as the convenience of water, feed and grass will admit of, and, if necessary, effectually to prevent a passage of hostile Indians with or without horses, he will erect a sufficient cover of logs or earth. It will be his duty to guard the pass effectually, and if necessary to send out armed parties, either on foot or mounted, to defend the ranchos in the vicinity, or to attack wandering parties of wild Indians.

"(2) The assistant commissary of subsistance, will take measures to provision this post until further orders.

"P. St. George Cooke,
"Lieut. Col. Commanding.

Agreeably with the foregoing order, Company C took up the line of march for the Cajon Pass on the 12th.

CHAPTER XXXII.

Efficiency of the Battalion—John Allen Excommunicated—Colonel Cooke Orders the Horses, Purchased by Soldiers, Sold at Auction—Fort Erected—War Imminent—Detachments all Called In—Dragoons our Champions—Privilege to Re-enlist Declined—Death of Captain Hunter's Wife—Colonel Stevenson Appointed to Supersede in Command—Letters from Families—News of a Battle—Arrival of General Kearny—He Compliments the Battalion—Skirmish with Indians—A Barbarous Practice Abolished—General Kearney's Address to the Battalion—Detachment to Accompany him to Fort Leavenworth.

From the daily practice in which the Battalion engaged while in garrison, the most of the officers and men became very proficient in military tactics. Colonel Mason, of the 1st dragoons, an experienced officer, gave the Battalion the credit of excelling any volunteers he had ever seen in going through the manual of arms.

On the 18th of April, the members of the various quorums of Seventies, stationed at Los Angeles, assembled about one mile from camp and organized into a mass quorum, with Stephen M. St. John as president, and, among other business, unanimously excommunicated John Allen from the Church of Jesus Christ of Latter-day Saints. He was the hunter mentioned as being lost near the summit of the Rocky Mountains, who joined the Church to get to California as a soldier. His conduct did not entitle him to a place in respectable society of the world, much less in the Church of the Saints.

The labors required of the detachment stationed at Cajon Pass being essential, and the services of company C required at Los Angeles, the following was issued:

"(Orders No. 8.)

"HEAD QUARTERS, SOUTHERN MILITARY DISTRICT,
"LOS ANGELES, April 22nd, 1847.

"(1) 1st Lieutenant Pace, of Mormon Battalion, will march to-morrow morning with twenty-seven non-commissioned officers and men, with rations for thirty days, to the Cajon Pass, where he will relieve Company C, Mormon Battalion, and occupy the same position and perform the same duties of defending the pass from the passage of hostile Indians. He will detach on his arrival a non-commisioned officer and six men, mounted on the horses now at that post, at Mr. Williams' rancho, where they will operate under the guidance of Mr. Williams, on the occasion of hostile Indians showing on the ranchos in the vicinity. This party will take with them their rations and will be supplied with beef by Mr. Williams.

'(2) Lieutenant Rosecrans, commanding Company C, having turned over to Lieutenant Pace the horses, saddles and his instructions, will march with his company the morning after the arrival of the detachment, with all diligence to this post.

"P. ST. GEORGE COOKE,
"LIEUT. COL. Commanding."

A few of Lieutenant Pace's detachment having purchased horses to ride upon the expedition to the Cajon Pass, the Colonel ordered the animals taken from them and sold to the highest bidder. The journals kept by the men which mention this circumstance do not say whether the avails of the sale were given to the owners of the horses or not. The order, although admissible under the military regulations, was looked upon as arbitrary.

Company A was paid off on the 23rd as was also the detachment of Lieutenant Pace, which started the same day to relieve company C. The next day the following was issued:

(Orders No. 9.)

"HEAD QUARTERS S. M. DISTRICT,
LOS ANGELES,
April 24, 1847.

The Mormon Battalion will erect a small fort on the eminence which commands the town of Los Angeles. Company A will encamp on the ground to-morrow forenoon. The whole company will be employed in the diligent prosecution of the labors for one week, but there will be a daily detail of a non-commissioned officer and six privates for the camp guard, which, with the cooks absolutely necessary, will not labor during their detail. The hours of labor will be from half past six o'clock until 12 o'clock, and from 1 o'clock until 6 o'clock. The guard will mount at half past 5 o'clock.

(2) Lieutenant Davidson, First Dragoons, will trace to-morrow on the sight selected, his plan, which has been approved of, a fort with one small bastion, front for at least six guns in barbette, assisted by the company officers. He will have the direction, as superintendent, which pertains to an officer of engineers. As assistant quartermaster, he will procure the necessary tools.

P. ST. GEORGE COOKE,
LT. COL. Commanding."

The 25th of April being Sunday, the Colonel's ever lucky day, or general day to commence marches, company A moved on to the hill, in obedience to the Colonel's order. There were various rumors afloat about an expected attack from the Spaniards and Indians that night. Colonel Cooke directed our officers, especially Captain Hunt, to have the Battalion ready to form a line of battle, at a moment's notice, with loaded guns and fixed bayonets.

We were up most of the following night, owing to the Colonel believing we would be attacked. The enemy did not appear, however, and the remaining portions of the Battalion were ordered to remove to the hill as fast as the companies received their pay.

Company C arrived from the Cajon Pass, having received orders from Colonel Cooke, by express through a dragoon

Corporal, stating that another war seemed imminent. The detachment under Lieutenant Pace also arrived, having been ordered back by an express, the Colonel very properly withdrawing all protection until he had assurance that the conditions of the armistice, already detailed, would be kept by the Californians, and until they and Fremont's men ceased their threats. They were also given to understand that in case they came upon us no prisoners would be taken. They, of course, understood what that meant. The instructions to the Battalion were to the same effect: "Take no prisoners—show no quarter, nor ask any."

Our position on the hill commanded Los Angeles, upon which our artillery would have played to good advantage, and the city would doubtless have been destroyed; but with the prospect of the Mexicans again rising and the low murmurings of civil war hardly ceasing to salute our ears, what the end would have been is difficult to say.

What few dragoons there were, were true to their country and to the Battalion, and none of the latter could be insulted with impunity in the hearing of the former. When bullies came into the town and began to impose upon the "Mormon boys," the dragoons would not allow them to take their own part if they could avoid it, but would say: "Stand back; you are religious men, and we are not; we will take all of your fights into our hands," and with an oath would say: "You shall not be imposed upon by them." Several instances of the kind might be named, but it is not deemed necessary.

Company A commenced work immediately upon their arrival at the new camping place, at excavating the ground for the fort, and the work was afterwards prosecuted by twenty-eight men from each company, who were relieved every fourth day.

On the 29th, twenty-eight volunteers came in from Santa Barbara, bringing us some ammunition.

On the 4th of May, an order was read from Colonel Cooke, giving the Battalion the privilege of being discharged on condition of enlisting for five years as U. S. dragoons; but under the circumstances, the generous proposition could not consistently be accepted.

On the 5th, news arrived of the death of the wife of Captain Jesse D. Hunter, at San Diego, which sad event occurred on the 27th ult. The funeral discourse was preached by Elder Wm. Hyde. She was a very estimable lady and faithful Latter-day Saint. She left a male child about two weeks old.

An order was read the same day from General Kearny, appointing Colonel Stevenson, of the New York volunteers, to the command of the southern district of California, thus relieving Colonel Cooke, that he might return to the United States with General Kearny. We also learned that two companies of Stevenson's command were ordered to Los Angeles.

On the 8th, an express arrived from Santa Fe and the United States, bringing some letters to the Battalion from Nauvoo and Council Bluffs; also news of a severe battle between United States dragoons and Navajo Indians, which lasted three days. Twenty-eight dragoons were reported killed. Governor Bent, of Santa Fe, was also reported killed. The Indians were defeated with heavy loss.

This day we received the following order, which was promptly executed:

(Orders No. 3.)

"HEAD QUARTERS, LOS ANGELES,
May 8, 1847.

Lieutenant Thompson, with twenty men of the Mormon Battalion, rationed for three days, will march immediately to a rancho, within six miles of the foot of the mountain and use every effort to destroy the hostile Indians reported to be in the vicinity. A guide will be furnished.

P. ST. GEORGE COOKE,
LT. COL. Commanding."

On the 9th, General Kearny arrived at Los Angeles from Monterey. A salute of twenty-one guns was fired. Colonel Stevenson and other officers of note accompanied him. The General came to our camp and gave some good advice to those with whom he conversed.

He remarked to an officer, that history might be searched in vain for an infantry march equal to that performed by the Battalion, all circumstances considered, and added: "Bonaparte crossed the Alps, but these men have crossed a continent."

The following order explains itself:
(Order No. 10.)

"HEAD QUARTERS,
SOUTHERN MILITARY DISTRICT,
LOS ANGELES,
May 9, 1847.

The commanding officer at San Diego will employ a physician for attendance on that garrison. Assistant Surgeon I. S. Griffin, U. S. A., will report himself for duty at this post, without unnecessary delay.

P. ST. GEORGE COOKE,
LT. COL. Commanding."

Lieutenant Samuel Thompson, of company C, and party, who had proceeded to rout the Indians, according to the Colonel's order, surprised a small band in a cove in the mountains, killing six of them. F. T. Mayfield and George Chapin, two of his men, were slightly wounded—Mayfield in the groin, Chapin under the eye, both with arrows. One Spaniard, who accompanied them, was also slightly wounded. The Spaniard ran, unobserved, and scalped and took off the ears of the dead Indians. Under the California rule, a premium was given for wild Indians' scalps. This barbarous custom, however, was there and then abolished, and the Alcalda forbidden to pay any bounty on those referred to, or any others in the future. The Lieutenant commanding, as well as the men, were horrified and disgusted at the Spaniard's atrocity.

On the 10th, the Battalion was addressed by General Kearny. He dwelt at some length upon our arduous journey, our patriotism to the Government, obedience to orders, etc. In short, no commander ever did or could eulogize or give a greater meed of praise to any corps of veterans than was given this little band by the commander of the Army of the West. He sympathized with us in the unsettled condition of our people, but thought, as their final destination was not definitely settled, we had better re-enlist for another year, by which time the war would doubtless be ended and our families settled in some permanent location. In conclusion, he said he would take pleasure in representing our patriotism to the President and in the halls of Congress, and give us the justice our praiseworthy conduct had merited.

Three men were detailed from each company as an escort, to accompany the General to Fort Leavenworth, the names of whom, it is to be regretted, are not available, and cannot, therefore, be here given.

CHAPTER XXXIII.

Company B at San Diego—Building a Fort—Religious Services—Literary Club—Cheap Animals—"Herding Stallions"—Death of Albert Dunham—"Stocks"—Miserable Mobocrat—Fossil Remains—Wedding—Immoral Priest—Soldiers Seeking Work—News of General Taylor's Victory—Colonel Stevenson's Arrival and Address—Lieutenant Clift Appointed Alcalde—First Brick Made in California—Fourth of July Celebrated—Citizens of San Diego Petition to have the "Mormon" Soldiers Remain—Song—Return to Los Angeles.

The General, and party, started on their return trip on the 13th.

Leaving the main army on the hill, it will now be in order to give an account of company B, who left the Battalion at San Luis Rey, on the 15th of March. This company was ordered to relieve the dragoons, about thirty in number, under the command of Lieutenant Stoneman, to garrison the place until further orders. The company arrived and the dragoons left for San Luis Rey on the 17th.

Next day Sergeant Hyde was appointed to take eighteen men and quarter in the fort built by the marines, on an eminence about one-fourth of a mile from the town. This fort was constructed by digging a trench on the summit of a hill, and placing a row of large logs around the same. Against these gravel and rock were thrown up, thus forming a barricade, which was thought to be invulnerable. Seventeen pieces of artillery were so arranged as to command the town and surrounding country.

Religious services were held by the detachment every Sunday, which were generally well attended by strangers, and Lieutenant Wm. Hyde, and others, delivered a number of excellent discourses and lectures, which gave general satisfaction to all parties. A society was also organized, entitled the Young Men's Club, for the purpose of lecturing, reciting, declaiming, debating, etc., a kind of Young Men's Mutual Improvement Association.

A report being in circulation that the people of Sonora were landing arms on the coast and making other preparations for war, and that a large army was on the north side of the Colorado river, the frigate *Congress* sailed about the 29th to prevent their encroachments.

On the 4th of May, the company received six months' pay, the most of which was expended, by each individual, in purchasing animals, clothing, etc., as an outfit for the return trip. It was exceedingly fortunate for the Battalion that horses and mules were so very cheap. Wild mares were from three to four dollars each, those broken, to ride, from six to twelve dollars. Gentle mares, however, seldom brought more than seven or eight dollars. Horses, unbroken, were from six to eight dollars, horses, broken to ride, from ten to twenty dollars. Good herding stallions were worth about fifty dollars each, and mules were worth about double the price of common horses.

It may be well here to explain what is meant by "herding stallions." Each band of horses running at large in a semi-wild state usually had one powerful stallion—a leading spirit among his fellows, which fought the battles for the band and also kept the animals together by chasing and biting those that lagged behind or attempted to stray away. It sometimes occurred that lame or decripid animals were bitten and kicked in a most shocking manner and occasionally even killed by these stallions. The band presided over by a stallion usually numbered about two hundred.

At 1 o'clock a. m., on the 11th, private Albert Dunham died; his death was caused by an ulcer on the brain. His sickness was only of two or three days' duration. He was buried beside Captain Hunter's wife.

The Indians, who were located about San Diego, occasionally stole each other's wives. When caught, they were put in the stocks for a few days, and sometimes weeks, as a punishment. The stocks consisted of two hewn logs, one above the other, with semicircles cut in each so as to form a round hole, when joined together, large enough to go around the neck, and another smaller on each side in which to place the legs. To put culprits in, the top log had to be raised, and, after the head and feet had been put in place, it was again lowered and secured, leaving the head and feet on one side and the body on the other, resting on the ground. Sometimes only the head, and at others, only the feet, were put in the stocks.

Many of the Californian ladies dressed in silks and satins, and were exceedingly fair. As a rule, however, their reputation for morality and virtue was not the best.

Near the foreigners' burying ground resided a miserable specimen of humanity, who stole and begged from door to door. He was one of the most forlorn of human beings. He acknowledged to having been engaged in the Haun's Mill massacre, and begged our people to forgive him. He claimed to have been one of Fremont's party, and said he had been among the Rocky Mountains for the last seven years.

Samuel Miles, of the Battalion, was selected as a man of legal ability and some knowledge of American law, while he remained at San Diego, to aid the Mexican alcalde, or justice of the peace, in administering the laws of the United States by getting up papers, etc., which he did to the satisfaction of the Governor, to whom all legal proceedings were submitted for approval. This is understood to have been the first administration of civil law in lower California.

An interesting fossil discovery was made on the beach by H. W. Bigler and others—the skeleton of a whale; the ribs of which were nine feet long and ten inches broad. They were bleached white, hence were very light. Two were taken to the garrison and used for seats.

On the 18th, a marriage occurred in the town, the parties to which were a sea captain and a Spanish lady. The ceremony was performed by a Catholic Priest. Cannon and musketry were fired, while the wedding procession was marching. Feasting and drinking were kept up all night. Sometimes such parties were kept up three or four days and nights in succession, and the newly married couple not allowed to sleep during that time. Such weddings frequently cost from $300 to $800. The bridegroom had all the expenses to pay.

The priest of San Diego was said to have no wife, but was the father of seventeen children. He also had the reputation of being a drunken sot, and profane in his language.

The company being permitted to take jobs of work, such as making adobes, burning brick, building houses, digging wells, and performing various other kinds of mechanical labor, many availed themselves of the chance to earn something.

A letter from San Francisco to Sergeant Hyde, received on the 30th, stated that the Saints who sailed from New York, on the ship *Brooklyn*, had arrived and sown 145 acres of wheat, and that Samuel Brannan had gone to meet the Saints at or near the Great Salt Lake.

On the 14th of June, news of General Taylor's victory in Mexico arrived, and twenty rounds of artillery were fired, and the General cheered long and loud.

On the 22nd, Colonel Stevenson arrived from Los Angeles, and the following day addressed the company. He spoke in the highest terms of the industry and morals of the Battalion and of their good reputation among the Californians, and expressed a great desire to have the men re-enlist, especially the young ones. Captain Hunter followed in a short speech, in which he offered to re-enlist, for six months, on condition that the Colonel would grant the company, at the expiration of the term, pay and rations to San Francisco Bay or Bear River Valley, which proposal the Colonel readily accepted, also promising that a small detachment should be sent to meet the families, and act as pioneers for them if necessary. He further promised, that those who remained in San Diego should have the privilege of continuing to obtain work and earn money whenever off duty.

On the 24th, Lieutenant Robert Clift was appointed alcalde for the post.

On the 29th, H. W. Bigler and others cleared the first yard for moulding brick in San Diego, and, indeed, the first in

California. The labor was performed for a Californian, named Bandena. Philander Colton and Rufus Stoddard laid up and burnt the kiln. About this time, G. W. Taggart made a quantity of pack-saddles for the return trip.

On the 4th of July, the roar of cannon at daybreak announced the seventieth anniversary of our nation's birth. Henry W. Bigler's journal of this date, in substance, says of the celebration: "These demonstrations pleased the citizens so well that they brought out all the wine and brandy we wanted, and a hundred times more."

In the evening, Captain Jesse D. Hunter and Colonel Stevenson, with Sergeant Hyde and Corporal Horace M. Alexander, who had been to Los Angeles, arrived and were heartily cheered. The prominent citizens of the town were also enthusiastically greeted, which pleased them much. They sincerely regretted that the company were going to leave them. Mrs. Bandena, one of the most prominent ladies of the town, in an address, requested that the company take the American flag with them, as there would be no one left to defend it. Her's was a brief, but touching and patriotic speech.

SONG.

BY AZARIAH SMITH.

Composed when quartered at San Diego, in the service of the United States.

In forty-six we bade adieu
To loving friends and kindred too:
For one year's service, one and all
Enlisted at our country's call,
    In these hard times.

We onward marched until we gained
Fort Leavenworth, where we obtained
Our outfit—each a musket drew—
Canteen, knapsack, and money, too,
    In these hard times.

Our Colonel died—Smith took his place,
And marched us on at rapid pace;
O'er hills and plains, we had to go,
Through herds of deer and buffalo,
    In these hard times.

O'er mountains and through valleys too—
We town and villages went through;
Through forests dense, with mazes twined,
Our tedious step we had to wind,
    In these hard times.

At length we came to Santa Fe,
As much fatigued as men could be;
With only ten days there to stay,
When orders came to march away,
    In these hard times.

Three days and twenty we march'd down
Rio Del Norte, past many a town;
Then changed our course—resolved to go
Across the mountains, high or low,
    In these hard times.

We found the mountains very high,
Our patience and our strength to try;
For, on half rations, day by day,
O'er mountain heights we made our way,
    In these hard times.

Some pushed the wagons up the hill,
Some drove the teams, some pack'd the mules,
Some stood on guard by night and day,
Lest haplessly our teams should stray,
    In these hard times.

We traveled twenty days or more,
Adown the Gila River's shore—
Crossed o'er the Colorado then,
And marched upon a sandy plain,
    In these hard times.

We thirsted much from day to day,
And mules were dying by the way,
When lo! to view, a glad scene burst,
Where all could quench our burning thirst,
    In these hard times.

We traveled on without delay,
And quartered at San Luis Rey;
We halted there some thirty days,
And now are quartered in this place,
    In these hard times.

A "Mormon" soldier band we are:
May our great Father's watchful care
In safety kindly guide our feet,
Till we, again, our friends shall meet,
    And have good times.

O yes, we trust to meet our friends
Where truth its light to all extends—
Where love prevails in every breast,
Throughout the province of the blest,
    And have good times.

Orders were immediately given for the company to be in readiness to march to Los Angeles and join the remainder of the Battalion, preparatory to being discharged on th 16th.

It is proper to state here that the company, having greatly improved the town, as well as being peaceful, honest, industrious and virtuous, the citizens plead with them in the strongest terms not to leave. They had dug from fifteen to twenty good wells, the only ones in the town, several of which were walled with brick, besides building brick houses, including a court-house, to be used for courts, schools, etc. They had paved some of the sidewalks with brick, while some, being house carpenters, had done the finishing work on the inside.

On the 6th, the citizens of San Diego sent an express to P. St. George Cooke, commander of the southern military district, requesting that another company of "Mormons" be immediately sent to take the place of Company B, stating that they did not wish any other soldiers quartered there.

Up to the time of the company leaving San Diego, Philander Colton, Henry Wilcox, Rufus Stoddard and William Garner had burnt forty thousand brick. Sidney Willis had also made several log pumps and put them into wells, which gave universal satisfaction.

On the 9th, Company B took up the line of march for Los Angeles, at which place they arrived on the 15th, and took position in line.

It will now be proper to return to a consideration of the main army, which our narrative left on the hill on the 13th of May.

CHAPTER XXXIV.

Slaughter of Dogs—"Dancing Bill"—Detachment to San Pedro—Accident to John Spidle—Soap Factory—John Allen Drummed out of Service—Fate of Hastings' Company—Liberty Pole—Celebration of St. John's Day—Colonel Stevenson's Speech and Invitation to Re-enlist—Other Speeches Pro and Con—Conditions for Re-enlistment Rejected by Colonel Stevenson—Liberty Pole Raised—The Glorious Fourth—Bull Fight—Battalion Discharged—Paid Off—Some Re-enlist.

On the 4th and 5th of June, a number of the soldiers stationed at Los Angeles, by order of the Colonel, engaged in killing dogs, with which the town was overrun.

The 6th being Sunday, the Californians spent it, as they usually did the Sabbath, in horse racing.

On the 7th, "Dancing Bill," a prisoner at guard quarters, exchanged clothing with a squaw who brought him refreshments, and passed out at the door to make his escape. Henry Standage, who was guard No. 1, suspecting that all was not right, hailed the would-be squaw, in whose person he soon recognized the prisoner. He was turned over to the Corporal of the guard, who placed him in the back room, not, however, until he had made many threats and curses against the "Mormon" sentinel.

On the 10th, a small detachment was sent to San Pedro, to guard military stores.

On the 11th, letters were received by express from General Kearny's escort, advising us to purchase our animals at Los Angeles, they being much cheaper there than at Monterey. We also learned that the General had left Monterey for Washington on the 31st of May.

The same day, various orders were read, one relating to the case of John Allen, who had been several weeks in the guard house for deserting his post when on picket guard during the time of an expected insurrection. He was the man already mentioned as having been excommunicated from the Church of the Saints by the mass quorum of Seventies. On being court-martialed and found guilty of deserting his post, he was sentenced to have one-half his head shaved and be drummed out of the service and town at the point of the bayonet. He was also ordered by Colonel Stevenson, through Lieutenant George P. Dykes, not to return within two miles of the town during the existing war, under pain of being put in irons and retained thus until peace was declared. This order was given in consequence of personal threats of violence made by Allen, who was a notorious desperado.

On the 12th, John Spidle was thrown from his horse and badly hurt, but subsequently recovered.

At this period, several of the men were in the country on furlough, laboring for provisions for the return trip, mostly in the harvest field, this being the usual time for cutting grain in California. They were engaged by a Mr. Williams, who had about one thousand acres of wheat to cut. His staple crop was wheat, although he raised some barley, beans, peas, etc., and had large vineyards. He claimed to have owned about one thousand five hundred head of cattle at the commencement of the war. That number, however, was not extraordinary for ranchmen in that country. Owners of stock recognized their animals only by their brands. Common cattle sold for from one to five dollars per head, and good work oxen, well broken, from thirty to fifty dollars per yoke. Thousands of head of beef cattle were butchered merely for their hides and tallow, leaving the meat on the ground. A few years previous, the citizens turned out *en masse*, and killed cattle and horses by the thousands, leaving them upon the ground, because the country was so overrun with stock that they were compelled to lessen the number or have all die of starvation. They created an unbearable stench all over the country for months after the killing.

Much of the tallow obtained from the slaughtered animals was used in the soap factories, while the balance, with the hides, was shipped to the eastern and southern markets. Mr. Williams had a soap factory, conducted about as follows:

Over a furnace was placed a boiler about ten feet deep; and the same in diameter, the upper part made of wood. This was filled with tallow and the fattest of the meat. A little water was also poured into it and then the whole tried out, after which the grease was dipped into a box about ten or twelve feet square. The meat was then thrown away. Mineral earth was then leached like ashes, the lye obtained from it and the grease put together and boiled into soap. The best quality of soap, when made, was almost as white as snow. Indians usually did the work. Every ranchman had a general herdsman to look after his stock.

On the 14th, the sentence of the notorious John Allen was executed. He was marched between four sentinels, in charge of a corporal, with martial music in the rear. He was escorted through town at the point of the bayonet, while the musicians played the "rogue's march."

On the 25th, we received information of the terrible suffering of Captain Hastings' company of emigrants, many of whom perished in the Sierra Nevada Mountains the previous winter. The survivors subsisted for some time on the bodies of the dead.

On the 17th, John Allen was retaken prisoner at the ranchoree, a villa, about one mile-and-a-half from Los Angeles, and placed in the guard house, from which he subsequently escaped by digging a hole through an adobe wall.

On the 18th, a number of men returned from the mountains with a liberty pole for the fort. It consisted of two large pine logs, each fifty feet long; the hauling cost one hundred dollars, the cutting and other expenses about the same.

The same day, an order was read from the Colonel, calling for volunteers to re-enlist for six months. None responded. Fears were entertained by some that the Battalion would be pressed into the service for six months longer. Under the military regulations, this could have been done, if deemed necessary, to give the government time to bring on other troops.

The 20th being Sunday, meeting was held as usual. Excellent remarks were made by Father Pettegrew, Levi W. Hancock, Lieutenant Holman and others. One of the principal topics was our return to hunt up and relieve, as far as possible, our outcast, disfranchised families, and the Saints generally.

While Colonel Stevenson was absent at San Diego, visiting Company B, considerable anxiety was felt by the Battalion for his safety, as threats of personal violence had been made against him by some of the New York volunteers of his command.

The 27th of June being St. John's Day, was observed, as usual, as a holiday by Californians, or Mexicans, and Indians. Horce-racing bull-fighting, gambling, etc., were among the amusements of the day.

The same day, Lieutenants Andrew Lytle and James Pace were jointly elected by acclamation, as captains of hundreds, to lead back those who intended to return to their families that year.

On the 28th, Colonel Stevenson returned From San Diego, accompanied by Captain Hunter, Sergeant Hyde and Corporal Alexander.

On the 29th, at 8:30 a. m., the assembly call was beaten and the Battalion responded. An address was then delivered by Colonel Stevenson, in substance as follows: "The Spaniards are whipped but not conquered. Your term of service will soon close. It is of the utmost importance that troops be kept here until others can be transported. I have the right to press you into the service for six months longer, if deemed necessary, and have no doubt but I would be sustained in so doing, but believing, as I do, that enough, if not all, will re-enlist without, I have decided not to press you to serve longer. I am required to make a strong effort to raise at least one company, and the entire Battalion if possible. If the whole Battalion, or even four companies, enlist, you shall have the privilege of electing your own Lieutenant Colonel, Major and all subordinate officers. Your commander will be the third in rank in California. Should either of his superior officers die or be removed, he would be second in command, and should both be removed, he would be first—military governor and commander-in-chief of California. I sympathize with you in the condition of your families. I am a father—I have been a husband. Should you re-enlist, you shall be discharged in February with twelve months' pay, and in the meantime, a small detachment shall be sent, if necessary, to pilot your families to any point where they may wish to locate. Your patriotism and obedience to your officers have done much towards removing the prejudice of the government and the community at large, and I am satisfied that another year's service would place you on a level with other communities."

The Colonel, in this last remark, might be compared to the heifer that gave a good bucketful of milk and then kicked it over. It was looked upon as an insult added to the injuries we had received without cause. We could challenge comparison with the world for patriotism and every other virtue, and did not care to give further sacrifice to please pampering demagogues.

At the close of the Colonel's remarks, we were dismissed into the hands of our officers to hear speeches from them at such time and place as might be designated. We met at ten a. m., on a barren point, a quarter of a mile west of the fort.

Captain Hunter supposed he was looked upon by the brethren as a recruiting officer; he believed it to be the duty of the Battalion to re-enter the service and serve another term, giving various reasons.

Captain Hunt endorsed the remarks of Captain Hunter. He urged the necessity of maintaining the ground we had gained. As an oppotunity was now presented to gain still more, we should embrace it, by electing from our number an officer, who would be third in command in California, with a chance of his becoming first, through Colonel Mason and Colonel Stevenson being called away. His speech was in the main, a reiteration of that of Colonel Stevenson already given.

Captain Davis, in a brief speech, gave his assent to all that had been said on the subject.

Lieutenant Canfield, thought we had better enlist, in order that we might have some means to take to our families, as at present, it would take all of our pay for an outfit, and on finding the Church, we would have nothing. Some thought they could live on faith, but he believed that if we did not have something to live on besides faith, we would perish.

Lieutenant Dykes, sanctioned all that had been said, and, then, illustrating by his actions the fable of the heifer kicking over the good pail of milk, argued that all we had done, would be lost unless we served another term.

Father Pettegrew made a few remarks, stating that he thought it our duty to return and look after our outcast families; others could do as they thought best, but he believed we had done all we set out to do, and that our offering was accepted and our return would be sanctioned by our Church leaders.

The sun beat down so heavily upon us, that the meeting adjourned to "the big tent" in the fort. After a few brief speeches were made, Captain Hunter, Captain Davis and Father Pettegrew were chosen a committee to draft conditions of re-enlistment. The last named, asked to be excused from acting, as his views were well understood as not favoring the move, but those who had treated lightly his fatherly counsels, of whom there were a few, both officers and men, insisted that he should remain. The articles were soon drafted, and a few more speeches were made.

Sergeant Hyde, in a mild yet forcible manner, said we had made one offering, which he felt assured was accepted, and he thought we should now return and be ready for any sacrifice which might be necessary to make in the future. All, so far as we had any knowledge, were satisfied with our past year's service, and he believed God was satisfied.

Sergeant Tyler, reviewed some of the leading remarks of Colonel Stevenson, Captain Hunt and other officers on the point of first, second and third in command in California. He referred to the pledges of Colonel Allen, who repeatedly assured the Battalion that in case of his death or removal, the command would fall upon the senior officer of this corps. The sad event of that noble officer's death, had shown the Battalion that while a senior officer might be removed by death or otherwise, *our* commander might also be removed, and we be left without any rank in the command of California, and the chances were two to one against us. Where was the realization of those pledges? So far as our officers taking the command was concerned, instead of that, were not our noses put upon the grindstone, and were they not still there? Those who wished, could remain, but he felt it a duty he owed the Church as well as his family to return.

After a few other remarks were made, mainly by way of personal explanations, the meeting adjourned *sine die*. At the close of the meeting, a call was made for volunteers, and some fifteen or sixteen names were given, after which the terms were presented to Colonel Stevenson, and were by him rejected.

On the 1st of July, the liberty pole was raised, without an accident or any inebriety.

On the 4th, the entire command of the place assembled under Colonel Stevenson, in the fort, at sunrise. The "Star-Spangled banner," was played by the New York volunteer band, while the colors were being raised. Nine cheers were given for the stars and stripes, and "Hail Columbia" was played by the band, after which thirteen guns were fired by the first dragoons. The companies were then marched back to their quarters.

At eleven a. m., the command was again called out, under arms, and the dragoons and the Battalion paraded inside the fort. Many Californians and Indians were present to witness the ceremonies. The Declaration of Independence was read by our worthy quartermaster, Lieutenant Stoneman, of the 1st dragoons, "Hail Columbia," was again played by the band, and Colonel Stevenson made a brief and appropriate speech, giving the fortification the name of Fort Moore, in honor of the brave Captain, whose unfortunate death has already been mentioned. The band then played "Yankee Doodle," followed by a patriotic song by Musician Levi W. Hancock, of the Battalion and a march tune by the band, after which Colonel Stevenson proposed to have the Declaration of Independence read, if the Californians desired it, in the Spanish language, but the offer was respectfully declined.

The soldiers were each treated to a glass of wine, marched to their quarters, and dismissed. Thus ended the ceremonies of the day.

On the morning of the 6th, the Battalion, on invitation, attended the funeral services of a soldier of the 1st dragoons, who died the previous evening at the hospital. He was buried with the honors of war. Being a member of the Catholic church, he was interred in the cemetery belonging to that sect.

On the evening of the 9th of July, the town was illuminated in honor of Roman Catholic festivities, and the next day a Mexican bull fight occurred on the flat near the town. It was supposed to be a ruse on the part of the Californians to draw the Battalion from the fort, that they might obtain possession, secure the arms and ammunition and gain control of the country. The Battalion, accordingly, remained in the fort, from which point the men could view the sports below the hill, almost as well as if they had been present. At night the cannons were loaded and placed in position, and the men lay on their arms, prepared to form a line of battle at a moment's warning. Besides the bull fight, a grand ball was gotten up and the Battalion especially invited to attend. The best music and seemingly every other attraction was offered to induce us to leave the fort, but we did not take the bait.

The bull fight also continued during the 11th, and closed on the 12th. Expert Californians, mounted on spirited horses, fought the bulls with spears or lances. Several horses were killed and their riders saved by their comrades throwing blankets over the bulls' heads to blindfold them while the dismounted men escaped from the corral. Two men were considerably hurt, and a little boy of Captain Daniel C. Davis', a spectator of the scene, was thrown about twenty feet by a bull, but not seriously injured. This bull had broken from the corral, and caught the boy on his horns and threw him out of his way while making his escape. General Pico took an active part in these exercises, and the barbarous scenes were witnessed by several hundred people.

On the 15th, Company B arrived from San Diego, preparatory to being discharged, and the next day at three o'clock, p. m., the five companies of the Battalion were formed according to the letter of the company, with A in front and E in the rear, leaving a few feet of space between. The notorious Lieutenant, A. J. Smith, then marched down between the lines in one direction and back between the next lines, then in a low tone of voice said: "You are discharged." This was all there was of the ceremony of mustering out of service this veteran corps of living martyrs to the cause of their country and religion. None of the men regretted the Lieutenant's brevity; in fact, it rather pleased them.

On the 17th and 18th, some of the companies drew their pay and, on the 20th, one company made up from the discharged Battalion, re-enlisted for six months and elected Captain Daniel C. Davis, former Captain of Company E, to command them. The object of their enlistment was to garrison the post of San Diego.

CHAPTER XXXV.

Travels of General Kearny's Escort to Monterey—Kearny's Arrival—Fremont Under Arrest—Overland Journey Commenced—Incidents of Travel—Costume of Digger Indians—Losses in Fording a River—Visits from Brethren—Sacramento Valley—Remains of the Ill-fated Emigrants—A Horrible Scene—Bury the Bones—Accidental Shooting—Nude Indians—Boiling Springs—Pass Soda Springs and Bear Lake Valley—Meet Companies of the Saints—Arrival at Fort Leavenworth and Discharge—Fremont Put in Irons.

Leaving this company now for awhile, as well as the balance of the discharged Battalion, we will follow the fortunes of General Kearny and his escort.

General Kearny left Los Angeles on the 13th of May, 1847, accompanied by Colonel Cooke and three men of the escort chosen, to proceed by water to Monterey. The other nine men of the escort, under Lieutenant Stoneman, were left to proceed overland and meet them at Monterey.

The party traveling by land, made twenty miles the first day and encamped by two springs, which were about six feet apart, one of which was hot and the other cold. The fifth day out, they arrested a soldier, and the next day another, both deserters from Monterey. On the 18th, they ascended a mountain through a rain cloud to fair weather above. No other incidents of importance occurred during the journey to Monterey, at which place they arrived about noon on the 25th. They were immediately quartered in a building formerly occupied by Colonel Stevenson's regiment. They found that General Kearny and party who sailed from San Diego, and who expected to reach Monterey before them, had not yet arrived, and that Colonel Fremont was held there under arrest, though not in confinement, for disobedience to the orders of his superiors, and assuming the title of commander-in-chief and governor of California.

Sergeant Jones, one of the party, mentions in his diary an instance of the sagacity of goats, that came under his observation during his stay in Monterey. While walking along the wharf, he noticed two of these animals, which ran bleating from vessel to vessel until they reached their own boat, which they appeared to recognize at once.

To pass away the time, the detachment went on board of the man-of-war, *Columbus*, which carried seventy-four guns and seven hundred sailors and mariners. The frigate, *Congress*, arrived there on the 27th, as did also the sloop *Lexington*, bearing among her passengers, General Kearny and Colonel Cooke.

The next day the detachment drew seventy-five days' rations, and on the 31st took up its line of march. The journey, during the first few days, lay through beautiful valleys, abounding with luxuriant grass, including the varieties known as timothy and clover, in their wild state, also wild oats. Numerous bands of wild horses were found, and many streams difficult to cross were encountered. In some instances, the men carried their packs on their heads while crossing the rivers to keep them from getting wet. In other cases, they rowed the luggage across the streams in a rawhide boat, which they carried along for the purpose, packing it upon a mule between the streams. As they advanced, they found the grass become more scant and dry, in consequence of the drouth. While traveling, on the 9th of June, they learned of a company of Saints, some of those who sailed on the ship *Brooklyn*, being located only six miles from their line of travel, but the men did not have time to visit them. The Digger Indians abounded in the region through which they traveled, and they saw many of them. These natives lived mainly on seeds and roots, and their only clothing consisted of a wisp of grass fastened around the loins.

While crossing a river on the 11th, Colonel Cooke lost everything he had except the clothing he wore, including a journal of five hundred pages, containing a diary of the travels of the Battalion from Sant Fe to Los Angeles, one hundred dollars in gold and his entire outfit of rations. One of his men also lost everything. The Colonel's journal was subsequently found by an Indian.

The next day, they entered the most beautiful valley they had seen in California, where a few American families were located, and where they found the first field of corn they had seen in the country. They learned that an express from the Church to the Saints in that country, had arrived in Upper California. The few Saints referred to, had sailed around Cape Horn from New York, on the ship *Brooklyn*. It was also learned that Samuel Brannan had started east across the Sierra Nevada and Rocky Mountains to meet the Pioneers and pilot them through to California. A Brother Rhodes, who emigrated to California the previous October, from Missouri, visited the General's camp in the evening.

On nearing the Sacramento river, on the 13th, they were also visited by another brother. A number of American settlers were located in the Sacramento valley. Sutter's Fort, at which about twenty-five soldiers were stationed, was about one mile and a half from the crossing of the river.

On the 14th, they received one additional horse each for the journey. During that day and the next they also dried some beef and baled some flour and pork. The Sacramento valley, at that time, had a very inviting appearance, and the soil appeared as good as any in the world. Mechanical and other labor was very high-priced and scarce. Good land could be obtained for twenty-five cents per acre under Mexican title, and a great proportion of the land was open to squatters. Wheat was worth one dollar per bushel.

On the 20th, while traveling over mountains which, in many places, were covered with snow they found vegetation just starting upon patches of bare ground. Passing through Bear valley, they found a deserted cabin which had been built by Missouri emigrants the previous fall, and in which they had left many of their goods.

On the 21st, they traveled through snow from two to twelve feet deep and over rough mountains before reaching the Truckee river. There a small lake was found about one mile wide and three miles long, now called Lake Tahoe. In the vicinity of this lake were several cabins built by that portion of Captain Hastings' company, which was snowed in the previous fall. Their numbers were estimated at about eighty souls, who all perished except about thirty.

The General ordered a halt and detailed five men to bury the dead that were lying upon the ground. One of the men was said to have lived four months on human flesh and brains. Their bodies were mangled in a horrible manner. This place is known as Cannibal Camp. Colonel Fremont passed the General and party at this place. It was the first time the party had seen him since leaving Sutter's Fort. After they had buried the bones of the dead, which were sawed and broken to pieces for the purpose of obtaining the marrow, they set fire to the cabin and left the horrible place.

From that point the party traveled seven miles farther, and encamped within one mile of another cabin, where more dead bodies were found. The General did not, however, order them buried.

On the 22nd, —— Quigley, one of the party, accidentally shot himself through the arm, inflicting a severe wound.

On the 26th, the party encamped by an Indian village, which consisted of wigwams of brush. The Inhabitants numbered about two hundred, some of whom fled to the mountains and others skulked in the brush. Some of them came to the camp a short time afterwards. Both men and women were naked.

The next day, after traveling a considerable distance over a sandy desert, a hot spring was reached, which threw up a column of boiling water from four to six feet high. The water boiled up and ran off at the rate of about one barrel per minute. The ground underneath seemed to be hollow, and the sound of the water was as if poured upon red-hot rocks; it could be heard for a considerable distance. The ground was more or less heated for about a half mile from the spring in each direction. A mule broke through the surface, nearly half a mile from the spring, and steam immediately issued forth from the hole made. The rocks and sand for miles around, as well as the ashes, all looked as though they had undergone the action of fire. After leaving these springs, great scarcity of good water, feed for the animals, and wood, was experienced. Most of the water found was either salty or bitter, and much of the country was a barren waste. Some of the mules gave out from hunger, thirst and fatigue.

On the 7th, while traveling up the Humboldt, or St. Mary's river, another boiling spring was passed, the steam from which could be seen for several miles.

The next day, four horses were stolen from the party by the Snake Indians. Colonel Fremont was at this time traveling in the rear of the General and his party, but the next day he overtook them, and they afterwards journeyed together.

On the 14th, emigrants on their way to Oregon were met and the next day the party reached Fort Hall, where a supply of bacon was obtained.

July 16th, one year from the day of the Battalion's enlistment, found the party a short distance from Soda Springs, which place they reached and nooned at on the 17th.

Following up Bear River, very cold nights were experienced, there being considerable frost. Emigrants, bound for Oregon, were occasionally seen, and, on the 19th, a man named Smith, who had come from California with Samuel Brannan, was met, and from him the party obtained much valuable information concerning the migrating Saints, etc. That night they encamped near an Indian village consisting of twenty lodges, and the next day traveled twenty-five miles across the mountains and found another Indian village, where a number of fresh horses were obtained.

Green river was reached on the 22nd, and the Big Sandy the next day, and during that day the party was overtaken by a thunder shower, the first, according to the diary of Brother N. V. Jones, one of the party, which he had seen for nearly a year.

While encamped on the Platte river on the 29th, they met the first company of Saints they had seen on the road, and obtained their first reliable information with regard to their families and the Church. John Binley, one of the General's escort, stopped with the company met, on account of ill health.

On the 3rd of August, having learned that a company of the Saints, journeying westward, would soon be met, the General gave permission to N. V. Jones and two other brethren of his escort, to go on in advance of him and meet it. They accordingly proceeded with all practicable haste, and met the company on the 4th. They found many acquaintances, spent a happy time with them before the General overtook them, and Brother Jones received a letter from his wife, the first he had seen from her from the time he had left Fort Leavenworth—almost a year. It had only been written about two months previously, and was therefore considered quite fresh for that age of slow transit.

During the journey from this place to Fort Leavenworth, very little of interest occurred. On arriving at the latter post, the mules and other public property were turned over to the proper officers, and the men received $8.60, each as payment for the time which they had served in excess of the year for which they had enlisted. On receiving their discharge, they proceeded immediately to join their families in the region of Kanesville (now Council Bluffs City), Iowa.

At Fort Leavenworth, General S. F. Kearny, "Commander of the Army of the West," ordered Colonel J. C. Fremont put in irons, and, in that condition, took him to the national capital for trial, which resulted in his conviction upon the charges alleged against him, and in depriving him of his office. The disabilities thus incurred were, however, subsequently removed, owing to his many hardships as an explorer and, probably, on account of benefits which the nation had derived from his services. His trial, which was quite lengthy, created much excitement, and was a subject of national interest.

CHAPTER XXXVI.

Discharged Soldiers at Los Angeles—Their Morality, etc.,—Organize for the Return Trip—Journey Commenced—A Remarkable Dream and its Fulfillment—Difficult Mountain Trail—Animals Lost—Beef Cattle Slaughtered—A Memorial of a Mountaineer's Death—The Hottest Day—Vain Search for Walker's Pass—Ecstatic Dance of an Indian—Sacramento Valley—News of the Pioneers—Some of the Men Decide to Remain and Work in California.

Let us now return to the discharged Battalion left in that center of sedition and profligacy—Los Angeles, a town which could boast, perhaps, of more lewdness than any other upon the coast. Though stationed for such a length of time in that sink of iniquity, the character of the Battalion for sobriety and virtue was maintained. As a proof that the men did not partake of the immorality of the place, it may be remarked that a hospital surgeon was heard to say that among over seventy soldiers which he treated at Los Angeles for a loathsome disease, only one was a "Mormon." And if it be any palliation of the sin in the case of that one, it may be said that he was led to pollute himself while intoxicated. That same surgeon gave it as his opinion that, for virtue, the Mormon Battalion were without a parallel among soldiers.

On the 20th of July, the majority of those who did not re-enlist were organized into companies for traveling, after the ancient and modern Israelitish custom, with captains of hundreds, fifties and tens, as follows: Lieutenants Andrew Lytle and James Pace, of company E, captains of hundreds; Sergeants William Hyde, Daniel Tyler and Redick N. Allred, respectively, captains of fifties. Elisha Averett, musician, was appointed captain of ten pioneers.

It is to be regretted that the names of the other captains of tens are unknown to the author. None of the diaries to which he has had access in compiling this history furnish them, and during the lapse of thirty-five years they have escaped from his memory.

This fact may be accepted as one of the many evidences that the compilation of the history of this arduous and highly important campaign was not commenced any too soon. Many exceedingly interesting events have doubtless been buried with the departed veterans.

On the 21st, the pioneers advanced, scarcely knowing whither they went, only that they had been told that by traveling northward, mainly under the base of the mountains, Sutter's Fort, on Sacramento river, might be reached in about 600 miles, while the sea-shore route would be 700 miles.

Captain Allred's fifty took up the line of march on the 23rd, and traveled twenty miles to General Pico's rancho, which seemed to have been an old deserted Catholic Mission. There were two large gardens, including vineyards. One of these covered about 200 acres of ground. There was no grain in these enclosures, but fruit in abundance, such as grapes, figs, pears, apricots, cherries, plums, peaches, apples, olives, dates, etc.

The next day, after eighteen miles travel, over a rugged, steep and high mountain, where two pack-animals lost their footing and rolled twenty or thirty feet before they could regain it, Francisco's rancho was reached. Here this company remained some four days, awaiting the arrival of the other two fifties, who had tarried to complete their outfit of animals, provisions, etc.

Beef cattle were purchased at this place for all the members of the Battalion who purposed returning to their families that year.

On the 27th, the other companies arrived at Francisco's rancho. When within four or five miles, the author recognized the place and surrounding country, having seen it in a dream prior to the Battalion's discharge. At the time of this remarkable dream, the intention of the Battalion was to take the southern route *via* Cajon Pass, reaching the Great Salt Lake from the South. It may not be entirely uninteresting to relate a portion of the dream.

First, I thought a man clothed in white came to my tent door, having a bottle in his hand, filled with a liquid resembling olive oil. Reaching it to me he said: "take this and drink of it; it is the pure love of God, that casteth out all fear and causeth men to draw nigh unto God." I drank two swallows, and returned the bottle. The eyes of my understanding were then opened and I was filled with the glory of God throughout my whole system. I saw that we traveled northward and subsequently eastward, instead of south and east as anticipated. On arriving at this rancho, I thought we had passed all of the wild animals that sought to destroy us or impede our progress, which it appeared were numerous and strong, the last being a lion, which I instructed the company to pass without halting or seeming to notice.

On arriving at the creek, I dismounted and drank of the water, and received strength to pursue my journey, which many feared I would be unable to do. I was then caught away in the spirit to the valley of the Great Salt Lake, and saw myself with many others in a holy Temple, where the Twelve Apostles presided. The house was filled with the glory of God, and in a room adjoining the main one in which I sat was Jesus, the Redeemer of the world. I did not see Him, but knew He was there. Lucifer also appeared, claiming to be the Christ, and offering free salvation to all who would accept him as their ruler without any church obligations. He was finely dressed, in black, and very genteel, until he discovered that no one paid any attention to his sophistry, when he became enraged and threatened to "tear down the Temple and destroy the kingdom of God," when, as commanded, he left the house. All was calm as a summer's morning and no one seemed to fear any of the threats made or to believe he would have power to do any harm. I awoke and the main features of my dream were repeated in open vision, especially as relates to the Temple. From that time I never doubted but Salt Lake Valley would be the final destination of the outcast Saints.

When I awoke and found that it was only a dream, the reality of facts did not seem to lessen, but I found my whole being filled with joy and rejoicing, a thrill of gladness pervading my soul from my crown to the ends of my fingers and toes. As to the wild beasts, they represented the many obstacles thrown in our way to hedge up our departure, prominently among them being the Californians selling us animals stolen from their fellows, who claimed, proved and took them from us, or, perhaps, the parties divided the spoils. When the officers saw so few re-enlist we were also threatened with being pressed into the service; at least it was rumored that such a move was under serious consideration.

On overtaking Captain Allred's company, I predicted that we would have no further trouble from those sources, which proved literally true, for no further attempt at claiming animals or other trouble of like nature, came in our way. On arriving at the creek I purposely fulfilled a portion of my dream, by alighting from my horse, lying down and taking a good drink at the very place seen in the dream, and received health and strength in so doing.

Many of my comrades will doubtless recollect the relation of the foregoing dream and vision.

We left Pico's rancho with our beef cattle in front, passing over a rugged mountain, very high and almost perpendicular. It made our heads swim to look down it. In crossing this and other steep mountains, we lost twelve head of our beef cattle.

The next day we traveled over other rough mountains and lost three more of our beeves, and then concluded to rest and kill our remaining beef cattle and dry the meat.

On the 31st, the pioneers advanced to look out the road, while the company remained in camp and finished curing the meat.

On the first of August, we traveled fourteen miles and encamped in a beautiful valley where we found, cut in the bark of a tree, the name of Peter Lebeck, who was killed by a Grizzly Bear on the 17th day of October, 1837. The skull and other bones of the bear, which was killed by Lebeck's comrades, were still lying on the ground near by.

The next day, a ride of fifteen miles brought us to Tulare River. Finding it impassable, we traveled five miles up it and encamped.

On the 3rd, Elisha Averett returned from an Indian village, bringing with him several Indians, including a chief. A guide was procured from among them, and we continued twelve miles farther up the river.

The following day, we traveled six miles farther up the stream, where a raft was made to carry over a portion of our goods, while some forded the stream with their luggage on their heads, and still others crossed a half mile below, at a new crossing discovered by an Indian. All were over by about two o'clock.

On the 5th, our new guide left us because we could not hire his entire lodge. We had but little water that night, and it took us all night to water our animals out of a few bog holes we had dug in damp places.

On the 9th, we arrived at a large stream of water in a beautiful valley, and the next day made a raft and took our baggage over the stream, while our animals were forced to swim.

On the 11th, our journey lay across a dry plain. It was pleasant traveling in the forenoon, but in the afternoon the weather was excessively hot, with but little air stirring, and when a little breeze came, it was hot and suffocating. Two men gave out and could not ride or travel; others made but little progress, and it almost seemed that all must perish. Those who reached camp first, drank, filled their canteens and returned to revive their thirsting comrades. All finally revived and reached camp. We had no thermometer, but all agreed that this was the hottest day they ever experienced in any country.

Having no guide, the company remained in camp during the 12th, for the pioneers to explore the route, and, if posible, find Walker's Pass over the mountains. One of the men had procured an old map at Los Angeles, in the hope of defining the different localities, but it proved of no avail to us, as we could not even tell the names of the streams of water we were traveling on.

On the 13th, we made ten miles up the river, with the hope of finding Walker's Pass. Our pioneers, however, returned, informing us that there was no pass at that point.

After crossing the river and retracing our journey for a distance of twelve miles, we decided to seek no farther for a pass over the mountains, but continue northward to Sutter's Fort, on the Sacramento River, situated about one-and-a-half miles from where the great city of Sacramento now stands, but which was then a lone military post in a wilderness. Our aim was to follow Fremont's trail. Indians came into our camp that night, and had what we took to be a religious dance, one getting the "power" much like what we had seen in Methodist revival meetings. While another Indian beat time with a split stick, he danced, sang and talked, until he swooned away in right old-fashioned Methodist style. However, at this juncture, the nude savages, whose clothing consisted of a breech-clout, exhibited more good sense than many of our civilized Christians would have done under similar circumstances, for a leading spirit among them, instead of allowing the unconscious man to lay in a senseless swoon for hours, lit his cigarette and blew the smoke into his ears and mouth, and slapped the pulse of his wrists sharply, until consciousness was restored.

After traveling twenty-two miles on the 15th, we encamped on what was supposed to be the San Joaquin River. Continuing on, we did not follow any trail for any great distance, but kept near the western base of the California Mountains, and still supposed that we were on the San Joaquin River.

On the 20th, we arrived at the Sacramento River and encamped. There were several small farms in this region, mostly planted to corn, and cultivated by Indians.

On the 22nd, after crossing a beautiful valley and camping on a fine mountain stream, three men were sent ahead to Sutter's Fort, to engage our supply of provisions.

During our next day's travel, we passed some Indian wigwams. The men being absent, the women and children fled and hid in the brush, like young partridges; a few of the males having returned, visited our camp at night.

On the 24th, we reached a settlement of white people, and were almost overjoyed to see a colony of Americans, the first we had seen since leaving Fort Leavenworth, about a year previous. But the best of all was, the news brought by a man named Smith, who said he had accompanied Samuel Brannan to meet the Church, and who informed us that the Saints were settling in the Great Salt Lake Valley, and that five hundred wagons were on the way. This was our first intelligence of the movements of the Church since the news brought by Lieutenant Pace and Brothers Lee and Egan, at the Arkansas crossing. One must have our previous sad experience to appreciate our feelings on this occasion.

The following day, we rested and held meeting in the evening, as we had frequently done since our discharge. Some having but a poor fit-out, wished to remain here and labor until spring, wages being good and labor in demand; besides, a settlement of the New York Saints was within a few miles. President Levi W. Hancock made some appropriate remarks on the union that had been and was among us, and thought that a few might remain and labor until spring and all would be right. He then asked the company if, in case any felt to remain, they should have our prayers and blessings. All voted in the affirmative. Good remarks were also made by others on the same subject. A few remained. Wages were said to be from twenty-five to sixty dollars per month, and hands hard to get at any price, as there were so few in the country.

CHAPTER XXXVII.

Get Horses Shod and Procure an Outfit—Johnson's Mill—Nude Indians—Mrs. Johnson's Story—Horrible Account of Suffering—Human Beings Living on the Flesh of their Fellows—Taste Developed for such Food—Meet Samuel Brannan Returning to California—Doleful Account of Salt Lake Valley—Captain James Brown Met—Epistle from the Twelve Apostles—Letters From Friends.

On the 26th, we traveled twenty miles and encamped on American Fork, two miles from Sutter's Fort. Here the animals that had become tender-footed, were shod, at a cost of one dollar per shoe. We also purchased our outfit of unbolted flour at eight dollars per hundred. In those days, California and every other western territory had but little bolted flour, except such as was transported from the United States or the Sandwich Islands. Those were days of vigor, health and long life.

On the 27th, the pioneers and about thirty others advanced, while the bulk of the company remained to get horses shod. The advance made about eighteen miles, from which point, our course changed from northward to eastward.

On the 28th, we arrived at Captain Johnson's mill, on Bear Creek. This man had Indians laboring for him, who were entirely naked. I noticed one large man, probably six feet in height, come and stand by the door, an unabashed picture of nature unadorned. He was apparently waiting for the young woman of the house—the captain's wife—to give him something to eat. Captain Johnson passed in and out of the house while the savage stood by the door, without taking any exceptions to his nude appearance, from which we inferred that he was used to seeing the Indians in such a condition. Indeed, we were informed that those he hired, went without clothing, and the Indian we saw there was probably one of his employes.

Captain Johnson was said to have been one of Fremont's battalion, and his young wife was one of the survivors of the ill-fated company who had been snowed in at the foot of the Sierras, already alluded to. Her mother, Mrs. Murray, who was a Latter-day Saint, was among the number who perished in that horrible scene of death. The circumstances under which she became a member of that company were explained to us by her daughter, Mrs. Johnson.

"The lady being a widow, with several children dependent upon her for support, while residing in Nauvoo, heard of a chance of obtaining employment at Warsaw, an anti-"Mormon" town, thirty miles lower down the Mississippi. Thinking to better her condition, she, accordingly, removed to Warsaw, and spent the winter of 1845-46 there. In the spring of the latter year, a party about emigrating to Oregon or California, offered to furnish passage for herself and children on the condition that she would cook and do the washing for the party. Understanding California to be the final destination of the Saints, and thinking this a good opportunity to emigrate without being a burden to the Church, she accepted the proposition, but, alas! the example of Sister Murray, although her motives were good, is an illustration of the truism, that 'it is better to suffer affliction with the people of God' and trust in Him for deliverance, than to mingle with the sinful 'for a season,' and be lured by human prospects of a better result!

"The company crossed the plains during the summer of 1846, under the guidance of Captain Hastings. They passed through Salt Lake Valley, around the south end of the lake, and proceeded on westward. Lacking that union which has characterized companies of Saints, while traveling, they split up into factions, each party determined to take its own course. The few who remained with the persevering Captain, pushed through to California, while the others were caught in the snows of the Sierra Nevada Mountains.

"The party Mrs. Murray was with was next in rear of that of the Captain, and, of course, nearest the source of relief. After their food was exhausted, in fact, after several had succumbed to death through hunger and others were subsisting upon their flesh, a few of them, one of whom was Mrs. Murray's eldest daughter (afterwards Mrs. Johnson), in desperation, resolved to make an attempt to cross the mountains and obtain relief. Fitting themselves out with snow shoes, they started, and, after proceeding some distance, they met Captain Hastings and a party from the Sacramento Valley, coming with provisions to relieve them. On reaching the camp of the starving emigrants, the relief party found Mrs. Murray dead and others perfectly ravenous from starvation. Children were actually crying for the flesh of their parents while it was being cooked. There was good reason to suspect that Sister Murray had been foully dealt with, as she was in good health when her daughter left her, and could scarcely have perished from hunger during the brief period of her absence.

"Leaving Captain Johnson's mill, we proceeded on, following the trail of General Kearny. On arriving at Bear Creek, in Bear Valley, we found three wagons and a blacksmith's forge, which had been abandoned by the emigrants who were snowed in the previous winter. We rested there one day, to recruit our animals, the feed being good, and found plenty of huckleberries, which were a fine treat.

"During the 3rd of September, we passed other wagons at the place where General Kearny's party had buried the remains of the famished emigrants, and at night reached the place where the rear wagons of the unfortunate Hastings company were blocked by the snow, and were horrified at the sight which met our view—a skull covered with hair lying here, a mangled arm or leg yonder, with the bones broken as one would break a beef shank to obtain the marrow from it; a whole body in another place, covered with a blanket, and portions of other bodies scattered around in different directions. It had not only been the scene of intense human suffering, but also of some of the most fiendish acts that man made desperate by hunger could conceive.

"It seemed that on reaching that point on their journey, the unfortunate emigrants were divided into several different parties. Some lagged behind because there was work required to make a road for their wagons, and they were determined not to do it themselves; others were in favor of stopping to recruit their animals, all of which were turned out to grass when the storm came, and scattered and buried them up. In this terrible delemma their provisions were soon exhausted, and they began to subsist upon the bodies of their dead relatives. Those who had no deceased relatives borrowed flesh from those who had, to be refunded when they or some of their relatives should die. In some cases, children are said to have eaten their dead parents, and *vice versa*. Some were supposed to have been murdered as we would butcher an ox.

"When relief came, one man had a trunk packed full of human flesh and two buckets full of human blood, stored carefully away. When questioned about the blood, he professed to have extracted it from the veins of two women after they were dead, but the seemingly well-founded opinion was that there had been foul play. Some were caught in the act of eating human flesh for a lunch, as a matter of choice, while they were passing over the mountains with the relief party, after they had obtained plenty of other food. And when their pockets were examined, they were found to contain chunks of human flesh, which were taken from them and thrown away. One man had even acquired such a mania for that kind of food, that after he had been in Sacramento Valley some months, where food was plentiful, he admitted to having a longing for another such a meal, and expressed to a stout, comely lady a desire for a roast from her body. This cannibal, whose name might be given were it not for shame's sake, was, when we passed through Sacramento Valley, being watched for by the lady's husband, who swore he would shoot him on sight.

"Leaving the tragic scene on the morning of the 6th of September, we resumed our journey, and in a short time met Samuel Brannan returning from his trip to meet the Saints. We learned from him that the Pioneers had reached Salt Lake Valley in safety, but his description of the valley and its facilities was anything but encouraging. Among other things, Brother Brannan said the Saints could not possibly subsist in the Great Salt Lake Valley, as, according to the testimony of mountaineers, it froze there every month in the year, and the ground was too dry to sprout seeds without irrigation, and if irrigated with the cold mountain streams, the seeds planted would be chilled and prevented from growing, or, if they did grow, they would be sickly and fail to mature. He considered it no place for an agricultural people, and expressed his confidence that the Saints would emigrate to California the next spring. On being asked if he had given his views to President Brigham Young, he answered that he had. On further inquiry as to how his views were received, he said, in substance, that the President laughed and made some rather insignificant remark; 'but,' said Brannan, 'when he has fairly tried it, he will find that I was right and he was wrong, and will come to California.'

"He thought all except those whose families were known to be at Salt Lake had better turn back and labor until spring, when in all probability the Church would come to them; or, if not, they could take means to their families. We camped over night with Brannan, and after he had left us the following morning, Captain James Brown, of the Pueblo detachment, which arrived in Salt Lake Valley on the 27th of July, came up with a small party. He brought a goodly number of letters from the families of the soldiers, also an epistle from the Twelve Apostles, advising those who had not means of subsistence to remain in California and labor, and bring their earnings with them in the spring.

"Henry W. Bigler received a letter from Elder George A. Smith, of the Apostles, stating among other things, that President Brigham Young, with one hundred and forty-three Pioneers, arrived in Salt Lake Valley on the 24th day of July.

It also mentioned the arrival of the Pueblo detachment of the Battalion, and stated that some were very busy putting in garden and field crops, while others were making adobes to build a temporary fort as a safeguard against Indians. The letter also stated that President Young and the Pioneers would return to Council Bluffs, and Father John Smith, Patriarch, would preside until the Twelve returned the next season.

CHAPTER XXXVIII.

Many Return to California—Death of Henry Hoyt—Money Providentially Provided—Clothing Lost—Pants Worn Out—Skins Purchased for a New Pair—Arrival in Salt Lake Valley—Destitute Condition of Men—Clothing Donated for Them—Seeds Brought by Battalion—Prolific Yield of Peas—Characteristics of Peas Change.

"From the last-named encampment, many, probably over half of the company, returned in accordance with the instructions from the Twelve, to spend the winter in California. We were also overtaken there by a portion of the company left at Sutter's Fort and a few others who had remained behind our party to travel slowly with Brother Henry Hoyt, who was sick. Brother Hoyt had gradually failed since our separation, and finally died on the 3rd of September, 1847. He would not consent to tarry, but insisted on pursuing the journey. He had several times been taken from his horse in sinking spells, received strength through the ordinance of laying on of hands, and again continued his journey. A short time prior to his demise he was asked if he did not wish to stop and rest. He answered "No, go on." These were the last words he ever spoke. Growing more faint directly afterwards, he was aided by Sergeant R. N. Alred and other companions from his horse, and laid upon the ground under the shade of a tree, where, in a few moments, he expired without a struggle or a groan. He was buried in the best manner the company could afford, although in the absence of proper utensils his grave was rather shallow. Timbers and brush were piled upon it to hide his remains from the wolves. He died as he had lived, a faithful Latter-day Saint. This last remark, to the best of the author's knowledge and belief, holds good with regard to all members of the Battallion who died in the service, and when "all who lay down their lives for Christ's sake shall be crowned," it may be presumed that not one of them will be missing from the number.

After leaving the place last mentioned, an incident worthy of note occurred. The author, before leaving Los Angeles, expended all his cash and borrowed a trifle to complete his outfit. While sitting by the camp fire, one evening, looking at a paper he had taken from his pocket, he noticed something bright drop between his feet. Picking it up he discovered it was a two dollar Mexican gold piece, looking as new and bright as though it had just come from the mint. Mentioning the circumstance to some of his friends, among whom was President Levi W. Hancock, the latter replied: "Keep it, Brother Tyler, you will need it." Considering it a gift from the Almighty, as upon no other principle could he account for its falling in the air and alighting between his feet, he kept it, as Brother Hancock advised.

Probably two or three days after that, by accident, the pack containing the author's change of wardrobe, as well as his provisions, got a little turned and frightened his half-wild mule, which ran away and lost off the pack. All was recovered except the sack of clothes, which could not be found, although diligent search was made. The only pants he had left were of cotton and already thread-bare in several places. On reaching Fort Hall he purchased a large deer-skin and a young elk-skin with the two dollars which he had found. These were taken to Salt Lake, where Sister St. John and her daughter Harriet made a pair of pantaloons, of which the author had been destitute for several days, having to wrap himself in a Pima blanket.

Few incidents of importance occurred during the journey to Salt Lake Valley, where we arrived on the 16th of October, and were overjoyed to meet so many of our friends and relatives. We found them living in a fort consisting of a row of buildings running at right angles around a ten acre block. The rooms all opened into the enclosure, and had small windows or port holes looking outward, for purposes of defense and ventilation. The entrance to the enclosure was through a large gate in the centre of the east side or row of buildings running north and south. The gate was locked at night. The site of that first structure, which is in the Sixth Ward of Salt Lake City, is known still as "the old fort." The walls, however, have long since been removed; hence the temporary fortification now exists only in name.

" Many of the men, on arriving in the Valley, were extremely destitue of clothing, but their necessities were somewhat relieved by some of the influential brethren taking up a collection among the families of the settlers of such articles of wearing apparel as they could spare for the benefit of the "Battalion boys." Nothing that was donated seemed to come amiss; anything that would cover the nakedness of the men or help to keep them warm was acceptable. True, the men presented rather a motley, and, in some instances, almost a ludicrous appearance, on account of the disparity in the color and fit of their several garments, but comfort with them was the first consideration, and they were thankful to get anything that would tend to that object. President John Taylor and Presiding Bishop Edward Hunter, were foremost among those who made the collection of clothing for the destitute soldiers.

Different members of our company brought various kinds of garden and fruit seeds, as well as grain, from California, which were found very useful in this inland valley, situated a thousand miles from any source of supply, as the mass had little or none of them, though a few may have been reasonably supplied.

Lieutenant James Pace introduced the club-head wheat. The author, and perhaps some others, the California pea, now so general and prolific as the field pea of Utah. The detached soldiers who wintered at Pueblo, near the headwaters of the Arkansas River, brought the variety of wheat known as the *taos*, common in our Territory.

These with the other varieties in connection with those brought by the emigrants, although insufficient to supply the demand, did much towards relieving the temporary wants of the people. I left six quarts of the California peas with Brother Seely Owens, who proposed to raise them on shares, giving me one-half of the proceeds on my arrival the next year. On my arrival in the fall of 1847, with my family, Brother Owens delivered to me half a bushel of dry peas, stating that while they were the best and most prolific peas he ever saw, these were all he had saved. Some of them were ready for use as green peas about June. His provisions being exhausted, he and his family had mainly subsisted upon them until the late heavy frosts stopped their bearing. Up to that time, a new crop had come on as fast as the first was picked off. He proposed to make compensation for what he had used over the portion due him, adding that he would like a few for seed if I could spare them, as he did not wish to be out of the prolific variety. I informed him if he would take one-half of what was left, the matter would be satisfactorily settled. I gave to others two quarts, leaving myself six quarts for the next spring's planting. The same result followed as the previous year. My provisions ran short and I had to fall back on the peas for my family's supply of food. Emigrants from the States for California came in hungry for vegetables, anxious to pay cash or other provisions for them. I picked and sold as well as used all we needed and gave some to my neighbors until almost winter, when the frost finally stopped their growth, after which I harvested three bushels. Of course, every family wanted some of the new variety. I found no difficulty in disposing of all I desired. But, kind reader, now for the sequel: Provisions became more plentiful, and, instead of continuous crops of the California peas, when the first were matured the vines died, so that instead of a November harvest they ripened and began to shed from the dead vines towards the end of July and early in August, and this has been their history ever since. Some argue that they must have been sown at some particular stage of the moon. That may have been so, but I can assure my friends that they were planted in the ground on our own little planet, and that while the moon may have looked complacently on, it was the same kind Providence who said, "It is my business to provide for my Saints in the last days" that caused these unusual results. I may add, also, that many in those days of scarcity, testified that the flour increased in their boxes to their great joy and surprise.

CHAPTER XXXIX.

Eastward Journey Resumed—No Flour to be Obtained for the Trip—Disappointments at Bridger and Laramie—Scant Fare—Episode with Indians—Diet of Rawhide Saddle Bags—Providential Freezing of the River—Reach Winter Quarters—Kindness of Friends.

" A few of the members of the Battalion found their families in Salt Lake Valley on our arrival there, and, of course, had no farther to go; some others were so worn down with fatigue and sickness that they were unable to proceed eastward at that time, and still others preferred to remain in the valley until the following spring and endeavor to prepare a home for their families. Thirty-two out of the number, however, were eager to meet their wives and children, and therefore did not hesitate about continuing their journey another thousand miles, even at that late season of the year. We expected to obtain flour in the valley for the remainder of the journey, but found that the people, as a rule, had not enough to subsist upon until they could harvest a crop. We were informed, however, that plenty of flour could be obtained at Fort Bridger, only 115 miles distant, so, relying upon that prospect, we left the valley in good spirits on the 18th of October, 1847, and started eastward.

"We arrived at Fort Bridger during a rather severe snow storm, the first of the season, and, to our chagrin, learned that the stock of flour which had been kept there for sale had all been bought up by emigrants to California and Oregon. Bridger informed us that he had not even reserved any for those located at the post, and they were then living solely upon meat. He thought, however, we could get all we wanted at Laramie, upon reasonable terms.

" On leaving Salt Lake Valley, we had about ten pounds of flour to the man, hence we were not entirely without when we reached Bridger. We purchased a little beef there to serve us until we could find game, and pushed on. We killed two buffalo bulls before reaching Laramie, and jerked the best of the meat. We had an occasional cake until we reached the upper crossing of the Platte, 100 miles above the fort. There we baked our last cake, on the 4th of November, having made our ten pounds of flour, each, last sixteen days. Of course, during that time we had eaten considerable buffalo and other beef and occasionally had some small game, including one elk killed by Wm. Maxwell.

"It was, probably, about the 10th of November when we reached Fort Laramie. There, as at Fort Bridger, we were again disappointed about getting flour, the only bread-stuff purchased being one pound of crackers by Captain Andrew Lytle, for which he paid twenty-five cents. We obtained a very little dried buffalo beef of good quality. The post trader advised us not to kill any buffalo when we reached their range, as it would offend the Indians. He considered it would be a safer and better plan to employ the Indians, should we meet any, to kill some buffalo for us.

"Those who had a little money purchased what meat they could afford and divided with the company. Twelve miles below Laramie we found an Indian trader on the south side of the Platte river. A few of the men crossed over and purchased 100 pounds of flour, which cost only $25. There being but about three pounds to the man, it was decided to use it only for making gravy, or for thickening soup, as we had still about 500 miles of our journey to travel.

"When about sixty or seventy miles below the fort, our meat was exhausted. We were now among a few scattering buffalo, but as we had been informed that it would be dangerous for us to kill any of them, we were in somewhat of a dilemma what course to pursue to obtain food. However, we decided that He who owned "the cattle upon a thousand hills" had a claim on these, and, being His offspring, we would venture to take one. Besides, there had been no Indians in sight for several days, and, last but not least, we might as well die in battle as of hunger, as in the former case our sufferings would be of shorter duration.

"The hunters succeeded in killing one bull and a calf. While skinning the former we saw a smoke and discovered Indians on the south side of the river, opposite to where we were. We consulted as to the best course to pursue. Some thought we had better go on and leave our booty, but Captain R. N. Allred suggested, very properly, that with our worn-down animals, this would be useless, as in case they were in for fighting, they could soon overtake us; hence, we decided to stand our ground. We dressed our beef and reached camp on the river, from the foot-hills some time after dark. We were not molested.

Near that point, Captain R. N. Allred traded a small worn-out mule to an Indian for a pony. About fifteen miles below we passed, perhaps, 300 lodges of the Sioux tribe. There a stalwart Indian came out and seized the pony by the bridle bit. Captain Lytle and the author, being on the lead, returned to relieve Brother Allred, by which time many other Indians, squaws and papooses had gathered around.

The writer wore a broad-brimmed Panama hat, having undressed elk-skin depending from the under side of it, with the hairy side inward, to shield his ears and face from the cold. His body was covered with a large dressing gown, which had been donated to the company by our venerable Presiding Bishop, Edward Hunter. The reader can imagine how a man weighing not more than 135 pounds would appear attired in the capacious folds of such a garment, made to fit a person several inches taller and upwards of one hundred pounds heavier than himself. His unique appearance, when mounted upon a mule, was not very inviting to a white man, and it actually seemed to strike terror to the hearts of the "reds," so that, at his approach, all scattered and left Brother Allred, except the stalwart fellow who held the horse by the bit. He maintained his grip and stood firm as a statue, evidently determined on having the pony at all hazards. The mystery of the movement was soon solved by another brave leading out the decrepit mule which Brother Allred had recently traded for the pony, thus proving that the Indian had rued his bargain. The Indian also indicated, by his gestures, that he considered himself cheated, and, having no interpreter we were unable to let him know that the mule only required a little rest and a chance to recruit, when he would be much the more valuable animal of the two. There seemed no other way but for Brother Allred to yield up the pony and take back the mule, which the Indians had almost used entirely up in hurrying to overtake us, and the exchange was accordingly made, and all disputes settled.

"About 150 miles below Laramie, we awoke one morning to find ourselves under about twelve inches of snow. From this point to Winter Quarters, about 350 miles, we had to travel and break the trail through snow from one to two feet in depth.

"Just before and after crossing the Loup Fork river, we lost a few animals, supposed to have been stolen by Pawnee Indians. Near the crossing of the river, the head of a donkey was found, which Adjutant P. C. Merrill's company had killed some time before for beef. It was supposed to have belonged to Sergeant D. P. Rainey. Captain Allred took an ax and opened the skull, and he and his messmates had a fine supper made of the brains.

"Near the same point Corporal Martin Ewell opened the head of a mule killed by Captain James Pace's company only the day before, with the same result.

"The day we reached the Loup Fork, we divided and ate the last of our food, which in the main consisted of rawhide "saddle-bags" we had used from California to pack our provisions in. This was during a cold storm which lasted several days. Our next food was one of Captain Lytle's young mules, which had given out and was unable to travel. This was the first domestic animal our little company had killed since our beef cattle in California, although we had several times looked with a wistful eye upon a small female canine belonging to Jos. Thorne, who, with his wife and one or two children, in a light wagon, had accompanied us from Fort Bridger. Friend Joseph, however, removed the temptation by trading her to the Pawnee Indians for a small piece of dried buffalo meat. Of this family pet, they doubtless made a rare treat, their greatest feasts being composed mainly of dog meat.

"Owing to floating ice, we were unable to cross the Loup Fork for five days, in which time we traveled a few miles down the river and found Captain Pace's company just in time to save them from the danger of being robbed by Pawnee

Indians who came over in considerable numbers. The remnants of the two companies afterwards remained together.

In hopes of procuring some corn from an Indian farm on the opposite side of the river from us, a few of the men ventured to ford the stream, but the corn had been gathered and twice gleaned from the field by other travelers, so that all they could find were a few scattering, rotten ears. Captain Pace and William Maxwell, also visited an Indian camp some distance away, to try to purchase food, but failed to get any, as the Indians had none to spare. They, however, stayed all night with them and obtained a good supper and breakfast and were otherwise treated kindly.

The cold became so intense that the river froze entirely over, and on the morning of the sixth day of our stay upon its banks, we commenced to cross upon the ice. The ice bent and cracked, and holes were soon broken in it, but we persevered until everything was over, the last article being Brother Thorne's wagon. The weather began to moderate when the sun appeared above the horizon, and the ice had become so rotten before we finished crossing that the last few trips were extremely dangerous. But a short time had elapsed after we had safely gained the other shore before the ice broke away and the river was again covered with floating fragments.

A kind providence had made the congealed water bridge for our special benefit, and removed it as soon as it had filled its mission. From the killing of Captain Lytle's mule until we reached Winter Quarters, probably ten day's travel, we subsisted upon mule meat alone, without salt. On arriving at Elk Horn River, thirty miles from Winter Quarters, we found a ferry-boat with ropes stretched across, ready to step into and pull over, which of course we did.

It was understood that this boat was built by the Pioneers, and was first used by them. It afterwards served the companies who followed on their trail; was then used by the Pioneers and Lieutenant Merrill's company on their return; and last, but not least, by us, for whom it had been last left. We crossed on the 17th of December, 1847.

The next morning, we arose early and took up the line of march, and the foremost men arrived in Winter Quarters about sundown, while the rear came in a little after dark.

Thus, it will be perceived that we were just two months in making the journey from Salt Lake to the Missouri River, a distance which is now traversed by the cars in a little over two days. Some of the company found their families in the town of Winter Quarters, while others were across the Missouri River, at or near Kanesville, now Council Bluffs, Pottawatomie County, Iowa. The reader can more easily imagine our joy and that of our families and friends than it can be described.

The kindness of friends, brethren and sisters, on our arrival at Winter Quarters, now Florence, Nebraska, is deserving of special mention. All the soldiers, although in some instances they were highly respectable, were unavoidably dirty and ragged; yet they found only warm-hearted, sympathetic brethren, sisters and friends among the people, from President Young and the Twelve Apostles to the least child who knew what the words "Mormon Battalion" meant. They had been taught to know that that valiant corps had been offered like Isaac, a living sacrifice for the Church as well as the nation.

CHAPTER XL.

"Mormon Volunteers"—Quartered in San Diego—Detachment Sent to San Luis Rey—Death of Sergeant Frost and Neal Donald—Extra Work Done by the Soldiers—Serve Longer than They Enlisted for—Immorality Among their Successors—Journey to Salt Lake Valley by the Southern Route.

It will now be proper to return to a consideration of the members of the discharged Mormon Battalion who re-enlisted.

On the 20th of July, 1847, one company, known as "Mormon Volunteers," made up from the rank and file of the Battalion, was mustered into the service of the United States at Cuidad de Los Angeles, California, by First Lieutenant A. J. Smith, First Dragoons, of Battalion notoriety, for a term of six months. Daniel C. Davis, former Captain of Company E, Mormon Battalion, was elected Captain of this company. The names of all officers and soldiers will be found upon the following roll which has been preserved intact:

OFFICERS.

Daniel C. Davis, *Capt.*
Cyrus C. Canfield, *1st Lieut.*
Ruel Barrus, *2nd Lieut.*
Robert Clift, *3rd Lieut.*
Edmund L. Brown, *1st Sergt.*
Samuel Myers, *2nd Sergt.*
Benjamin F. Mayfield 3rd *Sergt.*
Henry Packard, *4th Sergt.*
Thomas Peck, *1st Corpl.*
Isaac Harrison, *2nd Corpl.*
Hiram B. Mount, *3rd Corpl.*
Edwin Walker, *4th Corp.*
Richard D. Sprague, *Musicn.*
Henry W. Jackson *Musicn.*

PRIVATES.

Boyle, Henry G.
Baily, Addison
Baily, Jefferson
Beckstead, Orin
Bowing, Henry
Brass, Benjamin
Brown, William
Beckstead, Gordon S.
Brizzee, Henry
Byrant, John
Calahan, Thomas
Calkins, Edwin
Carter, Philo I.
Clark, Riley P.
Clawson, John R.
Clift, James
Condit, Jeptha
Covil, John A.

ROLL OF "MORMON VOLUNTEERS."

Donald, Neal
Dayton, Willard Y.
Dutcher, Thomas P.
Earl, Jacob
Earl, Jessie
Evans, William
Fatout, Ezra
Fellows, Hiram W.
Fletcher, Philander
Hart, James
Harmon, Ebenezer
Harmon, Lorenzo F.
Harmon, Oliver
Hickenlooper, William
Kibbey, James
Lemmon, James
Lance, William
Maggard, Benjamin
Morris, Thomas
Mowry, James
McBride, Harlem
Mowry, John
Neal, Conrad
Nowler, Christian
Peck, Isaac

Peck, Edwin M.
Park, James
Riter, John
Riser, John J.
Runyan, Levi
Richards, Peter F.
Sexton, George S.
Shumway, Aurora
Smith, William
Smith, Lot
Steel, George
Steel, Isaiah
Steers, Andrew
Thompson, Miles
Watts, John
West, Benjamin
Wheeler, John L.
Wheeler, Henry
Williams, James V.
Winter, Jacob
Workman, Andrew J.
Workman, Oliver G.
Young, Nathan
Zabriskie, Jerome

The following order was given four days after the company was mustered:

"HEADQUARTERS SOUTHERN MILITARY
DISTRICT, CALIFORNIA,
CUIDAD DE LOS ANGELES,
July 24, 1847.

Captain—

You will proceed to San Diego with your company and garrison that post. San Diego, San Luis and the surrounding country, will be under your command. You will be watchful and vigilant, and especially have a strict eye upon all persons passing in and out of the country, and by every mail give me such information as regards the state of the country, as well as deportment of the people towards your command. You are, whenever called upon by the civil authorities, to sustain them in the execution of the laws, and in all things to act with prudence and discretion in the performance of your duties.

Respectfully, your obedient servant,

J. D. STEVENSON,
Col. Commanding S. M. District, Cal.

Captain D. C. Davis."

On the 25th, the company took up the line of march for San Diego, on the Gulf of California, where it arrived on the 2nd of August. It was intended as a kind of provost guard, to protect the citizens from Indian raids and to watch the movements of belligerent parties, until information of a treaty between the two governments should be received.

Soon after his arrival at San Diego, Captain Davis received the following order:

"HEAD QUARTERS S. M. DISTRICT, CALIFORNIA,
"SANTA BARBARA, August 4, 1847.

"Sir:

"You will immediately upon the reception of this, post at the mission of San Luis Rey twenty-seven men of your company, with one sergeant and one corporal, the whole under the command of Lieutenant Barrus, who will take charge of and prevent any depredations being committed upon the mission property. The detachment will remain at that post until further orders from district head quarters. You will receive by this mail a garrison flag which please return receipt for.

"CAPTAIN D. C. DAVIS, J. D. STEVENSON,
"SAN DIEGO. Commanding S. M. DISTRICT,
"CALIFORNIA."

This company had very little military duty to perform. By virtue of agreement with the military commander, made before enlistment, the most of the men, when off duty, immediately turned their attention to common and mechanical labor, and San Diego again began to awake from her slumbers and deadness to life and thrift.

With a view to the sanitary and moral regulation of the garrison, the following order was issued:

"MILITARY STATION, SAN DIEGO,
August 6, 1847.

(1) A daily detail of four men and one non-commissioned officer, will be made for police, whose duty it shall be to clean the quarters and the yard in front, also the parade ground.

(2) Strict attention of all must be given to cleanliness of person and clothing, as well as a proper regard for decorum of conduct.

(3) In no case will playing at cards be allowed in quarters, either by the men belonging to the garrison or others visiting it, and all non-commissioned officers are hereby required to report immediately any violation of the above regulations.

DANIEL C. DAVIS,
Commanding Officer."

It being necessary to again garrison San Luis Rey, the following order was issued:

"MILITARY POST AT SAN DIEGO,
"August 9, 1847.

"2nd Lieutenant R. Barrus, Mormon Volunteers, will proceed to-morrow, 10th inst., at 2 p. m., with twenty-five men and one sergeant and one corporal to San Luis Rey, and take charge of the mission and all other public property there, and prevent any depredation being committed by the Indians or others upon the same, and will report to me by every mail anything that transpires which at all affects the public good. You will be vigilant and act with prudence and discretion in the performance of your duties. You will make requisition upon the quartermaster for twenty days' provisions. The wagon and team which transports the provisions, etc., you will retain at the mission until further orders.

"LIEUT. R. BARRUS,   DANIEL C. DAVIS,
   "1st Company,   CAPT. Commanding,
      "Mormon Volunteers.   SAN DIEGO."

On the 8th day of September, 1847, Sergeant Frost, the former brave Corporal, on whose memory the Battalion love to dwell, succumbed to the fell monster death. No eulogy on his character is needed; suffice it to say, he was a man of few words, but abundant in good deeds. His remains were interred a half mile south-east of town.

A vacancy being caused by the death of Sergeant Frost, the folllowing order was issued to fill it:

"(Order No. 3.)

"SAN DIEGO,
"September, 11, 1847.

"Private Henry Packard, of Company A, Mormon Volunteers, is hereby appointed Sergeant of said company, to fill the vacancy occasioned by the death of Sergeant Lafayette Frost. He will be obeyed and respected accordingly.

"Approved: By order of
"(Signed) J. D. STEVENSON, DANIEL C. DAVIS,
"COL. Commanding CAPT. Commanding
"S. M. DISTRICT, CAL. SAN DIEGO."

On the 5th of November following, Brother Neal Donald, another worthy veteran, departed and was buried by the side of Sergeant Frost. The following order appears in connection with the record of the company, but without date:

"Private Thomas Morris, of the Mormon Company of Volunteers, stationed at San Diego, is hereby appointed hospital steward for that post, *vice* Waddell, 7th New York Volunteers, reduced. He will be obeyed and respected accordingly.

"By order of COL. STEVENSON,
"J. C. BONNYCASTLE,
"1st LIEUT. and ADJT. NEW YORK Volunteers."

The time for which the company of "Mormon Volunteers" enlisted, expired on the 20th of January 1848, but they were not mustered out for almost two months after that. In the meantime, they were very busily employed when not on duty. One of the men, Brother Henry G. Boyle, writing of their labors, says: "I think I whitewashed all San Diego. We did their blacksmithing, put up a bakery, made and repaired carts, and, in fine, did all we could to benefit ourselves as well as the citizens. We never had any trouble with Californians or Indians, nor they with us. The citizens became so attached to us that before our term of service expired, they got up a petition to the governor of California to use his influence to keep us in the service. The petition was signed by every citizen in the town. The governor tried hard to keep us in the service another year. Failing in that, he tried us for six months longer." This latter offer was declined, and other volunteers took their place. The social evil spread among the soldiers under the new regime, and their condition is reported as having been simply horrible. Brother Boyle sums up the matter by saying that *"civilization was fully established."*

On the 14th of March, 1848, the company's time of enlistment having overrun nearly two months, it was disbanded at San Diego. These veterans drew their pay the day following, and, on the 21st, a company of twenty-five men, with H. G. Boyle as Captain (Captain Daniel C. Davis having declined a "third term"), started for Salt Lake Valley.

On the 31st they arrived at Williams' ranch, and fitted out for the journey by the southern route. Those who did not join the home-bound company mostly went up the coast to the mines, towns and farms, and some of them died in that land; others returned the year following, while some still remain in California.

On the 12th of April, the little company having obtained a proper outfit, again took up the line of march. Orin Porter Rockwell and James Shaw, who had traveled the route the previous winter, were chosen pilots by and for the company. They started with only one wagon and 135 mules. Of course they were packers. They arrived at Salt Lake on the 5th of June, 1848.

Theirs was the first wagon that ever traveled the southern route. This is the only feasible route from Salt Lake, and all Utah for that matter, to travel by wagons in the winter season, to Southern California. Thus another great national wagon road was pioneered by the enterprise of a portion of this indomitable Battalion of "Mormons," or Latter-day Saints; nor, as we shall soon discover, was this the last of their numerous pioneering successes. Like Joseph in Egypt, whatever they put their hands to prospered.

Having safely landed this little company at the capital city of the Saints, we will now bid them adieu and return and hunt up those we left on the Truckee river to return to California, and raise some money, and then come on to Salt Lake Valley in the spring or summer of 1848.

CHAPTER XLI.

Men who Returned to California for Work—Employed by Captain Sutter to Build Mills—Discovery of Gold in the Mill Race by Mr. Marshall—Other Discoveries—Effects of the gold fever.—

Nothing of note transpired among those who started back on the 7th or 8th of September, 1847, to find labor for the fall and winter, until they reached Sutter's Fort, on or about the 14th of September, 1847.

The next day, a stipulation for all who wished labor was entered into, as follows, to wit: Captain John A. Sutter being desirous of building a flouring mill, some six miles from the fort and a saw-mill, about forty-five miles away, proposed to hire all the men, about forty in number, either by the job or month, at their option, to dig the races. Twelve and a half cents per yard, and provisions found, was finally agreed upon, the men to do their own cooking. Their animals were also to be herded with the Captain's, free of charge.

Captain Sutter advanced one-half of the prospective cost in gentle work oxen. A portion of the men obtained plows, picks, spades, shovels and scrapers and moved up to the designated point for the saw-mill, while the balance went to dig the race for the grist-mill. The former commenced labor about the 17th, clearing $1.50 each the first day. They subsequently earned more. The frame of the flouring mill, a short distance from the subsequent site of Sacramento City, was raised the latter part of December, 1847, and the saw-mill probably a little later. To the credit of "Mormon" labor, be it remembered, is California indebted for the erection of these mills. Much credit is due Captain Sutter and his partner, Mr. Marshall, for starting these enterprises and their gentlemanly bearing towards the discharged soldiers. But aside from these discharged "Mormons," there were no laboring men worth naming in the State, and but for them the mill enterprise and the consequent discovery of gold in that region might have been long delayed.

The following have been handed in as the names of those who dug the head and tail race of the saw-mill, some of whom also worked on the frame under the superintendence of Mr. Marshall, who did some of the mill-wright work, to wit: Alexander Stephens, James S. Brown, James Barger, William Johnston, Azariah Smith, Henry W. Bigler, of the Battalion, and Peter Wimmer, William Scott, and Charles Bennett, not members of the Battalion nor of the Church of the Saints, but honorable "outsiders," who, from the days of Nauvoo, have been more or less with the Church.

On or about the 24th of January, 1848, the water was turned into the race above the saw-mill. The race was found good, but the water, in leaving the flume and reaching the head of the tail race, having considerable fall, washed a hole near the base of the building. Being turned off, Superintendant Marshall went below to ascertain what effect the wash was likely to have. While thus examining, his eyes caught sight of yellow shining metal, which he picked up, not knowing what it was, but believed it to be gold. A subsequent assay proved his conjecture to be correct. The nuggets were in value from twenty-five cents to five dollars each.

It is detracting nothing from Captain Sutter or his partner, Mr. Marshall, to say that although the latter was the "lucky man" in making the first discovery of gold, the uncovering of the precious metal was the result of the labor of a portion of the members of the Mormon Battalion, hence it may very properly be said that "Mormon" labor opened up and developed one of the greatest resources of our nation's wealth. The "Mormon" discharged soldiers "shook the bush," and friend Marshall, unexpectedly, "caught the bird." Like most great and useful discoveries, this was unexpected and probably unthought of, and, from a mere human standpoint, was purely accidental. To the author, however, the hand of an all-wise providence is plainly visible in it.

"The intelligence of the discovery of gold was shortly after confidentially conveyed to Wilford Hudson, Sidney S. Willis and Ephraim Green, who subsequently came to the mill and learned the foregoing facts.

"They examined the rock at the bottom of the wash and found a few additional specimens. After stopping and resting a few days, they returned to the flouring mill, thence to an island in the Sacramento river, subsequently known as "Mormon Island."

On that island, or sand-bar, was found gold in paying quantities, but, strange to say, only a little company of nine persons out of about forty could be persuaded that it was a reality, although the dust was exhibited and the fact stated that men were digging and washing from twenty to thirty dollars of pure gold nuggets and dust per day. This order of things, however, lasted only a few weeks, until its opposite was realized. The secret was made public and such fabulous reports were circulated that "In the settlements along the coast and on the rivers, lawyers closed their offices, doctors forsook their patients, schools were dismissed, farmers allowed their grain to fall to the ground uncared for, and almost everybody of every description came in every conceivable way and manner, in one grand, wild rush to the 'gold diggings'; on horses, mules, with wheelbarrows, with packs on their own backs, and some with nothing but the dirty rags they stood up in, and in a few weeks, the mountain wilderness was turned into busy mining camps, and the whole face of the country seemed to change as if by magic."

It may also be very properly stated here that the excitement of the late war with Mexico now subsided and the malcontent Californians, who had sought a favorable opportunity to re-take the country, relinquished all idea of another conquest, and, true to the Spanish instinct, turned their attention to mining, thus closing and healing the bloody chasm. While Texas opened the gory conflict, with the Mexicans, to the patriotism and unflinching industry of the Mormon Battalion is due the honor of closing the Mexican war in California.

CHAPTER XLII.

Attempt to Explore a New Route to Salt Lake Valley—Forced to Return on Account of Deep Snow—Three Men Grow Impatient and Make Another Attempt, and are Murdered by Indians—The Company Follow and Discover their Remains—Animals Alarmed—Scattered by the Firing of a Cannon.

According to previous arrangements, a company of eight persons started on the 1st of May, 1848, Sergeant David Browett being elected Captain, to pioneer, if possible, a wagon road over the Sierra Nevada Mountains eastward, the Truckee route being impracticable at that season of the year. This company consisted of David Browett, Captain, Ira J. Willis, J. C. Sly, (known as Captain Sly), Israel Evans, Jacob G. Truman, Daniel Allen, J. R. Allred, Henderson Cox and Robert Pixton.

Three days' travel brought this company to Iron Hill, where they found the snow so deep they could travel no farther. A donkey belonging to one of the men was com-completely buried in the snow, except his ears. On this occasion, these appendages were not to be despised, ugly and unique as they usually appear, for one or two of the men got hold of them and dragged Mr. Donkey on to terra firma and saved his life. None of that company will be very likely to wonder why those animals are made with large ears.

Brothers Willis, Sly and Evans ascended to the summit of a mountain. Seeing nothing but snow-capped mountains in advance of them, it was decided not to abandon but to postpone the enterprise until a later period. So far as they could judge, a wagon road would at least be possible and perhaps a success. One day's travel in descending took them back from winter's cold, snowy regions to a warm, spring atmosphere, where flowers bloomed and vegetation was far advanced.

"The balance of May and the month of June were spent in digging gold, buying wagons and a full outfit for a wagon train, and making a rendezvous in Pleasant Valley, a beautiful place, about fifty miles east of Sutter's Fort.

" About the 24th of June, Captain Browett, Daniel Allen and Henderson Cox, desired to cross the mountains on a second exploring tour, but their friends, or at least a portion of them, thought the undertaking risky, owing to the wild Indians. They, however, being fearless and anxious to be moving, decided to brave all dangers and make the effort. They started, and the sequel will show that the fears of their friends were but too well founded.

" By the 2nd of July, the company were again on the march; two days' travel from Pleasant Valley, brought them to Sly's Park, a small valley or mountain dell, thus named for Captain James C. Sly, who first discovered it. Here the company made a halt. Ten men on the 4th, took up the line of march to pioneer the way over the summit of the mountains. Four days' travel over rough and rugged mountains took them across, and they found themselves safely landed at the head of Carson Valley, Nevada. As they returned to their comrades, they spent six days endeavoring to find a more practicable route, but failed.

" On the 16th of July, the company again broke camp, and the next day arrived at Leek Springs. Here, in the absence of Captain Browett, the company again organized, with Jonathan Holmes President, and Lieutenant Samuel Thompson Captain.

" The company numbered about thirty-seven individuals, all told, with sixteen wagons and two small Russian cannon, which they had purchased before leaving Sutter's, one a four, the other a six-pounder. The cost of these guns was four hundred dollars.

" This little band, like most of the Battalion, had great confidence in Divine interposition in their behalf, believing that a kind Providence would second their efforts to return to their families and friends.

Israel Evans, a representative member of the company, to whom the writer is indebted for a journal of their travels, says: "We had an abiding faith in God, that inasmuch as

He had opened unto us the treasures of the hills to help us to means for our return, He would also show unto us the way by which we could travel home."

In addition to the outfit already named, they subsequently obtained about one hundred and fifty head of horses and mules, with about the same number of horned stock, consisting of work oxen, cows and calves. This camp was kept one day after the return of the explorers, to work the road which they had pioneered. They had no guide, nor, so far as known, had the foot of white man ever trod upon the ground over which they were then constructing, what subsequently proved to be a great national highway for the overland travel.

Some four or five miles took them to what they named Tragedy Springs. After turning out their stock and gathering around the spring to quench their thirst, some one picked up a blood-stained arrow, and after a little search other bloody arrows were also found, and near the spring the remains of a camp fire, and a place where two men had slept together and one alone. Blood on rocks was also discovered, and a leather purse with gold dust in it was picked up and recognized as having belonged to Brother ~~Daniel~~ Allen. The worst fears of the company: thatced the three missing pioneers had been murdered, were soon confirmed. A short distance from the spring was found a place about eight feet square, where the earth had lately been removed, and upon digging therein they found the dead bodies of their beloved brothers, Browett, Allen and Cox, who left them twenty days previously. These brethren had been surprised and killed by Indians. Their bodies were stripped naked, terribly mutilated and all buried in one shallow grave.

The company buried them again, and built over their grave a large pile of rock, in a square form, as a monument to mark their last resting place, and shield them from the wolves. They also cut upon a large pine tree near by their names, ages, manner of death, etc. Hence the name of the springs.

After the darkness of night had gathered around them and they were sadly conversing by the camp-fire, Indians or wild animals came within smelling or hearing distance of their stock, which became so frightened that they rushed to within a few rods of the camp-fire, forming a circle around it, with their eyes shining like balls of fire in the darkness. As quick as possible, a cannon was loaded and fired. The belching forth of fire in the darkness, accompanied by the terrific report, echoing many times across the little valley, so terrified their animals that they scattered in every direction, and it was not until late the second day that all were recovered, some having been overtaken at a distance of twenty-five miles on their back track. If, as was thought, Indians were in the vicinity, intending to make a raid upon the camp, the report of the cannon so frightened them that they fled, as nothing was seen of them. The Digger Indians, at that time, were almost entirely unacquainted with the use of fire arms, and the effect, upon them, of the roaring of a cannon, in the stillness of the night, may easily be imagined.

While some were hunting the stock, others were working the road, and the balance removing camp to Rock Springs, only about four miles from the place where the men were murdered.

CHAPTER XLIII.

Make a Road to Carson Valley—Meet Emigrants—Their Joy at News of Gold—Enter the Valley by the Deep Creek Route—"Mormon" Enterprise in San Francisco—Adventurous Trip from San Francisco to Council Bluffs.

" At Rock Springs the company halted two or three days, and with the entire force were only able to work the road for a distance of three miles to another opening, after which the camp marched only five miles, which took them over the highest mountains, though not over the main dividing ridge.

' This was about the first of August, and yet, strange to tell, those prairie farmers of the Middle and Western States, with their wagons, had to be hauled over various banks of "the beautiful snow," in some places from ten to fifteen feet deep. On this short day's march, two wagons were upset and two broken, the spokes in the hind wheel of one being all broken. New spokes were, however, soon made from a dry pine tree near at hand, which did such good service that the wheel required no further repairs until the company reached Salt Lake Valley.

" Other work was required upon the road, and then a journey of about five miles brought the company near to the summit of the dividing ridge of the Sierra Nevada mountains.

· The next morning, the wagons were lightened by the heaviest freight being packed upon mules over the ridge and down the steep descent of the mountain. They camped near the eastern base, giving the place the name of Hope Valley; the spirits of the explorers who first discovered it reviving when they arrived in sight of it.

" The next day's travel, took them to the lower end of the valley. Before they could advance farther, four days more were spent in working the road. They then traveled five miles down the canyon to the head of Carson Valley. Here, like the Puritan fathers upon landing at Plymouth Rock, they tendered thanks to God who had delivered them, not from the dangers of the sea, but the far more dreaded merciless savages, the ferocious wild beasts that abounded in that region, and from being dashed to pieces while traveling over and around the steep precipices of the everlasting snow-capped mountains. They had no idea of the magnitude of the work they had performed, nor did it once enter their minds that in less than twelve months many thousands of their fellow countrymen would gladly avail themselves of this road to reach a land they had so cheerfully and recently left.

" They traveled down the Carson river a few days, but not feeling satisfied to go farther in that direction, they halted, and Israel Evans, with a few others, went on another exploring tour. They sighted a grove of cottonwood trees several miles to the northward. They returned to camp, and the next day, after toiling all day, as they had done several previous days, through sage brush and sand, the grove was reached. On arriving, they were almost overjoyed to find themselves in the emigrant road, near the lower crossing of the Truckee river. They now knew where they were and about the distance they had to travel, and governed themselves accordingly. They soon met a few trains of California emigrants, who, on learning that they were fresh from a new Eldorado, were anxious to learn what the prospects were.

" One of the men began to explain, and, taking his purse from his pocket, poured into his hand perhaps an ounce of gold dust and began stiring it with his finger. One aged man of probably over three score years and ten, who had listened with intense interest while his expressive eyes fairly glistened, could remain silent no longer; he sprang to his feet, threw his old wool hat upon the ground, and jumped upon it with both feet, then kicked it high in the air, and exclaimed, 'Glory, hallalujah, thank God, I shall die a rich man yet!' Many very interesting and somewhat similar scenes occurred as the tidings were communicated to other trains, this company having brought over the snow-capped Sierra Nevada Mountains, the first news of the discovery of gold in California.

" When this enterprising little company reached Goose Creek mountains, instead of following the old emigrant road *via* Fort Hall, on Snake river, some two hundred miles more or less out of their way, they struck across the country, by what is now known as the Deep Creek route, crossing the Malad and Bear rivers a few miles above their junction. They arrived in Salt Lake Valley about the 1st of October, 1848, feeling happy and thankful that they had exchanged the land of gold for wives, children and friends—the home of the Latter-day Saints.

In all of the travels of the Battalion, making in the round trip about five thousand miles, often in close proximity to far superior forces of the enemy, as well as passing through several strong nations of wild and ferocious Indians, there was "no fighting except with wild beasts." Taking into consideration their many hardships and privations, there were but few deaths, and it may be safely stated that no portion of the veterans of the Mexican war of the same number, did more effective service, or accomplished as much in the way of filling the coffers of the nation's wealth as did the MORMON BATTALION.

To the members of the Mormon Battalion, who remained in California after their discharge, to seek work, is also due considerable credit for improvements made and enterprises established in San Francisco and the surrounding region. Zacheus Cheeney and James Baily, of the Battalion, were the first persons to make brick in San Francisco. They commenced the kiln in April, after which Brother Cheeney went to the mines, and Brother Baily burned the bricks—50,000, in June, 1848. Some tiles had previously been burned, and possibly some bricks may have been imported as ballast, but none had ever been made there.

Among those of the Battalion who remained in California until 1848, were William Hawk, his son Nathan Hawk, Silas Harris, Sanford Jacobs, —— Slater and another whose name is forgotten, who, together with four men who were not Latter-day Saints, were employed by Samuel Brannan to carry private mail from California eastward to emigrants journeying to California and Oregon, also to Salt Lake and Council Bluffs. They left San Francisco on the 1st of April, 1848, and passed Sutter's Fort on the 15th. On reaching the Sierra Nevada mountains, they had some trouble with the Digger Indians, who ran off seventy-five of their horses, but all were recovered. They also encountered deep snow, which, in some places, was very soft. On reaching the Truckee river, they found it very high and rapid, with rocky, dangerous bottom, but they crossed in safety. They were twenty-three days in traveling about forty miles. On reaching Salt Lake, Silas Harris remained there, and the others continued on. They had difficulty from high water more or less all the way to the Platte river. When near the east end of Grand Island they had eighteen head of horses stolen by the Pawnee Indians, and, when in pursuit to recover them, had a skirmish in which several shots were exchanged and one Indian was supposed to have been killed. William Hawk, one of the pursuing party, was miraculously saved by the guns of the Indians failing to go off, when several aimed at him while only a few feet distant and attempted to fire. One Indian, also, tried to shoot him with an arrow, which Brother Hawk parried off, upon which the Indian struck him a heavy blow across the forehead with his bow, the mark of which he bears at the present time. He was stunned for the moment, and bled profusely, but otherwise escaped uninjured. No other members of the company were harmed, and the animals were all recovered.

CHAPTER XLIV.

President Young Requested by the Military Commander of California to have Another Battalion sent there—President Young's Address to the "Battalion Boys" in Salt Lake Valley—Why the Call was Made for the Battalion—Opposed to their Re-enlisting.

President George Q. Cannon, in his "History of the Church," alluding to that period immediately succeeding the arrival of the Battalion in Salt Lake Valley, says:

"By direction of Col. R. B. Mason, Military Governor of California, Col. J. D. Stevenson wrote to President Young that he was instructed to authorize Captain Jefferson Hunt to raise a volunteer battalion of "Mormons." He alluded to the "severe persecution" endured by the Saints, and attributed much of the prejudice existing in California to the exclusiveness of the Saints, as well as the bad reports which had preceded them; but he said that the intercourse with the men of the Battalion since their arrival had dispelled the prejudices, and that having had occasion to visit all the prominent places from Santa Barbara to San Diego, he had found a strong feeling of respect entertained for the Mormon people, both by the native and foreign population, and an earnest desire expressed that they should be retained in service during the war and finally become permanent residents of that section.

"After the arrival of President Young in the Valley he called the brethren of the Battalion together and blessed them in the name of the Lord for their fidelity to the kingdom of God. He told them it was not generally understood why the Battalion had been raised. The Latter-day Saints had friends and enemies at Washington. When President Polk could do them a favor he was disposed to do it, but there were those around him who felt vindictive towards the Saints and kept continually harping against them, and who thought themselves wise enough to lay plans to accomplish their destruction. The plan of raising a Battalion to march to California by a call from the War Department was devised with a view to the total overthrow of the kingdom of God and the destruction of every man, woman and child, and was hatched up by Senator Thomas H. Benton. The enemies of the Saints firmly believed they would refuse to respond to the call, and they told President Polk this would prove to him whether they were friends to the Union; and they further advised the President that when the call would be rejected, to say to the States of Missouri and Illinois and the mobocrats: "The Mormons are at your mercy." When Captain Allen, who had been appointed by the government to call upon the Latter-day Saints to raise a battalion for the war, read his papers, the power of the Almighty was upon President Young and his brethren, and it overshadowed Allen, and he straightway became the friend of the people, and had he lived, President Young said, he would have remained their friend.

"It was to the praise of the Battalion, President Young said, that they went as honorable men, doing honor to their calling and to the United States, and he was satisfied with all of them. If some had done wrong and transgressed and been out of the way, President Young exhorted them to refrain therefrom, turn to the Lord and build up His kingdom. Who could say, he asked, he was without sin?

"President Young said he felt glad that their conduct had proved to their commanders and generals that they were the best and most reliable soldiers; and although there were, perhaps, no people in the Union who would have responded to the call under the circumstances the Saints were in, still it was the best course that they could have pursued. President Young further remarked that he saw the whole plan concocted as plainly as he saw the faces then before him, and he felt within himself that his faith in God would out-general the wickedness of their enemies. The Battalion was formed, it started, and the sword fell on the other side. If the Battalion had not gone, they would not have been in the Valley then. He alluded to feelings which existed between those who had been in the army and those who had not; such feelings, he said, were wrong. His fellowship was as pure for one person as for another who had been preserved in the gospel covenants.

"He said he did not want the Battalion to re-enlist for another six months. He regretted that he did not have clothing for them; but he would rather wear skins, he said, than go back to the United States for clothes."

CHAPTER XLV.

First General Festival of the Mormon Battalion in Salt Lake Valley—Speeches by Father Pettegrew, Presidents Young, Kimball and Grant, Sergeant Hyde, Captain Brown, Lieutenants Clark and Thompson and Brothers Huntington, Williams, Wilkin, King, Garner, Durphy, Hess and Hawk.

Some items connected with the first general festival of the Battalion, which was held in the Social Hall, in Salt Lake City, on the 6th and 7th of February, 1855, will be interesting as a part of this history.

On this occasion, all the members of the Battalion who were in the Territory, who could possibly attend, with the First Presidency of the Church and a number of other friends, met together to enjoy a social reunion. The Social Hall was tastefully decorated, the best of music was in attendance and a number of tables were spread with all the delicacies and luxuries which the country afforded in the shape of edibles, to tempt the appetites of the assembled guests.

During the course of the proceedings, a number of speeches were delivered, which were replete with interesting reminiscences of days of service, and fatherly counsel from the First Presidency of the Church and others.

Father Pettegrew being called upon by the committee, came to the front of the stage, and said:

"Fellow-soldiers of the Mormon Battalion, and ladies—the wives and daughters of those men who were offered a sacrifice for the Church of Jesus Christ of Latter-day Saints: When the time had arrived for the Church to take its flight into the wilderness, according to the predictions of the Prophets, a demand was made by the Government of the United States for five hundred able-bodied men to go and fight for the rights of the people before whom they were fleeing. I say it was at the time when we were fleeing from the persecution, oppression and tyranny exercised against us in our own country, the land in which we were born. This order came at the very time we were escaping into the wilderness to seek protection and liberty among the mountains of the western wilds. It was not long after the order came before we were on the march for the West, to help the United States against Mexico, and I can assure you, brethren and sisters, that when I look upon this lively assemblage and contrast it with the scenes I have passed through in twenty-three years' experience in this Church, and think of what has taken place, things past come to mind with great vividness, as though they were still before my eyes, and I have indeed cause to rejoice in the present scenery before me, and also in the anticipations of the future.

"My father was a soldier and fought under General Washington, and when a boy I heard nothing else, scarcely, but the accounts of the war, and my father's views respecting the prosperity, success, and triumph of those early warriors, and the liberty that was gained for all. I for years enjoyed many of the benefits of that liberty, until truth sprang out of the earth, and the light of revelation dawned; then the liberty and freedom purchased by our forefathers were taken from me and my brethren. Hundreds and thousands of acres of good land, that we paid our money for, has been taken away from us by the wicked, while we, only some of the vast number of the robbed and plundered, escaped with our lives and but little else. I rejoice when I think of the scenes through which I have passed, and then behold so many of those men who were sick through fatigue, (for many of our noble band were sick on their way to Santa Fe,) when upon a long march, and for two or three days and nights without water, and suffering from fatigue such as is only known to these, my fellow soldiers. Although their hardships were numerous, I think there were only two of our brave men fell victims to the monster death before reaching Santa Fe. When I think of this, I feel truly grateful to our God this day for His many blessings, and to see so many of those generous-hearted men who have offered their lives for the cause of Christ."

President H. C. Kimball, then addressed the audience as follows:

"Brethren, keep as still as you can, I suppose you ain't in a hurry are you? (The congregation all replied to the question in the negative.) I motion you stick to it till you get satisfied, if it takes the whole week; this world was not made in a day, neither will our victory be obtained in one day, but it will take many years, for it is a great work. Brethren, these are some of my feelings respecting you. You know I was one of the recruiting officers; President Young and myself went round recruiting, so I consider myself one of the superior officers of this company; and I feel that I have considerable of a right here; in fact I felt that I could not stay away.

"You all know my feelings about you; I have not anything in my heart but the very best of feelings toward you; and there is not anything in the world causes my feelings to be aroused sooner than to see any one take a course to put a stop to the influence of this people, either in one shape or another. I want to see you all honor yourselves, and make your Priesthood honorable in the sight of high heaven. I wish to see you honor God and your calling as you did in the campaign when you went to California. I verily believe and know, that you did then, generally speaking, and I know that resulted in the salvation of this people, and had you not done this, we should not have been here.

"I want to tell you, gentlemen, that we'll have times and seasons yet, and you will be brought into closer quarters than you were on those occasions. I feel to warn you, and forewarn you of these things. Don't sell your guns, but if you have not good ones, see and get them, and rub up your swords and be ready; but fear not, for the Lord will prepare a ram in the thicket, and he will save his people and overthrow the wicked, if it takes every one of those boys who were in Zion's Camp and this Battalion to do it. Brother Grant was in Zion's Camp, and it was said in a revelation given to the Prophet Joseph, that we then offered a sacrifice equal to that of Abraham offering up Isaac, and Isaac's blessing shall be upon you, brethren.

"I hope you will stay together till you are satisfied with your enjoyments, and myself and Brother Grant will sustain you;

and do not for a moment get it into your hearts that we are anything but your friends, for we have the best of feelings towards you all. Our prayers are lifted up by day and by night in your behalf, and you will be blessed indeed, every man and every woman. But every man that lifts his hand against you shall fall, and every nation, and president, and king that lift their hands against you and this people, cannot prosper; but the curse of the Almighty will rest upon them. These are my views and feelings upon that subject. May God bless you forever and ever. Amen."

President J. M. Grant came to the front of the stage, and made the following remarks:

"I see before me men, and I believe the principal part, if not all of you whom I now behold, were in the renowned Mormon Battalion.

"I have read many narratives of the valor of men, and the service they had rendered to their country; but I here see a set of men that rendered service to their country—not such service as was rendered by the men who first raised the ax to break up the wild timber and clear the ground for cultivation; neither do I see that class of men who labored and fought to remove the obstacles that once existed in the United States; but I see men who have stood in defense of their country, under the most heartrending circumstances that human beings could be placed in; men having families and friends to leave on the open prairie; and, as our forefathers fought under General Washington and saved the country from the enemy, so did this Mormon Battalion save a large tract of land from being taken by the enemy, and they saved this people from being pounced upon by the militia of several States; for heartless villains had concocted plans to have all this people murdered while upon the western frontiers.

"You will all remember that I went to Washington, and I know from what I there learned, that the Hon. Thomas H. Benton advocated the necessity of raising troops and cutting off all the 'Mormons' from the face of the earth. Notwithstanding you had rendered your services, and offered your names to go and serve your country in the war with Mexico, yet, while you were doing this, one of the senators, and one of the principal men in the Senate, too, did endeavor to induce the Senate, the Cabinet, and the House of Representatives, to raise a force sufficiently strong to go out against the poor defenseless 'Mormon' women and children who were left upon the wild prairie unprotected. Yes, Mr. Thos. H. Benton wanted to take troops and pounce upon your wives and children when upon the banks of the Missouri River, and sweep them out of existence. And when the case was argued, the question was asked: 'Supposing you cut off the men, what shall be done with the women and children?' 'O,' said Benton, 'if you argue the case, and wish to know what shall be done with the women, I say wipe them off, too.' 'Well, then,' was asked, 'what shall be done with the children?' 'Why,' said Benton, 'cut them off, men, women and children, for the earth ought to drink their blood;' and the feeling was so strong upon the question that it came within a little of magnetizing the whole nation. What should we have done if we could not have argued that we had five hundred men upon the plains, engaged in the service of their country, and their wives and their children left without protection? What, I say, would have been the consequence if we had not had this plea? Israel must have been put upon the altar. And if we could not have raised the complement of men, what would have been the fate of this people? Israel must have been put in the tomb, unless by the interference of high heaven a ram had been found in the thicket. Yes, brethren, had it not been for this Battalion, a horrible massacre would have taken place upon the banks of the Missouri River. Then, I say, notwithstanding your hardships and the difficulties you passed through, you rendered service to the people of God that will ever be remembered, and such service as will bring blessings upon your heads in time and in eternity. And if your friends fell by the wayside; and if any of you lost your families, your wives or your children, and you sustain the people of God, you can depend upon a reward for all that you suffered, for you are the sons of God. This is the real relationship of this Battalion, to the Lord Almighty. Our motto is, to sustain the constitution of the United States, and not abuse it; and we intend to live by it, and this is no chimera as some of our enemies might be pleased to call it. You have done a good work, and I say, may God bless you all, and may you honor God as you have honored your country, and all will go well with you from this time henceforth.

"When Isaac went to the altar, he was called a lad, and was twenty-five years old (and some of you are not much older than that now), he went cheerfully, because he knew it to be right; but he had no more of a task to perform than this Battalion, for you had to live upon what you could get; eat hides, blood and all; and you had to eat your mules, and walk over the scorching plains, and be days and nights without water. I would as soon have carried Isaac's burthen as yours. These things are remembered by all those who see and feel in the kingdom of God; but I am fully aware that many of those who are rather careless and wild do not realize the important service that you rendered on that memorable occasion. The burthen laid upon you was hard to bear, and it was harder than there was any need for it to be.

"We are friendly to our country, and when we speak of the flag of our Union, we love it, and we love the rights the Constitution guarantees to every citizen. What did the Prophet Joseph say? When the Constitution shall be tottering we shall be the people to save it from the hand of the foe.

"I have as much love and respect for the Constitution of '76, as any other man, and I have as much right to the liberty and privileges it guarantees as any other man. Do I think as much of a federal government as I ought? I believe I have as much respect, and am as loyal as any other man, and I believe in giving the rights that are guaranteed by that Constitution to all, not excepting the degenerate children of our forefathers.

"Brethren, you have been called upon to defend not only the Church of God, but your country; and you have many times been called upon to defend your leaders, and it is possible that you may be called upon again. You say that you had but little fighting to do, but that does not prove you never will have it to do. You may yet see the day when the interests of the Church of God will call you into the field of battle, and hence I say, brethren, be ready for whatever may come.

"I have not come here to dance, nor feast, but I have come to mingle my voice with yours, and to say God bless you; and also to say, you are a good set of men—servants of the people of God. I came here to say, you deserve credit, and to offer you my thanks for your services in that Battalion."

"After dinner, President Brigham Young came upon the stage, and beholding the company full of life and merriment, he exclaimed: "Well, I declare, this beats all the parties I have ever seen here." He stood and watched the company then upon the floor go through a few figures, after which the house was called to order by the committee, when President Brigham Young made the following

REMARKS:

"I intend to occupy your attention but a very short time.

"I now behold a part of the men who left their wives, children, fathers, mothers, sisters, and brothers, cattle, horses, and wagons, upon the prairie, in a wild and savage country, and took up their arms and marched forth to the defense, I would be glad to say, of our beloved and happy Republic. The men now before me, (for I presume there are but few here who do not belong to the Battalion,) are men who have constantly had a goodly share of my faith, prayers, and sympathies from the time they volunteered to go into the service of the United States, at least as much as any other set of men who do, or ever did belong to this kingdom.

"Some have imagined, as I have been informed, that the Battalion was not looked upon with sufficient favor, by the balance of the community. Owing to this misunderstanding, I take the liberty of expressing my feelings in part. Perhaps, in a few instances, there may have been remarks made about some members of the Battalion, from which it may be inferred that there might be persons who rather lightly esteemed those who went into the service of the United States. I presume that some of those now present have this idea, and do not wish to be looked upon lightly by their brethren, but wish to be favorably considered by the Saints.

"At the departure of the Mormon Battalion, I am sure that no set of men, or people, ever had more faith exercised for them than this people then had. Perhaps, also, there have been no people on the face of the earth, who, according to their knowledge, possessed more faith than did those very men, when they left their families at the Bluffs.

"What gave rise to the brethren being called upon to go into the United States service? I will tell you some things about it. Suppose it had been shown to you, that there were men in Washington, and influential, too, men who held control of the affairs of the nation, to a great degree, who had plotted to massacre this people, while on the frontiers in an Indian country, you would doubtless have gone to work to circumvent their plans; consequently, all we had to do was to beat them at their own game, which we did most successfully. I was, and am fully persuaded that a senator from Missouri did actually apply for, and receive permission from President Polk, to call upon the militia of Iowa, Illinois and Missouri, and if he wished more he had also authority to go to Kentucky and raise a force strong enough to wipe this people out of existence, provided that those men who had been driven from their homes should refuse to comply with the unjust demand upon us for troops. This circumstance you are all well acquainted with, and I need not speak more about it. It was most thoroughly and incontrovertably proven that we were on hand, and that our loyalty was beyond question.

"Doubtless the spirits who surrounded the senator alluded to, said that this people were hostile to the government; and the President gave him permission to call upon the governors of the States I have mentioned (if we did not fill the tyrannical requisition for five hundred of our men) and get troops enough to march against us, and massacre us all. Without doubt, this was decreed in Washington, and I was moved upon to forestall it. As quick as this idea entered my mind it came to me, I will beat them at their own game. Did we not do it? I think we did.

"The brethren who went with the Battalion went with as good hearts and spirits, according to the extent of their understanding, as ever men went upon missions to the world, and they manifested a readiness to do anything required of them.

"I will say to you, that, according to the best knowledge I have of you, the course and conduct of many were not justifiable before the Lord, and a knowledge of these facts caused me to weep. But you went upon your journey, were faithful to your officers, and faithful to the Government; and perhaps no other set of men, under the same circumstances, would have done better; and the character that you bear, among the officers whose opinion is of any value, is good.

"I will briefly allude to Colonel Doniphan. After his return, and in a party made by his friends, in St. Louis, at which Mr. Benton was present, he made a speech, and in his remarks, said: 'I can take one thousand MORMON BOYS, and do more efficient service against Mexico, than you can with the whole American army.' This I have been told by those who heard him make the assertion. That was his testimony, and I presume he gave it openly and publicly. I suppose he felt like giving Benton a challenge, for he was always opposed to him in politics; but Benton was not disposed to say anything in reply to it, at least I have heard of no reply.

"The Battalion went on and performed their duties, and fulfilled their mission; and every person who has the spirit of revelation, can see that to all human appearance this people must have perished, had not these men gone into the service of their country. So far as human nature can discern, I say that these men now before me, were the saviors of this people, and did save them from carnage and death. I have always felt an interest in their welfare, and the Lord knows it; and my feelings towards them have always been good, and I do not know that I ever thought of them, but that the feeling burst into my heart 'God bless them!' I bless you now, and pray every good being to bless you, for I have always felt to bless you from morning till evening, and from evening till morning.

"I see your motto there, 'The Mormon Battalion—a ram in the thicket!' Yes, and well caught too. This Battalion made every sacrifice required — they offered their lives to save this people from the evils designed by their enemies. They did everything that was required by the Government of the United States, and I am sorry to say, that some few of them lost their lives in the service. I will tell you one thing, brethren and sisters, which is as true as the Lord Almighty lives; if that Battalion had done as I told them in every particular, there would not a single man have fallen while in that service; I know that such would have been the result. Most of them did live and acted well; but they had the world, the flesh, and the devil, to contend with, and their circumstances were of a very peculiar nature. Some of the most heart-rending and cutting scenes that men could pass through, this Battalion was called to endure, and hence it is no wonder to me that they should manifest their weaknesses in those trying times. On the contrary it would have been unprecedented if they had not in some shape or other, manifested the weakness and frailty of human nature. Many of them are with us, some are in California, and some scattered to the nations of the earth to preach the gospel, and a few have died and gone to another sphere; but we ought to be thankful that so many are here to-day, to participate in the enjoyments of this festivity.

"Brethren, you will be blessed, if you will live for those blessings which you have been taught to live for. The Mormon Battalion will be held in honorable remembrance to the latest generation; and I will prophesy that the children of those who have been in the army, in defense of their country, will grow up and bless their fathers for what they did at that time. And men and nations will rise up and bless the men who went in that Battalion. These are my feelings, in brief, respecting the company of men known as the Mormon Battalion. When you consider the blessings that are laid upon you, will you not live for them? As the Lord lives, if you will but live up to your privileges, you will never be forgotten, worlds without end, but you will be had in honorable remembrance, for ever and ever.

"We were accused of being of all people the most dangerous. We were said to be aliens from our Government, and from the pure institutions of our country. But what are the facts? It has been currently stated that while the volunteers under Colonel Stevenson, and other troops from different parts of the Union, were in California, United States Army officers had to seek protection at the hands of these my brethren, against other United States Army officers who proved treacherous, and the Battalion continued steadfast to their trust, and saved that region of the country to the United States. These things they did most faithfully, and to the great benefit of our common country.

"What is said about the treacherous? They could go back, mingle in society, drink and carouse, and it was all right. But the poor Mormon Battalion, the true friends of the country—the true patriots of liberty, had to seek a home in the mountains, and their services were but little thought of. Does this make you feel badly? No, their praise would be a shame, and their presence a disgrace to these 'Mormon' boys.

"I have watched with interest the whole movements of this Mormon Battalion from the beginning, and I will now ask where is there in the whole United States, a more loyal and patriotic band of men? Where is there another set of men like them, anywhere outside of this Church? Others do not know what the principles of a free government are, or should be; but this people do comprehend them, and know what they are, or what they ought to be, therefore, I shall not blame them so much as I should you were you to go astray.

"I thank the Lord that you are here under such favorable circumstances as the present. I do not wish to detain you, and hope you will enjoy yourselves, though I am sorry to see you so crowded, but pleased to see you so good-natured about it.

"You are welcome to the use of this hall; I do not know when the next party wish to occupy it; but if you are not through by the time that others want it, I will tell them to wait, therefore, take your time; and when you get through, you cannot get one cent into my hands for its use. If you have any money that you do not know what to do with, give it to the Perpetual Emigrating Fund to help the poor."

Elder William Hyde was invited to make some remarks. He came forward and said:

"I am truly happy, brethren, sisters, and fellow soldiers, to meet with you in this capacity. These are the best days of my life; I feel that we are a happy people. I have not language to express my feelings on this occasion.

"My brethren around me feel that I, with them, have made a free-will offering of all that was earthly, and of all that was near and dear unto us, and this offering for the salvation of the aged fathers, mothers, wives, and children of the Latter-day Saints; and in a temporal light, it seemed that we sacrificed all.

"At the time we were called upon to enlist in the service of our country, I was in a feeble state of health, and every natural feeling would say, brother William, you are not fit to undertake such a task; and yet the spirit would say, you must not withhold. We passed through it; the scenes were trying; and what emotions of gratitude would come up in our minds when reflecting upon the goodness of our heavenly Father! And ever since the day of our discharge, I have looked for a time like this—a day of enjoyment.

"I have been separated from my brethren in Zion for a long time, thousands of miles of sea and land have lain between us, and I have never forgotten you. You will be in my mind, and I shall be in yours, and we shall reflect and speak of each other in the gratitude of our souls in a time to come, for then, having overcome and proven valiant to the cause of God, (for I feel we shall be valiant, and be saved in the kingdom of God,) we shall think of past times, and the day of trouble and hardships.

"I say I have been looking for a day of this kind ever since we left the service, but it has seemed as though we never should have a chance of meeting all together again. Sometimes a few have met, but now a large majority have the privilege of meeting to join in the dance, in the music, the feast, the song, and to mix and mingle our joy and rejoicing all together, and have a good time. I cannot express the joy of my heart on this ever-to-be remembered day; it is a glorious day to me.

"It has been my lot to travel many thousand miles, and I have been ready to give up many times, but the Battalion would come into my mind, and the thought would give me fresh courage, and my faith would increase, and the Almighty would bless and strengthen me, so that I would soon recover. And I know, brethren, we were accepted in the course we pursued; I feel to rejoice in having the approbation of my brethren who stand at the head of affairs.

"I have been thinking of a toast to-day, which I will here give:—President Young and all others who offered their assistance in the day of trouble—the recruiting officers of the Mormon Battalion: May they never want for a ram in the thicket. And if we should not live may we have children to live and be as ready as we were at Council Bluffs to go forth in the defense of our counry and our religion.

"May God bless us and save us, and may we live to His glory while upon earth, and throughout eternity. Amen."

Captain James Brown came to the front of the Orchestra and said:

"Brethren, sisters, and fellow-soldiers; as has been remarked by Brother William Hyde, this is one of the happiest days I have had since I enlisted in the Mormon Battalion; and I have not language to express the feelings of my mind, in meeting with the Battalion on this occasion. When I look at this happy company and contrast the present scenes with those we witnessed when we left Council Bluffs, Fort Leavenworth, Santa Fe, and from there to California, and to this city, it fills my heart with gratitude to God. And I can say that the time has come, notwithstanding the trials and scenery around looked gloomy then, for the Lord to favor Zion.

"We have in a measure extricated ourselves from our enemies, and thank God for it. When we were in trouble, the Lord extended his mercies to us, and we had cause to rejoice; and we now are free from the claws of those who were our oppressors; and this is through obedience to those whom God has set in his kingdom to govern and regulate all things for our eternal welfare. Let us rejoice, and officers and all be ready to go forth in defense of the principles of righteousness; for, as we stated yesterday, we have been the means of redeeming our brethren; and our sacrifice is tantamount to that of Abraham offering Isaac. The members of the Battalion left their wives and children, their friends and everything that was near and dear to them upon the earth, excepting only the counsel received from the authorities of the Church, and that they went to fulfill.

"I do not suppose there is an individual in the Battalion, who, had he been left to his own thoughts and feelings, independent of counsel, would have enlisted. I would have felt very reluctant under the circumstances had it not been for the counsel of my brethren whom God authorized to dictate the affairs of His kingdom.

"We have accomplished the work required of us, redeemed our brethren, and helped to place the Church in the valleys of the mountains, where the kingdom of God will roll forth with mighty power, and it shall fill the whole earth.

Lieutenant Clark said:

"I wish to relate a circumstance that transpired when the Battalion were about leaving for California. A lady who belonged to the Battalion was in conversation with another lady, and when interrogated about her husband going to California, and asked how she felt, the reply was, that she would rather be a soldier's widow than a coward's wife. My toast is, may this spirit be in all the wives of the Mormon Battalion.

"My heart is filled with joy and rejoicing on this festive occasion, and I feel the same spirit that has rested upon me from time to time since we left the service. I have many times looked forth to the day we could meet together and see better times, when we should see our brethren in peace, and of which we have a small sample to-night. My faith is that the time will come when the offspring of this Battalion will become as numerous as the sand upon the sea shore. And I pray that we may ever feel the spirit that will prompt us to act whenever called upon in defense of our country. Brethren, may the Almighty bless us and save us all in His everlasting kingdom. Amen.

Lieutenant Thompson said:

"With peculiar feelings I arise to make a few remarks. I am very grateful for this privilege of meeting with my brethren. I am one of those who helped to lift out the wagons when almost embedded on the sandy plains, and my spirit is glad within me when I think of the privileges we enjoy as a people in this lovely valley, and I hope we may live still further to rejoice together. My prayer is that we may live to see each other's faces again and enjoy ourselves as we are doing here, and as we did on the plains."

D. B. Huntington said:

"I feel like saying a word or two, although I am sensible I have not language at command, whereby to express my feelings. It does my heart good to see such an assembly as this, and it seems to me that there never was such a spirit of faith and good feeling among this body as at the present time; and this is only the commencement. This festival will long be remembered in the hearts of this people, and it will be regarded as an item of important history in this kingdom.

"It is, indeed, a pleasing thought with me that there has not been a word of jarring in the whole of our proceedings in this festival.

"I wish to say a few words for the benefit of all, respecting trials. I feel to say every one will have as hard a time of trial as any of these my brethren had when we shook hands with our wives and bid farewell. I and my wife never saw a darker day; she said to me, Dimick, I fear I shall never see you again. I laid my hands on her head and blessed her in the name of the Lord, and told her we would live to see each other again, and spend many happy years together.

"Brother Brigham and Brother Heber asked me to go, and if they had told me that I should not return any more, I do not think I should have felt it any more than I did that trial. Probably you may have to make as great a sacrifice within a few years to come.

"Brethren, read the Book of Mormon, for nothing will make a man feel more deeply than to leave his family under those circumstances, and by reading that book you will get comfort by referring to the trials of the ancients. There is not a man here but will be tried in one way or another, therefore be faithful or not many will stand the trying day; but never let it be said that one of this noble band has fallen through transgression. There are a few that go into error like G. P. Dykes, and who will not do right. Brother Dykes has gone into error and is damned; he has the curse of his brethren upon him for his follies and missdoings."

Brother Tippets observed:

"I never expect to see a day when I shall feel worse than when I left my family at Winter Quarters. If I had known where I was going, and the trials I would have to pass through and endure, I could not have felt worse.

"My toast is, may every one of the 'Mormon' boys become the father of a great kingdom, and every wife a mother.

Thomas S. Williams said:

"Fellow soldiers, I will take the liberty of detaining you a short time. I have never experienced a happier time in my life than within the last forty-eight hours. I do not know where to begin to unbosom my thoughts and feelings on the present delightful occasion; but brethren, I am one with you, in heart, mind, and soul, and in everything else in this kingdom. I can say with those who have spoken, that a more gloomy day nor time never surrounded me than when we took our line of march. Though I have been in prison and suffered considerably, but never was the day so dark with me as the one before named. I was a mere boy as many others were, from sixteen to twenty-five years of age, when we enlisted in the service of the United States. I started as a private soldier, and when we raised the liberty pole I had but a yoke of oxen, and an old wagon. My wife and children I left with only about five days' provisions, and not having the least idea where they would get the next. The day following I ascertained that Brother Higgins was going to fetch his wife and family. I therefore determined that if we could raise means any way I would take my wife with me, and I made up my mind to do it if I had to tramp all the way and carry my knapsack. I was there a private soldier, without a dime in the world, but the blessings of prosperity and peace had been pronounced upon the Mormon Battalion, and I, of course, knew that it was right for me to take care of my family, and hence I determined to take them with me. I am proud to say, that I have my wife and daughters and sons here this evening.

"What could be more gratifying than what we enjoyed of the blessings of heaven while passing through these trying scenes? It would be impossible, and therefore it is useless to attempt a description of what we passed through; for never since the days of Adam did a set of men live, and I may say perhaps never will live and pass through such a scene as we did in the Battalion; leaving our wives and children to the care of Him who careth for all, out upon the broad plains, and nothing to preserve them from the cold, searching winds; they were in the care of their heavenly Father. But brethren, what was their faith and confidence in God? They had a promise from our leader that He would protect them, and they were satisfied that all would be well.

"After all this we are assembled together among the mountains, to worship our God, and do that which our consciences teach us is right in the sight of high heaven.

Mr. David Wilkin said:

"If I should undertake to express my feelings this evening, I should make a complete failure; for I feel far more than I can express. I am full of pleasure and delight when I look upon so many with whom I had the honor of walking, with the knapsack and musket. I say that a braver set of men never lived, and thank heaven that we live and enjoy what the United States by its liberal constitution has bequeathed to us. We are the living monuments of our Father's mercy; He has made us to participate in the rich blessings of His kingdom, and may He prolong our lives to a good old age. I did not think of occupying two minutes when I got up here, for I know my brethren's hearts are full to overflowing, and I feel assured that if a vote was called, every one would readily manifest their full and entire satisfaction with the enjoyments of this festival. Brethren, while I look upon the countenances before me I feel to rejoice in the joy and pleasure that seem to beam forth from them; I contrast the scenery with the past, and compare it with what we have previously experienced.

"The motto before us—the richest gem that we can transmit to our children and children's children. This people appreciate the sacrifice and offering of the "ram in the thicket." Ancient Israel had their paschal lamb, and so have modern Israel."

J. M. King was then called upon to make a few remarks; he said:

The last two days have been the happiest I ever spent upon the earth, and as has been said by others respecting the time when we parted, I also felt it to be a trying time. I left my wife and family at Pisgah, one of the sickliest parts in that district of country, and indeed it was a trying time to me. I can truly say that I feel to rejoice in the present company, in the society of my brethren and sisters.

"It was my lot to return to the States and tarry there four years before I could get to this place again, but I now rejoice that I have the privilege of being with those who have waded through "thick and thin."

"I have proved the leaders of this kingdom to be prophets of the most high God, and I am ready to support and uphold them. I well remember the evening that Brother Brigham called for recruits, and I also recollect that he promised inasmuch as we would go forth and do the best we could we should live to enjoy the society of the Saints again, and I feel to rejoice that we have the oportunity of realizing a fulfilment of the promise.

David Garner said:

"I feel thankful for this opportunity of meeting with you. I have not had such a happy time in my life as this. I will sing a few verses to cheer up your hearts." Mr. Garner then sang "Come, come away" with much spirit and energy.

Brother Durphy said:

"I wish to present one of the blest of the Mormon Battalion before you. There are but a very few that know me now, I presume, owing to the great change that has taken place in me since we were in the service of the United States, for there is now more health and strength, and nerve in me than there was at that time, or ever was before. You all know that I was a poor hump-backed, peaky-faced, long, scrawny, kind of a man, and when we were about to leave the Bluffs, I was told that I should never see California, but thank God I have been and returned, and am now full of life and spirit, and I feel that I am one of the blest of the Lord in every respect."

Brother Tippets next addressed the company:

He rejoiced in the pleasures of this festival, and often thought of what the brave men of the Battalion had endured. He spoke of Brother and Sister Williams' boy being raised up from sickness by the power of God. When he went in the service of the United States, he was supposed to be in a consumption; at that time he only weighed one hundred and twenty-three pounds, but after traveling and passing through trials for nine months with the Battalion he weighed upwards of one hundred and fifty pounds.

Brother John Hess said:

"'There is a feeling within me that I cannot express, but it has got my coat off. I feel to rejoice insomuch that I cannot find language to express the feeling of gratitude in my heart. I am thankful for what I enjoy from the hands of our heavenly Father. Could this feeling be bought? No, money would not begin to buy what I enjoy were it possible to sell it.

"We have felt and experienced during this festival, (saying nothing of what we have passed through in days gone by,) that the Lord is with us by his power, to protect us and do us good. It is true it was not always pleasant to have to pass through those trials, but it was for our good, and will be in future, therefore, let us be determined to never flinch so long as there is a button to the coat. I say I have rejoiced beyond anything that I could express while in the society of my brethren, and I do hope that this will not be the last time the members of this Battalion will have to mingle together."

Singing and dancing were then freely indulged in, a spirit of charity, order and peace, governing and controlling the whole proceedings. The house was next called to order, when William Hawk came forward and made the following remarks, with much spirit and energy:

"Brethren and Sisters—I want to bear testimony to one saying that has been thrown out here, *viz:* that the President promised this Battalion, that inasmuch as they would go forth and do right there should not be a ball shot at them; and I can say for one, that I realize the truth of that saying; I have experienced it—I have seen those words fulfilled and that promise verified to the very letter, when placed in the midst of my enemies with nothing but these little MALLETS to defend myself with, (the speaker here exhibited his fists,) and they were well armed with bows and arrows, knives and rifles, but they burnt the priming, the powder flashing in the pan, and not a gun aimed at me went off, and their arrows broke.

"When Brigham Young said he wanted us to go I put my name down to go for one, and the Indians did not kill me. I had to leave my family at the Bluffs, my wife in a very weakly state of health. I had five children, and the oldest went with me to California, and he is now in Sacramento city. On my return, I brought my wife and was coming to this place, and she got killed at Ash Hollow, in a stampede, and her body is laid by the road side. I wish to make honorable mention of her, for she was a noble woman. The rest of my family are here and rejoicing in the truth, and I feel thankful for the blessings that have attended me; and I feel to wish I may ever pour out my soul to God for a continuance of His blessings. And I do not wish my services in that Battalion to be the last good deed of my life; I want to be ready, and to be on hand come what will."

CHAPTER XLVI.

Synopsis of a Lecture by James Ferguson—Correspondence Between Ferguson and Cooke—Cooke's Deference to the Mormon Battalion when Passing Through Salt Lake City in 1858—Survivors of the Mormon Battalion—Song.

The following from a lecture by Sargeant Major James Ferguson, delivered before an assembly of Elders, including the Presidency of the Church in Europe, at 36, Islington, Liverpool, Nov. 7, 1855, is an interesting review of some of the most striking incidents of the Battalion's experience:

"Although on the subject of the Mormon Battalion much has been said and written, I cheerfully comply with the request of our much-loved President, brother Franklin D. Richards to speak upon it now. It may seem strange to you that such a subject should be called up in these lands; but when you call to mind that there is no portion of the kingdom of God with which the interests of that Battalion are not now interwoven, it cannot seem strange to you that it should be talked of wherever that kingdom has an interest.

"We were mustered into service on the 16th of July, 1846. A few hurried preparations, and the gray haired old men and striplings marched off merrily as our commander ordered the music to play a hasty farewell to 'the friends we left behind us.'

"Deprived of the rights granted to other volunteers, of choosing our own officers, Captain Allen, of the regular dragoons, was commissioned by the President of the United States to command us. But he was a gallant and brave officer. The rigid discipline and rough service of the army had failed to smother the better impulses of his generous heart. He was ever ready to befriend us, and but for his stern and willing interference, we would have been compelled to submit to, or avenge, various and repeated insults as we passed down the frontiers of Missouri to our place of outfit, Fort Leavenworth.

"But our bright hopes in him had an end here. Scarcely had we resumed our march, when the sad news of his death overtook us. A gloom overspread our whole camp, for there was not a heart but loved him.

"At Council Grove, we were halted to deliberate how to proceed. The command of the Battalion was here given to Lieutenant Smith, of the First Dragoons. Letters were despatched to President Polk, praying for the privilege due to us, of electing our commander. And now commenced a series of the most trying cruelties. Our commander was not of himself cruel and wicked, but he was weak, and became, to a great extent, the creature of Doctor Sanderson, a rotten-hearted quack, that was imposed upon us as our surgeon. The hospital wagons, designed for our use by Colonel Allen, were left behind. These abuses continued and increased until, when we mustered at Santa Fe, and on the Rio Grande, one hundred and fifty of the Battalion were pronounced unable to continue the march to California. These were ordered back to winter quarters at the Pueblo near Taos, where, in the midst of much suffering and exposure, their term of enlistment nearly expired. Some of them died there; and among the number, young Richards, to whom I have before referred, and Blanchard, an only son of aged depending parents.

"On our arrival at Santa Fe, instead of the favorable answer we had a right to expect from the government, we found Captain Cooke appointed to take command—an officer also of the First Dragoons, famous, in his own corps, for the tyrannical strictness of his discipline. Not a murmur was heard at this fresh indignity.

"With a sorry outfit of jaded mules, famished beeves, and scabby sheep, we resumed our march. While yet in the settlements of New Mexico, our rations were reduced a quarter; and for our comfort, we learned that for a march of a hundred days, over an undiscovered country, we had fifty days' scanty rations.

"Leaving the Rio Grande, about the southern boundary of New Mexico, without a guide who knew the country before us, we turned in a westerly course. We threaded our way through the Sierra del Madre, cutting a road through the

"Pass of the Guadaloupe," alternately pulling our ponderous wagons up the sandy hills, and lifting them down the rocky descents. The various incidents of our travels, each day presenting something new, are materials for a long history. I can only glance hastily at some scenes as I pass along.

"Descending the Sierra del Madre, as we came in sight of the valley of the San Pedro, the vast prospect before us made us for a moment forget our fatigues and sufferings. Fresh hope seemed to enliven every heart. It seemed like a new world ready for population. Parched, and fainting with thirst, the waters of the river were before us, and the shade trees on its banks.

"While marching down this river, a scene occurred, which, while it afforded amusement to some and suffering to others, manifested the kind watch-care of our Heavenly Father. Our beeves had dwindled down to a few sickly skeletons. Our camp was threatened with scurvy, and many attacked with diarrhœa; and there seemed no hope for us. Surprised, and some of them wounded by our hunters, a herd of wild cattle made their appearance on all sides of us. Some, more furious than the rest, made a dash at our train. One pitched a poor fellow into the air, severely wounding him. Another tossed a mule on its horns, and tore his entrails, while another lifted a wagon out of its track.

"The troops of four "Presidios," having learned of our approach, had assembled at Tucson to interrupt our march. Heedless of the threats of the Mexican commandante, we advanced, and, as the troops retreated with their artillery, we marched through their walled town.

"A desert of seventy miles brought us to the Gila. We were welcomed by the rude hospitality of the Pimas. An old chief, at the head of his warriors, squaws, and little ones met us in the path, and presenting his cakes of sweet corn-meal, invoked upon us the protection of the Great Spirit as we passed on.

"On the 10th of January, 1847, we crossed the Colorado. An unsuccessful attempt to raft our provisions down the Gila had deprived us of a great part of them, although we were already reduced to quarter rations. Without a chance for rest, we entered upon the 'Tierra Calienta, the Big Desert of the

Colorado. Ninety miles without water, save in the deep wells we dug but had no time to drink from, brought us to the end of our deserts. Those alone who endured them can conceive the sufferings experienced on this desert. It was well named the Hot Land. In vain was our rear guard ordered to prevent the men from lagging behind; the stoutest staggered, and one after another fell fainting. They would revive, advance, and fall again; and many, when at last water and grass were found, fell down exhausted, unable to reach the camp. The clear stream appeared to laugh at them in mockery, and there they lay gasping till some feeling messmate returned with the replenished canteen.

"A few days brought us to the rancho of the American Warner. Unlike the hospitable Pimas, he hid his bread and drove his cattle into the mountains. Here we learned of the retreat of the Californians from Los Angeles. Without a pause for rest, we changed our course to meet them, but they concealed themselves till we had passed.

"Thus, despite of every attempt to bring us to an engagement, we reached our destination at San Diego, on the 31st of January, fulfilling the prediction of our President, that we should not fight a battle. God fought our battles for us, and our victories were not bought with blood. Garrison duty, drills, and entrenching the camp at Los Angeles, made up the balance of our service.

"Many attempts were made by Fremont to excite the people of the country against us. He had attempted to retain the governorship of California, against General Kearny, when our arrival put a stop to his insubordination. Our entry into the Pueblo, starved, ragged, and weary, seemed to testify to the inhabitants to the truth of his accusations against us of cannibalism, barbarity, plunder, and rapine.

"When he came into our midst at a subsequent period, how different his reception. He was starved, dismounted, and weary. His party sick and dying daily. We gave him shelter, fed him, furnished him with horses, and healed his sick. A dog will show gratitude to the hand that feeds him. But *he* is silent, or snaps like a wolf.

"His attempts were all in vain. The people soon learned that we were their friends and protectors. They petitioned for our re-enlistment, and wept at our discharge. We had made many friends. Lieutenants Smith and Stoneman parted from us with regret. They had with others been taught to despise us. But they soon found, that though 'Mormons,' and many of us from other lands, we had the hearts of men and Americans. And our brave Colonel—he was rigid in his discipline, and often cross and exacting. But beneath it all, he had a kind, manly heart, and while sometimes he would curse us to our face, he would defend us as his own honor in our absence. Major Cloud, our pay master, also of the regular army, was our true and devoted friend to the last. He, too, is gone, among the few friends who shone out for a little while, like bright stars on a stormy night, then set in the midst of thick clouds. Many who had once been our enemies became our friends. But none of our friends have ever become enemies. The most warlike of the many tribes of the red men that we passed, met us in kindness and parted from us in peace, because we did not abuse their hospitality.

"Thus ended a campaign unparalleled in any history. The drill succeeded the weary march in cheerfulness. The song and dance made a glad echo on the bleakest desert, and the prayer of gratitude was never smothered by murmuring complaint. While one company remained an additional year in service, and husbands and fathers endured another long march to join their suffering families, a few sought employment on the Sacramento, and there, to crown the campaign, opened those inexhaustible mines which have drawn so many adventurers to the rich shores of the Pacific."

The following written and published about eleven years subsequent to Colonel Cooke's connection with the Mormon Battalion, and at a time when, if ever, he would have thought and spoken ill of that brave band of soldiers, is significant of his sense of justice towards them:

"Great Salt Lake City,
"August 25, 1858.

"*Editor Deseret News:*

"Having been requested by numerous friends to publish the accompanying letters, and obtained the permission of Colonel Cooke to do so, I shall feel obliged by your insertion of them in the *News*.

"Very respectfully,
"Yours in Christ,
"JAMES FERGUSON."

"GREAT SALT LAKE CITY, U. T.,
"May 4, 1858.

"SIR:

"In looking through files of eastern papers, lately received, I saw a letter purporting to have been written by you, and dated at Camp Scott, November 29th, 1857. In that letter you assert that the 'Mormons' are a set of cowards, like all assassins and bullies.

"I am what is generally termed a 'Mormon,' and as such served my country honorably under your command. Your statements I consider most unwarranted, and a very ungenerous return for the sincere respect entertained for you by the Mormon Battalion, and indeed the whole 'Mormon' people.

"I sincerely trust that you have it in your power to disclaim the authorship of that letter. If not, as an American citizen and a gentleman, spurning the epithets hurled at me in connection with a people of whom in the midst of their worst misfortunes I am proud, I ask you, kindly and with respect, to make that apology which your own sense of honor will suggest is due.

"I have the honor to remain,
"Most respectfully, etc.,
JAMES FERGUSON,
Brig. Gen. U. T.
Adj. Gen."

"LT. COL. P. ST. GEO. COOKE,
"2nd Dragoons, U. S. A.,
"Camp Scott.

The following is Cooke's reply:

"HEAD QUARTERS, 2nd DRAGOONS,
"CAMP FAULKNER, June 8, 1858.

"SIR:

"I have this day received your letter of May 4th, respecting the authenticity of a letter, which you say, was published in an eastern newspaper, purporting by, and in which I 'assert the Mormons are a set of cowards, like all assassins and bullies.' I wrote no such letter: I wrote no letter for publication. I never wrote or spoke such a sentence. I left Camp Scott November 26th, and did not return: the letter, you say, was dated there November 29th.

"I never saw such a letter in the papers, or heard of its existence, until lately as a rumor from Salt Lake City.

"I thank you for informing me of this mysterious forgery. My sense of the performance of the Mormon Battalion was expressed at San Luis Rey, in an order, which you remember, and which stands printed in a Senate document; and I can only refer to my connection with you, on the Battalion staff, as a satisfactory and pleasant one.

"Very respectfully,
"Your obedient servant,
"GEN. JAMES FERGUSON,   P. ST. GEORGE COOKE.
"Salt Lake City,   Lt. Col. 2nd Dragoons.
"Utah Territory."

When Colonel Cooke wrote the foregoing letter he was on his way to Utah, with the U. S. Army, under command of the late rebel general, Sidney A. Johnston, for the purpose of suppressing the imaginary "Mormon Rebellion." When the army passed through Salt lake City on the 26th of June following, Colonel Cooke, out of deference to the brave men who had served under him in the Mormon Battalion, took off his hat and rode through the deserted city with his head uncovered.

The following are the names, addresses, occupations and offices of the surviving members of the Battalion, so far as known at the present time (March, 1882):

Adams Orson B. (Sergt), Harrisburg, Washington Co., Utah; Farmer and Stock Raiser.
Adair Wesley, Arizona; Farmer.
Allen Rufus C., Paragoonah, Iron Co., Utah; Farmer.

SURVIVING MEMBERS OF THE BATTALION. 371

Allred Redick N. (Q. M. Sergt.), Chester, Sanpete Co., Utah; Bishop, and Col. of Militia.
Averett Elisha (Musician), Kanab, Kane Co., Utah.
Allred J. T. S., Spring City, Sanpete Co., Utah; Farmer.
Averett Juthan, Springville, Utah Co., Utah.
Allred Reuben W., Kanarra, Kane Co., Utah.
Barrus Ruel (Lieut.), Grantsville, Tooele Co., Utah; Farmer.
Bybee John M.; Farmer.
Barney Walter, Monroe, Sevier Co., Utah; Farmer.
Brizzee H. W., Mesa City, Arizona.
Boyd G. W., Salt Lake City; Stock Raiser.
Bunker Edward, Santa Clara, Washington Co., Utah; Bishop.
Buckley Newman, Springville, Utah Co., Utah; Book-canvasser.
Bates Joseph, Payson, Utah Co., Utah.
Bird Wm., Paris, Bear Lake Co., Idaho.
Bigler H. W., St. George, Washington Co., Utah; Employed in the Temple.
Barrowman John, Nephi, Juab Co., Utah; Farmer.
Brimhall John, Orderville, Kane Co., Utah; Farmer and Mechanic.
Boyle H. G., Payson, Utah Co., Utah; Missionary, and Chaplain of Utah Legislature.
Brown John, Leeds, Washington Co., Utah; Farmer.
Butterfield Jacob K., Taylorsville, Salt Lake Co., Utah.
Brunson C. D., Box Elder Co., Utah.
Beckstead Gordon S., South Jordan, Salt Lake Co., Utah.
Brown James S., Salt Lake City; Home Missionary.
Buchanan John (Corpl.), Manti, Sanpete Co., Utah; Carpenter.
Brown Alexander, Lynne, Weber Co., Utah.
Brown Jesse S., Promontory, Box Elder Co., Utah.
Clark Lorenzo (Lieut.), St. George, Washington Co. Utah; Tanner.
Caldwell Matthew, Huntington, Emery Co., Utah; President of Seventies, and Farmer.
Cazier John, Nephi, Juab Co., Utah.
Curtis R. F., Newton, Cache Co., Utah; Farmer.
Curtis Dorr P.; Farmer.
Cox Amos, Manti, Fremont Co., Iowa.
Chase Hiram B., Nephi.
Casper Wm. W., Mill Creek, Salt Lake Co., Utah; Major in Militia and Farmer.
Cole James, Springville, Utah Co. Utah.
Casto Wm., Big Cottonwood, Salt Lake Co., Utah; Horticulturist and Farmer.
Casto James.
Collins R. H. (Corpl.), Huntington Emery Co., Utah.
Chase John D., Nephi, Juab Co., Utah; Member of High Council.
Carpenter W. H., St, George, Washington Co., Utah; Broom Maker.
Cheeney Zacheus, Centerville, Davis Co., Utah; Farmer.
Dykes Geo. P. (Lieut.), Arizona.
Dalton Henry S., Centerville, Davis, Co., Utah.

Dalton Edward, Parowan, Iron Co., Utah; Member of Utah Legislature and Probate Judge.
Dalton Harry; Farmer.
Dodge Augustus E., Toquerville, Kane Co., Utah; Agriculturist.
Decker Zechariah, Emery Co., Utah.
Dunn Thomas, Goose Creek, Cassia Co., Idaho.
Earl Jacob.
Evans Israel, Lehi, Utah Co., Utah; Farmer.
Fairbanks Henry, Payson, Utah Co., Utah; Farmer.
Forsgreen John, Salt Lake City.
Follett Wm. T., St. George, Washington Co., Utah.
Follett Wm. A., Arizona.
Frederick David, Beaver, Beaver Co., Utah.
Forbush Lorin.
Garner David, North Ogden; Farmer.
Hunter Jesse D. (Capt.), California.
Higgins Nelson (Capt.), Elsmore, Sevier Co., Utah; Farmer.
Hulett Sylvester (Lieut.), Manti, Sanpete Co., Utah.
Hanks Ebenezer (Sergt.), Parowan, Iron Co., Utah; Miner.
Hunsaker Abraham (Sergt.), Brigham City, Box Elder Co., Utah; Farmer and Bishop of Honeyville.
Hancock Levi W. (Musician), Washington, Washington Co., Utah; One of the First Presidency of Seventies.
Hatch Meltiar, Panguich, Iron Co., Utah; Ranchman.
Hatch Orin, South Bountiful Davis Co., Utah; Farmer.
Harmon Lorenzo F.
Harrison Isaac, Sandy, Salt Lake Co., Utah; Postmaster and Justice of the Peace.
Hendricks William D., Richmond, Cache Co., Utah; Railroad Contractor.
Howell T. C. D., Clifton, Oneida Co., Idaho; Farmer.
Harmon Oliver N., Hoytsville, Summit Co., Utah; Home Missionary.
Hess John W., Farmington, Davis Co., Utah; Bishop.
Hunter Edward, Grantsville, Tooele Co., Utah; Bishop.
Hinckley Arza E., Cove Creek, Millard Co., Utah; Ranchman.
Hickenlooper Wm. F., Ogden, Weber Co., Utah.
Holdaway Shadrach, Provo, Utah Co., Utah.
Hunt Marshall, Snowflake, Apache Co., Arizona.
Hawk Wm., Salt Lake City.
Hudson Wilford, Grantsville, Tooele Co., Utah.
Henrie Daniel, Manti, Sanpete Co., Utah.
Harris Silas, Glendale, Kane Co., Utah; Farmer and Stock Raiser.
Huntsman Isaac, Wellsville, Cache Co., Utah; Blacksmith.
Ivie Thos. C., Scipo, Millard Co., Utah; Farmer.
Ivie Richard,   "   "   "   "   "
Jamerson Charles, Minersville, Beaver Co., Utah.
Judd Zadock K., Kanab, Kane Co., Utah.
Jackson H. J.
Kelly Wm., American Fork, Utah Co., Utah; Farmer.

SURVIVING MEMBERS OF THE BATTALION.

Keysor Guy M., Richfield, Sevier Co., Utah.
Luddington Elam (Lieut.), Sugar House Ward, Salt Lake Co., Utah; Merchant.
Landers Ebenezer, Salem, Utah Co., Utah; Farmer.
Lewis Samuel, Panguich, Iron Co., Utah; Stone Mason.
Lawson John.
Lake Barnabas, Franklin, Oneida Co., Idaho.
Layton Christopher, Kaysville, Davis Co., Utah: Counselor to Stake President, and Farmer.
Larson Thurston.
Lemon James W., Weston, Cache Co., Utah; Farmer.
Merrill Philemon C. (Adjt.), St. David, Arizona; Patriarch.
Muir Wm. S. (1st Sergt.), West Bountiful, Davis Co., Utah; Farmer.
Miles Samuel (Q. M. Sergt.), St. George, Washington Co., Utah; High Counselor and Justice of the Peace.
Morris Thomas, Farmer's Ward, Salt Lake Co., Utah; Market Gardener.
Murdock John R., Beaver, Beaver Co., Utah; President of Stake and Councilor in Legislature.
Merrill Ferdinand, Salt Lake City, Utah; Farmer.
Murdock Orrice C., Republic City, Republic Co., Kansas; Farmer.
McCullough Levi H., Fillmore, Millard Co., Utah.
Moore Calvin H., Spring City, Sanpete Co., Utah.
Martin Edward, Salt Lake City; Hackman.
Mesick Peter, West Weber, Weber Co., Utah.
Mead Orlando F., Spanish Fork; Shoemaker.
Myers Samuel, Glendale, Kane Co., Utah; Carpenter and Joiner.
Martin Jesse B., Scipio, Millard Co., Utah; Farmer.
McArthur Henry, " " " "
Mowrey Harley, Paris, Bear Lake Co., Idaho.
Maxwell William B., William's Valley, Secora Co., New Mexico; Ranchman.
Naile John C., Toquerville, Kane Co., Utah; Farmer and Pomologist.
Oakley James, Springville, Utah Co., Utah.
Olmstead Hiram, Ogden, Weber Co., Utah.
Pace James (Leiut), Washington, Washington Co., Utah; Farmer.
Packard Henry, Springville, Utah Co., Utah.
Peck Edward, Provo, Utah Co., Utah; Blacksmith.
Prows Wm, C., Kanosh, Millard Co., Utah.
Pulsipher David, Concho, Arizona.
Park James, Cedar Valley, Utah Co., Utah.
Rainey David P., (Sergt., not Corp. as erroneously appears on the roll), Richmond, Cache Co., Utah; Farmer.
Shipley Joseph, American Fork, Utah Co., Utah.
Roberts Levi, Kaysville, Davis Co., Utah; Farmer.
Rowe Wm., Mendon, Cache Co., Utah; Farmer.
Rollins John, Springville, Utah Co., Utah.
Roe C. C., Sanpete Co., Utah.
Riser John J., Centerville, Alameda Co., California; Farmer.
Rogers Samuel H., Snowflake, Apache Co., Arizona.

Rust Wm., Payson, Utah Co., Utah; Doctor.
Strong Wm., Salt Lake City.
Smith John G., Draper, Salt Lake Co., Utah; Farmer.
Stoddard Rufus, Piute Co., Utah.
Shupe James, Ogden, Weber Co., Utah; Blacksmith.
Shepherd M. L. (Corp.), Beaver, Beaver Co., Utah; Counselor to President of Stake, Farmer and Stock Raiser.
Smith Azariah, Manti, Sanpete Co., Utah.
Smith Albert (Q. M. Sergt.), Manti, Sanpete Co., Utah.
Standage Henry, Arizona.
Savage Levi, Toquerville, Kane Co., Utah; Vine Gardener.
Smith Willard G., Littleton, Morgan Co., Utah; Stake President and Probate Judge.
Sprague R. D. (Musician), Brigham City, Box Elder Co., Utah.
Sanderson Henry W., Fairview, Sanpete Co., Utah; Mayor, and Major in Militia.
Stephens Lyman, Orderville, Kane Co., Utah; Carpenter and Joiner.
Smith Lot, Sunset, Apache Co., Arizona; President of Stake.
Steele John, Toquerville, Kane Co., Utah; Farmer.
Sessions John, Provo Valley, Wasatch Co., Utah; Farmer.
Thompson Samuel, (Lieut.), Spanish Fork, Utah Co., Utah; Farmer.
Tyler Daniel (Sergt.), Beaver City, Beaver Co., Utah; President of High Priests' Quorum, and Magistrate.
Terrill Joel J. (Sergt.), Ogden, Weber Co., Utah; Farmer.
Tuttle L. T. (Sergt.), Manti, Sanpete Co., Utah; Merchant.
Taggart G. W. (Musician), Richville, Morgan Co., Utah; Member of High Council.
Tanner Myron, Provo, Utah Co., Utah; Bishop.
Thompson John C., Riverdale, Weber Co., Utah; Farmer.
Twichel Anciel, Beaver, Beaver Co., Utah; Farmer.
Tippets John H., Sanpete, Co., Utah.
Thompson James L.; Farmer.
Thomas Elijah, Leeds, Washington Co., Utah.
Wriston John P.
Wade Edward, Ogden, Weber Co., Utah.
Workman Andrew J., Virgen City, Kane Co., Utah; Farmer.
Workman Oliver G., Salt Lake City.
Walker Wm. H., Big Cottonwood, Salt Lake Co., Utah; Farmer.
Wilson George D., Hillsdale, Iron Co., Utah.
Wilson A. G., Moab, Emery Co., Utah.
Weaver Franklin, Cache Co., Utah.
White S. S., Pleasant Grove, Utah Co., Utah.
Webb C. Y., Parowan, Iron Co., Utah.
Winn Dennis, Richmond, Cache Co., Utah.
Williams James V., Monroe, Sanpete Co., Utah.
Wilkin David, Pioche, Lincoln Co., Nevada.
Zabriskie Jerome, Minersville, Beaver Co., Utah; Farmer and Stock Raiser.

MORMON BATTALION SONG.

BY THOMAS MORRIS.

All hail the brave Battalion!
  The noble, valiant band,
That went and served our country
  With willing heart and hand.
Altho' we're called disloyal
  By many a tongue and pen,
Our nation boasts no soldiers
  So true as "Mormon" men.

O'er many a barren desert
  Our weary feet have trod,
To find, where, unmolested,
  The Saints can worship God.
We've built up many cities—
  We're building temples, too;
Which prove to all beholders
  What "Mormon" hands can do.

We settled here in Utah,
  Upon a sterile soil,
And by our faith and patience
  And hard, unflinching toil,
And thro' the daily blessings
  Our Father, God, bestows,
The once forbidding desert
  Now blossoms as the rose.

What tho' the wicked hate us,
  And 'gainst our rights contend;
And, through their vile aggressions,
  Our brotherhood would rend!
The keys of truth and knowledge,
  And power to us belong;
And we'll extend our borders
  And make our bulwarks strong.

Our sons are growing mighty,
  And they are spreading forth,
To multiply our numbers
  And beautify the earth.
All hail, the brave Battalion!
  The noble, valiant band,
That went and served our country
  With willing heart and hand.

www.ingramcontent.com/pod-product-compliance
Lightning Source LLC
Chambersburg PA
CBHW030403230426
43664CB00007BB/730